Microsoft® Works 4.5 6-in-1

by Jane Calabria and Dorothy Burke

®

A Division of Macmillan Computer Publishing
201 West 103rd Street, Indianapolis, Indiana 46290 USA

Jane and Dorothy would like to dedicate this to some of our family members: Jim Abel, Midge and Steven Klotz. Good luck with Works!

Library of Congress Catalog Card Number: 97-68088

ISBN: 0-7897-1357-8

99 98   6 5 4 3 2

Interpretation of the printing code: the rightmost double-digit number is the year of the book's first printing; the rightmost single-digit number is the number of the book's printing. For example, a printing code of 97-1 shows that this copy of the book was printed during the first printing of the book in 1997.

Screen reproductions in this book were created by means of the program Collage Complete from Inner Media, Inc, Hollis, NH.

Printed in the United States of America

President
Roland Elgey

Senior Vice President/Publisher
Don Fowely

Publishing Director
Karen Reinisch

General Manager
Joe Muldoon

Acquisitions Editor
Lisa Swayne

Senior Product Director
Lisa D. Wagner

Product Development Specialist
Melanie Palaisa

Production Editor
Tom Lamoureux

Strategic Marketing Manager
Barry Pruett

Webmaster
Thomas H. Bennett

Product Marketing Manager
Kristine R. Ankney

Assistant Product Marketing Manager/Design
Christy M. Miller

Assistant Product Marketing Manager/Sales
Karen Hagen

Technical Editor
Sherry Kinkoph

Technical Support Specialist
Nadeem Muhammed

Acquisitions Coordinator
Tracy M. Williams

Software Relations Coordinator
Susan D. Gallagher

Editorial Assistant
Virginia Stoller

Book Designer
Dan Armstrong

Cover Designers
Glenn Larsen
Kim Scott

Production Team
Marcia Deboy
Maribeth Echard
DiMonique Ford
Kay Hoskin
Laura A. Knox
Christy M. Lemasters

Indexers
Nadia Ibrahim
Craig Small

Composed in *Helvetica* and *Palatino* by Que Corporation.

About the Authors

Jane Calabria and Dorothy Burke have teamed up successfully on several Que books, including the *10 Minute Guide to Lotus Notes Mail 4.5*, and *Windows 95 6-in-1*. Both are independent consultants, trainers, and authors and they travel the United States teaching and consulting.

Jane has authored or contributed to 12 Que books, which include the *Professional Developer's Guide to Domino 4.5*. She has a long history of training and consulting in operating systems, databases, word processing, electronic mail, the Internet, Lotus Notes, and Domino. She is heard weekly in the Philadelphia area on KYW News Radio 1060 AM, giving reports on computing and computer news as "JC on PCs." Her reports are also found on AOL.

Dorothy is a contributing author to *Special Edition, Using Power Point* and has spent many years consulting and training in desktop publishing, operating systems, spreadsheets, graphics programs, Lotus Notes, and Domino.

Acknowledgments

We would like to thank "The Godfather," Karen Reinisch, and Don (or is it Dom?) Essig for this opportunity and for their hard work and good humor. Our gratitude to Tom Lamoureux, our Production Editor, who makes silk pages from total chaos.

A special thanks and warmest wishes to Melanie Palaisa, our Product Development Specialist. There was a time we thought Melanie taught us everything we know, but now we realize that Melanie is just beginning to teach us!

Thanks to Laurie Ulrich for her many contributions throughout this book.

We consider ourselves fortunate to work with the finest and most talented professionals in the publishing world. We are also fortunate to have such loving and supportive spouses and we thank Rob and Tom for putting up with us, and for putting up without us.

We'd Like to Hear from You!

As part of our continuing effort to produce books of the highest possible quality, Que would like to hear your comments. To stay competitive, we *really* want you, as a computer book reader and user, to let us know what you like or dislike most about this book or other Que products.

You can mail comments, ideas, or suggestions for improving future editions to the address below, or send us a fax at (317) 581-4663. The address of our Internet site is **http://www.quecorp.com** (World Wide Web).

In addition to exploring our forum, please feel free to contact me personally to discuss your opinions of this book: I'm **73353,2061** on CompuServe, and I'm **mpalaisa@que.mcp.com** on the Internet.

Thanks in advance—your comments will help us to continue publishing the best books available on computer topics in today's market.

Melanie Palaisa
Product Development Specialist
Que Corporation
201 W. 103rd Street
Indianapolis, Indiana 46290
USA

Trademarks

All terms mentioned in this book that are known to be trademarks or service marks have been appropriately capitalized. Que Corporation cannot attest to the accuracy of this information. Use of a term in this book should not be regarded as affecting the validity of any trademark or service mark.

Contents

Part II: Introduction to Works   113

Part III: Word Processing 133

xvii

Part V: Databases   389

Appendixes   555

Introduction

If you're using a computer at home, odds are great that it came with Microsoft Works. Odds are good that you are reading this introduction while standing in a bookstore, trying to decide if you need this book. If you knew all there was to know about Microsoft Works, you probably wouldn't be standing there, reading this. This Introduction will help you to determine if you should invest in *Microsoft Works 4.5 6-in-1*.

What Can This Book Do for You?

You'll definitely learn to use Microsoft Works. Beyond that, many of the skills you will learn in this book will apply to other software programs. Learning basic computing, word processing, database, spreadsheet, and Windows 95 skills can increase both your productivity and your market value in the workforce.

Can You Learn to Use a Computer Program from a Book?

A book allows you to learn at your own pace. Using this book, alone, at your computer, no one can see you when you make a mistake. You can concentrate more on the lessons and worry less about being embarrassed. With this book, you learn the basic concepts and navigation of Microsoft Works as well as some of the more advanced features.

Do You *Need* This Book?

We haven't really found any software that is as *intuitive* as the software publishers would like us to believe. As an adult sitting at a computer for the first time, you're more likely to experience an intuitive *headache* than an intuitive program. Working at a computer for the first time can make an intelligent and reasonable adult feel like a ten-year-old child. No, we take that back; there's a good chance a ten-year-old knows her way around computers! Yes, this book can help you learn your way around Works, to use Works productively, to increase your computer skills, and to learn quickly, with each lesson taking about 10 minutes of your time.

Why This Book Rather than Another?

We present to you, in a reasonable and concise method, the tools and information you need to make Microsoft Works *work* for you (not against you) without filling the pages with useless computing trivia. We've dedicated an entire section to "Real World Solutions" that is project-oriented. It even tells you how to use the *Wizards,* those supposedly no-brainer automated miniprograms that help you create newsletters, mailing lists, and mass mailings. We help you answer the Wizard and show you the results of those answers before you make your selections.

We use a teaching formula that is comprised of two parts. The first is Que books and the popularity of their 10 Minute Guide Series. Over four million 10 Minute Guides have been sold on various software titles! This book is written using that very successful 10 Minute lesson format. The second part is our life's work—we teach basic skills to those who are new to computers and we teach advanced skills to programmers. We have very successful careers. Our secret? We are *you.* We remember our first computer (and we were a lot older) and like you, we learned to use a computer and software when we were *adults.*

Why You Should Use This Book

Microsoft Works 4.5 6-in-1 is for you if you want a jump-start to using Microsoft Works at home or at the office to create documents, write letters, keep personal or small business records, create lists of clients, or home or office inventory. It will also help you to understand and grasp the basic skills of word processing, spreadsheets, databases, and Windows 95.

How This Book Is Organized

Microsoft Works 4.5 6-in-1 has lessons ranging from the basics to some more advanced features. You can work through the book lesson by lesson, building upon your skills, or you can use the book as a quick reference when you want to perform a new task.

Following is a brief description of each part of *Microsoft Works 4.5 6-in-1*:

- **Part I, Windows 95 and Internet Explorer**   The book begins with the basics of using Microsoft Windows 95. You'll learn how to use a mouse, print, create folders and manage files, and how to use the Internet Explorer and Internet mail.

- **Part II, Introduction to Works**   You'll learn how to use Help and how to launch and exit Microsoft Works. You'll become familiar with the Works Task Launcher and each of the Works Tools.

- **Part III, Word Processing**   Here, you learn basic word processing skills as well as the capabilities of Works' word processing features. You learn how to create basic documents, format text, and enhance documents with graphics and drawings. You'll also learn how to create envelopes and labels and how to use some of the TaskWizards.

- **Part IV, Spreadsheets**   From the most basic of spreadsheet skills to some more advanced formula writing, Spreadsheets teaches you the features of Works' spreadsheet capabilities and helps you to develop skills applicable to other programs. You also learn how to create impressive charts and graphs.

- **Part V, Databases**   This section teaches you how to build basic databases and also why and when you need a database. Here, you learn how to create fields, use formulas, create forms and reports, and sort, search, and manipulate data. Databases can help you to increase your record-keeping productivity, and this section shows you how.

- **Part VI, Real World Solutions**   This section is projects-oriented, giving you step-by-step instructions on how to complete a project. Here, you learn how to create a small business plan and how to make a household inventory.

- **Appendix A: Importing and Exporting**   You can import and export files to and from Works and other programs. Here, you will learn how to import graphics files and export spreadsheet files.

- **Appendix B: Using the Communications Tool**   Works includes a tool that enables you to connect to other computers. Here, you learn how to add a modem, configure phone settings, and prepare to communicate with other computers.

Conventions Used in This Book

Commands, directions, and explanations in this book are presented in the clearest format possible:

Titles of windows and dialog boxes are capitalized to distinguish them from regular text. For example, the Custom Conventions box refers to an on-screen box whose title bar reads "Custom Conventions."

A series of menu selections that you must click will be separated by commas. For instance, "Select **Start**, **Programs**, **Excel**" means that you click the Start button, the Programs menu choice, and then the Excel option.

As a further help, commands you are directed to select will also be in **bold** so you can see them clearly.

You might also be directed to hold down several keys simultaneously, as in the command "Press **Ctrl**+**F2.**" The two keys that you press will be connected with the plus sign (+).

Some information is offset to draw your attention to it:

Tips   Provide timesaving shortcuts and workarounds to potential trouble spots.

Cautions   Warn you of situations that can land you in trouble.

Terms   Give definitions for jargon that you are not expected to know but which will be useful as you master Works 6-in-1.

Skills Transfer Tips   Highlight procedures that you learn in Works or Windows, but can apply to other Windows programs.

Windows 95 and Internet Explorer

Navigating the Windows 95 Desktop

In this lesson, you learn to start and shut down Windows, how to work with the parts of the Windows desktop, and how to use a mouse to manipulate items on the desktop.

Starting Windows 95

To start Windows 95, you simply turn on your computer and monitor. As your computer boots, Windows loads the files it needs to run. You'll notice the Windows 95 logo screen and several black screens with white type.

After the operating system is loaded, a password dialog box appears asking for your user name and your password. If you are a member of a network, you must use the exact user name and password assigned to you by your network administrator; if you are not sure of what to enter in this dialog box, ask your administrator. You should use the same user name and password each time you log on to Windows so that your desktop, applications, and customization settings will always be the same. By default, Windows displays the log on dialog box if you're on a network. If you don't see a logon dialog box, you don't have to enter a user name or password to work in Windows.

Boot   A term used to describe a computer's starting-up process, during which the operating system and configuration files are loaded into the computer's memory.

User Name and Password   Identifies you to your computer and/or to the network server, and protects your computer from illegal entry.

Log On   Attaching to the network so you can use its resources—files, printers, and so on.

Follow these steps to open the Windows program, if you're on a network:

1. Enter the following information:

User Name—The name by which you are identified by your computer or the network.

Password—Your personal watchword for logging in to the computer or network.

2. Press **Enter** to start Windows.

CAUTION

Error Message!   Many different errors could occur at this point. For example, a message might appear on your screen telling you a connection could not be restored or that you're not a valid user. First, make sure you've typed your password correctly and you used the appropriate case when typing. If you have a problem connecting to the network, see your network administrator for help.

TIP   **Should I Press Enter or Click OK?**   Pressing **Enter** in a dialog or message box is the same as choosing the **OK** button; pressing the **Escape** key is the same as choosing the **Cancel** button.

Understanding the Windows Desktop

After Windows appears, you will see various items on the screen, as shown in Figure 1.1. The items you see enable you to open applications, manage files, send and receive mail, and perform many other tasks throughout your work-day. Depending on your installation, you may or may not see all of the items shown in the next figure.

The components of the Windows screen include:

- **Desktop**   This is the background on which all other elements appear. You can think of the Windows desktop like the top of your own traditional office desk. Just as you can move papers around, hide certain items in drawers, and add and remove things on your desk, you can manipulate things on your Windows desktop.

- **Icons**   Icons are pictures that represent programs (The Internet, Word for Windows, Excel, and so on), folders, files, printer information, computer information, and so on, in both Windows 95 and Windows applications. Most often, you use icons to open folders and files.

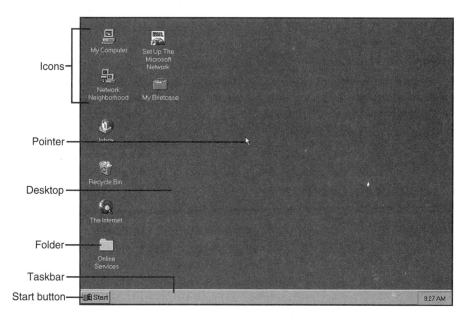

Figure 1.1 Common components of the Windows screen.

- **My Computer** The My Computer icon represents the contents of your computer, including the hard drive, floppy and CD drives, applications, folders, files, and so on. Double-click an icon to open it and view its contents.

- **Network Neighborhood** This icon displays other computers connected to your computer on a Microsoft or other type of network, such as NT or NetWare.

- **Inbox** The Inbox represents Microsoft Exchange, a program you can use to fax and e-mail other computers.

- **The Internet** If you have access to an Internet Service Provider, you can use the Internet Explorer to access the Net, including Web pages and e-mail.

- **Recycle Bin** The Recycle Bin is a place in which deleted objects remain until you empty the trash. You can retrieve items—files, programs, pictures, and so on—from the Recycle Bin after you delete them. Once you empty the trash, however, you can no longer retrieve items from the bin.

- **My Briefcase** My Briefcase is a feature you can use for copying and transferring files from your computer to a notebook or other computer. My Briefcase enables you to easily transfer and update your files.

- **Online Services** This folder icon enables you to quickly and easily sign up for any of the online services it contains, including America Online, AT&T WorldNet, and CompuServe. You must have a modem connected to your computer and configured before using one of these services.

- **Set Up The Microsoft Network** A step-by-step guide to configuring your computer and connecting to Microsoft's special Internet network. Again, you'll need a modem to use this feature.

- **Taskbar** The Taskbar contains the Start button, any open application or window buttons, and the time. You can click a taskbar button to open the window or application it represents. Use the Start button to open programs, documents, help, and so on.

- **Start Button** The Start button displays a menu from which you can choose to open an application, open a document, customize Windows, find a file or folder, get help, or shut down the Windows 95 program.

- **Folder** A folder contains files, programs, or other folders on your computer; for example, the Online Services folder contains programs that let you sign up for an online service like CompuServe. A folder is the same thing as a directory.

- **Pointer** The pointer is an on-screen icon (usually an arrow) that represents your mouse, trackball, touchpad, or other selecting device. You use it to select items and choose commands. You move the pointer by moving the mouse or other device across your desk or mousepad. You'll learn how to use the mouse in the next section.

Using the Mouse

You use the mouse to perform many actions in Windows and in Windows applications. With the mouse, you can easily select an icon, folder, or window, among other things. Selecting involves two steps: pointing and clicking. You also can open icons and folders by double-clicking them, and you can move an item by clicking and dragging that particular article.

To *point* to an object (icon, taskbar, Start button, and so on), move the mouse across your desk or mouse pad until the on-screen mouse pointer touches the object. You can pick up the mouse and reposition it if you run out of room on your desk. To *click*, point the mouse pointer at the object you want to select, and then press and release the left mouse button. If the object is an icon or window, it becomes highlighted. When following steps in this book, click the left mouse button unless the directions specify otherwise.

The right mouse button can be used when you want to display a shortcut, or a quick menu. To *right-click*, point the mouse pointer at an object—folder, taskbar, desktop, and so on—and click the right mouse button. A shortcut menu that presents common commands relating to the object appears. If, for example, you right-click a folder, the menu might offer these commands: Open, Explore, Create Shortcut, and Properties. The items on the menu depend on the object you're right-clicking.

When you *double-click* an item, you point to the item and press and release the left mouse button twice quickly. Double-clicking is often a shortcut to performing a task. For example, you can open a folder or window by double-clicking its icon.

You can use the mouse to move an object (usually a window, dialog box, or icon) to a new position on-screen. You do this by *clicking and dragging* the object. To drag an object to a new location on-screen, point to the object, press and hold the left mouse button, move the mouse to a new location, and release the mouse button. The object moves with the mouse cursor as you drag it. If you want some practice with the mouse, open the Solitaire game and play a round or two; choose **Start**, **Programs**, **Accessories**, **Games**, and then **Solitare**.

You also can perform certain actions, such as selecting multiple items or copying items, by performing two additional mouse operations. *Shift+click* means to press and hold the **Shift** key and then click the left mouse button while pointing to various objects; *Ctrl+click* means to press and hold the **Ctrl** key, and then click the left mouse button. The result of either of these actions depends upon where you are in Windows.

Using the Start Button

The Windows Start button provides access to programs and documents, the help feature, the find feature, and many other elements in Windows 95. You'll use the Start button to perform most tasks in Windows. For more information about using menus, see Lesson 3.

To use the Start button, follow these steps:

1. Point the mouse at the **Start** button, located on the taskbar, and click the button. The Start menu appears (see Figure 1.2). Your Start menu may display more options than the one in the figure, depending on what is installed to your computer.

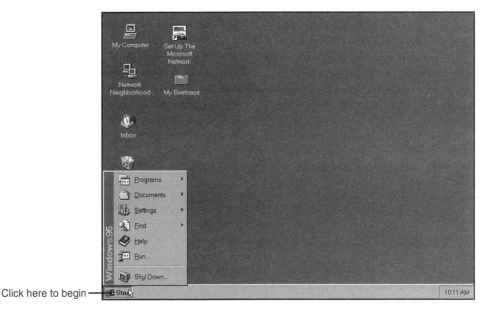

Figure 1.2   The Start menu provides easy access to programs.

2. Click the task or command you want to display, as follows:

- **Programs**   Displays a secondary, or cascading, menu that includes Windows Accessory programs, Online Services, the Internet Explorer, and other programs on your computer.

- **Documents**   Displays up to 15 of the most recently opened documents; for quick and easy access, click the document name and the application. The document opens and is ready to work.

- **Settings**   Displays a secondary menu that includes the Control Panel Printer folders, and the Taskbar command for customizing your Windows setup. For more information, see Part I, Lesson 24.

- **Find**   Enables you to search for specific files, folders, or computers. You can search your own hard drive or the network drive.

- **Help**   Displays help for performing tasks and procedures in windows. For more information, see Part I, Lesson 5.

- **Run**   Enables you to enter a command line (such as a:\install) to run a program from hard, floppy, or CD disks.

- **Shut Down**   Displays the Shut Down dialog box in which you prepare your computer before turning it off.

 TERM   **Secondary or Cascading Menu**   An arrow after any menu command designates another menu, called a cascading or secondary menu. It will appear if you choose that command. Windows supplies as many as four cascading menus starting from the Start menu.

Using the Taskbar

In addition to the Start button, the taskbar displays buttons representing open windows and applications. You can quickly switch between open windows by clicking the button on the taskbar. Figure 1.3 shows the taskbar with two buttons: My Computer (representing the open My Computer window) and Exploring (representing the hidden, or minimized, Windows Explorer).

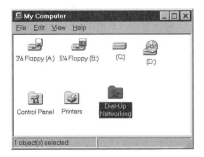

Figure 1.3   Open and minimized windows are represented on the taskbar by buttons and the window's name.

You can move the taskbar to the top, left, or right side of the screen to customize your workspace. Additionally, you can hide the taskbar until you need it.

To move the taskbar, click the mouse anywhere on the bar (except on a button) and drag the taskbar to the right, the left, or the top of the screen. As you drag, the taskbar relocates to that area. You can easily drag the taskbar back to the bottom if you prefer it there.

To hide the taskbar, follow these steps:

1. Click the **Start** button.
2. From the **Start** menu, click **Settings** and then click **Taskbar**.
3. Choose the **Auto Hide** check box by clicking that box; then press **Enter** to close the dialog box. The taskbar slides off of the screen.

When you need the taskbar, move the mouse to where the taskbar was; you may have to slide the mouse off of the screen. The taskbar reappears.

Can't Display the Taskbar! If you move the mouse to where the taskbar should be and the taskbar doesn't display, press **Ctrl+Esc** to display the taskbar and open the **Start** menu.

CAUTION

To show the taskbar all the time, click **Start**, **Settings**, **Taskbar** and click the check box so no check mark appears. Press **Enter** to close the dialog box.

Shutting Down Windows 95

Before you turn off your computer, you must shut down Windows to ensure you don't lose any data or configuration. You also can shut down Windows and restart the computer, in MS-DOS mode, for example, or to log on to the network under a different name. Following are the Shut Down options available to you in the Shut Down Windows dialog box:

- **Shut Down the Computer** Choose this option when you're finished using your computer for the day. When Windows displays a message telling you to shut off your computer, you can safely turn off the machine.

- **Restart the Computer**   Choose this option to shut down and then restart the computer in Windows mode. You'll use this option when you've changed configuration in the Control Panel, for example, and you want that configuration to take effect.

 TIP   **This Takes Forever!**   If you want to restart *Windows only* and not reboot the PC, hold down the **Shift** key while selecting Restart the Computer.

- **Restart the Computer in MS-DOS Mode**   This option shuts down Windows and starts the computer back in DOS mode, with a black screen, white type, and a C-prompt, or *command* prompt. From the command prompt, you can enter many familiar DOS commands or install DOS applications. See Lesson 17 for more information.
- **Close All Programs and Log On as a Different User**   Choose this option when you're sharing a computer with someone and they are already logged onto the network. When you choose this option, the network logon dialog box appears in which you can enter your user name and password.

To shut down Windows, follow these steps:

1. From the Desktop, click **Start**, **Shut Down**.
2. When the **Shut Down Windows** dialog box appears, choose one of the options previously described. To quit working on the computer, choose **Shut Down the Computer**. Then choose **Yes**.
3. Do not turn off the computer until Windows displays the message telling you that it's okay to turn off your computer.

In this lesson, you learned to start and shut down Windows, work with the parts of the Windows desktop, and use a mouse to manipulate items on the desktop. In the next lesson, you learn to work with windows.

Working with a Window

In this lesson, you learn to open, resize, move, view, and close a window, and how to use scroll bars to view more of a window.

What Is a Window?

A *window* is a boxed area in which you view files, folders, drives, hardware icons, or other elements. Figure 2.1 shows the components that make up a window. Many of these components are the same for all windows in Windows 95 and Windows applications, which makes it easy for you to manage your work. Keep in mind that although most windows are similar, you'll run across some windows that don't have all of the following components.

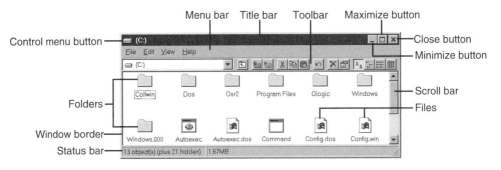

Figure 2.1 The elements of a typical window.

You can open and close a window, reduce and enlarge a window, and move a window around—which is what this lesson is all about. In addition, you can open more than one window at a time, stack one window on top of another, and otherwise manipulate windows as explained in Part I, Lesson 7. Table 2.1 briefly describes the common elements of a window.

Table 2.1 Window Elements

Element	Description
Title bar	Contains the window's name, the Control menu, and the Minimize, Maximize, or Restore, and the Close buttons.
Menu bar	Contains menus with related commands and options that help you control the window and its contents. See additional information about menus in Part I, Lesson 3.
Control menu button	Contains commands that help you manage the window itself.
Toolbar	Graphic tool buttons that represent shortcuts to various menu commands you use in your work.
Minimize button	A button that reduces the window to a button on the taskbar.
Maximize button	A button that enlarges the window to fill the screen.
Close button	A button that closes the window.
Folders	Icons within windows that represent directories; folders can hold other folders and files.
Files	Document, spreadsheet, database, program, and other components stored in folders on a drive in your computer.
Windows border	A rim around a restored window that you can use to resize the window.
Status bar	A bar across the bottom of the window that describes the contents of the window, such as free space, number of objects or files in a window, and so on.
Scroll bar	A vertical and/or horizontal bar that enables you to view hidden areas of a window.

TIP **No Toolbar or Status Bar Showing?** If a window doesn't display the toolbar, choose the **View** menu, and the **Toolbar** command; to display the Status bar, choose **View**, **Status Bar**.

Windows Contents

Windows 95 is made up of a series of windows that often contain different items. When opened, each icon on your desktop, for example, displays different contents just as various folders, files, and applications display various contents.

Additionally, after you open a window, you can usually open items within the window, such as icons, folders, programs, and documents. Often, you can open a window within a window within a window, and so on, until your desktop is filled with windows.

The following is an example of a set of windows you can open from the My Computer icon:

- **My Computer window** Displays hard drive icons, floppy disk or CD icons, Control Panel folder and the Printers folder; often this window also includes the Dial-Up Networking icon.
- **Hard drive icon** Displays all folders (or directories) on that drive, plus any files found on the root directory (usually the C drive).
- **Program Files folder** Displays folders representing programs included with Windows, such as the Accessories, Internet Explorer, Online Services, and so on.
- **Internet Explorer folder** Includes the Internet Explorer program and files needed to run the program, plus several text files you can read to get more information about the Internet Explorer.

Opening a Window

To open a window from an icon, double-click the icon. For example, point at the **My Computer** icon and double-click. If you do it correctly, the My Computer icon opens into the My Computer window.

Having Double-Click Trouble? If you have trouble opening a window by double-clicking, you need to practice the double-click movement. You can also change the speed of the double-click to better suit your "trigger" finger; see

CAUTION Part I, Lesson 25.

There is another method you can use to open a window. Just point to the icon and right-click once, and a shortcut menu appears. Select **Open** from the menu.

Sizing a Window with Maximize, Minimize, and Restore

You may want to increase the size of a window to see its full contents, or you may want to decrease a window to a button on the taskbar in order to make room for other windows. One way to resize a window is to use the Maximize, Minimize, and Restore commands found on the Control Menu. If you use the mouse, you will use the Maximize, Minimize, and Restore buttons located at the right end of the window's title bar. The buttons and commands work as described here.

Select the Maximize button, or command, to enlarge the window. A maximized hard drive window, for example, fills your entire screen, thus hiding any of the desktop in the background. Clicking the Maximize button of a program, document, or other window enlarges that window to fill the screen.

Select the Minimize button, or command, to reduce the window to a button on the taskbar.

Select the Restore button, or command, to return a window to the size it was before it was maximized. (The Restore button and command are available only after a window has been maximized; the Restore button replaces the Maximize button in a maximized window.)

Figure 2.2 shows the hard drive window (opened from My Computer) maximized; it fills the entire desktop. At full size, the hard drive window's Restore button is available. When the window is at any other size, you see the Maximize button instead of the Restore button.

To maximize, minimize, or restore a window with the mouse, click the appropriate button in the title bar of the window. To maximize, minimize, or restore a window using the Control menu, follow these steps:

1. Click the **Control menu** button to open the window's Control menu; alternatively, press **Alt+Spacebar**.
2. Click the command (**Restore**, **Minimize**, or **Maximize**) you want to initiate. Alternatively, use the down-arrow to move to and highlight the command, then press **Enter**.

Hard drive's title —

Minimize and Restore buttons

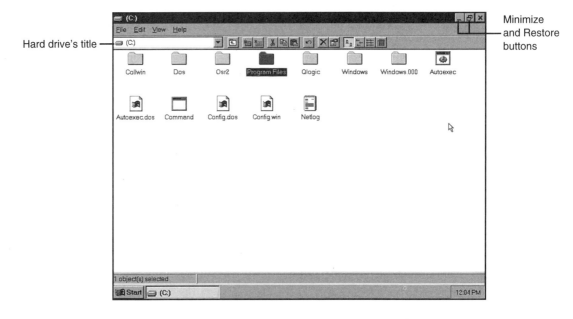

Figure 2.2 The hard drive window enlarges to fill the screen.

Sizing a Window's Borders

At some point, you'll need a window to be a particular size to suit your needs. For example, you might want to fit two or more windows on-screen at the same time. You can drag the window's frame, or border, to change the size of the window. A window's border appears only on a restored window, not on a maximized or minimized window.

To use the mouse to size a window's borders, follow theses steps:

1. Place the mouse pointer on the portion of the border that you want to resize: left or right side, top or bottom. When the mouse is positioned correctly, it changes shape to a double-headed arrow.

Use the vertical double-headed arrow (on the top or bottom of the window border) to resize the window's height by dragging the frame up or down.

Use the horizontal double-headed arrow (on the left or right window border) to resize the window's width by dragging the frame left or right.

Use the diagonal double-headed arrow (on any of the four corners of the window border) to resize the window's height and width proportionally by dragging the corner diagonally.

2. Click and drag the border toward the center of the window to reduce the size of the window, or away from the center to enlarge the window.

3. When the border reaches the desired size, release the mouse button.

Using Scroll Bars

Scroll bars appear along the bottom or the right edge of a window when the window contains more text, graphics, or icons than it can display.

Using scroll bars, you can move up, down, left, or right in a window. Figure 2.3 shows an example. Because all of the hard drive window's contents are not fully visible in the window, the scroll bars are present on the right side and the bottom of the window.

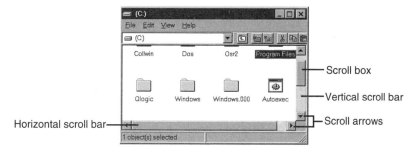

Figure 2.3 Use scroll bars to move within the window.

What Is a Scroll Bar? A scroll bar is a bar that contains three items: two scroll arrows and a scroll box. You use the scroll arrows and the scroll box to move around in the window, scrolling a line at a time, or even a page at a time.

The following steps teach you how to use the scroll bars to view items not visible in the window:

1. To see an object that is down and to the right of the viewable area of the window, point at the down-arrow located on the bottom of the vertical scroll bar.

2. Click the arrow, and the window's contents move up.

3. Click the scroll arrow on the right side of the horizontal scroll bar, and the window's contents shift to the left.

By its placement within the scroll bar, the scroll box depicts how much of a window is not visible. If you know approximately where something is in a window, you can drag the scroll box to get there quickly. To drag the scroll box and move quickly to a distant area of the window (top or bottom, left or right), use this technique:

1. Point to the scroll box in the scroll bar and press and hold the left mouse button.

2. Drag the scroll box to the new location.

3. Release the mouse button.

On the other hand, sometimes you may need to move slowly through a window (to scan for a particular icon, for example). You can move through the contents of a window one screen at a time by clicking inside the scroll bar on either side of the scroll box.

Empty Windows?   Don't worry if text, graphics, or icons don't appear in a window. Use the scroll bar to bring them into view. Items in any window appear first in the upper-left corner.

CAUTION

Moving a Window

When you start working with multiple windows, moving a window becomes as important as resizing one. For example, you may need to move one or more windows to make room for other work on your desktop, or you may need to move one window to see another window's contents. You can move a window easily with the mouse.

TIP   **Don't Lose the Title Bar!**   Be very careful that you do not move a window so far off the screen that you cannot see the title bar. If you lose the title bar, you may never be able to move the window back into full view.

To move a window, point at the window's title bar, press and hold the left mouse button, and drag the window to its new location.

Viewing a Window's Contents

Windows displays the contents of a window in icon form; for example, the elements in the My Computer window are represented by pictures of a hard drive, floppy drive, and folders. Other windows, such as your hard drive window, display elements as folders and files.

You can display the contents of any window in various ways so you can better see the contents. The default, or standard, view in most windows is by Large Icons (refer to Figure 2.3). Large icons help you quickly identify the contents. You also can view the contents of a window as follows:

- **Small Icons**   Contents are displayed with a small icon next to the file or folder name; small icons represent the application in which a file was created, folder, or executable program.

- **List**   Similar to small icons but the icons are even smaller.

- **Details**   Lists icon, file or folder name, file size, file type, and last date modified. When in Details view, you can click the heading button—Name, Size, Type, or Modified—to automatically sort the contents by that heading. For example, click Name and folders list in alphabetical order followed by file names listed alphabetically.

Figure 2.4 shows four windows, each with a different view of the window's contents: Large Icons, Small Icons, Details, and List.

To change views of the window's contents, choose **View**, and then select **Large Icons**, **Small Icons**, **List**, or **Details**.

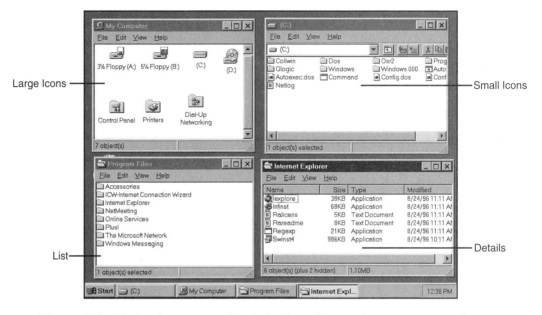

Figure 2.4 Display the contents of a window in a different view so you can easily identify files or folders.

Closing a Window

When you're finished working with a window, you should close it. This often helps speed up Windows, conserves memory, and keeps your desktop from becoming cluttered.

To close a window, you can do any of the following:

- Click the **Control menu** button and choose **Close**.
- Click the **Close** button in the Title bar.
- Press **Alt+F4**.
- Choose **File**, **Close**.
- Double-click the window's **Control**-menu button.

TIP **Quick Close** To quickly close several related open windows, hold the **Shift** key while clicking the **Close** button on the last window you opened.

In this lesson, you learned to open, resize, move, view, close a window, and how to use scroll bars to view more of a window. In the next lesson, you learn to use menus and toolbar buttons.

Using Menus

In this lesson, you learn how to use toolbar buttons, select menus, open menus, choose menu commands, and use menu shortcuts.

Using Toolbar Buttons

Most windows and applications offer a toolbar containing various buttons you can use as shortcuts. Toolbar buttons represent common commands you often use in Windows, such as cut, copy, undo, and so on. The tools that are available to you depend on the window or application you're using. Figure 3.1 shows the toolbar for the My Computer window.

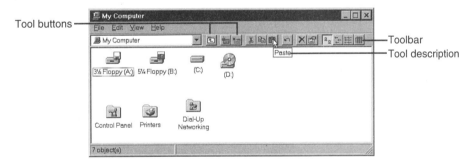

Figure 3.1 Use tool buttons to speed up your work.

 TIP **Handy Helpers** Most Windows applications provide helpful descriptions of the tools on a toolbar. Position the mouse pointer over any tool button and wait a second or two. A small box or bubble containing the button's name or a description of its function appears. When you move the mouse pointer, the description disappears. To activate the tool button, click it with the mouse.

To use a tool button, click it. Just like commands, any of a variety of results may occur. If, for example, you select a folder or file and choose the Copy tool button, a duplicate of the folder or file moves to the Windows Clipboard for pasting to another area later. If you choose the Undo tool button, the last action you performed is reversed.

What Is a Menu?

A *menu* is a list of related commands that you use to perform tasks in Windows and in Windows applications (tasks such as copying or deleting selected items in a window). Menu commands are organized in logical groups. For example, all the commands related to arranging and opening windows are located on the Windows menu. The names of the available menus appear below the Title bar of any window or application that uses menus.

Lost with No Idea of What to Do?   Anytime you're not sure what to do next or how to perform a specific task, click each menu in the application and read each command. Generally, you can find what you want this way; if not, you can always choose the Help menu (as described in Part I, Lesson 5).

CAUTION

In this book, I will use the format menu title, menu command to tell you to choose a command from a pull-down menu. For example, the sentence "choose File, Properties" means to "open the File menu and select the Properties command."

TERM

Pull-Down Menu   A menu that appears to "pull-down" from the menu bar. You access the menu by clicking its name in the menu bar. You then have several options to choose from within the pull-down menu.

Choosing Menu Commands

To choose a menu command with the mouse, follow these steps:

1. Click the menu title in the menu bar. The menu opens to display the available commands.

2. To choose a particular command, simply click it. For example, to see the View commands available for the My Computer window, click the **View** menu in the menu bar. The **View** menu appears (see Figure 3.2).

Click here to
display the menu

Figure 3.2. Click any menu to view its contents.

3. To make the menu disappear, click anywhere outside the menu.

To choose a command on the menu, move the mouse to that command and click. What happens next depends on the menu and the command.

TIP **Want to Use the Keyboard?** If you want to use the keyboard to choose menu commands, press the **Alt** key to activate the menu bar of the active window. Use the left and right arrow keys to highlight the menu you want; then use the up and down arrows to highlight the command you want. Press **Enter** to activate the highlighted command. You could, alternatively, press **Alt**+ the underlined letter to activate a menu; press **Alt+F**, for example, to open the **File** menu and then press the underlined letter in the command you want to activate.

Reading a Menu

Windows menus contain a number of common elements that indicate what will happen when you choose a command, provide a shortcut, or limit your choice of commands. Some menus, for example, may contain commands that are dimmed or grayed out. However, most commands perform some sort of task when you select them.

CAUTION **Unavailable Commands** If a command appears grayed out, you cannot currently use that command. Grayed-out commands are only available for use under certain circumstances. For example, you cannot choose the **Copy** command or the **Delete** command if you have not first selected an object to copy or delete.

Depending on the type of command you select, one of four things will happen:

- An action will take place. For example, choosing **File**, **Delete** erases the selected icon or file.
- A dialog box will appear. Any command followed by an ellipsis (...) displays a dialog box containing related options (see Part I, Lesson 4 for more information).
- A secondary menu will appear. A command followed by an arrow displays a second (cascading) menu offering related commands.
- A feature will be turned on. A check mark or bullet appears to the left of the option on the menu and that option remains active until you either select a different bulleted option in the same menu or deselect the checked option by clicking it a second time.

 TIP **Separator Lines Give You a Clue** Commands on most menus are grouped together and divided by separator lines. When (bulleted) option commands are grouped, you can select only one option in the group. When check mark commands are grouped, you can choose as many or as few options as you want.

Figure 3.3 shows common menu elements: the ellipsis, the check mark, and option bullet, an arrow with cascading menu, and separator lines.

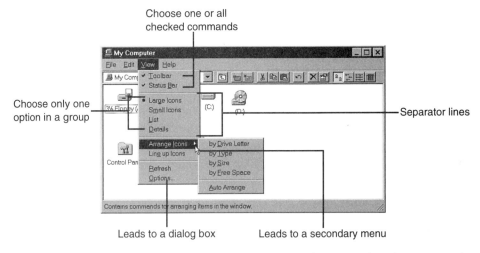

Figure 3.3 Indicators let you know what will happen before you select the command.

To practice using menu commands, follow these steps:

1. In the My Computer window, choose **View**, **Toolbar**. The Toolbar displays, if it was not already displayed.

2. Choose **View**, **Options** (notice the ellipsis after the Option command). A dialog box appears.

3. To cancel the dialog box, choose the **Cancel** button.

Using Shortcut Keys Instead of Menus

Until you become familiar with Windows and your various Windows applications, you'll need to use the menus to view and select commands. However, after you've worked in Windows for a while, you'll probably want to use shortcut keys for commands you use often. Shortcut keys enable you to select commands without using the menus. Shortcut keys generally combine the Alt, Ctrl, or Shift key with a letter key (such as Alt+W). If a shortcut key is available, it is listed on the pull-down menu to the right of the command.

For example, Figure 3.4 shows the Edit menu from the hard-drive window on My Computer. As you can see, the shortcut key for Cut is **Ctrl+X**. You cannot use the shortcut key while the menu is open; you must either choose a command or cancel the menu. You can, however, remember the shortcut key and use it instead of opening the menu the next time you need to cut a file or folder.

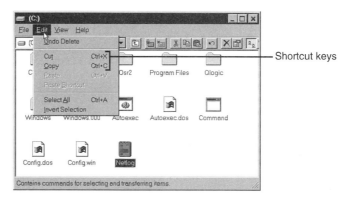

Figure 3.4 Use shortcut keys to save time.

Using Shortcut Menus

Windows supplies a variety of shortcut, or quick, menus that contain common commands you often use. You can display a shortcut menu by right-clicking an object—the desktop, a window, a folder or file, and so on. The commands a shortcut menu displays depends on the item and its location.

To display and use a shortcut menu, point the mouse at the object you want to explore, cut, open, or otherwise manipulate, and right-click the mouse. The **shortcut** menu appears; move the mouse to the command and click again. Cancel a shortcut menu by clicking the mouse anywhere besides on the menu.

Figure 3.5 displays a shortcut menu resulting from right-clicking a hard-drive icon.

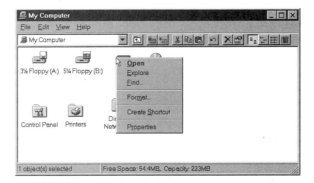

Figure 3.5   Quickly access a command with a right-click.

In this lesson, you learned how to use toolbar buttons, select menus, open menus, choose menu commands, and use menu shortcuts. In the next lesson, you learn to use dialog boxes.

Using Dialog Boxes

In this lesson, you learn how to use the various dialog box components.

What Is a Dialog Box?

Windows and Windows applications use dialog boxes to exchange information with you. As you learned in Part I, Lesson 3, a menu command followed by an ellipsis (…) indicates that a dialog box will appear. A dialog box asks for related information the program needs in order to complete the operation.

Windows also displays dialog boxes to give you information. For example, Windows might display a dialog box to warn you about a problem (as in "File already exists, Overwrite?") or to confirm that an operation should take place (to confirm you want to delete a file, for example).

CAUTION

Box Won't Go Away If a dialog box won't go away and your computer beeps at you when you try to continue your work, don't worry. That beep is Windows' way of telling you that you must always respond to a dialog box before you can continue. You can press **Enter** or choose **OK** to accept the message or changes in the dialog box, or you can press the **Esc** key or choose **Cancel** to cancel the message or changes in the box.

Using the Components of a Dialog Box

Dialog boxes vary in complexity depending on the program, the procedure, and the number of options in the actual box. Some simply ask you to confirm an operation before it is executed, others ask you to choose, for example, a drive, folder, file name, file type, network path, or any of numerous other options.

The following list briefly explains the components of a dialog box. Not all dialog boxes contain all components.

- **Text box**   A text box provides a place to type an entry, such as a file name, path (drive and directory), font, or measurement.

- **List box**   A list box presents a slate of possible options from which you can choose. Scroll bars often accompany a list box so you can view the items on the list. In addition, a text box is sometimes associated with a list box; you can either choose from the list or type the selection yourself.

- **Drop-down list box**   This box is a single-line list box with a drop-down arrow button to the right of it. When you click the arrow, the drop-down list box opens to display a list of choices. You can often scroll through a drop-down list as you do a list box.

- **Option buttons**   Option buttons present a group of related choices from which you can choose only one. Click the option button you want to select and all others become deselected.

- **Check box**   A check box enables you to turn an option on or off. You might find a single check box or a group of related check boxes. A check mark appears in the box next to any option that is active (turned on). In a group of check boxes, you can choose none, one, or any number of the options.

- **Command button**   When selected, a command button carries out the command displayed on the button (Open, Help, Quit, Cancel, or OK, for example). If there is an ellipsis on the button (as in Option...), choosing it will open another dialog box.

- **Tabs**   Tabs represent multiple sections, or pages, of a dialog box. Only one tab is displayed at a time, and each tab contains related options. Choosing a tab changes the options that appear in the dialog box.

Using Text Boxes

You use a text box to enter the information that Windows or a Windows application needs in order to complete a command. This information is usually a file name, folder name, measurement, style or font name, or other information related to the original menu and command. Figure 4.1 shows a text box and list boxes in the Open dialog box (accessed from the Windows WordPad File menu).

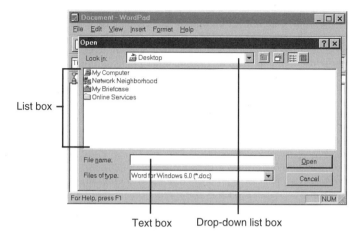

Text box   Drop-down list box

Figure 4.1 Use text boxes and list boxes to specify your preferences.

TIP **Save Time and Trouble** If you want to replace text that's already in a text box, drag your mouse I-beam over the text (to highlight text) and start typing. When you type the first character, the original text is deleted. Often when you first open a dialog box containing a text box, there is already text present and highlighted; if you start typing, you automatically delete the current text.

To activate a text box by using the mouse, position the mouse over the text box (the mouse pointer changes to an I-beam) and click. The I-beam pointer shape indicates that the area you're pointing to will accept text. Look for the I-beam when you want to enter text in a dialog box. Notice that the insertion point (a flashing vertical line) appears in the active text box.

To activate a text box by using the keyboard, press **Alt+selection letter**. (The selection letter is the underlined letter in a menu, command, or option name.) After you have activated a text box and typed text into it, you can use several keys to edit the text. Table 4.1 outlines these keys.

Table 4.1 Editing Keys for Text Boxes and Other Text

Key	Description
Delete	Deletes the character to the right of the insertion point
Backspace	Erases the character to the left of the insertion point

continues

29

Table 4.1   Continued

Key	Description
End	Moves the insertion point to the end of the line
Home	Moves the insertion point to the beginning of the line
Arrow keys	Moves the insertion point one character in the direction of the arrow
Shift+End	Selects the text from the insertion point to the end of the line
Shift+Home	Selects the text from the insertion point to the beginning of the line
Shift+Arrow key	Selects the next character in the direction of the arrow
Ctrl+C	Copies the selected text to the Clipboard
Ctrl+V	Pastes the selected text from the Clipboard

Clipboard   The Clipboard is a tool provided by Windows that holds any cut or copied text for you so you can paste it to another location, document, or application. For more information, see Part I, Lesson 8.

Using List Boxes

You use a list box to select from multiple available options. For example, you use the Look In list box in the Open dialog box to select the drive that contains the file you want to open (refer to Figure 4.1).

To select an item from a list box by using the mouse, click the appropriate list item and click **OK**. You can also select more than one item in many list boxes by holding down the Shift key as you click. The item you select automatically appears in the linked box above the list box.

To select an item from a drop-down list box, open the list box by clicking the down-arrow, and then click the appropriate item.

Using Option Buttons

Option buttons enable you to make a single choice from a group of possible command options. For example, the Print Range options displayed in Figure 4.2 enable you to choose which pages of your document you want to print.

The active option (the All option in Figure 4.2) has a filled-in circle. The figure is from WordPad using the File, Print command. To select an option button, click the circle for the option you want.

Active selection ⟶
Option buttons ⟶

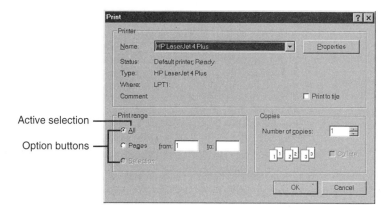

Figure 4.2 You can choose only one option in a group.

Using Check Boxes

For options that you can select (activate) or deselect (deactivate), Windows and Windows applications usually provide check boxes. When a check box is selected, an **X** or a check mark appears in the box, indicating the associated option is active (see Figure 4.3); this figure is from WordPad using the Format, Font command. To select or deselect a check box, click the box.

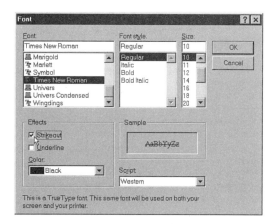

Figure 4.3 A check mark indicates the active, or selected, option.

31

Using Command Buttons

You use command buttons to either accept or reject the changes you've made in a dialog box, to get help, or to access another related dialog box. To select a command button, simply click it.

Figure 4.4 shows the two most common command buttons: **OK** and **Cancel**. Select the **OK** command button to accept the information you have entered or to verify an action and close the dialog box. Select the **Cancel** command button to leave the dialog box without putting into effect the changes you made in the dialog box.

 TIP   **Quick and Easy**   You can press the **Enter** key in a dialog box to quickly accept the changes and close the dialog box. Similarly, you can press the **Esc** key to cancel the changes made to the dialog box and close the box at the same time.

Accidents Happen   If you accidentally select the Cancel command button in a dialog box, don't worry. You can always reenter the changes to the dialog box and continue. However, you need to be more careful when you select OK CAUTION   in a dialog box. The instructions you enter in the dialog box will be executed and changing them back may be a bit harder than canceling changes.

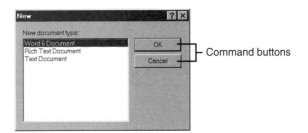

Figure 4.4   Use command buttons to control the dialog box.

 TIP   **Close Means Cancel**   Choosing the Close button in a dialog box is the same thing as canceling it.

Using Property Sheets and Tabs

As noted previously, property sheets are similar to dialog boxes in the components they contain: check boxes, list boxes, text boxes, command buttons, and so on. Figure 4.5 shows the Taskbar Properties sheet.

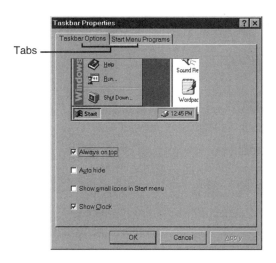

Figure 4.5 Choose a tab that represents the options you want to change.

In a property sheet containing more than one tab, choose options within the sheet and then click the **Apply** button to accept the changes. You can then select the other tabs and make other changes. Once you've chosen the **Apply** button, however, you cannot cancel those changes using the **Cancel** command button; you must go back to the tab and change the options. To select a tab, click the tab with the mouse pointer.

In this lesson, you learned how to use the various dialog box components. In the next lesson, you learn how to use Windows help.

Using Windows 95 Help

In this lesson, you learn how to get help, use the Help feature's shortcut buttons, and use the What's This? feature.

Getting Help in Windows 95

Windows offers several ways to get online help—instant on-screen help for menu commands, procedures, features, and other items. Online help is information that appears in its own window whenever you request it. Windows' Help feature offers three types of help: index, find, and contents features.

The Contents feature displays a list of topics (such as Introducing Windows and Tips and Tricks) as well as a 10-minute tour of using Windows. The Index feature enables you to access specific categories of topics—such as adapters, disk configuration, copying, and so on. Find lets you search for specific words and phrases—such as About, Mem, Printing, and so on.

 TIP **Setting Up Help** The first time you choose Find in Windows Help, Windows runs a Find Setup Wizard that compiles every word from the Help files into a database you will use to find subjects. Follow the directions and the Wizard will guide you.

 TIP **Fast Help** Most dialog boxes, including Help dialog boxes, include a Help button (a question mark in the title bar) that enables you to get help on items within the dialog box. Click the question mark and point the mouse at an area you have a question about. Windows displays a box with a definition or other information relating to your question. When you're finished reading the help, click the mouse to hide the information box.

Using the Contents Feature

You can get help with common procedures using Help's Contents feature. The Contents feature displays the top level groups of information covered in Help, such as How To and Troubleshooting. When you select a major group, a list of related topics appears, as shown in Figure 5.1.

Document represents help topics

Book represents major group

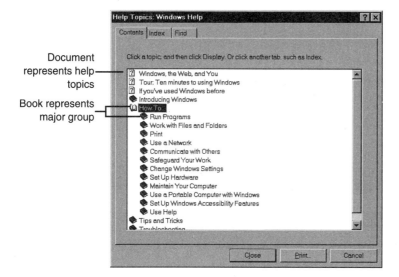

Figure 5.1   Choose from the list of topics for task-specific help.

Follow these steps to use Help's Contents feature:

1. Choose the **Start** button and then choose **Help**. The Help Topics: **Windows Help** dialog box appears; select the **Contents** tab if it is not already selected.

TIP   **Pick a Tab**   The last tab in the Help Topics window that you accessed is the one that appears the next time you open Help.

2. In the Contents list, double-click the book icon in front of the topic you want to view. The book opens and related topics appear either in a list of books or documents.

3. Double-click a document icon to view information about that topic (see Figure 5.2).

Figure 5.2 A Help window tells you what you need to know when you have trouble printing, for example.

4. When you finish with the Help topic, you can choose one of the following buttons:

Close (X) To close the Help window and return to the Desktop.

Help Topics To return to the Contents tab of the Help Topics window and select another topic.

Back To display the previously viewed Help window.

Options To copy, print, or otherwise set preferences for the Help window.

Using the Index Feature

Help's Index feature provides a list of Help topics arranged alphabetically on the Index tab of the Help Topics window. Either you can enter a word for which you are searching, or you can scroll through the list to find a topic. Figure 5.3 shows the Index tab of the Help Topics: Windows Help dialog box.

To use the Help Index, follow these steps:

1. In the Help Topics window, choose the **Index** tab.

2. Click the text box with the number **1** above it and type a topic you want to know about. As you type, Windows moves to the topics beginning with the first letters you enter.

TIP **Browse the List** You can scroll through the index list to see what other topics are available.

Figure 5.3   Use the Index tab to find specific words and phrases in Help.

3. In the list of topics, select the topic you want to view and choose Display, or simply double-click the topic. The Help topic window appears.

4. When you're finished with the Help topic, you can choose another option, or you can close the Help window by pressing **Alt**+**F4**.

Using the Find Feature

You can search for specific words and phrases in a Help topic instead of searching for a Help topic by category. The first time you use the Find feature, however, you have to instruct Windows to create a list that contains the words from your Help files. (You create this list only once.)

The Find feature is especially useful when you cannot find a particular Help topic in Help Contents or on the Index tab's list of topics.

To use the Find feature, follow these steps:

1. In the Help Topics window, choose the **Find** tab. If you have used Find before, skip down to the next set of steps. If you haven't previously set up the Help topics, the **Find Setup Wizard** dialog box appears. Continue with these steps.

2. In the **Wizard** dialog box, choose one of the following:

   Minimize Database Size   Creates a short, limited word list (recommended because it takes less hard disk space).

   Maximize Search Capabilities   Creates a long, detailed word list.

   Customize Search Capabilities   Enables you to create a shorter word list, including only the Help files you want to use. Use this option if you have limited disk space. If you select this option, choose **Next**, and then choose the topics you want to include.

3. Click the **Finish** button to create the word list.

When Windows finishes creating the word list, the **Find** tab contains a text box, a word list, and a topic list as shown in Figure 5.4.

Figure 5.4 Windows now has a word list to search through.

To search for words or a phrase in the **Find** tab, follow these steps:

1. Type the word or phrase you want to find in the first text box at the top of the dialog box. This enters the word for which you want to search, and Windows displays forms of the word in the word list in the middle of the **Find** tab.

2. If you see a word that applies to your topic, select that word to narrow your search. If you do not want to narrow the search, move on to step 3.

TIP **Topic List** Instead of typing something in the text box, you can scroll through the word list and select the word you want from the list. If you want to find words similar to the words in a Help topic, click the **Find Similar** button.

3. Click one or more topics in the topic list, and then click the **Display** button. Windows displays the selected Help topic information in a Windows Help window.

4. When you finish with the Help topic, you can close the Help window or select another option, as described in the next section, "Using Help Windows."

CAUTION **Rebuild the List** If you don't want to use the first list that Windows creates, you're not stuck with it. You can rebuild the list to include more words or to exclude words. Click the **Rebuild** button and choose a word list option to re-create the word list.

Using Help Windows

When you access a windows Help topic window, a toolbar appears at the top of the Help window and always remains visible. This toolbar includes three buttons: Help Topics, Back, and Options. Table 5.1 describes each button in the toolbar of a Windows Help window as well as the Options menu.

Table 5.1 Windows Help Toolbar Buttons and Menu

Button	Description
Help Topics	Opens the Help Topics: Windows Help window containing the Contents, Index, and Find tabs.
Back	Displays the previous Help topic window you viewed during the current session.
Options	Displays a menu containing the following commands: Annotate, Copy, Print Topic, Font, Keep Help on Top, and Use System Colors.

The following list describes the Options menu commands in more detail:

- **Annotate** Enables you to mark any text or topic in a Help window so you can easily find the topic later. A paper clip icon appears beside any annotated text in Help.

- **Copy**   Places a copy of the text in the Help window on the Windows Clipboard for pasting to another document, application, or window.

- **Print Topic**   Sends the text in the Help window to the printer for a hard copy.

- **Font**   Select from Small, Normal, or Large type to view the help text; Normal is the default.

- **Keep Help on Top**   Choose whether to always display the Help window on top of all documents and windows so you can easily follow directions as you work.

- **Use System Colors**   Choose this option to restart the Help feature and change the colors in the Help box.

Using the What's This? Feature

The What's This? feature provides a handy way for you to get more information about dialog box options. You activate this feature by selecting the **?** icon that appears at the right end of the title bar in some (but not all) Windows dialog boxes. Figure 5.5 shows a window with the What's This icon and a description you might see if you clicked that icon.

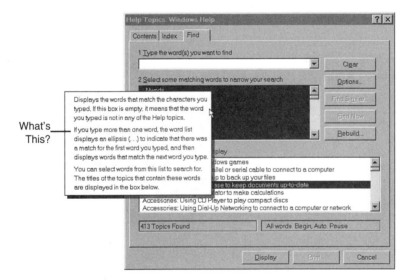

Figure 5.5   Use the What's This? feature to get help on certain dialog box elements.

The following steps tell you how to use the What's This? feature to display a description of most options in a Windows dialog box.

1. Click the **?** icon in the upper-right corner of the Windows dialog box. A large question mark appears next to the mouse pointer.

2. Click any option in the dialog box, and Windows displays a box containing a short description of the item you selected.

3. When you finish reading the Help information, click anywhere on the screen to close the Help box.

 TIP **Quick Description** If you right-click an option in a dialog box, a shortcut menu appears displaying one menu command: **What's This?** Click **What's This?** to view a description of the option. Note, however, that this works only if the dialog box contains a question mark in its title bar.

In this lesson, you learned how to get help, use the Help feature's shortcut buttons, and use the What's This? feature. In the next lesson, you learn to start and exit applications in Windows.

Starting and Exiting Applications in Windows 95

In this lesson, you learn to start and exit a Windows 95 application as well as how to view the common elements of Windows applications' screens.

Opening a Windows Application

Windows provides a Start menu from which you can perform many tasks, including starting Windows programs. To display the Start menu, click the **Start** button on the Windows taskbar. You can open the Help feature from the Start menu; you also can open various applications from the Start menu by choosing the Programs command. The menus you see stemming from the Programs menu will vary depending on your system setup (see Figure 6.1).

To open an application, follow these steps:

1. Choose the **Start** button.
2. Select **Programs** to display the Programs menu.
3. Choose the application you want to open, if it's listed on the Programs menu; alternatively, select the group containing the application you want to open.

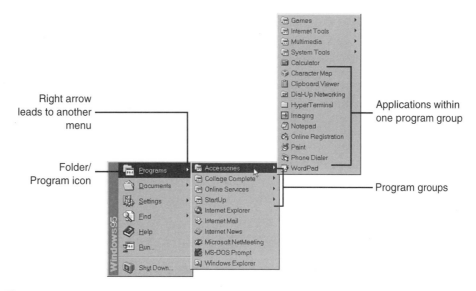

Figure 6.1 Access applications or other programs' menus from the Programs menu.

  Program Groups The Programs menu displays various group names—such as Accessories, Online Services, Startup, and so on—that display a menu of related applications when selected. You can identify a program group by the Folder/Program icon in front of it and the right-arrow following the command. Accessories, Online Services, and StartUp are installed when you install Windows. You may also have program groups for Microsoft Office, Lotus SmartSuite, or other applications you've installed on your computer.

  Open Documents If you have a specific document you want to open and you've recently worked on that document, you can click the **Documents** command on the **Start** menu to display a list; click the document you want to open and the source application opens with the document, ready for you to work on.

Viewing an Application's Screen

Depending on the application you open—whether it's a word processor, database, spreadsheet, or other program—the screen will include elements particular to the tasks and procedures used for that application. For example, the mouse may appear as an I-beam (for typing), an arrow (for pointing), or a cross (for selecting cells in a spreadsheet program); the "document" area may appear as a blank sheet of paper or a table with many cells.

Most applications, however, display the following elements: Title bar, Menu bar, Toolbars, Ruler, Scroll bars, a Document area, and a Status bar. Figure 6.2 shows the screen you see when you open the Windows accessory, WordPad.

 TIP   **There's Always Help**   If you need help with any applications, you can click the Help menu in that application and select a help topic.

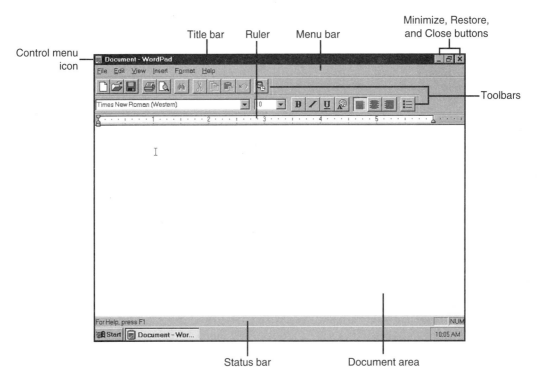

Figure 6.2   Most application screens contain similar elements.

Exiting an Application

You should always exit an application when you're done with it to ensure that your documents are saved before Windows shuts down. You can exit most

Windows applications in one of the following ways:

- Choose the **File**, **Exit** command.
- Click the **Close** button (X).
- Choose **Close** from the **Control** menu.
- Double-click the application's Control menu icon.
- Press **Alt+F4**.

CAUTION

If You Get a Message Before Closing If the application displays a message asking you to save the document before you close the program, choose **Yes** to save, **No** to close the application without saving the changes, or **Cancel** to return to the application. If you choose Yes, the application might display the Save As dialog box in which you assign the document a name and location on your computer's drive.

In this lesson, you learned to start and exit a Windows 95 application as well as how to view the common elements of Windows applications' screens. In the next lesson, you learn to work with multiple windows.

Working with Multiple Windows

In this lesson, you learn how to arrange windows, switch between windows in the same application, and switch between applications.

In Windows, you can have more than one application open at a time, and in each Windows application, you can work with multiple document windows. As you can imagine, opening multiple applications with multiple windows can make your desktop pretty cluttered. That's why it's important that you know how to manipulate and switch between windows. The following sections explain how to do just that.

Arranging Windows on the Desktop

When you have multiple windows open, some windows or parts of windows are inevitably hidden by others, which makes the screen confusing. You can use various commands to arrange your open windows. To access the cascade and tile windows commands, right-click the mouse in any open area of the taskbar and then select the command from the shortcut menu.

Quick! Clean the Desktop You can minimize all windows by choosing one command to quickly clear the desktop of open windows. Right-click the taskbar and choose **Minimize All Windows**. All open windows then become buttons on the taskbar.

Cascading Windows

A good way to get control of a confusing desktop is to open the taskbar's shortcut menu and choose the **Cascade** command. When you choose this command, Windows lays all the open windows on top of each other so that the title bar of each is visible. Figure 7.1 shows a cascaded window arrangement using WordPad, Solitaire, and Notepad. To access any window that's not on the top, simply click its title bar. That window then becomes the active window.

 Active Window   The active window is the one in which you are working. You activate a window by clicking its title bar, or anywhere inside the window, or by clicking its button on the taskbar. The active window's title bar becomes highlighted, and the active window comes to the front.

Other open windows
Active window

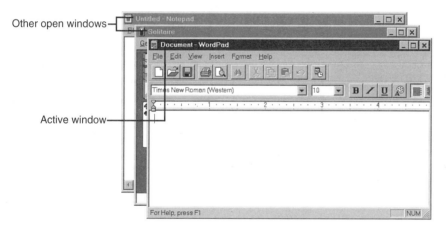

Figure 7.1   With cascaded windows, you can easily access the one you need.

You can still click and drag the title bar of any window to another location on the desktop and you can use the mouse to resize the window borders of any open window, even when it is cascaded with other windows.

Tiling Windows

If you need to see all open windows at the same time, open the taskbar's shortcut menu and select either the **Tile Horizontally** or the **Tile Vertically** command. When you choose to tile, Windows resizes and moves each open window so that they all appear side-by-side (vertically) or one on top of the other (horizontally), as shown in Figure 7.2.

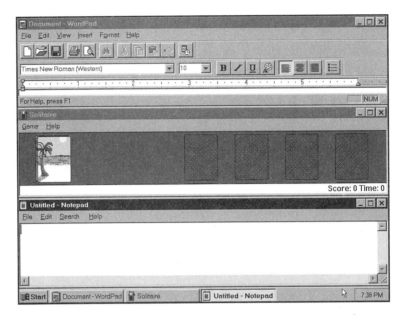

Figure 7.2 Tile windows so you can see a part of each window at the same time.

Moving Between Applications

Windows enables you to have multiple applications open at the same time. If the open application windows are not maximized, you might be able to see all of those open windows overlapped, on-screen. In this case, you can click any window to bring it forward. Often, however, it's easier to work in a single application by maximizing the application's window. Switching between applications then requires a different procedure. You'll most likely use the taskbar to switch from application to application by clicking the minimized application button on the taskbar.

After opening several applications—such as WordPad, Paint, and Solitaire, for example—you can use the taskbar by following these steps:

1. On the taskbar, click the button representing the application you want to bring forward (see Figure 7.3).

2. To switch to another open application, click its button on the taskbar. The open window minimizes back to the taskbar and is replaced by the next application you select.

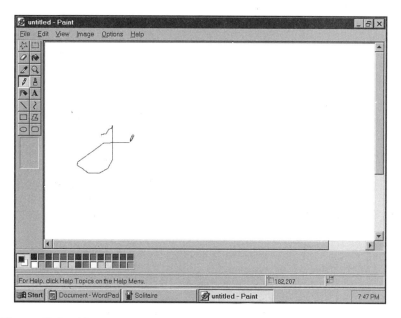

Figure 7.3   All open and minimized application windows appear on the taskbar.

Moving Between Windows in the Same Application

In addition to working in multiple applications in Windows, you also can open multiple windows within an application. Moving to a new window means you are changing the window that is active. If you are using a mouse, you can move to a window by clicking any part of it. When you do, the title bar becomes highlighted, and that particular window comes to the front so you can work in it.

Figure 7.4 shows multiple document windows open in Microsoft Word. You can switch between the windows, arrange windows, and open and close windows within the application, just as you can manipulate windows within the Windows 95 program.

Open multiple document windows using the **File**, **Open** command. By default, each window is maximized within the document area. To switch between open, maximized windows, click the Window menu and select the document from the list at the bottom of the menu. Alternatively, you can press **Ctrl** ⏐ **F6** to cycle through open windows.

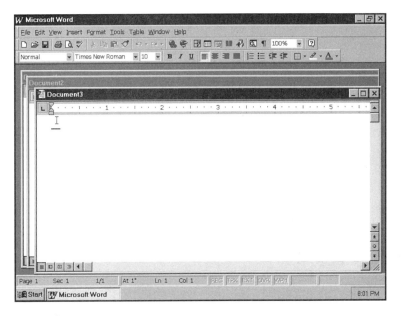

Figure 7.4   Three document windows are open within the program.

To view multiple document windows on-screen, follow these steps:

1. Restore the document window by clicking the document's **Restore** button. The open document windows cascade in the document area. The Restore button replaces the Maximize button.

2. To activate an open document window, click in the window's title bar or press **Ctrl+F6**.

3. To tile the windows, choose **Window, Arrange All**. Windows reduces each open document window and tiles them (horizontally) in the document area.

TIP   **They're All Just Windows**   You can use the window frames to resize each window. Likewise, you can minimize, maximize, open, and close the windows as you would any window. (See Part I, Lesson 2 for instructions.)

In this lesson, you learned how to arrange windows, switch between windows in the same application, and switch between applications. In the next lesson, you learn to copy and move information between windows.

Copying and Moving Information Between Windows

In this lesson, you learn about the Clipboard and how to copy and move information between windows.

What Is the Clipboard?

One of the handiest features of the Windows environment is its capability to copy or move information (text, graphics, and files) from one location to another. This feature enables you to share information between document windows, applications, and other computers on your network.

When you cut or copy data from an application, it's placed on the Clipboard and it remains there until you cut or copy again. You can paste the data from the Clipboard to a document or application. Note, however, that you don't have to open the Clipboard to use it—and 99 percent of the time, you won't. You'll just cut or copy your data, and then paste it to a new location.

Copy, Cut, and Paste When you copy information, the application copies it to the Clipboard without disturbing the original. When you cut information, the application removes it from its original location and places it on the Clipboard. When you paste information, the application inserts the information that's on the Clipboard in the location you specify. (The copy on the Clipboard remains intact, so you can paste it again and again, if necessary.)

You can view the information on the Clipboard viewer, if you want, by choosing **Start**, **Programs**, **Accessories**, and **Clipboard Viewer** (see Figure 8.1). In the Viewer, you can save the contents to a file name, add or remove text, edit the text, and open saved Clipboard files.

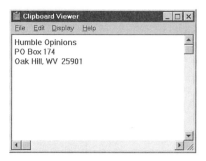

Figure 8.1 View and even save the contents of the Clipboard, if you want.

TIP **Without a Trace** When you turn off your computer or exit Windows, the contents of the Clipboard disappear. Be sure you save the contents of the Clipboard if you want to use the text or figures later.

Selecting Text for Copying or Moving

Before you can copy or cut text, you must identify the text by selecting it. Selected text appears in reverse video (highlighted). Figure 8.2 shows selected text in a WordPad document.

To select text, follow these steps:

1. Position the mouse pointer just before the first character you want to select.
2. Press and hold the left mouse button, and drag the mouse pointer to the last character you want selected.
3. Release the mouse button, and the selected text is highlighted.

TIP **Quick One-Word Selection** Quickly select one word of text by double-clicking the word.

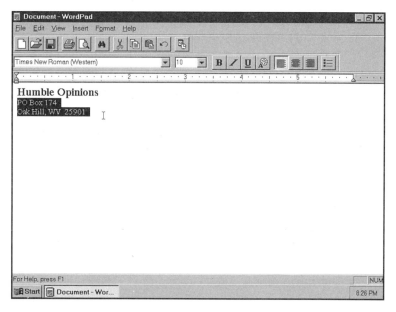

Figure 8.2 You must first select text before you can cut or copy it.

CAUTION

Where's My Selected Text? If you press an alphanumeric key (a letter, number, or any other character) while text is highlighted, Windows deletes the selected text and replaces it with the character you typed. Choose **Edit**, **Undo** or press **Ctrl+Z** (in most applications) to reverse the action.

Selecting Graphics

The procedure for selecting graphics depends on the Windows application you are using. In a word processing program, such as WordPad or Microsoft Word, you select a graphic by clicking the object. In a program like Paint, however, there are special tools for selecting shapes. Because the procedure may vary, you should refer to the instructions for each application. No matter how you select a graphic, however, when it's selected, small "handles" appear on the corners and sides of the graphic frame to indicate it is ready to copy or move.

Copying Information Between Windows

After you select text or graphics, the procedures for copying and pasting are the same in all Windows applications. To copy and paste information between windows of the same application, as well as between windows of different applications, follow these steps:

1. Select the text or graphic to copy.

2. Click the **Copy** button on the toolbar, or choose **Edit, Copy**. You can, alternatively, use a keyboard shortcut, such as **Ctrl+C** for copy. A copy of the selected material is placed on the Clipboard; the original selection remains in place.

3. Click to position the insertion point where you want to insert the selection. You can switch between document windows or between applications as learned in Part I, Lesson 7.

4. Click the **Paste** button, choose **Edit, Paste**, or press **Ctrl+V**. Windows copies the selection from the Clipboard to the insertion point.

 TIP   Multiple Copies   Because the selected item remains on the Clipboard until you copy or cut again, you can paste information from the Clipboard multiple times.

Moving Information Between Windows

After you select text or graphics, the procedures for cutting and pasting are also the same in all Windows applications. To cut and paste information between windows of the same application or windows of different applications, follow these steps:

1. Select the text or graphic.

2. Click the **Cut** button, choose **Edit, Cut**, or press **Ctrl+X**. Windows removes the selection from its original location and places it on the Clipboard.

3. Click to position the insertion point to where you want to insert the selection.

4. Click the **Paste** button, choose **Edit, Paste**, or press **Ctrl+V**. Windows copies the selection from the Clipboard to your document. (A copy remains on the Clipboard until you cut or copy something else.)

In this lesson, you learned about the Clipboard and how to copy and move information between windows. In the next lesson, you learn to view drives, folders, and files in the Windows Explorer.

Viewing Drives, Folders, and Files with the Windows Explorer

In this lesson, you learn how to use the Windows Explorer to view contents of a hard disk drive, floppy disk, or CD-ROM.

Starting the Windows Explorer

You use the Explorer to organize, rename, copy, move, delete, and otherwise manage your folders (directories) and files. Start the Explorer from the Start menu. Click the **Start** button and choose **Programs**, **Windows Explorer**. The Windows Explorer window opens.

Using the Explorer Window

At the top of the Explorer window, Windows gives the name of the drive whose contents you are currently viewing. In addition, the Explorer window is split into two panes. By default, the left pane displays your hard disk and the folders it contains. The right pane displays a list of the files stored in the selected folder. Figure 9.1 shows the Explorer window.

Table 9.1 describes the elements in the Explorer window. If you do not see a toolbar or status bar on your screen, open the **View** menu and select the item you want to display.

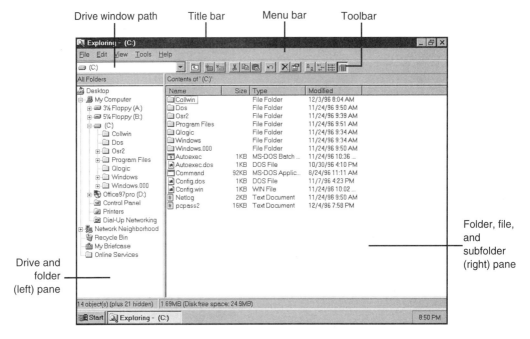

Figure 9.1   Use the Explorer to manage your drives.

Table 9.1   Explorer Window Elements

Element	Description
Title bar	Contains the window name (Exploring), the drive name, a Control menu, and the Minimize, Maximize, and Close buttons for the Explorer.
Menu bar	Displays menus related to disk, folder, file, and other operations.
Drive window path	Displays the current drive, and/or path, in the toolbar.
Drive and folder pane	Displays drives, folders, and subfolders as well as the recycle bin and the briefcase.
Folder, file, and subfolder pane	Displays the contents of the selected drive or folder in the left pane.
Toolbar	Provides various tools for navigating the Explorer.
Status bar	Displays such statistics as freespace on drive, number of files in a folder, and so on.

TIP   **Subfolders**   A subfolder is a folder within another folder—the same thing as a subdirectory.

TIP   **Folder and File Icons**   Each folder has a folder icon beside it, and each file has an icon that represents its file type (such as a sheet of paper for a document, window box for an executable program, and so on).

The Explorer also offers several tool buttons you can use to speed your work. Tool buttons represent common menu commands. Table 9.2 shows the tool buttons on the Explorer's toolbar and explains their functions.

Table 9.2   Toolbar Buttons

Tool	Name	Description
🖴 (C) ▾	Go to a Different Folder	Click to view a drop-down box of available drives and folders
⬆	Up One Level	Click to go to the parent folder of the current folder; for example, if you're in the My Documents folder, clicking this icon takes you to drive C
🖧	Map Network Drive	Use this tool to create a mapped drive to a network drive for quick access of a server's resources
🖧	Disconnect Net Drive	Click to disconnect from the network
✂	Cut	Cut the selected file or folder to the Clipboard
📋	Copy	Copy the selected file or folder to the Clipboard
📋	Paste	Paste the contents on the Clipboard to the current location
↩	Undo	Reverse the last action you performed; some actions cannot be undone
✕	Delete	Erases the selected file or folder
🖹	Properties	Displays the properties of the selected file or folder, including rights, name, size, date created, and so on

continues

Table 9.2   Continued

Tool	Name	Description
	Large Icons	Click to change the view of your files and folders to large icons with the names of the file or folder below the icon
	Small Icons	Click to change the view to small icons with the name of the file or folder
	List	Click to change the view to a list of the names of the files and folders
	Details	Click to change the view to a list of the file or folder name, the creation or modification date, size, and file type

To display drives, folders, and files, follow these steps:

1. In the left pane, scroll the list of drives and folders by using the scroll bar. The list displays floppy drives, hard drives, CD drives, the Network Neighborhood, and so on. Select the drive you want to view by clicking it.

2. In the left pane, double-click any folder to display its additional folders in the folder pane.

3. In the right pane, click a folder once to display its contents (files and folders).

Viewing Folders

Collapsed folders are represented by a plus sign (+) in the folders pane of the Explorer window; expanded folders are represented by a minus sign. Figure 9.2 shows both collapsed and expanded folders.

To expand a folder so you can view its contents, click the plus sign preceding the folder in the folders pane of the Explorer window. To collapse a folder to hide its contents, click the minus sign preceding the folder.

TIP   **Open Folders**   To open any folder: In the left pane, click the folder once; in the right pane, double-click the folder.

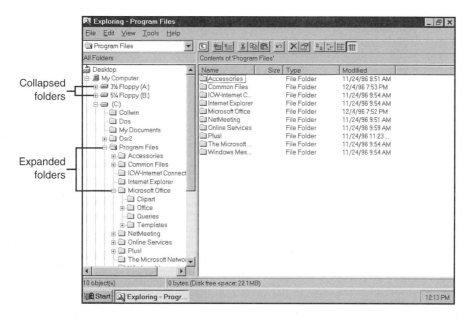

Figure 9.2   Expand a folder to see its contents; collapse it to hide its contents.

Viewing and Sorting Files

In addition to the file name, you can view various details about the files in a folder: the date created, file type, and file size.

To view file details, simply choose **View**, **Details**. Windows displays the file name, type, size, and creation or modification date (see Figure 9.3).

You also can use the heading buttons in the files pane to sort the files. To sort files, click one of the heading buttons shown in Figure 9.3 and described here:

Sort files by name   Alphabetically sorts files by name, A to Z on the first click and Z to A on the second click.

Sort files by type   Alphabetically sorts files by the file type (application, font, help, document, and so on), A to Z on the first click and Z to A on the second click. Notice that folders come first in the A to Z sort.

Sort files by size   Sorts files by size, largest to smallest on the first click and smallest to largest on the second click.

Sort files by date   Sorts files by date, earliest files created first on the first click and most recently created or modified files first on the second click.

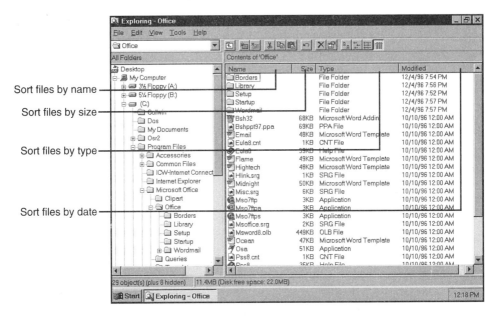

Sort files by name ──

Sort files by size ──

Sort files by type ──

Sort files by date ──

Figure 9.3 You might need to see the file details to determine files you want to copy, delete, or otherwise manipulate.

 TIP **Another Sort Method** You can choose the **View menu**, **Arrange Icons** command and choose to sort the files by **Name**, **Type**, **Size**, or **Date** by using the secondary menu.

Closing the Explorer

To close the Windows Explorer, choose **File**, **Close**, or click the **Close** button.

In this lesson, you learned how to use the Windows Explorer to view a disk's contents. In the next lesson, you learn to create and delete files and folders.

Creating and Deleting Files and Folders

In this lesson, you learn how to create folders, how to delete files and folders, and how to use the Recycle Bin.

Creating a Folder

Many folders are created automatically when you install a program. For example, when you install Word for Windows, the installation program creates a folder on your hard disk and places the Word for Windows files in that folder. You can use an application's designated document folder, or you can create folders yourself. For example, you might create a folder to hold any of the following groups of files:

- Subject-related files (such as all sales documents, whether they are word processing, accounting, or spreadsheet files, for example).

- Application-related files (such as all word processing files or, more specifically, all letters to customers).

- The files for an application that does not create its own folder during installation.

- All files you'll share with other network users.

To create a folder using the Explorer, follow these steps:

1. From the Desktop, choose **Start**, **Programs**, and **Windows Explorer**. The Explorer window opens.

2. In the Drive Window Path on the toolbar, click the drop-down arrow. From the drop-down list, select the drive on which you want to create the new folder.

3. In the left pane, select the folder in which you want the new folder located. This is often called the parent, or root, folder of your new folder.

 Root, Parent Folders   The root folder is the same as the drive. For example, C is the root folder of the hard disk. The root folder is also the parent of all folders on that drive, and any folder is the parent to all folders it contains.

4. Choose **File**, **New**, **Folder**, and a new folder appears in the right pane, with the name New Folder.

5. Type a name for the new folder in the highlighted text box (see Figure 10.1).

6. Press **Enter** to complete the process.

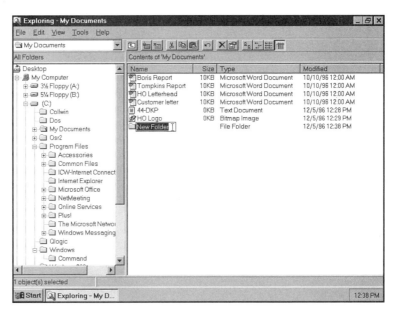

Figure 10.1   Add a folder to help organize your work.

TIP **Rename a Folder** To rename a folder, select the folder in the Explorer and choose **File**, **Rename**. The folder's name appears highlighted in a box; type the new name and press **Enter** to finish. You can, alternatively, click the folder name after selecting it to display the mouse I-beam, the highlighted word, and the box used for renaming; however, be careful not to double-click the folder's name or you'll open the folder instead of renaming it.

Deleting a File or Folder

You should delete a file or folder when you no longer need it, when your disk is getting full, or if you created the file or folder by mistake. Before you delete anything, however, it is a good idea to make a backup copy in case you discover a need for it later; copy to a floppy disk if you're trying to save disk space. See Part I, Lesson 11 for directions on how to copy files and folders.

In Windows, deleted items are moved to an area called the Recycle Bin and remain there until you empty the bin. Deleting items to the Recycle Bin does not provide any extra disk space. Those items remain on the disk until you empty the Recycle Bin. We'll talk more about the Recycle bin later in this lesson.

To delete a file or folder, follow these steps:

1. In the Explorer, select the file or folder you want to delete by clicking it. You can select multiple files or folders by holding the **Ctrl** key as you click the file you want to select.

TIP **Selecting More than One** For more about selecting files and folders, see Part I, Lesson 11.

Oops, Wrong Folder If you delete a parent folder, Windows also deletes everything in that folder as well. Be careful to delete only those files and folders you no longer need.

CAUTION

2. Choose **File**, **Delete** or press the **Delete** key. The Delete dialog box appears, asking you to confirm that you want to delete the specified item(s) (see Figure 10.2).

63

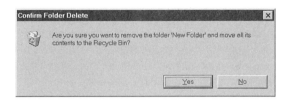

Figure 10.2 Delete unwanted files or folders.

> **3.** Select **Yes**, and Windows moves the item to the Recycle Bin.

Using the Recycle Bin

The Windows Recycle Bin holds deleted files and folders until you empty the bin or recover the files. You can open the Recycle Bin at any time to view the items in it.

Emptying the Bin

You can empty the Recycle Bin from Explorer or from the Desktop. You should check the Bin's contents before you empty it to be sure you're not deleting something you really want. You can view the Bin from the Explorer or from the Desktop.

To view and then empty the Recycle Bin, follow these steps:

> **1.** In the Explorer, scroll to the bottom of the left pane until you see the Recycle Bin.
>
> **2.** Click the Recycle Bin to display its contents in the right pane (see Figure 10.3).
>
> **3.** To empty the Bin, choose **R**. Windows displays a Confirmation dialog box.
>
> **4.** Choose **Yes** to delete the files.

 TIP **Empty the Bin from the Desktop** You can empty the Recycle Bin from the desktop at any time by right-clicking the Bin icon and choosing Empty Recycle Bin from the quick menu.

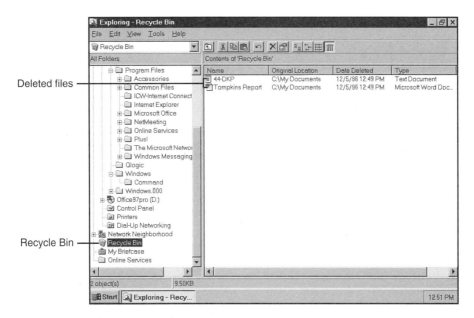

Deleted files

Recycle Bin

Figure 10.3 You can see which items will be deleted.

CAUTION

Permanently Deleted Files Once you empty the Recycle Bin, those files and folders are deleted and cannot be retrieved.

Recovering Deleted Files from the Bin

You can move files and folders to the Recycle Bin and then change your mind before deleting them completely from disk. When you recover a file or folder from the Bin, you're simply moving it back to its original drive and folder.

To recover files in the Recycle Bin, follow these steps:

1. In the Explorer, open the Recycle Bin so you can view the files and folders it contains.

2. Select any files or folders you want to recover and choose **File**, **Restore**. Windows moves the selected files and folders back to their original place on your hard drive.

In this lesson, you learned how to create folders, how to delete files and folders, and how to use the Recycle Bin. In the next lesson, you learn to move, copy, and rename files and folders.

Selecting, Moving, and Copying Files and Folders

In this lesson, you learn how to select multiple files and folders and how to copy and move them.

Selecting Multiple Files or Folders

To speed up operations, you can select multiple files or folders and then perform an action—such as copying, moving, deleting, or printing—on the entire group. For example, you may want to select several files to copy to a disk. Copying them all at once is much faster than copying each file individually. You select multiple files and folders in one of two ways, depending on whether they are contiguous or noncontiguous in the Explorer window.

 Contiguous   When the files that you want to select are listed next to each other in the Explorer without any files that you don't want between them, they are contiguous.

Selecting Multiple Contiguous Files or Folders

To select contiguous files or folders with the mouse, follow these steps:

1. In the Explorer, click the first file or folder you want to select, and it becomes highlighted.

CAUTION

It's Not Working! You cannot select multiple folders in the left pane; you can select multiple folders listed only in the right pane.

2. Hold down the **Shift** key and click the last file or folder that you want to select. Windows highlights all the items between (and including) the first and last selections. Figure 11.1 shows a selection of contiguous files.

3. To deselect all selected items with the mouse, click any file or folder. To deselect only one or two items, continue to hold down the **Shift** key, and then click the selected items you want to deselect.

Selected folders ⟶

Selected files ⟶

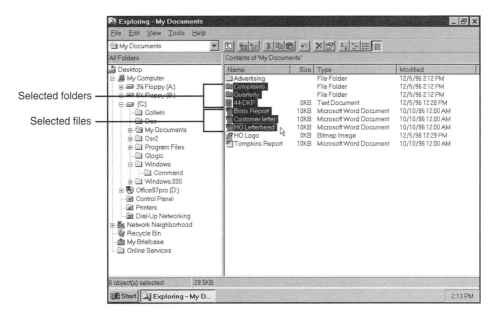

Figure 11.1 Select two or more contiguous files or folders by holding the Shift key as you click the files with the mouse.

Selecting Noncontiguous Files or Folders

Often, the files or folders you want to select are noncontiguous; that is, they are separated by several files you do not want to select. To select noncontiguous files or folders, you use the **Ctrl** key.

To select noncontiguous files or folders, follow these steps:

1. Select the first file or folder.

2. Hold down the **Ctrl** key and click the subsequent files or folders you want to select. Each item you select becomes highlighted and remains highlighted unless and until you deselect the items. Release the **Ctrl** key when you've completed your selection. Figure 11.2 shows a selections of multiple noncontiguous files and folders.

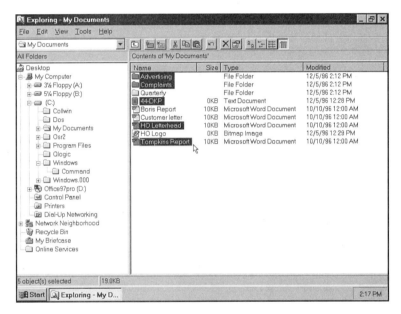

Figure 11.2 Select files that are not in sequence by holding down the **Ctrl** key when you click.

3. To deselect all selected items with the mouse, click any folder or file. To deselect only one or two items, continue to hold down the **Ctrl** key, and then click the selected items to deselect them.

TIP   **Selecting All Files**   If you want to select all of the files in the right pane of the Explorer, press **Ctrl+A** or choose **Edit**, **Select All**.

Moving or Copying Files or Folders

The time will come when you will want to rearrange files and folders on your system. For example, you might need to move a file from a folder of word processing files to a folder of files related to a particular subject. Or, you might want to copy files you've created into a folder to which certain other users have access. Windows provides you with two methods for doing this: menu commands and drag-and-drop.

Before you begin moving or copying files, take these warnings into consideration:

- When you copy or move a folder, you also copy or move the files and other folders within the folder.
- If you move application files to another folder, you may have trouble starting the application through the Start, Programs menu. Your best bet is to leave application files in their original locations.

Using Drag-and-Drop

The easiest way to move or copy files and folders to a new location in the Explorer is to use drag-and-drop. To drag and drop, you select the items you want from your source folder, hold down the mouse button, drag the mouse to the destination folder, and release the mouse button.

Specifically, follow these steps to use the drag-and-drop method of copying or moving files:

1. In the right pane, display the folder or file you want to move or copy.
2. Select the files you want to copy or move.
3. To copy the files, point to any one of the selected files, press and hold down the **Ctrl** key, press the mouse button, and drag the files to the folder or drive icon where you want the copy placed.

   To move the files, point to any of the selected files, press the mouse button, and then drag the files to the folder or drive icon to which you want to move the files.

CAUTION

Confirm File Replace If you attempt to copy or move a file or folder to a location in which a file or folder with the same name exists, Windows lets you know with a message that displays the selected file's and the original file's size and creation or modification date. Click **Yes** to replace the file, or **No** to stop the process.

Using the Menus

You can use the Copy and Cut commands on the Edit menu to move or copy files and folders. To use the menus to copy or move selected files or folders, follow these steps:

1. Select the files and/or folders you want to move or copy.

2. Open the **Edit** menu and select **Cut** or **Copy**. The selected items are either moved or copied to the Clipboard.

TIP **Quick Cut, Copy, Paste** As an alternative to using the Edit menu to cut, copy, and/or paste, you can click the **Cut**, **Copy**, or **Paste** tool button on the Explorer toolbar to accomplish the same task.

3. In the left pane of the Explorer, select the drive or folder in which you want to move or copy the selected files and/or folders.

4. Choose the **Edit** menu and the **Paste** command. Windows moves or copies the selected files or folders to the new location.

In this lesson, you learned how to select multiple files and folders and how to copy and move them. In the next lesson, you learn to find files and folders in Windows 95.

Renaming and Finding Files and Folders

In this lesson, you learn how to rename files and folders and how to find files and folders.

Renaming Files or Folders

You might rename a file or folder to reorganize or update your work; you might rename files to convert from the old eight-character names to longer, more descriptive ones. The more files and folders you create and use, the more likely it is that you will need to rename them at some point.

To rename a file or folder, follow these steps:

1. In the Explorer, select the file or folder you want to rename.
2. Choose **File**, **Rename**. The current name becomes highlighted and appears in a box with the mouse I-beam, as shown in Figure 12.1.
3. Enter the new name for the file or folder.
4. Press **Enter**. The new name appears beside the file or folder's icon.

CAUTION

But It Worked Yesterday!   Never rename program files (most have extensions EXE, COM, PIF, or BAT). Many applications will not work if their files have been renamed. Also, don't rename any files with the INI or DLL extensions; these are configuration files that Windows needs to properly operate.

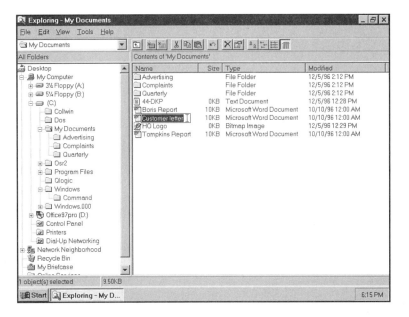

Figure 12.1   You can change the name of a file or folder quickly and easily.

Searching for a File

Using the Windows Find program (**Start** menu, **Find**, **Files and Folders**) works similarly to the Explorer's Find program. You can find a specific file, files with specific extensions, files for which you have a partial name, and more.

To search for a file, follow these steps:

1. From the Windows Explorer, choose **Tools**, **Find**, **Files** or **Folders**. The find dialog box appears with the Name & Location tab open (see Figure 12.2).

2. In the **Named** text box, type the name of the file or folder you want to find (use wild cards in place of unknown characters, if you want).

Wild Card   A character that fills in for other character(s) in a file name. When you're not sure of the file name you want to find or you're searching for more than one file with a similar extension of naming pattern, you can use the asterisk wild card (*) to replace multiple characters in the actual name, such as *.DOC (find all documents ending with the DOC extension). You can also use the question mark wild card (?) to replace one character in the file name, such as proj04??.doc. This search pattern will find files named proj04aa.doc, proj04ab.doc, or even proj0431.doc, for example.

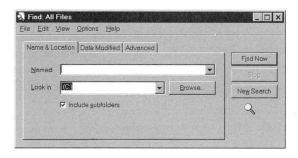

Figure 12.2 Tell Windows what to search for and where to begin the search.

3. In the **Look In** text box, enter the drive and/or folders you want to search. If you enter **C:**, for example, Windows searches all of drive C. You can, alternatively, choose the **Browse** button to select the drive or folder you want to search.

TIP **Browse?** When you click the Browse button, a dialog box appears in which you can choose the drive and folder you want to use. Double-click any drive or folder to open it and view its contents. Select the drive and folder you want to search and close the dialog box. The selected drive and folder appear in the Look In text box.

4. Click the Include subfolders option to put a check mark in it. This tells Windows to search all subfolders within the folders you've specified for the search.

5. Choose **Find Now**, and Windows searches for the files that meet your criteria. When it finishes the search, you see the results at the bottom of the Find dialog box. Figure 12.3 shows the results of the search C:*.doc. Notice that the title bar of the Find dialog box includes search criteria.

6. When you finish checking out the results, close the Find dialog box.

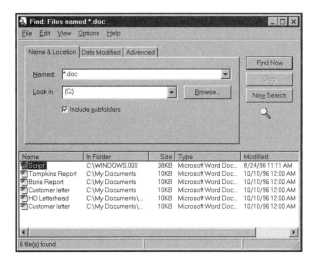

Figure 12.3 The results of the search for DOC files.

In this lesson, you learned how to rename files and folders and how to find files and folders. In the next lesson, you learn to install a printer and print.

Printing with Windows 95

In this lesson, you learn to print from an application, control the print job, and connect to a network printer.

Installing a Printer

You can easily install a printer to work with all of your Windows applications. Windows includes many *drivers* for various manufacturers' computers. To install a printer, you'll need your Windows CD-ROM or a disk containing printer drivers that came with your printer.

CAUTION

Printer Drivers Printer drivers are software programs you install to your computer. The drivers make the printer work with Windows 95 and your Windows applications.

To install a printer, follow these steps:

1. Choose the **Start** button, and then click **Settings**, **Printers**. The Printers window appears.

2. Double-click the **Add Printer** icon to display the Add Printer Wizard dialog box. Click **Next** to begin installing a new printer.

3. Choose whether to install a local printer or a network printer and then choose the **Next** button.

TERM

Local or Network Printer? A local printer is one connected directly to your computer; a network printer is one that may be connected to another computer on the network and is used by several workstations in addition to yours.

4. In the third Add Printer Wizard dialog box, choose the Manufacturer of your printer, such as Hewlett-Packard, and then the model of the printer, such as LaserJet 4, as shown in Figure 13.1.

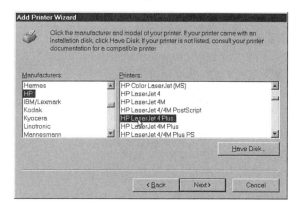

Figure 13.1 Choose the printer you want to install.

5. If you have a disk from the printer's manufacturer that contains Windows 95 drivers, insert the disk in the disk drive and click the **Have Disk** button; alternatively, insert your Windows 95 Setup CD-ROM and click the **Next** button.

6. Follow the directions on-screen. When Windows finishes setting up the printer, it returns to the Printers window.

Printing from an Application

The steps for printing from any Windows application are very similar. The biggest difference is that some dialog box options change from program to program. Most programs offer a Print icon on the toolbar that you can click to print one copy of the job; although in some programs, the print icon displays the Print dialog box. To print from a Windows application, follow these steps:

1. Choose **File**, **Print**, and the Print dialog box appears. Figure 13.2 shows the Print dialog box in the WordPad accessory program.

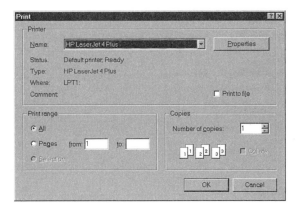

Figure 13.2 Use the Print dialog box to specify printing options.

2. Set any of the printing options described in the following list. Some applications will offer more specialized options; see a particular application's Help feature if you have questions:

- **Print Range** Specify the pages you want to print. For example, you can print all pages, the current page, a range of pages, or a selection of text (which you select before opening the Print dialog box).

- **Copies** Enter the number of copies to print. Often, you can choose a print order (front to back, for example) and whether to collate the copies or not.

- **Print to File** Prints the document into a file, which you can use to print your document from a computer that doesn't have the program you used to create it. (You then print the file by typing print file name at the DOS prompt of any computer. All document formatting is preserved.)

- **Printer** If you have several printers available, you can choose the printer to which you want to send the job.

- **Properties or Setup** Usually leads to a dialog box in which you can set paper size, orientation, paper tray, graphics resolution, and other options specific to your printer.

- **Collate Copies** Assembles the copies of a multiple-page document in order from 1, to 2, to 3, and so on.

3. When you're ready to print, choose **OK**. Windows sends the job to the printer.

CAUTION

Printing Errors   If your job doesn't print and you receive an error message from Windows, check to see that the printer is on and there is paper in it. Next, jiggle the cable at the printer's end and again at the computer's end, to make sure the cable is not loose. Try printing again.

TERM

Print Job   A print job is a document you're printing. Each time you choose **OK** in the Print dialog box, you're sending a print job to the printer (whether that document contains one page or forty).

Working with the Print Folder

When you print a document, the printer usually begins processing the job immediately. But what if the printer is working on another job that you (or someone else, if you're working on a network printer) sent? When that happens, there is a print queue that holds the job until the printer is ready for it.

TERM

Print Queue   A holding area for jobs waiting to be printed. If you were to open the contents of the queue, the jobs would appear in the order they were sent to the printer.

You can check the status of a print job you've sent by looking at the Print queue, found in the Printer's folder. Figure 13.3 shows a document in the Print queue. As you can see, the print queue window displays the information about the job.

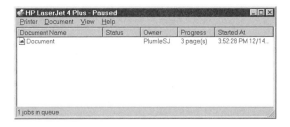

Figure 13.3   Use the Print queue to track your print jobs.

To display the Print queue, follow these steps:

1. From the Desktop, choose the **Start** button and then choose **Settings**, and **Printers**.

2. In the Printers folder, double-click the printer icon to which you are printing.

Empty Print Queue?   If no jobs appear in the Print queue, the job has already been sent to the printer.

CAUTION

Controlling the Print Job

It's hard to control just one or two jobs because they usually go to the printer too quickly. However, if there are several jobs in the print queue, you can control them. For example, you can pause and resume print jobs and you can delete a job before it prints.

Additionally, you can control the printer or just one particular document. You can, for example, cancel one document or all documents in the queue.

Pausing and Resuming the Queue

You may want to pause the queue and then resume printing later if, for example, the paper in the printer is misaligned or the printer is using the wrong color paper. Pausing the print queue gives you time to correct the problem. To pause the print queue, choose **Printer**, **Pause Printing**. To resume printing, choose **Printer**, **Pause Printing** a second time to remove the check mark beside the command.

Printer Stalled   If your printer stalls while it's processing your print job, Windows displays the word "stalled" in the printer status line in the queue. Choose Printer, Pause Printing to remove the check mark from the command and start printing again. If the printer stalls again, see if there's a problem with the printer (it might be offline or out of paper, for example).

CAUTION

79

Deleting a Print Job

Sometimes you'll send a document to the printer and then change your mind.
For example, you may think of additional text to add to a document or realize
you forgot to spell check your work. In such a case, deleting the print job is easy,
if you can catch it in time. Follow these steps:

1. Open the Print queue by choosing **Start**, **Settings**, and **Printers**; double-
   click the printer icon.
2. Select the job you want to delete.
3. Choose **Document**, **Cancel**.

 TIP   Clear the Queue!   To remove all files from the print queue, choose **Purge
Print Jobs**.

In this lesson, you learned to print from an application, control the print job, and
connect to a network printer. In the next lesson, you learn to adjust hardware
settings.

Controlling Hardware Settings

In this lesson, you learn how to change the date and time setting on your computer, modify mouse settings, and configure your modem.

Altering the Date and Time

You use the Control Panel to set your computer's system date and time, which is used to time-stamp files as you create and modify them. In addition, many applications allow you to automatically insert the date and time on-screen or when you print, so you'll want to be sure to have the right time on your computer.

Bad Battery?   If you set your time and date and then find that the date is wrong when you start your computer again, you probably have a bad battery. Check your computer's documentation for instructions on how to replace the battery.

CAUTION

To check or set the date and time, follow these steps:

1. From the Desktop, choose **Start**, **Settings**, and **Control Panel**.
2. In the Control Panel window, double-click the **Date/Time** icon. The Date/Time Properties dialog box appears with the Date & Time tab selected (see Figure 14.1).

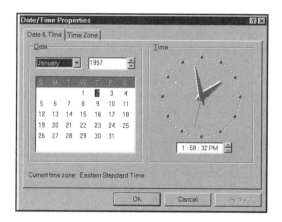

Figure 14.1   The Date/Time Properties dialog box enables you to set the date and/or time on your computer.

3. In the Date area, select the correct month and year from the drop-down lists; then click the day on the calendar.

4. To change the time, click the portion of the time you want to change and either enter the correct number or use the spinner arrows to increase or decrease the value accordingly.

5. (Optional) Choose the **Time Zone** tab and check the **Automatically Adjust Clock for Daylight Savings Changes** check box (put a check mark in it) if you want Windows to change the time automatically in the spring and fall.

6. Select **OK** or press **Enter** to accept the changes you have made.

 TIP   **Time Zone**   If necessary, use the Time Zone drop-down list to change your current time zone. You might use this option if you move or travel with your computer.

Modifying Mouse Settings

The mouse settings enable you to change tracking, to choose a double-click speed, and to swap the left and right mouse buttons. Figure 14.2 shows the Mouse Properties dialog box.

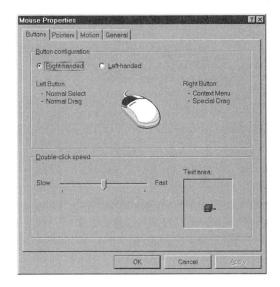

Figure 14.2 Adjust mouse settings to better suit your needs.

By double-clicking the **Mouse** icon in the Control Panel, you access the Mouse Properties dialog box, where you can modify the following settings for your mouse:

- **Pointer Speed (Motion tab)** Use pointer speed when you're working on a notebook or laptop computer. The speed adjusts the rate at which the pointer travels across the screen, making it easier to find your pointer on the small screen. Set the speed to **Slow** if you have trouble seeing the mouse pointer; set the speed to **Fast** if the "slow-motion" mouse is distracting.

- **Pointer Trail (Motion tab)** If you use a notebook or laptop computer, you can choose to display a trail, or echo the pointer, to help you find the pointer on a small, poor-resolution screen. Choose **Short** for a brief trail or Long for an extended trail.

- **Double-Click Speed (Buttons tab)** Adjust the speed to suit your finger's double-click speed. Slower means you can actually perform the two clicks more slowly. Adjust the speed and then test in the Text area.

- **Swap Left/Right Buttons (Buttons tab)** Check this box to switch buttons, if you're left-handed or just more comfortable with the switch.

To modify the mouse settings, follow these steps:

1. From the Desktop, choose **Start**, **Settings**, **Control Panel**.
2. In the Control Panel, double-click the Mouse icon to open the Mouse Properties dialog box.
3. Adjust the settings.
4. Choose **OK** to accept the changes you have made.

Configuring the Modem

If you have a modem attached to your computer, you can modify the settings. Additionally, you can add or remove modems easily by using the Modem Wizard.

Adding a Modem

Before adding a modem, connect the modem to your machine. If it's external, turn it on. If you've added an internal modem, make sure it's properly connected and that the computer's case is closed before turning your computer on.

To add a modem, follow these steps:

1. From the Desktop, choose **Start**, **Settings**, **Control Panel**.
2. Double-click the **Modem** icon to open the Modems Properties dialog box (see Figure 14.3).

Figure 14.3   Configure your modem in the Modems Properties dialog box.

3. To add a new modem, choose the **Add** button. The Install New Modem dialog box appears, as shown in Figure 14.4.

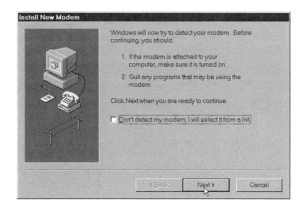

Figure 14.4 Adding a modem is as easy as following the directions.

4. Let Windows detect your modem by choosing the **Next** button; then follow the directions on-screen to complete the installation.

When Windows returns to the Modems Properties dialog box, you can configure the dialing properties, as described in the next section, or you can choose the **Close** button to return to the Desktop.

TIP **Too Many Modems?** To remove a modem you no longer use, open the Modems Properties dialog box and select the modem from the list. Choose the **Remove** button. Choose **Close** to return to the Desktop.

Modifying Dialing Properties

Dialing properties control how your calls are dialed. You may never need to modify these properties; however, if you're using a notebook and you use your modem from the road, hotels, and so on, you'll want to change dialing properties when you change locations.

To modify dialing properties, follow these steps:

1. In the Modems Properties dialog box, choose **the Dialing Properties** button on the General tab. The Dialing Properties dialog box appears with the My Locations tab showing (see Figure 14.5).

Figure 14.5 Use the dialing properties when you go on the road with your computer.

2. In the Where I Am area of the dialog box, enter the area code and choose the country from which you are calling.

3. In the How I Dial From This Location area, enter the following information, as required:

- **To Access an Outside Line, First Dial** If you must dial a number to access an outside line, as is often required at hotels or offices, enter that number in this area. Note you can enter a number to dial to access a local and/or long distance line.

- **Dial Using Calling Card** Select the check box and the choose the **Change** button to enter your calling card number.

- **This Location Has Call Waiting** If the location has call waiting, enter the code to disable that feature while you're calling with the modem.

- **The Phone System at This Location Uses:** Choose either **Tone** or **Pulse** dialing.

4. If this is a location you often make modem calls from, you can save these settings for the next time you need to make a call. At the top of the dialog box, choose the **New** button. The text in the I Am Dialing From text box becomes selected; enter the location name to save it, such as **Dartmouth Hotel** or **Bill's Office**. Press **Enter** to accept the changes and close the dialog box.

5. Choose **OK** to accept the changes and close the Modem Properties dialog box.

Changing Modem Properties

You also can modify certain modem settings as port, speed, and connection from the Modems Properties dialog box. The contents of a Modems Properties dialog box depends on the type and model of the modem, but generally, you'll find settings for such properties as port, speaker volume, maximum speed, and connection preferences.

To change your modem's properties, follow these steps:

1. In the Modems Properties dialog box, select the modem you are configuring from the list so the modem's name is highlighted.

2. Choose the **Properties** button. Make any changes in the dialog box according to your modem manufacturer's directions. If you have any questions about your modem's configuration, see the documentation that came with your modem.

3. Choose **OK** when finished setting the modem's properties. Choose Close to exit the Modems Properties dialog box.

In this lesson, you learned how to change the date and time setting on your computer, modify mouse settings, and configure your modem. In the next lesson, you learn how to work with the multimedia features of Windows 95.

Working with Multimedia

In this lesson, you learn how to use the CD Player, Media Player, and ActiveMovie.

Using the CD Player

You can use your CD-ROM drive on your computer to play music CDs. You must have a sound card installed and you may or may not use external speakers with your computer. With the CD Player, you can play CDs, switch the order in which you play tracks, and select specific tracks to play.

To use the CD Player, follow these steps:

1. Choose **Start**, **Programs**, **Accessories**, and **Multimedia**. From the Multimedia menu, choose **CD Player**. The CD Player appears; if you have a data CD or no CD in the CD-ROM drive, you'll see the message **"Data or no disc loaded"** (see Figure 15.1).

CAUTION

Still Won't Recognize the CD? If you insert a CD and your CD player still does not recognize it, you'll need to make sure you have a sound card installed in your computer and that you have a Windows 95 driver for the sound card installed. Double-click the System icon in the Control Panel and select the Device Manager tab. Double-click the sound, video, and game controllers device type to see if there is an installed sound card. If you see a yellow circle with an exclamation point in it or no sound card listed, you have a problem.

2. Insert the CD. Click the **Play** button to play, the **Pause** button to temporarily stop the CD, and use the **Stop** button to stop the music.

3. To change the order of the tracks that play, as opposed to playing the tracks in the order they fall on the CD, choose **Options**, **Random Order**.

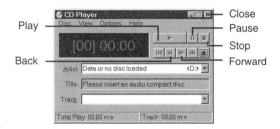

Figure 15.1 Use the CD Player to play music CDs from your computer.

 TIP **Not Loud Enough?** To adjust the volume of the CD Player, choose **View**, **Volume Control**. The Volume Control application appears from which you can turn up or down the volume.

Using the Media Player

Use the Media Player to play audio, video, and animation files in Windows 95. You can play a multimedia file, rewind the file, and fast forward the file. You also can copy a multimedia file into a document that you or someone else can play back. Video for Windows files have an AVI extension.

To open and use the Media Player, follow these steps:

1. Choose **Start**, **Programs**, **Accessories**, **Multimedia**, and then select **Media Player**. The Media Player opens (see Figure 15.2).

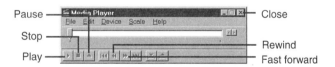

Figure 15.2 Play video and animation files with the Media Player.

2. From the Device menu, select the device type you want to play: **ActiveMovie** (animation), **Video for Windows**, or **CD audio**.

3. If you choose the ActiveMovie or Video for Windows option, an Open dialog box appears from which you can locate and choose the file you want to play. If you choose the CD audio option, then choose **File**, **Open** to select the file you want.

4. Choose the **Play** button to play the file.

Using ActiveMovie

The ActiveMovie player is similar to the Media Player; you can play animated clips or movies on both applications. Files you play using the ActiveMovie Control box include the following types: MPEG, MPE, MPG, MPA, ENC, and DAT. These extensions represent various file types of movies or animations that have been compressed somewhat because of their very large size.

To use the ActiveMovie program, follow these steps:

1. Choose **Start**, **Programs**, **Accessories**, **Multimedia**, and then choose **ActiveMovie Control**. The Open dialog box appears.
2. Choose the file you want to play and then click the **Open** button.
3. As the file plays, you can control the movie from the ActiveMovie Control box (see Figure 15.3).

Figure 15.3   Choose to play or stop the animation by using the ActiveMovie Control box.

Using a Multimedia File in a Document

You can place any multimedia file in a document so you or someone else can play the file at any time from within the document. You can copy the multimedia file and then paste it into the document.

To use a multimedia file in a document, follow these steps:

1. In the Media Player, open the **File** menu and choose **Open**.
2. Double-click the file you want to copy.
3. Choose **Edit**, **Options** and specify the options you want.
4. Open the document to which you want to paste the file and position the insertion point.
5. Choose **Edit**, **Paste**.

To play back a multimedia file from within a document, you double-click the icon representing the file.

In this lesson, you learned how to use the CD Player, Media Player, and ActiveMovie. In the next lesson, you'll learn to set up your system to connect to the Internet.

Configuring for the Internet

In this lesson, you will learn how to configure your settings to connect to the Internet.

How to Set Up for Internet Connection

You must have an Internet connection before you can use the Internet Explorer, Internet Mail, or Internet News. Windows makes it easy for you to configure your Internet connection. But first you'll need to get an Internet Service Provider (ISP) that is located in your area. An ISP provides you with all of the information—IP address, subnet mask, host name, and so on—you need to configure Windows 95 for the Internet.

After you set up your computer for using Internet Explorer, you can explore Web pages, send and receive e-mail, and access newsgroups on the Internet. Windows makes it easy to set up for using the Internet by providing a Wizard that guides you through the steps. This lesson shows you how to connect to the Internet. Lessons 17, 18, and 19 in this part will show you how to use the three Internet applications: Internet Explorer, Internet Mail, and Internet News.

To set up for the Internet, follow these steps:

1. Choose **Programs, Accessories, Internet Tools** and from this menu, select **Get on the Internet**. The Internet Connection Wizard appears. Choose the **Next** button to start the process.

2. Choose the **Manual** option if you have an account with an ISP and want to set up your computer with addresses and information your ISP has provided. Click the **Next** button to continue to set up. If you chose Manual, an introductory screen appears; choose **Next**.

TIP **Automatic for ISP** If you do not have an ISP and you want Windows to find an ISP for you, choose **Automatic** and follow the directions on-screen in the Wizard dialog boxes that follow.

3. The How to Connect Wizard box appears. Select the method you'll use to connect to the Internet. You'll most likely use the phone line to connect; however, if you're a member of a network, choose the LAN option instead. These instructions assume you're using a phone line. Click **Next**.

4. The Wizard next asks if you want to use Internet Mail; choose **Yes** and click the **Next** button. If you do not set up Internet Mail, you won't be able to send or receive e-mail messages over the Internet using Windows' Internet mail application.

5. The Installing Files Wizard dialog box appears. Click **Next** to continue the process. Windows may prompt you for your Windows CD-ROM; insert the disk and choose **OK** to continue.

6. When Windows is done copying files, it displays the Service Provider Information Wizard dialog box. Enter the name of your ISP and choose **Next**.

7. In the Phone Number Wizard dialog box, enter the area code (if applicable) and the phone number of your ISP. Choose the country code, if different from the U.S. Click the **Next** button.

8. In the User Name and Password Wizard dialog box, enter the User name and password assigned to you by your ISP. Notice the password enters as asterisks instead of characters, to protect your privacy. Click **Next**.

9. In the IP Address dialog box, choose the appropriate response and click the **Next** button. Your ISP may provide your IP address automatically through a special server, called a DHCP server; however, make sure you check with the ISP first before choosing that option. Generally, you enter an IP address that your ISP assigns you in this Wizard box.

10. In the DNS Server Address Wizard dialog box, enter the number(s) or name(s) for the name server(s) your ISP uses. This information, as well as all other you use in the wizard, should be obtained from your ISP. Click **Next**.

11. If you're configuring for Internet Mail, enter your e-mail address and your ISP's Internet mail server in the Internet Mail Wizard dialog box. Click the **Next** button.

12. The Complete Configuration Wizard dialog box appears to let you know that setup is complete. Click the **Finish** button. When you click the **Internet** icon on the desktop, the connection you just created will appear.

In this lesson, you learned how to configure your system for the Internet. In the next lesson, you learn to use Internet Explorer.

Using Internet Explorer

In this lesson, you learn how to use the Internet Explorer to browse the Internet.

Accessing the Internet

Depending upon your version of Windows, it comes with Internet Explorer 3.0, 3.02, or 4 that you can use for browsing the World Wide Web. The Internet Explorer enables you to access Web pages, download files, perform searches on the Net, and more. The browser displays pages complete with images, links, and text. This lesson assumes your Internet is set up and ready to go and that you are using Version 3.02.

Browser   Any software you use to view the Internet; in this case, the Internet Explorer.

Download   Transferring a file from the Internet to your own computer.

Links   Also called Hyperlinks, underlined text on Web pages that jump to other Web pages containing related information.

Set Up? Help!   In order to use Internet Explorer, you must have a connection through an Internet Service Provider and a modem attached to your computer or over the network. See Part I, Lesson 16, for information about configuring your computer for the Internet.

To start the Internet Explorer, follow these steps:

1. Choose **Start**, **Programs**, **Internet Explorer**; alternatively, you can double-click the **Internet** icon on the desktop.

2. The Connect To dialog box appears (see Figure 17.1). Choose **Connect** to dial and connect to the Internet. The Explorer dials your Internet Service Provider (ISP) and then displays the Internet Explorer window and the Microsoft home page.

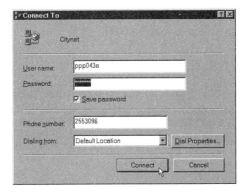

Figure 17.1 Connect to the Internet.

Internet Service Provider A vendor who provides you with a phone number you can use to connect to the Internet. The ISP also provides addresses and other information you'll need to configure the computer for the Internet.

Microsoft Home Page The first Web site you see after connecting to the Internet is the Microsoft home page, a Web page that tells you about Microsoft as well as other services you can access over the Net.

Using the Internet Explorer

The Internet Explorer opens to the Microsoft home page. You can use your mouse to scroll around the page and view the contents. When you see any underlined text, or the mouse pointer changes to a hand, you can click that link to see more, related information on a subject. For example, click **Today's Link** (see Figure 17.2) to view a link to another site that you may be interested in; this week, the link is to Hallmark's home page but the link changes from time to time, as do many links on the Web.

Go back to previous screen

Go back to the start page (Microsoft's home page)

Explore the Net!

Click a link

Figure 17.2 Surf the Web.

If you go to a link but want to return to the previous page, click the Back button on the toolbar.

Searching the Net

You can quickly find Web pages about any topic by searching for the topic. Internet Explorer provides several different search types you can use and experiment with.

To search for a specific topic on the Internet, follow these steps:

1. Choose **Go**, **Search the Web**; alternatively, click the **Search** button on the toolbar.
2. In the Search text box, enter the word or phrase for which you're searching.
3. Click the **Search** button.

TIP **Explore the Search Page** Scroll through the search page and see what other types of searching are available on the Web. Experiment!

97

4. The results of the search appear on-screen; you can scroll the page to see the topics found and click any underlined topic to view more information about it. Click the **Back** button to return to the Internet Searches page or choose link after link to just explore the Net.

Saving Favorite Places

You'll likely find Web sites that you will want to visit again. You can save the addresses to these sites so you can quickly go to them in the future.

To save a Web site to your Favorites folder, follow these steps:

1. While at the actual site, click the **Favorites** button on the toolbar to display the Favorites menu (see Figure 17.3).

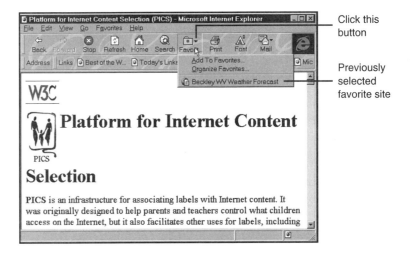

Figure 17.3 Create a menu of all your favorite places on the Web.

2. Select the **Add To Favorites** command and the Internet Explorer displays the Add to Favorites dialog box.

3. You can enter an alternate name in the Name text box to represent the site or you can accept the default name supplied. Choose **OK** and the site is added to your Favorites menu.

To access any of your favorite places, choose **Favorites**, **Open Favorites**, and select the site from the menu.

Going to a Specific Site

If you know the address of the Web site you want to visit, you can enter the address and go directly to that site. Follow these steps:

1. If the Address bar is not showing, click the **Address** button below the toolbar (refer to Figure 17.3).

2. Enter the address in the Address text box and press **Enter**. The addresses you visit during one session are listed in the drop-down address list so you can go back to any of the listings at any time during the session.

Exiting the Program

When you're done surfing the Web and you're ready to close the Internet Explorer, you can remain connected or disconnect from the Internet. If you remain connected, you can access Internet Mail or Internet News, as explained in the next two lessons. If you're finished with the Internet, you must use the Dial-Up Networking folder to disconnect.

1. To exit the Internet Explorer, choose **File**, **Exit**. If the Disconnect dialog box appears, confirming you want to disconnect from the Internet, choose **Yes** to disconnect or **No** to continue the session with Internet Mail or Internet News.

2. If the Disconnect dialog box doesn't appear, open the **Computer** window and double-click the **Dial-Up Networking** icon. The Dial-Up Networkng dialog box appears. Select your current connection and choose **File**, **Disconnect**. Close the open windows.

In this lesson, you learned how to use the Internet Explorer to browse the Internet. In the next lesson, you learn how to use Internet Mail.

Using Internet Mail

In this lesson, you learn how to open and close the Internet Mail program, read and reply to mail, and create mail.

What Is Internet Mail?

Internet Mail is an e-mail program through which you can exchange messages with others over the Internet. You can send a mail message to anyone for whom you have an address and you can receive messages in the Mail program.

Additionally, you can use the Internet Mail program to send files—such as reports, letters, spreadsheets, and so on—attached to a message to share with others.

In order to use Internet Mail, you must have a connection through an Internet Service Provider and a modem attached to your computer or over the network. See Part I, Lesson 16, for information about configuring your computer for the Internet.

Opening and Closing the Internet Mail Program

You can start the Internet Mail application from either Internet Explorer or from the menus. Similar to the Internet Explorer, exiting the program and disconnecting from the Internet are two separate procedures, as explained in this task.

To start the Internet Mail application, follow these steps:

1. Choose **Start**, **Programs**, **Internet Mail**. The Internet Mail window appears (see Figure 18.1).

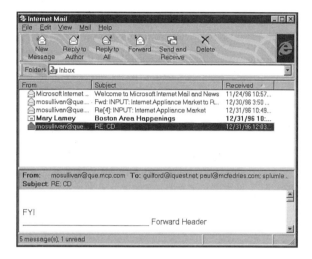

Figure 18.1 Send and receive mail over the Internet.

2. If you are not connected to the Internet, you can click the **Send and Receive** button on the toolbar to display the Connect To dialog box.

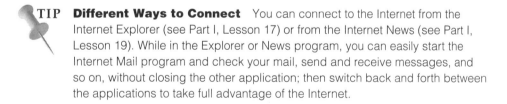

TIP **Different Ways to Connect** You can connect to the Internet from the Internet Explorer (see Part I, Lesson 17) or from the Internet News (see Part I, Lesson 19). While in the Explorer or News program, you can easily start the Internet Mail program and check your mail, send and receive messages, and so on, without closing the other application; then switch back and forth between the applications to take full advantage of the Internet.

3. Choose **OK** and the program dials your ISP and connects to the Internet. When connected, the program checks for new messages and sends any messages you may have written.

To disconnect from the Internet, follow these steps:

1. To exit the Internet Mail program, choose **File**, **Exit**.

2. Open the My Computer window and double-click the **Dial-Up Networking** icon. The Dial-Up Networking dialog box appears. Select your current connection and choose **File**, **Disconnect**. Close the open windows.

Reading Mail

The messages in your Inbox that are in bold type are messages that have not been read. Messages in regular type have been opened but remain in the Inbox until you either delete or move them to another folder.

To read a message, you can select it in the upper pane of the Internet Mail window and the message text is displayed on the lower pane. You also can double-click the message to open the window so you see the text in a better view (see Figure 18.2).

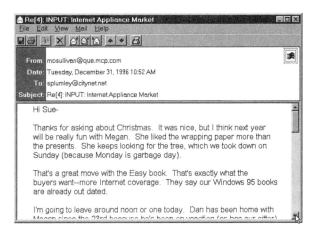

Figure 18.2   View the message in its own window.

Following are some other things you can do with open mail:

- To print an open message, choose **File, Print**.
- To delete a message, choose **File, Delete**.
- To close a message, choose **File, Close**.
- To read the next message in the list without closing the opened one, choose **View, Next Message**; to read the previous message, choose **View, Previous Message**.

Replying to a Message

You can reply to any message you receive, and Internet Mail automatically places a copy of the original message in your reply, separated from your text by a short, dashed line and identified with the > symbol preceding each line of the original message, including headers. When you reply to a message, the application also addresses the message to the original author and uses the subject of the original message as the subject of the reply, but with an RE: preceding the original subject.

To reply to an open message, follow these steps:

1. In the open message to which you want to reply, choose **Mail**, **Reply to Author**.

TIP **Want to Make Multiple Replies?** If the original message was sent to more than one person (i.e., carbon copies), you can send the reply to each person who originally received the message by choosing **Mail**, **Reply to All**.

2. In the Reply message window, add any names in the Cc area if you want to send a carbon copy of the message to someone else.

3. Enter the text of your message above the original text (see Figure 18.3).

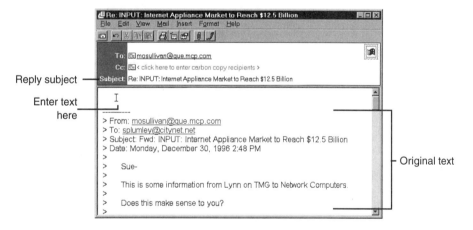

Figure 18.3 Reply to a message in Internet Mail.

4. When you're ready to send the message, choose **File**, **Send Message** or press **Alt+S**. If you're not connected to the Internet, Internet Mail stores your message in the Outbox and sends the message after you connect.

Creating Mail

You also can create a new message in Internet Mail. When you create a message, you'll need to know the recipient's Internet address. Then you add text as a subject and the message text. You send a new message the same way you send a reply.

To create a new mail message, follow these steps:

1. In Internet Mail, choose **Mail**, **New Message**; alternatively, click the **New Message** button.
2. In the New Message window, enter the address of the recipient in the To text box. Alternatively, click the address icon next to the To text box to display the Windows Address Book (see Figure 18.4).

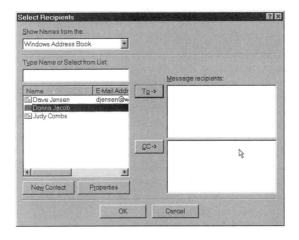

Figure 18.4 Use the address book to store addresses you often use.

3. If you want to add addresses to the address book, in the Select Recipients dialog box, click the **New Contact** button. Enter the name and e-mail address of the person in the Properties dialog box and then choose **OK**.

 TIP **Add More Info** You also can add information—such as a home phone number and address, business information, and notes—to the Properties dialog box about any recipient by clicking the various tabs and filling in the information.

4. To address the message to any person on your list, select the name and then click the **To** button; Internet Mail copies the name and address of that person to the To list box. You can add multiple names to the To list, or you can select any names and click the **CC** button to add them to the carbon copy list.

5. When you're done, click the **OK** button to return to the New Message window.

6. Click the **Subject** field and enter a topic for the message.

7. Click the message area and enter the text for your message.

8. Choose **File, Send Message** when you're ready to send the mail. If you're not connected to the Internet, Internet Mail stores your message in the Outbox and sends the message after you connect.

You can also do the following things before sending a message:

- To set a priority, or level of importance, for the message, choose **Mail, Set Priority**, and then choose either **High, Normal,** or **Low**. The default priority is Normal.

- To attach a file, choose **Insert, File Attachment**. In the Insert Attachment dialog box, select the file you want to attach and choose the **Attach** button. Internet Mail adds the file, represented by an icon, to your message.

- To format the message text, select the text and choose **Format, Font** or **Format, Align**. You also can create bulleted text in your message by selecting the text and choosing **Format, Bullets**.

In this lesson, you learned how to open and close the Internet Mail program, read and reply to mail, and create mail. In the next lesson, you learn how to use Internet News.

Using Internet News

In this lesson, you learn how to open and close the Internet News application in Windows, subscribe to a newsgroup, and download messages.

What Is Internet News?

Another Internet application included with Windows 95 is Internet News. With over 15,000 newsgroups on the Internet, you can use Internet News to exchange ideas and information about business, politics, hobbies, and many other interests. UseNet newsgroups (forums in which people exchange ideas on the Internet) enable you to contact others with similar, or completely different, ideas.

Newsgroup   A collection of related messages about a topic in which people have in common; for example, there is a computer consulting newsgroup, a dolphin newsgroup, an Irish music newsgroup, and so on.

Forum   An area of the Internet that enables people to exchange ideas about a topic of interest.

You can pose questions about your new computer, or state opinions about the best type of dog to use in hunting grouse. Discuss your home decorating ideas or meet people who write science fiction short stories. There are literally thousands of forums you can search, read about, and visit time and again. The Windows Internet News application enables you to browse a list of available UseNet groups, search groups for a topic or description, view a topic and related responses posted, and much more.

Opening and Closing the Internet News Program

When you open the Internet News program, Windows connects to the Internet. Initially, the program downloads a complete list of newsgroups.

To open and close the Internet News program, follow these steps:

1. Choose **Start**, **Programs**, **Internet News**. The Internet News dialog box appears.

If this is the first time you've used the program or if you've not subscribe to a newsgroup before, a dialog box appears asking if you want to view a list of available newsgroups. Choose **Yes** to continue.

CAUTION

Long Download Downloading an entire list of newsgroups may take quit some time; luckily, you download the whole list only once and then periodica add new lists to the current one.

After you've subscribed to one or more newsgroups, the Connect To dia box appears.

2. The Connect To dialog box appears. Choose **OK** to continue. Internet News dials your ISP and connects to the news server, downloading the available newsgroups for you.

CAUTION

How Do I Connect To? You must set up your computer to access the Internet before you can attach to Internet News. See Part I, Lesson 16, for information.

3. The Newsgroups dialog box appears, listing all available newsgroups (Figure 19.1). To view or subscribe to a newsgroup, see the next section.

4. To exit the Internet News program, cancel the Newsgroup dialog box t return to the Internet News window. Choose **File**, **Disconnect** and ther **File**, **Close** to close the program and disconnect from the news server.

CAUTION

The Modem Is Still Connected! If you're still connected to the Inter and want to disconnect, open the My Computer window and double-click the Dial-Up Networking icon. The Dial-Up Networking dialog box appears Select your current connection and choose **File**, **Disconnect**. Close the op windows.

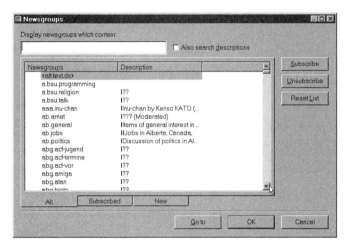

Figure 19.1   View the list of available newsgroups.

Viewing and Subscribing to a Newsgroup

You can view a list of current newsgroups at any time and subscribe to those you want to become a member of. When you view the newsgroup's messages, you can read those messages and respond to them. When you subscribe to a newsgroup, you simply make it easier to find the forum again when you connect.

To view the list of newsgroups in the Newsgroups window at any time, choose **News**, **Newsgroups** in the Internet News window or click the **Newsgroups** button. Scroll through the list of newsgroups to see what groups are available.

TIP   **So Many Newsgroups, So Little Time**   If you want to search for a specific newsgroup or topic, enter the topic in the Display Newsgroups Which Contain text box within the Newsgroups dialog box, wait just a second or two, do not press **Enter**. Internet Mail lists any newsgroups containing the topic you entered.

To view a newsgroup's messages and subscribe to a group, follow these steps:

1. In the Newsgroups dialog box, select the newsgroup whose messages you want to view.

2. Choose the **Go To** button near the bottom of the dialog box. Internet News lists the subjects of the messages in the Internet News window, as shown in Figure 19.2. To learn how to read and reply to messages, see the next section.

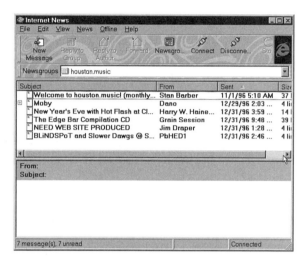

Figure 19.2 Scroll through the messages of any newsgroup.

3. To subscribe to a newsgroup, in the Internet News window after selecting a newsgroup and viewing its messages, choose **News, Newsgroups**. The Newsgroup dialog box appears. Alternatively, if you're already in the Newsgroups dialog box, go on to step 4.

4. Select the newsgroup you want to subscribe to in the list of Newsgroups. Click the **Subscribe** button to the right of the list. An icon appears next to the newsgroup. Subscribe to multiple newsgroups, if you want. When you're done, click **OK**.

You can view, in the Newsgroups dialog box, only those groups to which you've subscribed by clicking the **Subscribed** button located at the bottom of the Newsgroups list. You can, alternatively, click the **New** button to view only new newsgroups or click the **All** button to view all newsgroups.

Reading and Posting Messages

After you find a newsgroup in which you're interested, you can read the messages and post your own message at any time, if you want. Reading and posting messages is like talking to others about your similar interests.

 Posting   When you post a message, you're simply creating a message to send to the group or to reply to the author of a message you read, just as you would with e-mail. See Part I, Lesson 18, for more information.

To read and post messages in a newsgroup, follow these steps:

1. To read a message in the Internet News window, double-click the message in the upper pane. The message appears in a message window (see Figure 19.3).

 Easier to Read Message   If you select any message subject, its text appears in the lower pane of the Internet News window; however, if you double-click the subject to open the message window, it's easier to read and reply to the message.

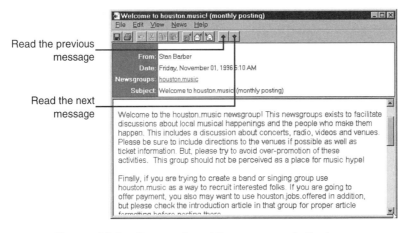

Figure 19.3   Open and read the messages in the forum.

2. You can continue to read messages from this same window by clicking either the **Previous** button or the **Next** button in the toolbar.

3. If you want to reply to a message, choose **News, Reply to Newsgroup**. The Reply message window appears with a copy of the original message and the message's topic in the Subject area of the header.

4. Enter your reply and choose **File**, **Post Message** to send it to the newsgroup.

To compose a new message to the group, choose **News**, **New Message to Newsgroup**. Complete the message as you would any e-mail message, by entering the newsgroup's address (you can get it from the Newsgroups dialog box), the subject, and the text. Choose **File**, **Post Message** to send it.

Downloading Messages

If you want, you can download the messages from a group so you can read and respond to them offline. Later, when you connect to the Internet again, you can send your replies to the group. You might want to download messages to save on your phone bill or your connect time, if your ISP limits your access to the Internet.

You can mark one message, all messages, or a thread for downloading.

Mark Marking a message is attaching a tag or label to it to indicate you want to save, download, read, or otherwise denote the message.

Thread A group of messages and replies about a specific topic within the newsgroup.

Download Copying message(s) to your computer's hard drive for use offline.

To download messages, follow these steps:

1. To mark one message for download, select the message in the Internet News window and choose **Offline**, **Mark Message for Download**.

To mark a thread, select the message with a plus sign in front of it in the upper pane of the Internet News window and choose **Offline**, **Mark Thread for Download**.

To mark all messages, choose **Offline**, **Mark All for Download**.

2. Choose **Offline**, **Post and Download and Internet News** to download the marked messages.

In this lesson, you learned how to open and close the Internet News application in Windows, subscribe to a newsgroup, and download messages.

Introduction to Works

Works Overview

In this lesson, you will learn what Microsoft Works is, the programs it contains, and how to launch and exit Works.

What Is Microsoft Works?

Microsoft Works is an integrated software program that combines the features of several tools to help you perform the functions of four different kinds of programs while working in only one program. Microsoft Works contains a Word Processor, a Spreadsheet, a Database, and a Communications Program. These programs, or *Works Tools*, can be used separately or together to help you perform tasks.

SKILLS TRANSFER

Program Similarities   Although Microsoft Works calls them *tools*, the Word Processing, Spreadsheet and Database functions of Works are actually scaled-down computer programs that fall in the software program categories of *word processing*, *spreadsheet* and *database*. Their function and design follow the basic function and design of other programs in the same category. For example, the Microsoft Works Word Processing tool is a similar program to Microsoft Word and Lotus WordPro. The Microsoft Works Spreadsheet tool is a similar program to Microsoft Excel and Lotus 1,2,3 spreadsheet programs. Basic skills that you will learn in these programs will apply to other word processing, database and spreadsheet programs.

Each program is designed to perform a specific function:

- Use the Word Processor to write letters or other documents.
- Use the Spreadsheet tool to create documents that contain numbers in rows and columns and perform calculations on those numbers.

- Use the Database tool to keep track of lists of names and addresses, or inventoried objects.

- Use the Communications tool to communicate with another computer, sending and receiving files (if you have a modem connected to your computer and if you have the rights to access the other computer).

Figure 1.1 shows the Works Task Launcher dialog box with the descriptions of the four tools found in Microsoft Works.

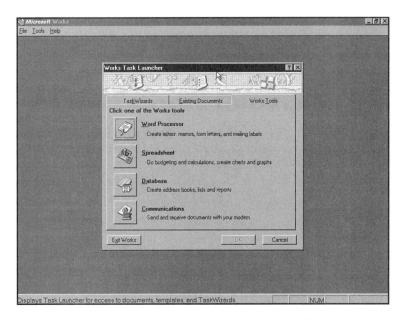

Figure 1.1   Microsoft Works has four tools which can work independently or together.

Table 1.1 lists tasks and projects that you might want to perform on your computer, and the tool you will use in Works to perform that task or create that project. The first column in the table is designed to help you quickly identify your project.

Table 1.1   Tasks you can perform in Works, and the tools you will use to perform them.

Category	Project	Use
Letters/correspondence	•Write a letter •Create a report for school	Word Processor tool

Category	Project	Use
Address/mailing lists	Maintain a list of vendors, friends or newsletter recipients	Database tool
Mass mailing	•Create a letter and/or envelopes •Create labels for envelopes.	Word Processor and Database tools
Newsletters/letterhead	•Create your own letterhead •Design a newsletter using columns and inserting graphics	Word Processor tool
Mortgage/loan analysis	See the payment schedule for a loan	Spreadsheet tool
Calendar	•Create a calendar for work or home •Keep a to-do list	Spreadsheet tool

Starting Works

To start Microsoft Works you must be in Windows 95 and Works must be installed on your computer.

For more information on starting Windows 95, using the Task Bar, or performing basic Windows skills, see Lesson 1, Navigating the Windows 95 Desktop, in Part I.

To start Works:

1. Click on the Windows 95 **Start** button.

2. Select **Programs**, **Microsoft Works**, **Microsoft Works** (see Figure 1.2).

3. The Microsoft Works Task Launcher dialog box appears as shown in Figure 1.3.

TIP   **Shortcut**   During installation Microsoft Works normally places a shortcut icon on your Windows 95 desktop. You can start Works by double-clicking on that icon.

TERM **Dialog Box** Microsoft Windows and programs designed to run under Windows (such as Works) use dialog boxes to exchange information with you. For more information on using Dialog Boxes, see Part I, Lesson 4, "Using Dialog Boxes."

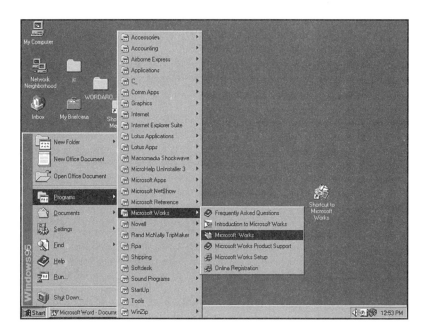

Figure 1.2 Starting Microsoft Works.

Figure 1.3 The Works Task Launcher.

The Task Launcher is the master control for works. It provides an easy-to-use menu, displaying all of Works features in one window.

The Works Task Launcher

There are three tabs on the Task Launcher:

- **TaskWizards**—Are mini programs that assists you in performing your task. For example, you can use the Letter TaskWizard to help you write a professional looking letter. Lesson 3 in this part will explain more about TaskWizards.

- **Existing Documents**—Displays a list of the documents you have created and saved. If you are using Works for the first time, this window will be empty. When you create Works documents you can reopen them by double clicking on the document in the list.

- **Works Tools**—Lets you access the Word Processor, Spreadsheet or Database tools without the help of Wizards. This allows you to create your own documents without assistance, but requires some knowledge in using these types of programs. The communications tool is also accessed from this page and does have Wizards to help you in sending and receiving files to and from other computers.

These tabs look and act like an index tab in a notebook and each contains different selections (refer to Figure 1.3).

Dialog Box Tabs   These are common among Windows dialog boxes. Each tab page displays different options you can apply. To see the contents of a tab, click once on the tab name.

To view the selections on each tabbed page, click once on the tab. The tabbed page on which you clicked will then appear in the front of the other tabbed pages as shown in Figure 1.4.

You'll learn more about the TaskWizards in Part II, Lesson 3, "Using the Works TaskWizard."

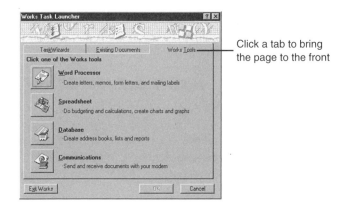

Click a tab to bring
the page to the front

Figure 1.4   Clicking on the Works Tools tab brings that page to the front.

Exiting Works

To Exit Works, click on the **Exit Works** button found in the Task Launcher.

CAUTION

Can't Exit?   An experienced Windows user may try to exit Works using **File**, **Exit Works** or by clicking on the Close button in the upper-right corner of the Window. These methods won't work if the Task Launcher is showing. The Task Launcher is a *dialog* box, and a Windows dialog box must be closed to access the windows and menus behind it.

In this lesson, you learned about the features of Works. You also learned how to start and exit Works. In the next lesson, you will learn how to access help.

Using Works Help

In this lesson, you will learn how to access and use the Works Help features.

Getting Help

Help is on the way! The Works help features are similar to other Microsoft products and products designed to run in Windows 95 that give the user a variety of ways to access help, using extensive help screens. If you are familiar with Windows 95, you might want to skip over this lesson because you access help in Works the same way as you do in Windows 95.

Using the What's This? Feature

The What's This? feature provides a quick method to get more information about dialog boxes. Since the Works program starts with a dialog box (the Task Launcher) this may be the first place you find yourself wanting or needing help. When activated, the What's This? feature will display a pop-up window with a short description of the item you point to with your mouse.

To activate What's This? help:

1. Click the **?** icon located in the upper-right corner of the Task Launcher dialog box. A question mark appears next to the mouse pointer (see Figure 2.1).

2. Click any list item, button or area of the dialog box. A short description of that option or item is displayed as shown in Figure 2.2.

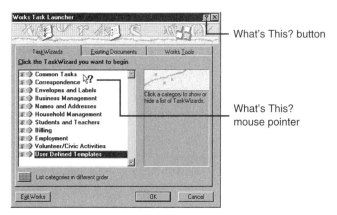

Figure 2.1   Click here for help.

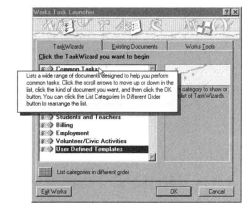

Figure 2.2   What's This? describes the Common Tasks category.

3. To clear the screen of the Help box description, click outside the Help box anywhere on the screen, or press the **Esc** key.

TIP   **What's Quicker than What's This?**   Right-click a dialog box area, option, or list and the Help box description will activate. Another quick method is to press the **F1** key. The F1 key will activate a description for whatever is currently highlighted in the dialog box.

The What's This?   This feature is found in the dialog boxes of Windows 95 and many Microsoft products and works in the same way you have learned here. The F1 key is a standard for software designed to run with Windows 95

and is used in many software programs, not just Microsoft programs. The next time you are playing a computer game, try the F1 key to see if it brings up help screens.

Using the Help Menu

To access the Help Menu, the Task Launcher dialog box must be closed. To close the dialog box, click the **Cancel** button. The Works Help window automatically appears, showing a list of topics for commonly used tasks such as how to create a document, how to open an existing document, and so on.

To access the Help Menu (and more detailed help information) click **Help** in the menu or press **Alt+H.** The menu drops down as shown in Figure 2.3.

Figure 2.3 The Help Menu.

Click the Menu selection you want and a dialog box, window or program will appear with the information you have requested. Table 2.1 lists the Help Menu items and a description of each.

Table 2.1 Help Menu Choices

Menu Selection	Description
Contents	Lists the contents of the Help database by category (word processor, spreadsheet, database, communications)
Index	Lists the entire contents of the database by keyword. Allows you to type in a word, action or item you want information about.
Introduction to Works	Activates a 10 minute introductory tour of Microsoft Works.

continues

Table 2.1 Continued

Menu Selection	Description
How to use Help	Opens a Help Window with a list of help features. Click on an item in the list to learn more about that item.
Hide Help	Closes Help windows (but not dialog boxes).
Launch Works Forum	Launches your Web browser and dials into the Works Forum at Microsoft. This option will not work if you do not have a modem. If you don't have a Microsoft Network account, the Microsoft Network registration screen appears and you can sign up for an account right there.
About Microsoft Works	Displays the About dialog box containing information about the version of Works you are using and copyright information. Almost every Windows program has a "Help About" dialog box and it is always the last item on a Help menu.

Using the Contents Feature

The contents feature of Works lists the available help topics by category. To access Help contents:

1. Click the Help menu and select **Contents**, or press **Alt+H** followed by **C**.

2. The Help Topics: Microsoft Works dialog box appears.

3. Expand a Help Topic category by clicking it. A list of topics displays under the category, with file folder icons for each topic. Click a file folder once to expand the topic as shown in Figure 2.4.

4. Continue opening file folders until you see a subject represented by a document icon as shown in Figure 2.4. You can use the scroll bar to scroll through the menu choices. Click the document icon and the Help information appears in the Help Window on the right of your screen as seen in Figure 2.5. See Part I, Lesson 2, "Working with a Window," to learn more about using scrollbars.

5. Expand as many file folders as you want. To collapse file folders, click the opened folder.

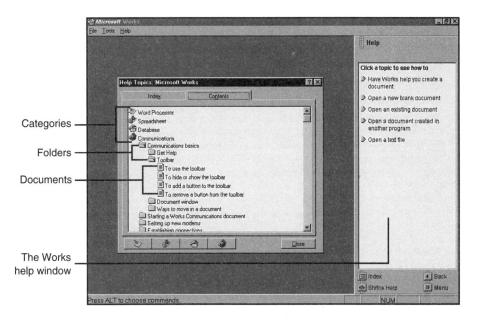

Categories

Folders

Documents

The Works
help window

Figure 2.4 Click a folder to expand it.

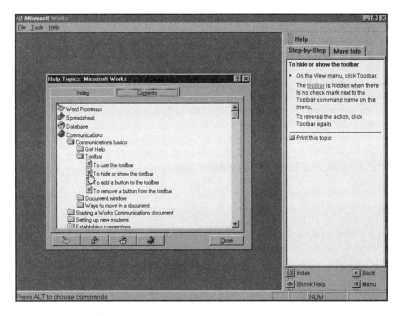

Figure 2.5 The Help Window displays the help document.

Using the Index Feature

The index feature of Help allows you to type a word or phrase and search the Help file for that word or phrase. You don't necessarily have to know the proper or technical phrase for your topic to find it. For example, if you didn't know how to change the way paragraphs align on your page, you could search for *paragraphs*, or even *changing*.

To access the index feature and search for a topic:

1. Choose **Help**, **Index** from the menu.

2. Type the word you want to search for in the text box as shown in Figure 2.6. As you type, the index entries in the bottom of the screen will change, matching the word you type as closely as possible.

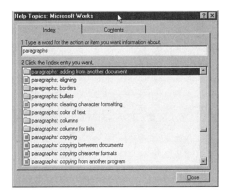

Figure 2.6   Using the Index feature of Help.

3. When you are finished typing, click the index entry you want to see. Works displays the selected topic information in the Help window.

4. To close the Index feature, click the **Close** button.

Using the Help Window

The Works Help window activates when you are working in the Contents feature of Help. It also activates when you create a new document. The Help window might list Works help topics or tabs with specific steps or information to help you perform a task. The Step-by-Step tab lists the steps necessary to perform a task. For example, Figure 2.7 shows the instructions found on the Step-by-Step tab page when the highlighting text document is selected in the Contents page of Help.

Figure 2.7 Help Step-by-Step tab.

The Help window can also contain *hypertext* (green, underlined text). You will see a pop-up description of the word in hypertext when you click it (see Figure 2.8).

The More Info tab contains overview, troubleshooting, and related information on your topic.

 To minimize the Help window, click the Shrink Help icon

To bring up the Help Index, click the Index button. Click the Back button to go to the previous Help screen, and click Menu to go back to the Main topics menu page of Help.

When you minimize the Help window, you will see two icons on the far right of the Works Windows—the Shrink Help button and the Index button. To restore help, click again on the Shrink Help icon. Restoring the Window restores the last topic you viewed in the window.

127

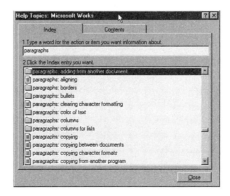

Figure 2.8   Hypertext reveals word definitions.

In this lesson, you learned ways to access Help and search for help. In the next lesson, you learn more about the Works TaskWizards.

Using the Works TaskWizards

In this lesson, you learn what TaskWizards are, how to find a brief description of each of the Taskwizards, and how to change the order of the wizard categories.

What TaskWizards Are

TaskWizards are the heart of the Works program. The purpose of Wizards is to help you to become productive in a short time and to produce professional-looking documents with limited—or no experience.

The TaskWizards page in the Works Task Launcher lists categories for types of tasks you can do with Works. Each task that you select runs a *Wizard*, a Microsoft term for a miniprogram that assists you in performing your task. For example, when you select **Letterhead** from the list of tasks, Works will start a program comprised of a series of questions that you will answer. The answers you provide instruct the program, and the program then designs the letterhead for you.

Viewing the TaskWizards Tab

When you first launch Works and click the TaskWizards tab, you'll see the wizards listed by category. (You'll learn how to change the order of these categories later in this lesson.) To view a category's contents, click once on the icon on the left of the category as shown in Figure 3.1. This expands the category. To collapse the category, click its icon again.

Icons at the left of the document names indicate which Works tool will be used to create that document as shown in Table 3.1.

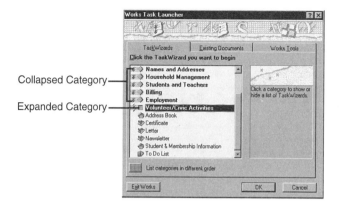

Figure 3.1   Categories can be expanded and collapsed by clicking their icons.

Table 3.1   Document Icons

Icon	*Function*
	Represents a document or task which will be created or performed using the Word Processing Tool.
	Represents a document or task which will be created or performed using the Spreadsheet Tool.
	Represents a document or task which will be created or performed using the Database Tool.

When you click one of the icons, a brief explanation of what you can do with that wizard is displayed in the right pane of the TaskWizard tab, as shown in Figure 3.2.

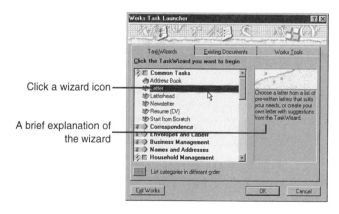

Figure 3.2   Select a wizard icon to learn more about it.

Changing the Order of Categories

As mentioned earlier, when you first see the TaskWizard tab, the wizards are listed by categories. However, if you'd prefer to organize the wizards another way, you can list wizards alphabetically, by the wizards most recently used, or by document type.

TaskWizards, Wizards, Tasks Much of what you can do in Works can be done in a TaskWizard. Throughout this book, you'll find the TaskWizards also referred to as Wizards, or simply Tasks. They all have the same meaning.

To change the order of the tasks in the TaskWizard window:

1. Click the **List categories in different order** button (see Figure 3.3) or use the shortcut keystrokes, **Alt+o**.

2. Indicate a new order for the tasks in the Works Task Launcher dialog box as shown in Figure 3.4.

3. Click **OK** to close the dialog box and return to the Task Launcher main window.

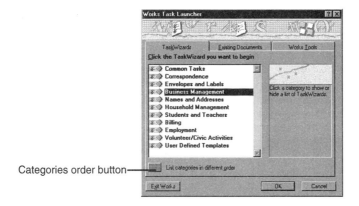

Categories order button

Figure 3.3 Click this button to list tasks in a different order.

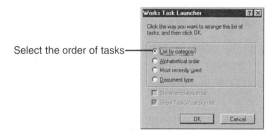

Select the order of tasks

Figure 3.4 Select the order of tasks.

Shortcut Keystrokes Are available through Windows 95 and Windows programs such as Works. If a menu selection or a selection in a dialog box contains an underlined letter (such as **List categories in different order**) you can make the selection by clicking it with your mouse, *or* by holding down the **ALT** key on the keyboard while pressing the underlined letter (O).

See Part I, Lesson 3, "Using Menus," for more information on Windows shortcut keystrokes.

Where Have the Categories Gone? You will only see categories for the tasks when you select **List by category** from the dialog box shown in Figure 3.4.

CAUTION

In this lesson, you learned what TaskWizards are, how to find out more information about them, and how to reorder the TaskWizard categories.

Word Processing

Word Processing Basics

In this lesson, you learn what a word processor is, the types of documents you can create, and the fundamental concepts of word processing with Works.

What Is a Word Processor?

A word processor is a tool for turning words into documents. A *document* is as any page or group of pages that you type and save as a file. You can create many different types of documents, such as:

- Letters
- Reports
- Proposals
- Résumés
- Brochures
- Newsletters

You'll learn to create several of these types of documents later in this Part and in Part VI, "Real World Solutions."

Launching the Word Processor

Microsoft Works has four tools that you can use: the word processor, the spreadsheet, the database, and the communication tools.

To begin using the Works word processor:

1. Click the **Start** button on the Taskbar.

2. Choose **Programs, Microsoft Works, Microsoft Works** from the Start menu.

3. The main Works window, called the Task Launcher, opens (see Figure 1.1). The Task Launcher is your starting point. There are three tabs across the top of the window. Click the **Works Tools** tab.

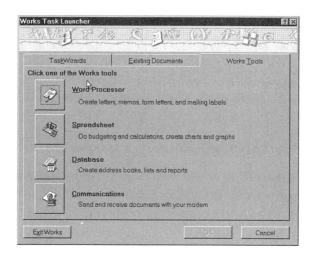

Figure 1.1   The Task Launcher.

4. The Works Tools tab offers you a choice of one of the main programs of Works:

   - Word Processor
   - Spreadsheet
   - Database
   - Communications

5. Click the **Word Processor** button. This opens a blank page, ready for you to begin typing.

Creating a Document

The blank page you see on-screen (see Figure 1.2) isn't really blank. The page is based on a *template,* a predesigned group of settings that enable you to just begin typing without making any adjustments. These settings are based on the requirements of a standard business letter:

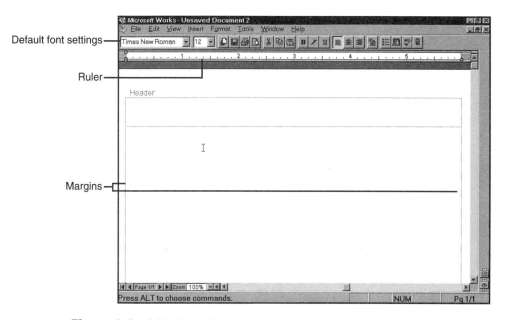

Figure 1.2 A blank word processing document

- The margins (edges of the page where you don't type) are set to 1 inch all around the page.
- There are tabs (for indenting text or typing lists in columns) set to every half-inch.
- Line spacing is set to single spacing.
- The font (typeface) is set to Times New Roman, 12 points.

Points Text is measured in *points,* a system devised by typographers for measuring and referring to text size. There are 72 points in an inch, so 12-point text is 1/6 of an inch tall.

137

Typing Text

Typing begins at the cursor, also known as the *insertion point*. It's the short vertical line you see blinking on your page.

Some typing basics:

- Don't press enter when your text is approaching the right margin. A feature called Word Wrap will make the text stop at the right margin and continue automatically on the next line.
- Do press the **Enter** key between items in a vertical list and to separate paragraphs. The Enter key is the same as the Return key on a typewriter.
- Don't use the Enter key to move down the page. Pressing Enter creates a new blank line, so you'll be adding blank lines as you go down the page. Use an arrow key instead to move down the page, or use the scroll bar.
- The Delete key erases the text to the right of the cursor.
- The Backspace key erases the text to the left of the cursor.
- Be sure to distinguish between a lowercase l and the number 1 Works can't calculate using numbers containing the letter l, because it won't recognize it as a numeral.
- Similarly, don't use a capital O as a 0 (zero). Works can't perform calculations on the letter O because it isn't a numeral.
- Don't use the Spacebar as a quick way to move across the page. Spaces are characters in a word processor, and they leave blank spots where you enter them. Instead, use the arrow keys to move across the page, or use the horizontal scroll bar.

Saving a Document

After you start typing your document, it's a good idea to save it. Don't wait until you've finished the entire document. Too many things can happen while you're working—a power outage or some computer hardware malfunction—and you could lose your work.

To save your document for the first time:

1. From the **File** menu, choose **Save** or **Save As**.
2. The Save As dialog box opens (see Figure 1.3), asking you to name your file and choose a location to store it.

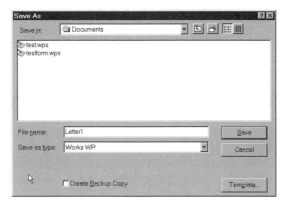

Figure 1.3   The Save As dialog box.

3. From the `Save in` box, choose the folder in which you want to save your file.

4. In the `File name` box, type a descriptive name for your document. Although Windows 95 allows up to 255 characters (including spaces) for a file name, keep your file names short and relevant. This will make it easier to find them later. Be aware that Windows 95 lists files in alphabetical order, so make the first word one that will help you find the file easily.

5. Click the **Save** button. Your document is saved, and you can continue working on it. Notice that the title bar of your Works window has changed. It now displays the file name you just assigned to the file.

As you continue to work on your document, you must save your changes and additions. To update your saved file to include any modifications:

- Choose **File**, **Save** from the menu
- Click the **Save** button on the toolbar
- Press **Ctrl+S**

Any one of these methods saves the file, including the latest changes. When using these methods after a file has already been saved, the Save As dialog box does not reopen.

To save your file and give it a different name or save it to a new location, choose **File**, **Save As**. This will open the **Save As** dialog box again, and you can assign a new name or choose a new folder or drive location for your file.

Saving with a new name creates a new version of your file, and the original file is left intact. The latest changes become part of the new file, and the original file is closed.

Previewing and Printing a Document

Although the screen shows your document very much as the printed version appears, it's sometimes difficult to get a real sense of how your final document will look. To see a preview of your document before printing, choose **File**, **Print Preview** from the menu. Works shows you a reduced view of your document, and provides buttons for zooming in closer to your preview and viewing subsequent pages. Figure 1.4 shows the Print Preview window and tools.

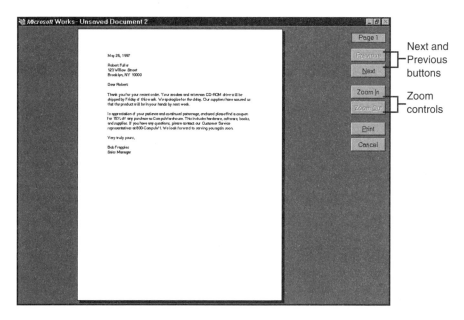

Figure 1.4   Print Preview.

To print your document, choose **File**, **Print** from the menu, or press **Ctrl+P**. Either of these techniques will open the Print dialog box, which is shown in Figure 1.5. The Print dialog box presents the following options:

- Print Range— You can choose to print All pages of the document, or to print a range of pages by entering page numbers into the From and To boxes. The default is to print All pages.

- Number of Copies—The default is one copy. You can enter any number you want, or use the up and down arrows to increase or decrease the number of copies.
- If you're printing multiple copies of a document with more than one page, you'll want to leave the default Collate setting On.

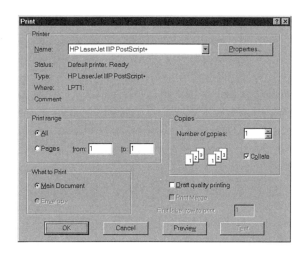

Figure 1.5   The Print dialog box.

The Print button on the toolbar will not open the Print dialog box. It will directly print one copy of every page in your document.

Closing a Document

When you want to stop working on a document, you can close the file. Choose **File, Close** from the menu. If you attempt to close your file without saving, the program will prompt you to do so.

Other methods you can use to close a file are (see Figure 1.6):

- Click the **X** (Close button) in the document window.
- Press **Ctrl+F4** or **Ctrl+W**.
- Click the **Control** icon once, and choose **Close** from the menu (don't confuse the document Control icon with the Program Control icon that closes the program—if the document window is maximized, the Control

icon appears just before File on the menu bar; otherwise, if the document isn't maximized, it appears on the title bar with the document name).

- Double-click the **Control** icon.

The Control Icon

File, Close

Keyboard shortcut

The Document
Close button

Figure 1.6   Closing a document.

Opening a Document

To open a previously saved and closed file, choose **File**, **Open** from the menu.

Following are other ways to open a file:

- Click the **Open** button on the toolbar.
- Press **Ctrl+O** on the keyboard.
- Choose the file from the most recently used files at the bottom of the **File** menu (see Figure 1.7). The last four files that you saved appear in this list, below the **Exit** command.
- From the Task Launcher, click the **Existing Documents** tab (see Figure 1.8). Select your file from the list, and click **OK**.

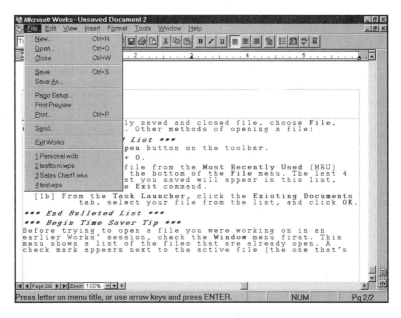

Figure 1.7 Opening a file.

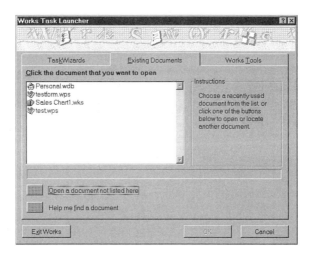

Figure 1.8 The Existing Documents tab.

TIP **Check to See If It's Still Open** Before trying to open a file you were working on earlier, check the **Window** menu first. If you didn't close the file before you started working on a new one, the name of the file shows at the bottom of the menu. If the file you seek is in the list, click it once to bring it to the top, making it the new active file.

Exiting Works

When you want to exit Microsoft Works, choose **File, Exit Works** from the menu. If you have made changes to the document since you last saved it, Works will ask if you want to save it. Click **Yes** if you want to save it, **No** if you want to exit without saving the document, or **Cancel** if you decide not to exit Works at this time. Figure 1.9 shows the Exit command and Task Launcher button.

TIP **But I Only Wanted to Get to the Task Launcher** Don't exit Works if you only want to go back to the Task Launcher. Click the **Task Launcher** button on the Toolbar, or choose **File**, **New** from the menu instead. That way, you don't need to close your document file. If you just need to open a file created in another Works Tool, choose **File**, **Open**, select the file from the Open dialog box, and then click **OK**.

The Task Launcher button

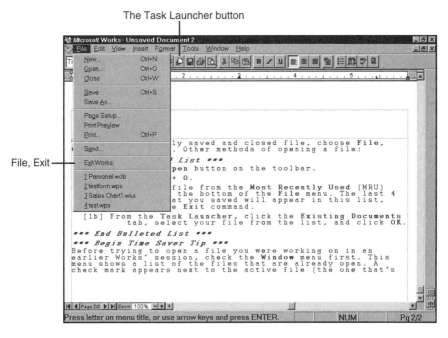

Figure 1.9 Exit Works or go back to the Task Launcher.

In this lesson, you learned what a word processor is, the types of documents you can create, and the fundamental concepts of word processing with Works. In the next lesson, you learn about the Works word processor window.

Understanding the Word Processor Window

In this lesson, you learn about the features found in the Works word processor window, including menus, toolbars, and methods of navigating a document.

The Word Processor Window Contents

The Works word processor window contains tools and features that assist you in creating a document (see Figure 2.1). It also has a Control icon and sizing icons for maximizing, minimizing, and closing the window as explained in Part I, Lesson 2, "Working with a Window."

To open a new document and view a blank document window, choose **File**, **New** from the menu. In the Task Launcher dialog box, click the **Works Tools** tab and choose **Word Processor**.

The main components of the word processor window are:

- The Title Bar—This strip across the top of any Windows application displays the name of the software you're using and the document name (if the document hasn't been saved, Works assigns a title such as "Unsaved Document 1").
- The Menu Bar—The menu bar contains a series of menus that contain commands for doing everything from saving your document to changing fonts.
- The Toolbar—The toolbar is a row of graphic buttons that represent the most commonly used commands that are also found in the menus.

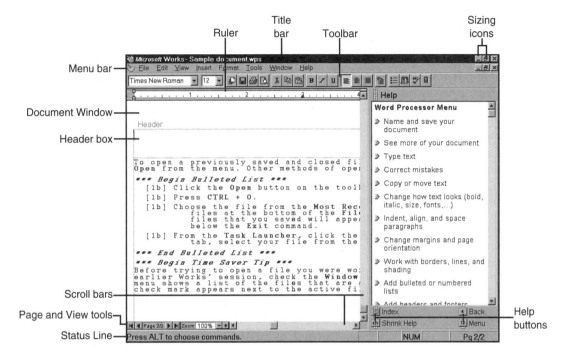

Figure 2.1   The Word Processor window.

- The Document Window—This is the "paper" you type on to create your document.

- The Scroll Bars—Found on the right side and across the bottom of your document window, these tools allow you to see the parts of your document that don't fit in the window.

- The Ruler—The ruler enables you to visually measure your document horizontally, and is used for setting tabs, indents, and adjusting the margins.

- The Page and View Controls—These tools appear on the lower-left corner of your document window. You can move forward and backward through a multi-page document, or choose to zoom in on the active page.

- The Status Line—This strip across the bottom of your screen tells you which page you're on, displays additional toolbar button information (when you're pointing to a button), and shows you if your Num Lock, Insert, or Caps Lock keys are on.

- The Help Window—The Help window is a separate window that can appear next to your document. You can shrink it out of view and open it only as needed.

The Word Processor Menu

The menu bar in Works word processor has eight menus. You can view the contents by clicking the menu name with your mouse, or pressing the **Alt** key plus the underlined letter in the menu name. The menus contain commands and keyboard shortcuts (listed on the right side of the menu) for every feature of the program. Menu items may appear dimmed (gray) at different times during the document-creation process. When a menu command is dimmed, it means that particular command would be inappropriate to use at the time. Figure 2.2 shows the File menu. To become familiar with the menus and their commands, take the time to look through each one.

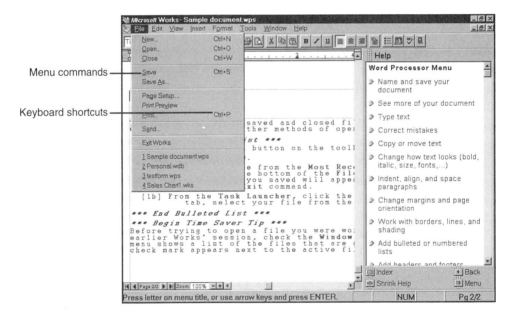

Figure 2.2 The File menu.

The Word Processor Toolbar

The word processor toolbar contains buttons for the most commonly used commands in the menus. Toolbar buttons represent commands such as Save, Print, and Spell Check. Many of the tools work like toggle switches—one click turns a feature on, a second click turns it off. When a toggle button is in use, it will appear depressed on the toolbar. Other toolbar buttons will open a dialog box.

The first two tools on the toolbar are drop-down list tools. To see the list of alternatives, click the drop-down arrow and select an item from the list. The item you select will appear in the box to the left of the drop-down arrow (this indicates that your selection is now the current setting). Figure 2.3 shows the Works word processor toolbar.

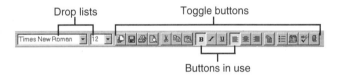

Figure 2.3   The Word Processor toolbar.

Moving Around in a Document

As you type your document, you may want to move quickly to the beginning of a previous paragraph, go to the next page, or move to the end of a line. To navigate and reposition your cursor within your document, you can use the scroll bars and then click your mouse on the document to place your cursor. You can also use these shortcuts:

- **Ctrl+Home** will take you to the top of the document.
- **Ctrl+End** will take you to the end of the document.
- The arrow keys on your keyboard will move you up or down one line, and left or right one character.
- Add the **Ctrl** key while pressing the arrows, and you will move up or down one full paragraph, and left or right one full word.
- The **Home** key will take you to the beginning of the line you're on.
- The **End** key will take you to the end of the line you're on.

- Press **Page Up** or **Page Down** to move up or down one full screen (a full screen doesn't always correspond to one printed page).
- Press **Ctrl+G** to open the Go To dialog box, and enter the page number you want to go to. This feature works only on documents of more than one page.

Although you can move around the document using the mouse and the vertical and horizontal scroll bars, Works provides an additional aid in the Page and View controls in the bottom-left corner of your screen. The Page controls show you which page you're on and how many total pages there are, plus provide buttons to move you to the beginning of your document, one page up, one page down, or to the end of the document. The Zoom control lets you magnify your view of the page, either by clicking the percentage and choosing a magnification from the list or by using the minus (-) and plus (+) buttons to zoom in or out.

TIP **Know Where Your Cursor Is** Using your scroll bars to view another section of your document will not automatically reposition your cursor. You must click your mouse in the document to place your cursor.

For this reason, it's very important that you can see your cursor on-screen before you begin typing or editing. If you don't, you could inadvertently add or delete text in the wrong place. Remember that wherever your cursor is, that's where your typing appears!

In this lesson, you learned about the features found in the Works word processor window, including menus, toolbars, and methods of navigating a document. In the next lesson, you learn to edit a document.

Editing Text

In this lesson, you learn to select and edit text, use the Clipboard to move and copy text, and to use Find and Replace and Easy Text to change the content of your document.

Selecting Text

You can select text with your mouse, the keyboard, or a combination of the two. Selecting text tells Works which text you want to edit. When selecting text with the mouse, your mouse pointer will change depending on its location in the word processor window:

- When your mouse is within your existing text, the mouse pointer looks like a capital I, and is called an "I-beam." You can use this pointer for selecting smaller portions of text, such as a word within a sentence, or a sentence within a paragraph.
- The mouse pointer turns to a right-pointing arrow when it is in the left margin of your document window. Use this mouse pointer for selecting large areas of text such as entire lines or paragraphs.
- Your mouse returns to a standard left-pointing arrow when it is on the menus, toolbar, scrollbars, or page/view controls.

Whether your mouse is an I-beam or a right-pointing arrow, clicking your mouse can select text:

- To select a single word, point to the word and double-click.
- To select a line of text, place your mouse pointer in the left margin next to the line and click once.
- To select an entire paragraph, place your mouse pointer in the left margin next to the paragraph and double-click.

To select text with the keyboard, use the **Shift** key and the arrow keys together:

- Use the **Shift** with the left and right arrows to select text one character at a time.
- Press **Ctrl+Shift** plus the left or right arrows to select entire words.
- Use **Shift** with the up and down arrows to select text one line at a time.
- Press **Ctrl+Shift** plus the up or down arrows to select entire paragraphs.

If you want to add more text to text that you selected with either the mouse or the keyboard, press the **Shift** key and click the mouse at the end of the text you want to select.

What Is the Clipboard?

The *Clipboard* is a temporary holding area in your computer's memory. The Clipboard allows you to move or copy text, graphics, or data from one document to another, between files, and between applications.

Here are some "ground rules" for the Clipboard:

- You can place only one selection on the Clipboard at a time. When you place a new selection on the Clipboard, the previous selection is removed from its memory.
- The Clipboard allows you to move or copy a selected item between any Windows-based applications. You aren't restricted to any particular type or brand of software.
- Exiting Windows empties the Clipboard. If you accidentally exit Windows or shut down your computer, you will lose whatever is stored in the Clipboard.

Moving and Copying Text

You can move or copy selected text to another location in your current document, to another document, or to a completely different application. To place text on the Clipboard:

1. Select the text that you want to move or copy.

2. From the **Edit** menu, choose **Cut** to move (this removes the selection from your document), or **Copy** to copy text. You can also use the **Cut** and **Copy** buttons on the toolbar. The selection is now held in the Clipboard, awaiting your command to place it in another location.

3. Position your cursor where you want to put the selection (the target location). If your target location is in another document, open the document and place your cursor where you want to put the Clipboard's contents.

 4. Choose **Edit**, **Paste** from the menu, or click the **Paste** button on the toolbar. The text appears in the target location.

In addition to the Edit menu and toolbar, you can issue Cut, Copy, and Paste commands from the keyboard:

- To Cut, press **Ctrl+X**.
- To Copy, press **Ctrl+C**.
- To Paste, press **Ctrl+V**.

Using Undo

You can reverse your last action with Works' Undo command. Choose **Edit**, **Undo** from the menu bar or press **Ctrl+Z** or click the **Undo** button on the Standard toolbar. As soon as you've undone an action, that action will appear on the Edit menu as an action that you can Redo.

 I Didn't Mean to Do That! If you've just made a mistake, you must use **Undo** immediately. Works' Undo command applies only to the very last action you took.

CAUTION

Finding and Replacing Text

You can search for a particular word or phrase in your Works document to assist you with proofreading, and you can replace the text you find with another word or phrase. This feature is especially useful in longer documents.

153

To simply find a word or phrase in an open document:

1. Choose **Edit, Find** from the menu.

2. In the Find dialog box (see Figure 3.1), enter the text you're looking for in the Find What box and click **Find Next**.

Figure 3.1   The Find dialog box.

3. If the text you're looking for appears more than once in the document, click **Find Next** again to go to the next incidence.

4. When you've come to the last occurrence of the text, you will be prompted, Works did not find a match. Click **OK**, and then click **Cancel** in the Find dialog box.

TIP   **Start at the Top**   If you start the Find program in the middle of your document, Works will stop at the end and ask you if you want to start looking again at the beginning of the document. To avoid this extra step, make sure your cursor is at the top of the document before you begin the Find process. You can get to the top of the document quickly by pressing **Crtl+Home**.

To replace the text you find with other text:

1. Choose **Edit, Replace** from the menu.

2. In the Replace dialog box (see Figure 3.2), enter the text you want to find in the Find What box.

3. Press **Tab** or click your mouse in the Replace With box. Enter the replacement text, exactly as you want it to appear in the document.

4. If you want to replace every occurrence of the text without seeing each one, click **Replace All**. Clicking **Replace** instead will allow you to skip some of the found items if you don't want to replace all of them. To skip an item, click **Find Next**.

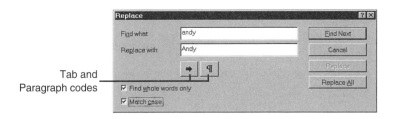

Tab and
Paragraph codes

Figure 3.2 The Replace dialog box.

The Find and Replace dialog boxes offer some extra features for customizing your search. You can specify that your search match the case of the text that you enter in the Find What box, and you can Find Whole Words Only. For example, a search that uses both of these options would keep you from finding "candy" when you're looking for "Andy."

You can also find and replace tabs and paragraph codes in your document by clicking the **Tab** and **Paragraph** buttons in the Find dialog box. The Tab code will appear as ^T, and the Paragraph code will appear as ^P.

What's a Paragraph Code? Every time you press the **Enter** key, you place a paragraph code in your document. Word processors consider a paragraph to be any text that is ended by the typist pressing the **Enter** key, also known as a "Hard Return." For more information on the basics of entering text, see Part III, Lesson 1, "Word Processing Basics."

TIP **See Where You Put Tabs, Spaces, and Hard Returns** You can choose to see your tabs and hard returns (paragraph codes) on-screen by choosing **View, All Characters** from the menu. Tabs, hard returns, and spaces will appear as symbols on your document (arrows for tabs, paragraph marks for hard returns, and dots for spaces). Don't worry; they won't print!

Using Easy Text

Easy Text is a Works feature that can save you time typing words, phrases, or whole paragraphs that you use often. For example, if you use the same closing paragraph in all your business letters, you can save the paragraph as Easy Text and never have to type it again.

To create and use Easy Text:

1. Type the name, phrase, or paragraph you want to save as Easy Text, and select the text.

2. Choose **Insert**, **Easy Text**. From the submenu, choose **New Easy Text**.

3. In the Easy Text dialog box, enter a short name for your Easy Text, such as "closing" for a closing paragraph. You can see your selected text in the Easy Text Contents box (see Figure 3.3).

4. Click **Done** to create your Easy Text and close the dialog box.

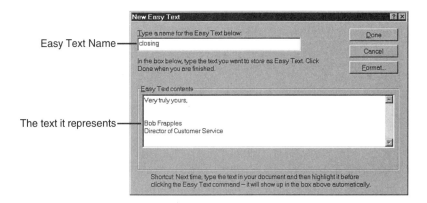

Figure 3.3 The Easy Text dialog box.

To use your Easy Text, place your cursor where you want your text to appear, and type the name you gave it. Press the **F3** key. You can also choose **Insert**, **Easy Text**, and choose your Easy Text name from the submenu.

TIP **Selecting Blank Lines** If you want a blank line to appear before and/or after your East Text when you use it later, be sure to select the blank lines above and below the paragraph when you create the Easy Text. It may help you to choose **View**, **All Characters** so that you can see the paragraph codes to select them.

In this lesson, you learned to select and edit text, to use the Clipboard to move and copy text, and to use Find and Replace and Easy Text to change the content of your document. In the next lesson, you learn to use the Spell Check and Thesaurus.

Using a TaskWizard to Create a Basic Letter

4

In this lesson, you learn to create a basic letter using Works' Common Tasks Letter Wizard.

Selecting the Letter

Works provides a TaskWizard to assist you in creating a letter. A Wizard is a program that takes you through the process of creating various documents, spreadsheets, and databases on a step-by-step basis.

To create a basic word processing document with the Letter TaskWizard:

1. If Works isn't currently open, open it by clicking the **Start** button, selecting Programs, **Microsoft Works, Microsoft Works**. Works opens and displays the Task Launcher (see Figure 4.1).

2. From the Task Launcher's TaskWizards tab, click **Common Tasks** to see a list of tasks. Choose **Letter** from the list. Click **OK** to select the Wizard and close the Task Launcher.

CAUTION

Another Dialog Box When you run any TaskWizard, a dialog box appears that asks if you want to create a new document using a TaskWizard or if you can work with an existing document. Choose **Yes, Run the TaskWizard** to continue with your task. If you don't want to see this dialog box every time you run a TaskWizard, deselect the **Always Show This Message** option.

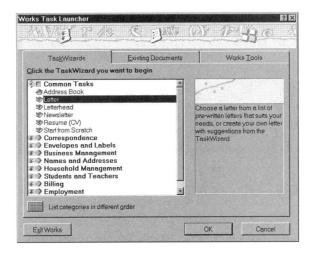

Figure 4.1 The Task Launcher.

3. The TaskWizard begins by offering you three different types of letters: Professional, Simple, and Formal (see Figure 4.2). As you click each one, you see a brief description of that particular type of letter and a sample appears.

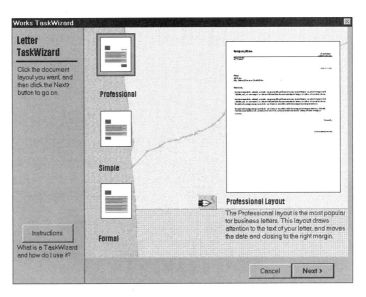

Figure 4.2 The Letter TaskWizard.

4. Choose the **Professional** letter, and click **Next**.

5. In the next dialog box, a series of five buttons offer you the chance to customize the letter (see Figure 4.3). To find out more about creating a customized letter, see Part VI, Lesson 7, "Creating Your Own Letterhead." To accept the Wizard's defaults and create a simple blank document that you can fill in with your own content, click **Create It!**

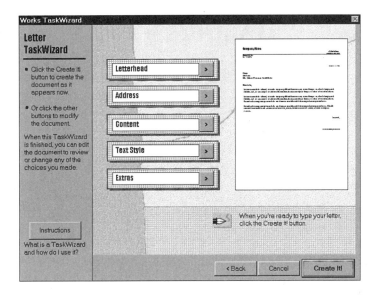

Figure 4.3 Letter Options.

 TIP **Let the Wizard Do the Work** Whenever possible, let the Wizard do the work for you! The TaskWizard creates your letterhead with the fonts, styles, and layout already designed for you. This is the purpose of a Wizard—to take the formatting and design decisions out of your hands.

6. The Wizard's Checklist appears (see Figure 4.4), showing the default settings for your letter:

- Professional style (based on your choice in the first dialog box)
- Wizard-designed letterhead
- Single Address
- Blank letter
- Prestige text style
- No extras

159

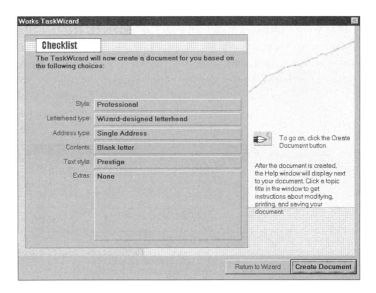

Figure 4.4   The Checklist.

7. To accept these settings, click **Create Document**. The Wizard will begin building the letter, and the resulting document will open in a new windo (see Figure 4.5).

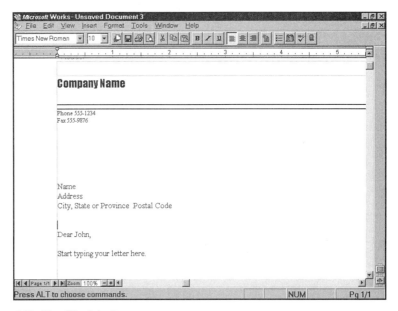

Figure 4.5   The Blank Letter.

160

Inserting Text

The Wizard creates a letter with example text built in, such as "Company Name" and a sample phone number to assist you in creating your letterhead information. To replace the example text, highlight it with your mouse and type your own text to replace it. The text you type will appear in the same font and style as the example text. Figure 4.6 shows the letter's example text replaced with a company name and other letterhead information filled in.

 TIP **See Where Tabs, Spaces, and Hard Returns Are** Seeing your paragraph, tab, and space codes can help you when you're inserting your text. To see these codes, choose **View**, **All Characters** from the menu (do the same thing to turn them off again).

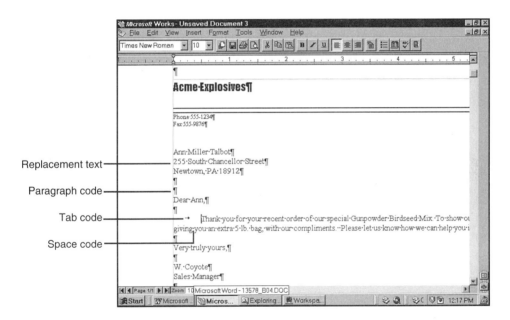

Figure 4.6 Inserting text.

Saving, Printing, and Closing the Letter

It's a good idea to save your document as early in the creation process as possible. The sooner you save it, the less chance you'll lose your work due to computer malfunctions or a power outage. Then you can update the file as you make changes by choosing **File, Save** from the menu or clicking the **Save** button on the toolbar.

When you print your file, click the **Print** button on the Standard toolbar if you want to print one copy without changing the defaults (you won't see the Print dialog box if you click the Print button). Otherwise, choose **File, Print** from the menu.

Remember to close your letter when you are finished with the file by choosing **File, Close**. If you forgot to save it before closing, a dialog box appears asking if you want to save the file. Click **Yes**.

For more information on saving, printing, and closing documents, refer to Part III, Lesson 1, "Word Processing Basics."

In this lesson, you learned to create a basic letter using Works' Common Tasks Letter Wizard. In the next lesson, you learn to Use the Spell Check and Thesaurus.

Using Spell Check and Thesaurus

In this lesson, you learn to use Works' Spell Check and Thesaurus.

Running Spell Check

You can check your document for misspelled words by using Works' spelling check program. A spelling check can be performed at any point in your editing process and can be done more than once. You can add your own words, such as people's names, peculiar terminology, and abbreviations to the Works dictionary.

CAUTION

Proofread! Spelling check programs work on the basis of a spelling dictionary. If a word doesn't appear in that dictionary, Works flags it as a spelling error. It may not be—it could be a proper name or jargon particular to your industry. Also, a spell checker will not catch misused words if they are spelled correctly (such as "form" when you meant "from"). It won't catch punctuation errors, either. You still need to proofread!

To run the spelling check on your document:

1. With your document open on-screen, choose **Tools**, **Spelling** from the menu or click the **Spell Check** button on the Standard toolbar.

2. The Spelling dialog box opens. Works displays each word that it doesn't find in its internal dictionary in the Change to box, one at a time. A list of alternate spellings appears in the Suggestions list box. Figure 5.1 shows the Spelling dialog box.

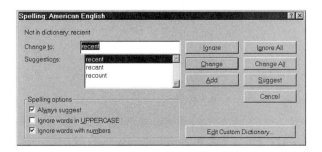

Figure 5.1 The Spelling dialog box.

3. You can choose from any of the following options:

- If one of the suggestions is appropriate, select it from the list and click **Change.** Click **Change All** if you've used the word more than once.

- If none of the suggestions is appropriate or there are no suggestions offered, type your own correction in the Change To box. Click **Change** or **Change All**.

- If the word is spelled correctly, click **Ignore** or **Ignore All**. Choose **Ignore All** if you know you've used the word again in the document.

- If the word is spelled correctly and you know you'll be using it in future documents, click **Add**. This will add the word to the Works custom dictionary, preventing it from appearing as misspelled the next time you use it.

- To set up how the spelling check works, you can select one of the three Spelling Options—**Always Suggest** to have the Spelling dialog box always present a list of proposed spellings, **Ignore Words in UPPERCASE** to have the spelling check ignore words in all capital letters (such as acronyms), or **Ignore Words with Numbers** to have the spelling check ignore words with numbers such as "Quarter1."

4. When the spelling check is completed, a dialog box appears telling you Spelling check finished. Click **OK** to return to your document.

 TIP **I Added a Misspelled Word to the Dictionary!**   You can remove words that you've added to the dictionary. In the Spelling dialog box, click the **Edit Custom Dictionary** button. Scroll through the alphabetized list of words, and when you find the one you want to remove, select it and click **Delete**. Click **Done** to close the dialog box.

Using the Thesaurus

You can use the Thesaurus to look up alternative words (synonyms) for words you feel you're using too often, or to get a word's definition by looking at other words that mean the same thing. To use the Thesaurus, select the word you want to look up, and choose **Tools**, **Thesaurus**. The Thesaurus dialog box displays your word, and two lists:

- A list of potential Meanings for your word appears on the left. In Figure 5.2, you see the meanings for the word "nice."
- A list of Synonyms (alternate words) appears on the right in the Replace with Synonym box. Depending on which meaning you choose, the list of synonyms changes.

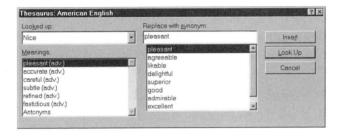

Figure 5.2 The Thesaurus.

If you want to know only what the word means, click **Cancel** to close the dialog box. If you want to replace your word with a synonym, select one from the list, and click **Replace**.

You can also use the Thesaurus to look up words that aren't in a document. In an open document with no text selected, choose **Tools**, **Thesaurus**. In the dialog box, type the word you want to look up in the Replace with synonym box, and click **Look Up.** The word you inserted moves to the Looked Up box. A list of meanings appears on the left, accompanied by synonyms on the right.

In this lesson, you learned to use the Spelling and Thesaurus programs. In the next lesson, you learn to format your text.

Formatting Text

6

In this lesson, you learn to change the appearance of your text by applying fonts and styles. You also learn to use WordArt.

Selecting a Font

You can format your text by changing its font, font size, and font style. These changes can be made from the toolbar or the Format menu.

To change your font from the toolbar:

1. With your document open, select the text you want to change.

2. Click the **Font** drop-down list on the toolbar. A list of fonts drops down. The fonts appear graphically, so you can tell what they will look like in your document (see Figure 6.1).

Figure 6.1 The Font button drop-down list.

3. Select a font that you like by clicking it in the list. Your selected text changes to that font.

Even though your font has changed, the text is still the same size. To increase or decrease your font size, click the **Font Size** drop-down list. A list of point sizes drops down. The higher the number, the bigger your text will be. Select a point size by clicking the number in the list.

Point Type is measured in points, a system devised by typographers for measuring and referring to text size. There are 72 points in an inch, so 10-point text is approximately 1/7 of an inch.

If you make your text Bold, Italic, or Underlined, you're changing its Font Style. The Bold, Italic, and Underline buttons on the toolbar work like toggle switches—one click and they're on, a second click and they're off. Figure 6.2 shows the toolbar with the Bold button turned on. To apply styles to your text, select the text and then click the button. You can apply one, two, or all three styles to any text.

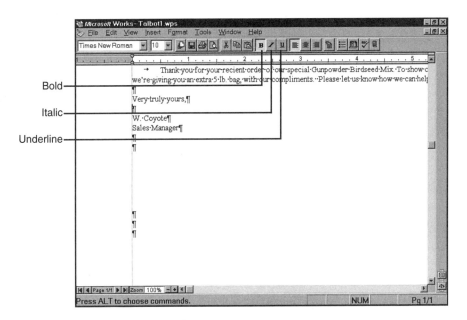

Figure 6.2 The Font Style buttons.

To change your text's font, size, and style from the menu, choose **Format, Font and Style**. The Format Font and Style dialog box is shown in Figure 6.3. The dialog box provides one location for you to change all of your text's visual attributes.

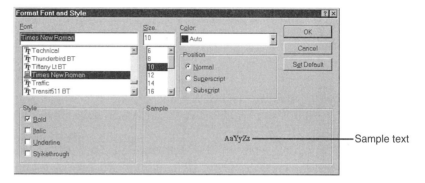

Figure 6.3   The Font and Style dialog box.

- Font—Select a font to use from the Font list. Use the list's scroll bar to see the different fonts available. The Sample area shows you sample text in each of the fonts you click in the list. You won't commit to a particular font until you click the OK button and exit the dialog box.

- Size—Select one from the list of point sizes. Use the list's scroll bar to see the larger sizes. The Sample area shows you what the selected point size looks like.

- Color—Click the drop arrow and scroll through 15 color choices. "Auto" is the default black text.

- Position—Choose from Normal, Superscript (text shrunken and raised above the baseline), and Subscript (text shrunken and lowered slightly below the baseline).

- Style—You can choose to make your text Bold, Italic, Underlined, or use Strikethrough to put a line through the text. You can use any combination of these styles.

 Baseline   As you type your Normal text, it is resting on an invisible line called a baseline. Think of it like writing on lined paper, except you can't see the line!

Changing the Default Font

Defaults are settings that are in effect automatically. Your default font in Works is Times New Roman, in 10 points. If you'd prefer to have a different font as your default, choose **Format**, **Font and Style** from the menu. Select your font, size, and style (you probably don't want colored text as a default), and click the **Set Default** button. Click **Yes** to change the default to your new settings.

Using WordArt

WordArt is a program, sometimes referred to as an *Applet*, that runs within Works and other Microsoft applications. You can use WordArt to create headlines and graphic text for newsletters, flyers, announcements, or any other type of document.

To insert WordArt into your open document:

1. Place your cursor where you want to place your WordArt text. Choose **Insert**, **WordArt** from the menu.

2. When WordArt is activated, its toolbar replaces the Works toolbar. Figure 6.4 shows the WordArt window and toolbar. A box appears in your document, with sample text that reads Type Your Text Here.

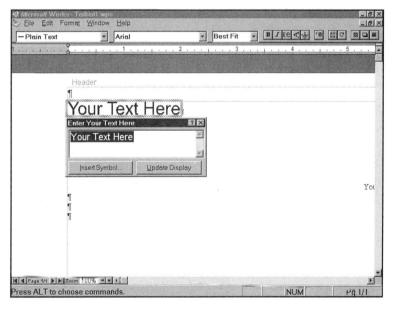

Figure 6.4   The WordArt window and toolbar.

3. Type your text and click the **Update Display** button. The WordArt text appears in your document, and the WordArt tools and text box remain on-screen.

There are many graphic effects that you can apply to your text with WordArt. Table 6.1 defines the WordArt tools.

Table 6.1   The WordArt Tools

Icon	Description
— Plain Text ▾	Click the drop-down list and choose a shape from the list. Your text will conform to the shape you select.
Arial ▾	Choose a font from the drop-down list.
Best Fit ▾	Click the drop-down list to choose a font size for your text. The default is Best Fit. Using Best Fit means that if your text box is enlarged or reduced, the text size will be automatically adjusted to fit the box.
B	Click this button to make your text Bold.
I	Make your text Italic with this button.
Ee	This button will convert your text to a combination of upper- and lowercase letters.
◁	Click this button to turn your text on its side.
A	This button will make your text grow vertically and horizontally to fit the text box.
≣	Click this button to choose your alignment, such as Center, Left, Right, and Justify.
AV↔	This button opens a dialog box with options for adjusting the space between your characters. Make your adjustments and click OK to close the dialog box.

Icon	Description
	Click this button to rotate your text. The Special Effects dialog box contains options for entering the degree of rotation, and the percentage that your text is skewed. Works refers to skewing as "sliding." Enter your rotate and slide settings and click OK to close the dialog box.
	Choose a shaded or patterned fill for your text, and click OK. The fill applies to the text, not the text box.
	Click this button to apply a shadow to your text. The Shadow dialog box contains options for selecting the direction of your shadow. After selecting your shadow style, click OK to close the dialog box.
	If you want your WordArt text box to have a border, click this button to select the border thickness and color. The default border is None.

For more information about aligning text, see Part III, Lesson 7, "Formatting Paragraphs."

When you're finished formatting your WordArt text, click anywhere outside the WordArt text box to deactivate WordArt and return to Works.

Once you've created WordArt, you can:

- Move the WordArt object by dragging it with your mouse. Your mouse pointer will change to a Move pointer (see Figure 6.5).
- Resize your WordArt object by clicking once on the text and then grabbing one of the handles and dragging outward to increase the item's size, or inward to make it smaller. The Resize mouse pointer is shown in Figure 6.6.
- Return to WordArt to reformat your text. Just double-click the WordArt object. The WordArt program is activated and the WordArt tools return to the screen.
- Delete a WordArt object by clicking it once to select it (the handles show) and then pressing the **Delete** key.

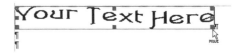

Figure 6.5 Moving a WordArt object.

Figure 6.6 Resizing a WordArt object.

In this lesson, you learned to change the font, size, style, and color of your text. You also learned to use WordArt to create graphic text. In the next lesson, you learn to format paragraphs.

Formatting Paragraphs

In this lesson, you learn to format paragraphs by using alignment, indents, and tabs. You also learn to create bulleted lists.

Aligning Text

You can align your text by the left and/or right margin, or from the center of the page. By default, your text is left aligned, meaning that when you type, your text starts on the left side of the page and the left side of your text stays even with the left margin. The right edge of the text doesn't have to stay even with the right margin (it's "ragged right").

Alignments can be applied to existing text, or set before you start typing. You can set your alignment from the toolbar or select **Format**, **Paragraphs** and use the Format Paragraph dialog box. Your four alignment choices are:

- Left—For paragraph text, this creates a ragged right edge with the left edge aligned with the margin. Left alignment is the default in new documents.
- Right—This alignment is often used for the date at the top of a letter. The right edge of a right-aligned paragraph is flush with the right margin, but the left edge is ragged.
- Center—You can use Center alignment for titles and headings. Center-aligned text is centered between the left and right margins.
- Justified—Justified alignment is available only from the Format Paragraphs dialog box. Use Justified alignment to align a paragraph from both the left and the right, eliminating the ragged right edge. Justified alignment is often used to create smooth text columns in newsletters.

To adjust the alignment of existing text in your open document, highlight the text and click the Left, Center, or Right alignment buttons on the toolbar. Figure 7.1 shows the Works toolbar and alignment buttons.

Figure 7.1   The Alignment buttons.

You can also adjust your alignment by choosing **Format**, **Paragraphs** from the menu. In the Format Paragraph dialog box (see Figure 7.2), click the button next to the Alignment style you want, and click **OK** to close the dialog box.

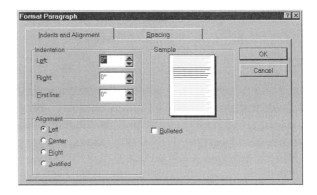

Figure 7.2   The Format Paragraph dialog box.

Using Tabs

Tabs are places on your document ruler where you place a mark (called a *tab stop*) that will control the movement of the **Tab** key. In a new, blank document, tabs are set by default to every half-inch starting at the left margin. You can set custom tabs at any place on the ruler and use them to indent the first line of a paragraph or for typing multi-column lists.

To set tabs, double-click the ruler or choose **Format**, **Tabs** from the menu. The Format Tabs dialog box is displayed as shown in Figure 7.3.

To set tabs in your open document:

1. Using the Format Tabs dialog box, choose a tab stop **Position** by typing the ruler location for your tab. You don't need to type the inch marks.

2. Select an Alignment for your tab. Choose Left, Center, Right, or Decimal.

3. Choose a Leader. The default is None, which works with most tabbed text.

4. Click **Set**. If you need to set more tabs, repeat steps 1 – 3, clicking Set after each one, and then click **OK** to accept your settings and close the dialog box.

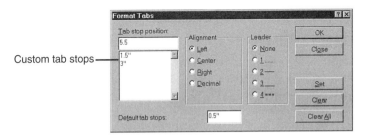

Custom tab stops

Figure 7.3 The Format Tabs dialog box.

Decimal Tabs These are particularly helpful for typing numbers with an irregular number of characters to the right of the decimal point but can also be used for currency where dollars and cents are involved (for whole numbers, use the Right alignment).

What's a Leader? A leader is a character, usually a dot, which fills the blank space between text and a tab. A table of contents is an example of the use of leader tabs. The page numbers are typed with a right-aligned, dot leader tab, creating a series of dots between the topic and the page number.

When tabs are set, they appear as small symbols on the ruler. Figure 7.4 shows the ruler with a series of tab stops.

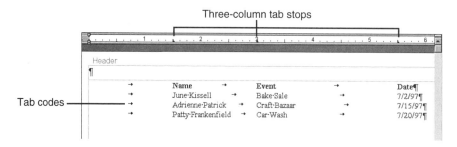

Figure 7.4 Tab stops on the ruler.

Editing Tabs

You can change tab settings that you've made in your document by moving the tab stops on the ruler with your mouse, or by making changes to your tab settings in the Format Tabs dialog box.

It is important to note that when you're entering your text, your tab settings apply from the cursor down in a document. If you set tabs when your cursor is at the top of a document, the tabs will stay in effect from the top down, until and unless you edit them. To set new tabs later in your document, reposition your cursor to the point where the new tab settings should take effect, and then set your new tabs. This works only as you're entering text.

To change your tab settings for text that has already been typed:

1. Select the text before opening the Format Tabs dialog box. (Choose **Format, Tabs** to display the dialog box.)

2. In the Format Tabs dialog box, select the tab you want to change by clicking the tab in the Tab Stop Position list box. To change the tab to a new setting, delete it and type in a new setting. Click **Set,** and then click **OK** to accept your changes and close the dialog box.

Clearing Tabs

To remove a tab stop, simply click the tab stop marker on the ruler with your mouse, and drag it down and off the ruler. When you release your mouse, the tab stop is gone. If you are removing a tab that applies to existing text, select the text before removing the tab. To remove a tab when you're in the Format Tabs dialog box, select the tab from the Tab Stop Position list box and click **Clear**. Click **Clear All** to remove all the tab stops and return to the default tab stops.

Indenting Paragraphs

Indenting a paragraph increases the distance between the text and the margin. You can set a variety of indent types, indenting the text from the left, right, or both. Paragraphs have two parts—a first line and a body. You can indent one or both of these parts. To set your paragraph indents:

1. In your open document, place your cursor in the paragraph you want to indent. You don't need to select any text unless you want to apply the indents to more than one existing paragraph.

2. Choose **Format**, **Paragraphs** from the menu. The Format Paragraph dialog box opens.

3. In the Indents and Alignment tab (refer to Figure 7.2), choose the Indentation you want:

   - Left Indent—The left edge of all the lines in the paragraph move to the left by an amount you specify.
   - Right indent—The right edge of all the lines in the paragraph move in a specified distance from the right margin.
   - First-line indent—The first line of the paragraph is indented by a distance you specify. The body of the paragraph remains at the left margin.

4. The Sample area of the dialog box shows how your indent settings will look in your document. Click the **OK** button to accept your settings and close the dialog box.

Figure 7.5 shows a variety of indented paragraphs.

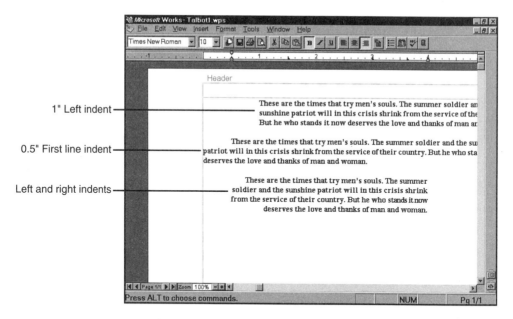

Figure 7.5   Paragraph indents.

Creating Bulleted Lists

You can type a list of single-line items or a series of paragraphs and put bullets in front of each one. The benefit of having Works do this for you (as opposed to you typing the bullets yourself) is that you can add items to your list and a new bullet will automatically appear.

To bullet an existing list in your open document:

1. Highlight the list of items or series of paragraphs that you want to bullet. Do not include the blank lines above or below the text in your selection.

2. Click the **Bullet** button on the toolbar.

Your text is bulleted with a generic dot bullet. If there were blank lines between your lines or paragraphs that are now bulleted, click each line individually and click the Bullet button on the toolbar. This will turn the bullet off for that line.

If you want to choose from a group of other symbols for your bullets, highlight your text and choose **Format, Bullets** from the menu. The Format Bullets dialog box is shown in Figure 7.6. Click the bullet symbol you want to use, and click **OK** to accept your selection and close the dialog box.

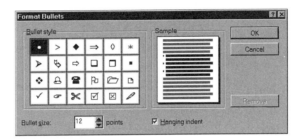

Figure 7.6 The Format Bullets dialog box.

 TIP **You've Changed the Default Bullet** Once you've selected a symbol for your bullet, that symbol becomes the default. The next time you bullet some text, if you want the generic dot bullet, you'll have to choose it from the Format Bullets dialog box.

In this lesson, you learned to format paragraphs by using alignment, indents, and tabs. You also learned to create bulleted lists. In the next lesson, you learn to use Easy Formats.

179

Using Easy Formats

In this lesson, you learn to use Works' Easy Formats feature to quickly apply a variety of text and paragraph formats to your document.

Applying a Format

To make it easier for you to format your documents, Works provides a tool called Easy Formats. *Easy Formats* are collections of formats that you can apply to any text. You can choose an Easy Format from the list of choices, or create your own. Existing Easy Formats can be edited to meet your specific needs. To apply an Easy Format to your open document:

1. Select the portion of your document to which you want to apply the Easy Format.

2. Choose **Format, Easy Formats** from the menu.

3. In the Easy Formats dialog box (see Figure 8.1), choose one of the formats from the list (the Sample box shows you how it will look and Description lists the formatting involved), and click the **Apply** button. Your text is automatically changed to the Easy Format style, and the dialog box is closed.

TIP **Know Your Easy Formats?** If you know what Easy Format you want to apply, save time by clicking the **Easy Formats** button on the toolbar. A list of available Easy Formats appears; click **More Easy Formats** if the format you want isn't on the list and then the Easy Formats dialog box appears.

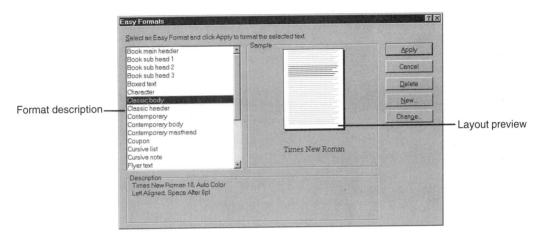

Format description

Layout preview

Figure 8.1   The Easy Formats dialog box.

Creating a Format

If the existing Easy Formats don't exactly meet your needs, you can create one that will. To create your own Easy Format:

1. Enter your text or use text in an existing document, and select the portion of it to which you want to apply your formats.

2. Choose **Format**, **Easy Formats** from the menu to open the Easy Formats dialog box, then click the **New** button, or click the **Easy Formats** button on the toolbar and choose **Create from Selection** from the drop-down menu.

3. Within the **New Easy Format** dialog box (see Figure 8.2), enter a name for your new Easy Format.

4. Using the six Format Settings buttons, you can assign fonts, indents, borders, and many other character and paragraph formats, and make them part of your Easy Format. Each Settings button opens the standard dialog box for that particular format.

5. After you've set your options in some or all of the formatting option areas, click the **Done** button. Your Easy Format name is added to the list of formats in the Easy Formats dialog box.

6. Choose your new Easy Format name from the list and click **Apply**. Your Easy Format will be applied to your selected text.

181

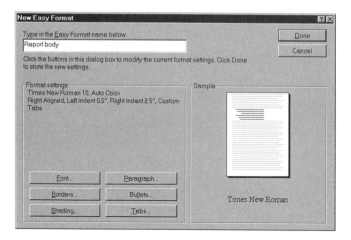

Figure 8.2   Create a new Easy Format.

For more information on applying character formats, see, Lesson 6 in this part, "Formatting Text." You can learn more about paragraph formatting in Lesson 7, "Formatting Paragraphs."

Changing and Deleting Formats

After you've created an Easy Format, you may decide you want to change something about it. You may also want to change something about the Easy Formats that Works provided. To edit an Easy Format:

1. Choose **Format**, **Easy Formats** from the menu.

2. In the Easy Formats dialog box, select the Easy Format name you want to edit and click the **Change** button. The Change Easy Formats dialog box opens. You'll notice that it looks just like the New Easy Format dialog box.

3. Using any or all of the six Format Settings buttons, change the aspects of the Easy Format that you need to, and click **Done** when your changes are complete.

4. Back in the main Easy Formats dialog box, you can choose your edited Easy Format and click **Apply** to format your selected text. If you have no text to apply it to at this time, click the **Close** button.

TIP **Applying to Existing Text** If you want to apply the edited Easy Format to existing text immediately after you've completed your modifications, select the text before beginning the editing process.

To completely remove an Easy Format from the list:

1. Choose **Format**, **Easy Formats** from the menu.

2. In the Easy Formats dialog box, select the Easy Format name you want to delete from the list. Click the **Delete** button. A prompt asks you to confirm your deletion. Click **Yes**.

3. To exit the Easy Formats dialog box, click **Close**.

In this lesson, you learned to use Works' Easy Formats feature to quickly apply a variety of text and paragraph formats to your document. In the next lesson, you learn to format your documents' pages.

Formatting Pages

In this lesson, you learn to format your documents by inserting page breaks, adding page numbers, setting margins, and using headers and footers. You'll also learn to create and format columns.

Inserting Page Breaks

Page breaks occur naturally every time your text exceeds the length of a page. As you're entering text and you reach the bottom margin of the page, Works creates a new page and the rest of the text flows onto it. However, you may need to "force" a page break where one would not occur naturally to keep text on a particular page or move the following text to the next page (for example, you want to keep a title page on one page and put the following text on the next page).

To manually create a page break, position your cursor where you want the page break to occur and do one of the following:

- Press **Ctrl+Enter**.
- Choose **Insert, Page Break** from the menu.

A page break that you create is different from one that occurs naturally as you type. A naturally occurring page break doesn't control where the text breaks between the preceding page and the subsequent page. If you delete text on the first page, text flows back from the second page. In the case of a forced page break, however, a code is inserted into the document, and the text that follows the page break cannot flow back unless the page break code is deleted.

To see your page breaks, make sure you're in Normal view by choosing **View, Normal** from the menu. It is only in Normal view that you can see and delete your page breaks. Page breaks appear as dotted lines running horizontally on the page. To delete your break, place the mouse in the left margin, on the same line as the dotted break line. Click the mouse to select the page break and press the **Delete** key.

 TIP   **Page Layout versus Normal View**   Works lets you view your word processing documents in two ways. The Page Layout view (the default view) shows you the edge of your pages, columns, footnotes, all pictures and objects, and headers and footers in the same position as they will appear on the printed page. The Normal view displays the document with formatting and objects but doesn't necessarily look the same as the final printed version: Headers and footers appear on the first page only, footnotes appear in a separate pane, columns appear below each other, and some pictures and objects may not display. However, it may be faster to type in Normal view, because you don't have to wait as long for the screen to refresh. To select a view, choose **View**, **Page Layout** or **View**, **Normal**.

Adding Page Numbers

It's a good idea to add page numbers to any documents that are longer than one page. Page numbers can make your collating job easier if you're producing multiple copies of the document, and they make it easier for your readers to keep the document pages in order.

To add page numbers to your document:

1. In an open, multi-page document, place your cursor in the header or footer area. It doesn't matter which page you're on. If you can't see the header and footer sections, choose **View, Page Layout** from the menu.
2. Choose **Insert, Page Number** from the menu.
3. The word *page* (between asterisks) appears on your document, in the upper-left corner. This is a page number code, also known as a place-holder. When the document is printed, the actual page number will replace the code.
4. To center or right-align your page number, highlight the code and click the appropriate alignment button on your toolbar.

5. To remove the page number from the first page of your document, choose **File, Page Setup** from the menu. Click the **Other Options** tab, and select the **No Header** and **No Footer on First Page** options. Click **OK.** Figure 9.1 shows the Page Setup dialog box.

6. To start your page numbering with a number other than 1, choose **File, Page Setup** from the menu. Click **the Other Options** tab, and enter a number in the `Starting page number` box (or use the up and down arrows to change the number). Click **OK.**

What About the First Page? Traditionally, the first page of a business or personal letter is not numbered.

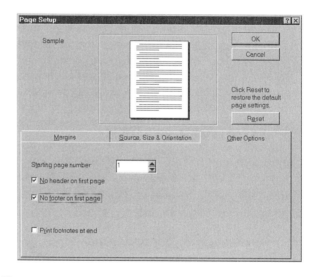

Figure 9.1 The page numbering options.

Page Number One If your page one is a cover page, you can make page two into page one by setting the starting page number to zero. The starting page number can also be set to negative numbers, so you can count the number of unnumbered pages that precede the page you want to be page one, and set the starting page number to that negative number. This can be useful if your document will have several introductory pages or a table of contents.

Using Headers and Footers

Just as page numbers help readers see which page they're on, headers and footers provide information to assist the reader in following long documents. A *header* is text that appears at the top of every page in your document, and a *footer* is text that appears at the bottom of every page in your document. You can place title, date, copyright, and other information in your header and footer.

Choose **View, Page Layout** from the menu to view the Header and Footer area on your document.

To insert header and footer text in your document:

1. Click your mouse to place your cursor in the header or footer area of your document. (You can also choose **View, Header** or **View, Footer** from the menu.) Figure 9.2 shows the header area in Page Layout view.

Figure 9.2   The header area with text inserted.

2. Type your text. You can format this text as you would any other text in the body of the document.
3. To switch between the header area and the footer area, use your scroll bars and reposition your cursor by clicking your mouse in the header or footer area, or **choose View, Header** or **View, Footer** from the menu.

Just as page numbers shouldn't be placed on the first page of a business or personal letter, headers and footers should not appear on the first page, either. To remove the header and footer sections from your first page:

1. Choose **File, Page Setup** from the menu.
2. Click the **Other Options** tab (refer to Figure 9.1).
3. Check **No header on first page** to remove the header from the first page. Check **No footer on first page** to remove the footer.
4. Click **OK** to accept your settings and close the dialog box.

Changing Margins

Your document margins are the area around the edge of the page where there is no text. Works' default margins are 1" from the top and bottom, and 1.25" from the left and right sides of the page.

To change your margins for your open document:

1. Choose **File**, **Page Setup** from the menu. Click the **Margins** tab. Figure 9.3 shows the Margins tab in the Page Setup dialog box.

2. You'll see four boxes for the **Top**, **Bottom**, **Left**, and **Right** margins of your page. Use the up and down arrows to increase or decrease the defaults, or select the contents of the boxes and type the new measurement. You don't need to type the inch marks.

3. Click **OK** to accept your changes and close the dialog box.

 TIP **Header and Footer Margins** In the Page Setup dialog box, you can also set how far from the edge of the paper you want to put the header or footer. Under From Edge, specify an amount in the `Header Margin` or `Footer Margin` text box.

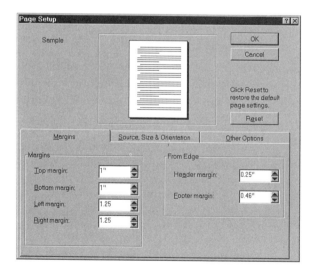

Figure 9.3 Setting margins from the Page Setup dialog box.

Setting the Paper Size

Most business and personal documents are "letter size," or 8.5" x 11," and this is the default paper size for a Works word processing document. If you want to print on another size paper, you can do so through the Page Setup dialog box.

To change the size of your open document's paper:

1. Choose **File**, **Page Setup** from the menu. This opens the Page Setup dialog box.

2. Click the **Source, Size & Orientation** tab (see Figure 9.4). This tab offers several options for changing or customizing your paper settings:

   - Orientation—Choose between Portrait and Landscape. These orientation settings can apply to any size paper. *Portrait* is the default and means that the paper is longer than it is wide. *Landscape* turns the paper on its side, so that it's wider than it is long.

   - Source—If you have more than one paper tray on your printer, you may keep preprinted stationery in one tray and blank sheets in the other. Use this drop-down box to select the tray that contains the paper you want to use.

   - Size—Choose from a list of several paper sizes, beginning with the commonly used Letter and Legal. There are also several envelope settings. You'll find out more about printing envelopes in lesson 15 in this section.

   - Width and Height options—Displays the measurements of the selected paper size. Use these option boxes to customize a paper size.

3. Choose the appropriate paper size, orientation, and paper tray. Click **OK** to accept your settings and close the dialog box.

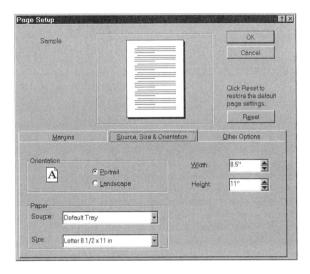

Figure 9.4 Paper Source, Size, and Orientation.

Creating Columns

When you create a newsletter or similar document, you can divide your page into columns like a newspaper. Although you can set up several columns per page, two or three columns are the easiest for you to use and your audience to read.

Column settings apply to your entire document. You can format existing text in columns or set up columns in a blank document before you begin typing.

To apply columns to your open document:

1. Choose **View**, **Page Layout** from the menu. You won't be able to see your columns unless you're in Page Layout view.

2. Place your cursor anywhere in the body of an open document. Choose **Format**, **Columns** from the menu. This opens the Format Columns dialog box shown in Figure 9.5. In this dialog box, you can enter up to three settings:

   • Number of columns—You can enter up to seven columns for portrait, letter-size paper. If you choose a higher number, Works will advise you that your number of columns and the paper size don't match.

- Space Between—This setting controls the space between columns. The default is 0.5". You may have to print your document before you can judge if this distance is too small or too large. Then adjust the gap between the columns by changing this measurement.

- Line Between Columns—Vertical lines serve two purposes—they can add a polished look to a newsletter, and they can help the reader follow the text.

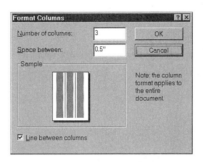

Figure 9.5   Formatting Columns.

3. After entering your selections, click **OK** to close the dialog box.

For more information on creating a newsletter, see Part VI, Lesson 8, "Creating a Newsletter."

At any point, you can change your column setup by choosing **Format, Columns** from the menu and modifying the dialog box settings. After you click **OK**, the text in your document will flow as specified in your new column setup.

What If I Want to Go Back to No Columns?   No columns and 1 column are the same setting. Change your number of columns to 1 in the Format Columns dialog box, and click **OK**.

CAUTION

In this lesson, you learned to format your documents' pages by inserting page breaks, adding page numbers, setting margins, and using headers and footers. You also learned to create and format columns. In the next lesson, you learn to create Tables.

Working with Tables

In this lesson, you learn to create tables, change table dimensions, and apply borders and shading to enhance the appearance of the table.

What Is a Table?

A table is a group of rows and columns added to a document for storing and organizing text. The intersections of the columns and rows in a table are called *cells*. Tables can be used to create multi-column lists, parallel paragraphs, and fill-in forms.

 TIP **Using Spreadsheets** If your table is going to contain a lot of calculations and will be filled with numbers rather than text, create a spreadsheet in Works' spreadsheet program. If you need to include the spreadsheet in your word processing document, you can always copy the spreadsheet to the Clipboard and then paste it into the document.

For more information about spreadsheets, see Part IV, Lesson 1, "Spreadsheet Basics."

Creating a Table

A Works word processing table is actually a simple spreadsheet that is added to your document. To create a table in an open document:

1. Place your cursor at the point in your document where you want to place the table.

2. Choose **Insert, Table** from the menu.

3. In the Insert Table dialog box, you can set the number of rows and columns and choose from a list of predesigned table formats (see Figure 10.1). The Example area shows what the selected format looks like.

4. Click **OK** to accept your settings and close the dialog box.

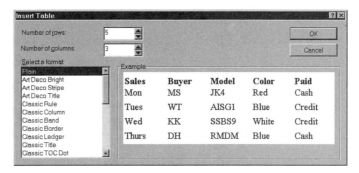

Figure 10.1 Inserting a Table.

TIP   **Context-Sensitivity**   When you're working in a table, your menus (all but File, Window, and Help) will change to contain spreadsheet-related commands. This is called *context-sensitivity*. If you click your mouse outside of the table, your menus return to normal. Click back inside the table and the spreadsheet commands reappear.

Entering Text into a Table

After you've inserted your table, you see a large rectangle appear on your screen. The first cell is active, and your cursor is blinking in the cell (see Figure 10.2). To enter text into the cell, simply type as you would any other text. Press the **Tab** key to move to the next cell (press **Shift**+**Tab** to move to the previous cell). You can also use the arrow keys to move from cell to cell or click in a cell to place the cursor there. Do *not* press **Enter** to move from cell to cell. Pressing Enter begins a new paragraph within the cell.

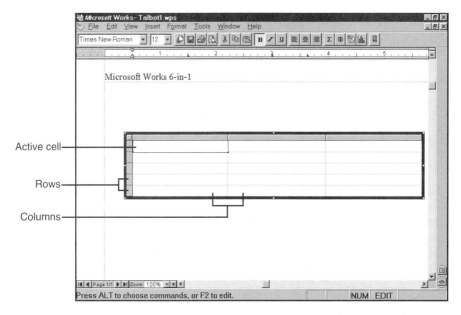

Figure 10.2 A new table.

Selecting Table Cells

In order to format your table cells or the text in your table, you have to select the cells first. To select cells in your table, click in the first cell you want to select, and drag your mouse through the remaining cells you want to select. You can also press your **Shift** key and use your arrow keys to select cells in any direction.

If you want to select an entire column or row, click the control cell at the top of each column or at the beginning of each row. Figure 10.3 shows the table control cells and a group of selected cells.

Figure 10.3 A group of selected cells.

Formatting Text in a Table

You can format text in table cells like any other text—you can change the text's alignment, fonts, style, and size. You can type paragraph text into a cell (the text will wrap within the horizontal dimensions of the cell) and set indents for the text. The only thing you can't do in a table cell is use the **Tab** key to indent text, since the Tab key moves you to the next cell. Figure 10.4 shows a document that was created with a table.

Invoice	Amount	Date Due	
B12789	$605.63	8/15/97	← Centered column headings
B12876	$1,500.00	9/21/97	
B13006	$56.95	10/5/97	
TOTAL	$2,162.58		

Text formatting (bold and italic) →

Figure 10.4 Formatted text in a table.

TIP **Having Trouble Navigating Through Your Table?** Turn on your gridlines so you can see each individual cell. To turn on or turn off gridlines, choose **View**, **Gridlines**.

For more information about formatting text, see Lesson 6, "Formatting Text," and Lesson 7, "Formatting Paragraphs," in this part.

In addition to character and paragraph formatting, you can format any numbers in your table. Choose formats such as currency (adds a dollar sign and a comma between thousands), percentages (multiplies the number by 100 and adds a percent sign), fractions (changes decimals to fractions), or dates (lets you change 1/23/97 to January 23, 1997). You can choose from 12 number formats in the Format Cells dialog box (see Figure 10.5). To format the numbers in your table:

1. Select the cell or group of cells you want to format.

2. Choose **Format**, **Number** from the menu to open the Format Cells dialog box, then click the **Number** tab (see Figure 10.5).

3. Choose your number format (check the Sample box to see how the number will look) and the number of decimal places you want to display.

4. Click **OK** to accept your settings and close the dialog box.

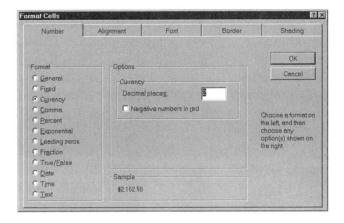

Figure 10.5 Number formats.

 TIP **Currency Button** Use the Currency button on the toolbar to format your cells that contain money amounts. Select the cells first, and then click the button.

Changing Table Dimensions

Before you create your table, you should think about what will go into it. For example, if the table will contain a list of employees and the hours they worked on a given day, think about how many columns that will require — one column each for the employee name, date, and hours worked. That's three columns. The number of employees plus your column headings will tell you how many rows you'll need.

Even if you plan ahead, you might need to make changes. After you've created the table and entered the text, you may decide that you want to add a column for the employees' Social Security numbers. If you forget to put in an employee and his or her hours, you'll need to add a row.

Adding Columns and Rows

To add a column, place your cursor in any cell in the column to the right of where you want to add your new column. Choose **Insert**, **Column** from the menu (or right-click the cell and choose **Insert Column** from the pop-up menu). A new column appears, sized to fit within your current table dimensions.

To add a row, click to place your cursor in any cell in the row below where you want to add your new row. Choose **Insert**, **Row** from the menu (or right-click the cell and choose **Insert Row** from the pop-up menu).

Changing Column Width

You can change the width of your columns to accommodate the width of the text in your cells.

To adjust column width from within the table:

1. Move your mouse pointer to the gray cells at the top of the column you want to widen or narrow.

2. Point to the seam between the column you want to adjust and the column to its right. You'll know you're in the right place because your mouse pointer will say Adjust, as shown in Figure 10.6.

Mouse pointer in Adjust mode

Invoice	Amount	Date Due
B12789	$605.63	8/15/97
B12876	$1,500.00	9/21/97
B13006	$56.95	10/5/97
TOTAL	$2,162.58	

Figure 10.6 Changing the column width.

3. Hold down the left mouse button and drag to the right to widen the column or to the left to narrow it.

To change column width from the menu:

1. Place your cursor in any cell in the column to be adjusted. Choose **Format**, **Column Width** from the menu.

2. In the **Column Width** dialog box, enter the number of characters wide your column should be. The default is 15 (see Figure 10.7).

3. Click **OK** to accept your setting and close the dialog box.

TIP   **Column Width**   If you're not sure how many characters across to make your column, click the **Best Fit** button in the Column Width dialog box. Your column width will be based on the widest entry.

Figure 10.7   Column width dialog box.

TIP   **Row Height**   Although the row height adjusts automatically depending on the size of type in the row, you can adjust the row height manually by dragging the seam between the gray cells at the beginning of the rows. You can also choose **Format, Row Height** from the menu to open the Format Row Height dialog box where you can specify the exact row height you want, click **Standard** to return to the standard row height, or click **Best Fit** to let Works fit the row height to the contents of the row. Click **OK** to exit the dialog box.

Applying Borders and Shading

Adding borders and shading to your table will enhance its appearance, and help to draw your readers' attention to specific columns, rows, or cells. Works supplies a series of preformatted table shading and border designs, which can make the process of enhancing a table much easier. To apply these formats to a table in your open document:

1. Place your cursor anywhere in the table. If you've clicked outside of the table, double-click the table to reactivate it.

2. Choose **Format**, **AutoFormat** from the menu. This opens the AutoFormat dialog box.

3. Scroll through the list of formats, and preview them by clicking them once. The Example area shows you a preview of the selected format. When you find one you like, click **OK** to accept your selection and close the dialog box. Figure 10.8 shows the AutoFormat dialog box.

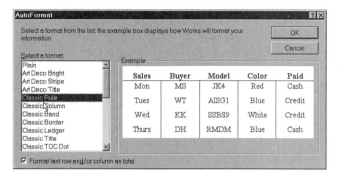

Figure 10.8 The Table AutoFormat dialog box.

If you'd prefer to apply your own borders and shading on a cell-by-cell basis, you can use the separate Borders and Shading commands in the Format menu. To apply borders and shading to individual cells:

1. Select the cell or cells you want to shade or border.

2. Choose one of the following menu commands:

- To apply shading, choose **Format**, **Shading** from the menu. Figure 10.9 shows the Shading tab in the Format Cells dialog box. Choose the shading pattern and foreground and background colors you want.

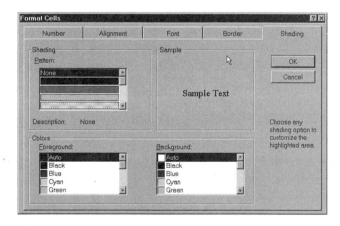

Figure 10.9 Apply shading to a table.

- To apply a border, choose **Format**, **Border** from the menu. Figure 10.10 shows the Border tab in the Format Cells dialog box. Choose the border type, color, and line style you want for your table.

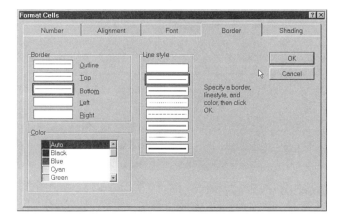

Figure 10.10 Applying borders to a table.

3. Click **OK** to accept your settings and close the dialog box.

TIP **Format Cells** You'll notice that if you choose Format, Border or Format, Shading, both commands take you to the Format Cells dialog box. You can click the Border or Shading tabs to do both jobs from one place, with one original command.

CAUTION **How Do I Remove a Table I Don't Want?** If you decide you don't need the table in your document, select the table by clicking it once. The table displays gray handles (if a solid border shows, click outside the table and the gray handles will appear). Press the **Delete** key.

In this lesson, you learned to create a table, enter text into table cells, and format the cell's appearance. In the next lesson, you'll learn to use Note It.

Using Note-It

In this lesson, you learn to use Works' Note-It program to add graphic pop-up text to your documents.

What Is Note-It?

Note-It is a program available through Works' Word Processor, Spreadsheet, and Database applications. A Note-It note is represented by a picture that you can place anywhere in your document, spreadsheet, or database form. When you double-click the picture, it displays a pop-up text message that you created. Note-It lets you pass comments or instructions on to readers or editors that can only be seen online.

Creating a Note

Creating a Note-It note requires some thinking ahead of time. First, you should decide where to place the picture that triggers your pop-up. Second, decide what your pop-up text will be. Note-Its are primarily used for comments and instructions for a reader who will be reviewing the document on-screen.

To create a Note-It in your open document:

1. Place your cursor where you want the picture to be.

2. Choose **Insert, Note-It** from the menu. The Note-It document window opens.

3. Select a picture from the Choose a Picture box that will represent your note. There are 20 graphics to choose from—you'll have to scroll horizontally to the right to see them all (see Figure 11.1).

4. In the Type Your Caption Here box (located beneath the pictures), enter an optional Caption for the graphic. The caption could read `Double-click here` or `Read this!` or something like that. If your readers are familiar with using Note-It, you can skip the caption.

5. In the Type Your Note Here box, select the instructional text and replace it by typing your note. The pop-up window will accept approximately 500 words, although a short note is the most effective use of this feature.

6. Choose the text size by clicking the button next to Big or Small.

7. Click **OK** to save your note and close the window. The Note-It picture and caption now appear in your document.

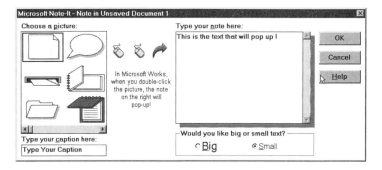

Figure 11.1   The Note-It window.

Moving and Copying Notes

If you've put your Note-It in the wrong place in the document, you can move it by using the Clipboard to cut and paste the Note-It picture. If you want to use the same Note-It in an additional location, use copy and paste to share the Note-It.

To use cut or copy:

1. Click once on your Note-It picture to select it. A thin, gray border and small handles will appear around the picture.

2. Choose **Edit, Cut** from the menu to move the picture, or **Edit, Copy** to duplicate it. This will put the picture, the caption, and the associated pop-up text on the Clipboard.

3. Position your cursor in the spot where you want to put the Note-It. Choose **Edit, Paste** from the menu. Your Note-It picture appears. If you double-click the Note-It picture, you see that the pop-up has come with it!

For more information about cutting and copying text with the Clipboard, see Part III, Lesson 3, "Editing Text," earlier in this part.

Editing and Resizing Notes

Change your Note-It by right-clicking the picture in your document. From the menu that appears, choose **Microsoft Note-It Object** and then choose **Edit** from the submenu. This reopens the Note-It document window, and you can choose a different picture, change your caption, and edit your pop-up text. Click **OK** in the window to accept your changes and close the dialog box.

To change the size of your Note-It picture, click once on the picture to select it. Place your mouse on one of the *handles* that appear on the object's sides or corners. The mouse pointer will change and the word Resize will display (see Figure 11.2). Your resizing options:

- To make the picture bigger, drag outward.
- To make it smaller, drag toward the middle of the picture.
- To increase or decrease its size but maintain its horizontal and vertical proportions (and thus avoid distortion of the picture), drag from a corner handle.

Handle   A handle is a small box that appears on the sides and corners of a selected graphic object, such as a Note-It picture. By clicking and dragging on the handles, you can resize a graphic.

Figure 11.2   Resizing a Note-It.

Deleting Notes

A Note-It is very easy to delete. Click the Note-It picture once to select it (don't display the pop-up) and press the **Delete** key.

CAUTION

I Didn't Mean to Delete That!   If you just deleted it, choose **Edit**, **Undo** from the menu, or press **Ctrl+Z**. Remember that Undo undoes only your last action!

In this lesson, you learned to create, edit, and delete a Note-It object. In the next lesson, you learn to add clip art and spreadsheet charts to a document.

Adding Clip Art and Charts

In this lesson, you learn to use Clip art and paste charts from a spreadsheet into your document.

What Is Clip Art?

Clip art are graphic images that you can add to your documents. Some are simple line drawings; others are complex graphics that use multiple colored and patterned fills. Works has a large group of its own clip art images that you can use, or you can use clip art from other Windows applications. Clip art collections are also available on CD-ROM at your local computer store. Most clip art images for Windows applications are interchangeable; others can be used with only one particular software program.

Inserting Clip Art

Works provides a Clip Art Gallery of just under 200 images. The images are broken down into categories, such as **Academic**, **Cartoons**, and **People at Work**. Many of them are full color, some are black-and-white.

To choose one of the images and place it in your open document:

1. Place your cursor where you want the clip art image. Choose **Insert**, **Clip Art** from the menu. The Microsoft Clip Gallery box opens (see Figure 12.1).

2. Choose a category on the left, and view the images for that category in the large box in the middle. If you want to see all of the available clip art images without changing categories, choose **All Categories**.

3. When you've found the image that suits your needs, you can either double-click to select it and close the dialog box, or you can click the image once and click **OK**. The image appears in your document.

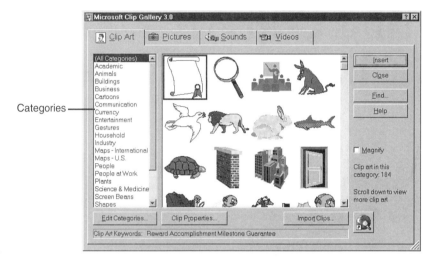

Categories

Figure 12.1   The Clip Art Gallery.

Resizing and Moving Clip Art

To change the size of your clip art, click once on the picture to select it. You'll know it's selected when a thin gray border and small boxes appear around the edge of the image. Place your mouse on one of the boxes (called *handles*) that appear on the sides and corners of the clip art. The mouse pointer will change and the word Resize will display (see Figure 12.2).

Your resizing options are:

- To make the clip art bigger, drag outward.
- To make it smaller, drag toward the middle of the picture.
- To increase or decrease its size in horizontal and vertical proportion (without distorting the image), drag from a corner handle.

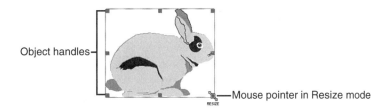

Object handles—

—Mouse pointer in Resize mode

Figure 12.2 Resizing Clip Art.

When you place clip art in your document, it is *Inline*, meaning it will move in your document as though it were text. You can center it with your alignment tools, for example, but you can't move it freely in the document. To be able to move it in any direction and have your text wrap around the image, you need to make the image *Absolute*. To change this setting, click once on the image to select it, and choose **Format**, **Text Wrap**. This opens the Format Picture dialog box, as shown in Figure 12.3. Click the **Absolute** button, and click **OK** to close the dialog box.

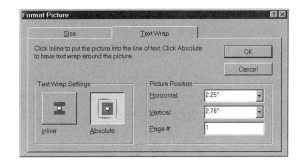

Figure 12.3 Text Wrap options.

Deleting Clip Art

Clip art is simple to delete. Click once on the clip art to select it and then press the **Delete** key.

I Didn't Mean to Delete That! If you just deleted it, choose **Edit**, **Undo** from the menu, or press **Ctrl+Z**. Remember that Undo undoes only your last action!

CAUTION

Importing New Clip Art

If you have clip art that "came with" another computer program or if you purchased a clip art collection on CD, you can import the clip art into your Works Clip Art Gallery. To add to the Gallery:

1. In an open document, place your cursor where you want the clip art image.
2. Choose **Insert**, **Clip Art** from the menu.
3. In the Microsoft Clip Gallery dialog box, click the **Import Clips** button.
4. In the **Add clip art to Clip Gallery** dialog box, choose the location of your clip art—Use the Look in box to select another folder on your hard drive or your CD-ROM drive (see Figure 12.4). When you go to the site where the clip art images are stored, the clip art files will appear in the list of file names.

Figure 12.4   Add Clip Art to the Gallery.

5. You can add the files one at a time, or hold down the **Ctrl** key as you click to select several at once. To add a clip art to your Gallery, select the file or files, and then click **OK** to select the files and close the dialog box.
6. The Clip Properties dialog box opens, and asks you to enter a keyword and to choose a category (see Figure 12.5). Both the keyword and category are optional. Click **OK** to add the clip art image to your Gallery and close the dialog box.

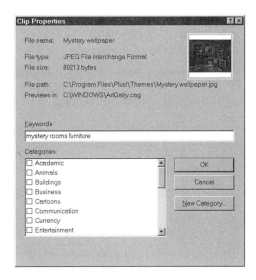

Figure 12.5 Clip Art Properties.

Your new clip art image is now on the Pictures tab in the Gallery.

What's a Keyword? Works' clip art images are each associated with one or more keywords. You can use the **Find** button in the Clip Art Gallery to search for clip art images by their keywords. For example, if you enter the keyword "Flower" in the Find dialog box, the Rose and the Sunflower images appear in the Gallery display.

Inserting a Spreadsheet Chart

Charts are a graphic representation of numeric data. You can add a chart that you've created in Works' spreadsheet program to your word processing document, or you can create a chart especially for your document.

To add an existing chart to your open document:

1. Place your cursor where you want to place the chart.

2. Choose **Insert, Chart** from the menu.

3. The Insert Chart dialog box opens (see Figure 12.6). Choose **Use an Existing Chart** and select your chart from the list of saved charts.

4. Click **OK** to accept your selection and close the dialog box. The chart is inserted into your document.

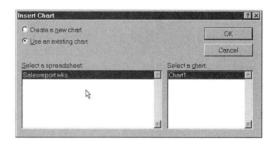

Figure 12.6 Inserting a Spreadsheet Chart.

TIP **Use the Right Tool for the Job** While you can create a chart from within Works' word processor, you're really using the spreadsheet program to do it. You'd be better off creating the chart in the spreadsheet program, where all the charting tools are available. After you create it, you can save it and access it as an existing chart in your current and future documents.

For more information on creating a chart with Works' Spreadsheet program, see Part IV, Lesson 18, "Chart and Graph Basics."

Moving, Resizing, and Deleting a Chart

To change the size of your chart, click once on the chart to select it. You'll know it's selected when a thin gray border and small boxes (called *handles*) appear around the edge of the image. Place your mouse on one of the handles. The mouse pointer will change and the word Resize will display. You have the following resizing options:

- To make the chart bigger, drag outward.
- To make it smaller, drag toward the middle of the picture.
- To increase or decrease its size in horizontal and vertical proportion (without distorting the image), drag from a corner handle.

To be able to move your chart in any direction, you must change its Text Wrap settings. To change this setting, click once on the image to select it, and choose **Format**, **Text Wrap**. On the Text Wrap tab, click the **Absolute** button, and click **OK** to close the dialog box.

To delete your chart, click once on it to select it and press the **Delete** key.

In this lesson, you learned to add clip art and charts to your document and change their size and location. In the next lesson, you learn to use Microsoft Draw.

Using Microsoft Draw

In this lesson, you learn to use Microsoft Draw to create shapes, lines, and graphic text to enhance your word processing documents.

What Is Microsoft Draw?

Microsoft Draw is a program that is available from Works' Word processor, Spreadsheet, and Database applications. It is used for creating geometric and freeform shapes, lines, and graphic text. You can use the Draw features to add diagrams to your documents or create a drawing that illustrates your text.

Starting Microsoft Draw

You can open the Microsoft Draw program by choosing **Insert**, **Drawing** from the menu. The Microsoft Draw program window opens on top of your document. The Microsoft Draw window is shown in Figure 13.1. After opening the program, you can maximize the window to increase your work area.

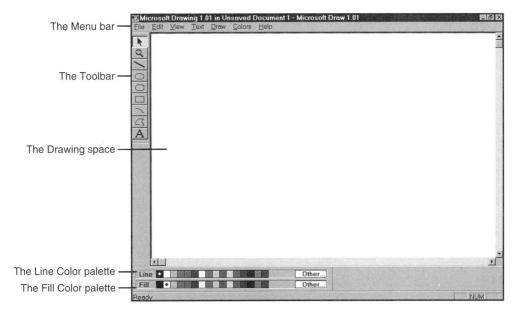

The Menu bar

The Toolbar

The Drawing space

The Line Color palette
The Fill Color palette

Figure 13.1 The Microsoft Draw window.

Understanding the Draw Window

The Microsoft Draw window contains four main components:

- The Drawing space—the area where you'll create your drawing.
- The Menu bar—seven menus give you commands for enhancing and controlling your drawn objects.
- The Toolbar—a series of eight tools for drawing and viewing circles, squares, freeform shapes, lines, and typing text.
- Two Color palettes—one for the object's fill color, the other for its outline color.

Understanding the Toolbar

There are nine tools on the toolbar—seven of them for creating objects, two of them for selecting and viewing objects you've already drawn. Table 13.1 shows each of the tools and describes their uses.

Table 13.1   The Microsoft Draw Tools

Icon	Description
▲	The Pointer is used for selecting an existing object. Click this tool and then click the object you want to select.
🔍	The Zoom tool will magnify an object, by "zooming in" on it. Click the tool, and then click your mouse on the object or portion of the drawing you want to magnify (hold down Shift to zoom out).
╲	The Line tool draws straight lines at any angle.
◯	The Oval tool draws ovals and circles. To draw a perfect circle, press and hold the Shift key while you draw the object.
▢	The Rounded Rectangle tool draws rectangles and squares with rounded corners. To draw a perfect square with rounded corners, press and hold the Shift key while you draw the object.
▢	The Rectangle tool draws rectangles and squares. Press and hold the Shift key while drawing to create a perfect square.
⌒	The Arc tool makes filled wedge shapes or arc lines. To draw a line only, select the object and turn off the Filled attribute in the Draw menu.
◿	The Freeform tool has three uses — to draw wavy lines, to draw wavy closed shapes, or to draw freeform polygons with straight sides. To draw wavy lines and shapes, select the tool and then drag your mouse on the drawing space. To draw polygons with straight sides, click and move the mouse rather than drag it as you draw each side of the polygon.
A	The Text tool allows you to type on your drawing. Select the tool and then click your drawing space to insert your cursor and begin typing.

Drawing Objects

Before drawing an object, you must select the appropriate tool. To select a tool, click the toolbar button with your mouse.

After you've selected the tool, move your mouse onto the drawing space. You'll notice that your mouse pointer changes:

- If you're drawing a shape or a line, the pointer turns to a crosshair (+). Click the mouse pointer to choose your starting point, and drag the mouse to create your object (see Figure 13.2). You'll drag diagonally, away from your starting point. The farther you drag, the wider your object will be.
- If you select the text tool, your pointer turns into an I-beam (see Figure 13.3). Click the mouse to place your I-beam, and begin to type.

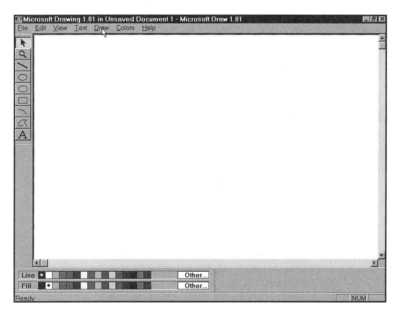

Figure 13.2 Drawing shapes and lines.

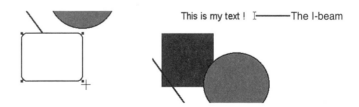

Figure 13.3 Typing text in a drawing.

TIP   **No Word Wrap**   There are no margins or Word Wrap in Microsoft Draw. If you want to type a paragraph, you will have to "fake" it by pressing **Enter** to force the text onto the next line. Microsoft Draw's text tool is best used for single words and short phrases.

Formatting Objects

You can change the appearance of an object after you've drawn it by using the menus and color palettes.

To change an existing object's fill or outline:

- Select the object by clicking it once. Four handles will appear on the object's corners.
- To change the object's fill or outline color, choose the desired colors from the fill and outline palettes.
- If you want to give the object a patterned fill, choose **Draw**, **Pattern** from the menu, and choose a pattern from the submenu.
- To accept the changes and deselect the current object, click away from the object on an unused spot in your drawing space.

 TIP   **Removing Fills**   To completely remove an object's fill attributes, choose **Draw**, **Filled** from the menu. Selecting **Filled** will remove the check mark next to the command and change the object to an empty shape.

If you draw an arc, freeform, or straight line, you can change the line's color from the line color palette. You can also apply a line style, such as dotted, dashed, or thick. To apply a line style to your selected line, choose **Draw**, **Line Style**. Select a style from the submenu, and your line takes on that style. Line styles can also be applied to the outline of a geometric or freeform closed shape.

Resizing and Moving Objects

You can make an existing object bigger or smaller by dragging its handles (see Figure 13.4).

To resize an object:

1. Select the item by clicking it once with your mouse. Four handles appear, one on each corner.
2. Point to a handle and press the mouse button. Drag the mouse outward to increase the object's size, toward the object's middle to decrease its size.
3. When the object is the desired size, release the mouse button.

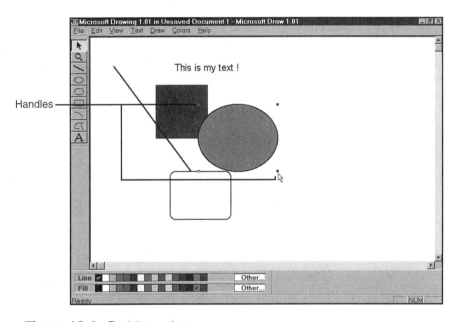

Figure 13.4   Resizing a shape.

TIP   Don't Distort as You Resize   Be careful how you drag the object's handles. If you want to increase or decrease an object's size and keep its horizontal and vertical proportions, drag the mouse diagonally from the corner.

To delete an object, click it once to select it. Press the **Delete** key on your keyboard.

Adding the Drawing to Your Document

After you've created a drawing, it doesn't automatically appear in your document. To place your drawing in your document, choose **File**, **Exit and Return** from the Microsoft Draw File menu, and then click **Yes** to insert your Microsoft Draw image into the document.

If you want to reedit your drawing later, double-click it in your document. Microsoft Draw is automatically reopened. You can edit the drawing as necessary, and then choose **File**, **Exit and Return**. Click **Yes** to insert the edited image back into your document.

In this lesson, you learned to use Microsoft Draw to create shapes, lines, and graphic text and place them in your Works document. In the next lesson, you learn the proper ways to create traditional and contemporary business letters.

Creating Business Letters

14

In this lesson, you learn about the three main styles of business letters and how to create them using the Works Word Processing Tool.

The Practice of Good Letter Writing

A good letter should be clear, concise, and its topics should follow a logical order. Correct spelling and grammar are essential. You can use Works' spelling checker and thesaurus to assist you in your proofreading process, but there's no replacement for rereading your document before you send it. The spelling checker won't find many things, such as using the wrong form or tense of a word. Works does not have a grammar-checking program.

For more information on using Spell Check and Thesaurus, see Lesson 5, "Using Spell Check and Thesaurus," earlier in this part.

Letter Styles

There are three main letter styles for business correspondence. The block style letter has become very popular in recent years, but the traditional indented style remains the standard in many conservative organizations. Modified block is a compromise between the other two styles.

For information on how to begin a word processing document, refer to Part III, Lesson 1, "Word Processing Basics." If you want to put your letter on your own letter, refer to Part VI, Lesson 7, "Creating Your Own Letterhead," to learn how to create your own letterhead.

Using Block Style

Block style has no indents, and all the text, including the date and closing, are left-justified. Figure 14.1 shows a block style letter. Unless the letter will be extremely short, you begin a block letter at the top margin by typing the date (for a short letter, look at it in Print Preview and then increase the top and bottom margins until it's approximately centered on the page).

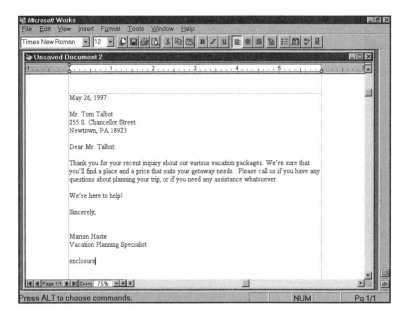

Figure 14.1   A block style letter.

To complete the letter:

1. Once you've opened the document (using the skills you learned in Part III, Lesson 1), enter the date, press the **Enter** key twice after the date, and type the recipient's name and address.

2. Press **Enter** twice again, and then type the salutation. It is currently acceptable to use either a comma or a colon at the end of the salutation.

3. Create a single blank line between the salutation and the beginning of the letter itself by pressing **Enter** once. Do not press the **Tab** key to indent your paragraphs.

4. Type your letter, pressing **Enter** twice after each paragraph. After the last line of the body of your letter, press **Enter** twice to create a couple of blank lines.

5. Type your closing, such as "Very truly yours" or "Sincerely." Follow it with a comma, and press **Enter** at least two times (if your signature is large, press the **Enter** key three or four times), and then type your name. Type your title on the next line.

6. If there is anyone who will receive a copy of the letter, press **Enter** twice after the closing and your name/title, and type **cc:** followed by their name.

7. If you are not the author of the letter, press **Enter** twice after cc:, and type the author's initials in capital letters, followed by a slash and then your initials. For example: "JS/mtk."

Using Modified Block Style

Modified Block style is the same as Block style, except the first line of each paragraph is indented ½". Figure 14.2 shows a modified block style letter. You can indent each paragraph by setting a 0.5" first-line indent in the **Format**, **Paragraph** dialog box before you type the body of your letter. You can also indent your paragraphs by pressing **Tab** at the beginning of each paragraph as you type.

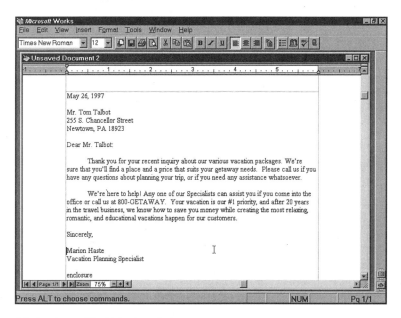

Figure 14.2 A modified block style letter.

For more information on setting indents, see Lesson 7, "Formatting Paragraphs," earlier in this part.

Using the Indented Style

The indented style is the traditional format for a business letter, although it's being replaced by the block style as the most accepted style. The date and closing are indented or right-aligned, and each paragraph has a first-line indent (see Figure 14.3).

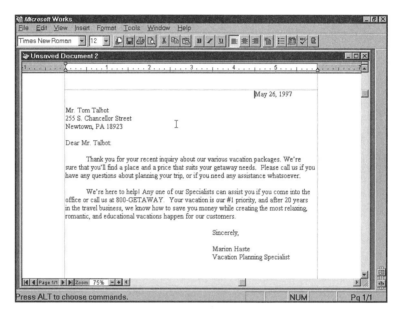

Figure 14.3 An indented style letter.

For more information on aligning your text, see Lesson 7, "Formatting Paragraphs," earlier in this part.

In this lesson, you learned about the three main styles of business letters and how to create them. In the next lesson, you learn to create envelopes and labels, and merge them with a database of names and addresses.

Using Envelopes and Labels

In this lesson, you learn to create and print envelopes and labels for a single mailing and to merge your envelopes and labels with a database for a mass mailing.

The Envelopes Task Wizard

The Envelopes Task Wizard is a tool that takes you step-by-step through the process of printing a single envelope or a large group of envelopes. You can provide a single address or use a database of names and addresses to create a mass mailing.

To learn how to set up an address book of frequently used names and addresses, see Part VI, Lesson 3, "Creating an Address Book." For mass mailings, you may want to refer to Part VI, Lesson 10, "Creating Form Letters."

To start the Envelopes Task Wizard:

1. Open the Works program by clicking the **Start** button on your Taskbar. Choose **Microsoft Works**, **Microsoft Works** from the **Programs** menu.

2. When Works opens, your first screen contains the **Task Launcher**. Click the **TaskWizards** tab.

3. Click **Envelopes and Labels** to display the list of related Wizards.

4. Choose **Envelopes** from the list (see Figure 15.1).

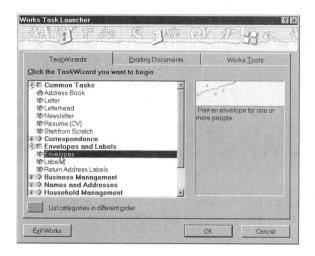

Figure 15.1 The Task Launcher.

5. Click **OK** to start the Wizard and close the dialog box. If an additional dialog box appears asking if you want to create a document using the TaskWizard or use an existing document, select **Yes, Run the TaskWizard**. To avoid seeing this dialog box in the future, deselect the **Always Show This Message** option.

The Envelopes Wizard opens with the **Instructions** tab as the active tab. The dialog box shows a list of the six steps involved in selecting, addressing, and printing envelopes. Figure 15.2 shows the Instructions tab.

TIP **Quick Envelopes** If you're already working in the Works word processor, you don't need to go to the Task Launcher to do envelopes. Choose **Tools**, **Envelopes** to open the Envelopes Wizard dialog box.

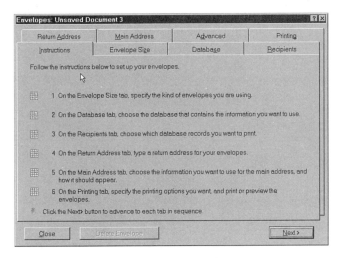

Figure 15.2   The Envelope Wizard Instructions.

Choosing an Envelope

The first step in the envelope process is to select the size of the envelope you want. The Wizard instructs you to click **Next** to go to the Envelope Size tab (see Figure 15.3). The Wizard offers a variety of standard envelope sizes to use. The default and most common business envelope is the #10. If you're using another size, scroll through the list to find it. If your envelope isn't listed, click the **Custom** button to enter your envelope's dimensions. After selecting your envelope, click **Next** to continue the process. The instructions direct you to the **Database** tab.

What If I Click Next Too Many Times?   If you go past a step and aren't sure where you are in the process, click the **Instructions** tab and review the steps. You can retrace your steps and pick up the process where you lost track. Click **Back** if you've advanced one step beyond where you should be.

CAUTION

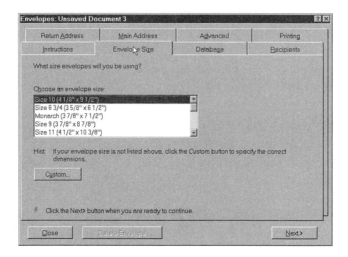

Figure 15.3 Setting Envelope Size.

Using a Database for Envelope Addressing

The next step in creating your envelopes is to choose the database that contains your names and addresses. The **Database** tab lists all of the databases you have in the Works Documents folder (see Figure 15.4).

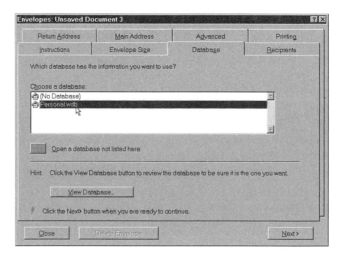

Figure 15.4 Select a database.

CAUTION

What If I Don't Know Where My Database Is?   If your database is in another folder, click the button **Open a database not listed here**. You can look through the other folders on your local and/or network drives to find your database.

What If I Don't Have a Database?   You need a database of names and addresses in order to create a group of envelopes. If you don't have a database, read Part V, Lesson 1, "Database Basics," Or Part VI, Lesson 3, "Creating an Address Book."

If you're not sure which database is the one you want to use, select a database and click View Database. Once you view the database, click **Go Back** to return to the Envelope TaskWizard.

Select your database file and click the **Next** button to continue the Envelopes Task Wizard, which is the **Recipients** tab.

CAUTION

What Do I Do If I Want to Print Only One Envelope?   When you want to address an envelope to one person or company, you don't need a database. Once you choose the envelope size, skip the step where you select the database. Follow the instructions below for entering your return address and then go to the Main Address tab. Instead of inserting fields, enter the address in the Main Address box. Then follow the instructions for printing.

Selecting Recipients

The Recipients tab (see Figure 15.5) allows you to choose which records in your database will be used for envelopes. You have four options:

- All records
- Current visible records
- Currently marked records
- Filtered records

If you want to Filter your database, see Part V, Lesson 10, "Working with Filters." To mark your records, click the **View Database** button and click the box next to each record you want to use. Click **Go Back to** return to the Envelope dialog box.

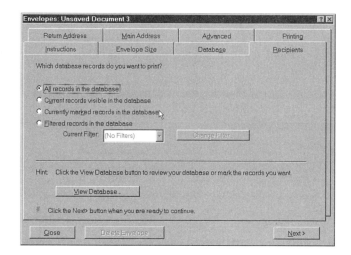

Figure 15.5   Choosing your recipients.

To print an envelope for every record in your database, leave the default option (**All Records**) selected. Click **Next** to move to the Return Address tab.

Setting Up Your Return Address

Type your return address in the large white box in the Return Address tab (see Figure 15.6). To format the font of the Return Address, click the Font button and choose your font, size, and style. If you will be using preprinted stationery, you can skip this tab, and click **Next** to move to the Main Address tab.

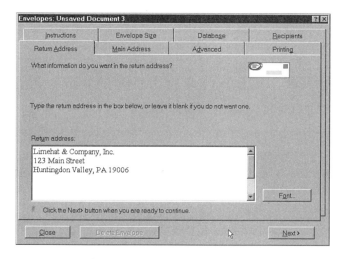

Figure 15.6   Setting up your return address.

Inserting Fields

The Main Address tab allows you to choose which fields from your database will print out on the envelope. To select your fields and place them in the Main Address box, click the field name in the list, and click the **Add Field** button. When you want to start a new line in your envelope (to insert your address fields, for example), click the **New Line** button. You can also double-click the field names to insert them, and press **Enter** when you want to start a new line. Figure 15.7 shows the Main Address tab with the address composed.

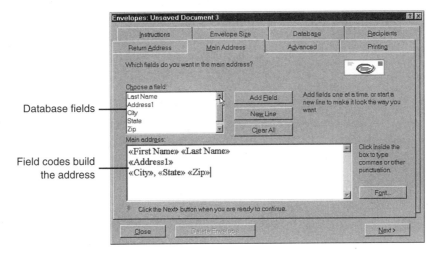

Database fields ——

Field codes build
the address

Figure 15.7 Inserting fields to create the Main Address.

Details, Details Remember to put spaces between your fields and a comma after the City field. The field names are the instructions that tell Works what data to put in your address. You must type any other text, punctuation, and spaces in the Main Address box.

If you want to format the font for your Main Address, click the **Font** button and choose a font, size, and style for your text. Click **Next** when you're ready to move to the Printing tab and create your envelopes.

Printing Envelopes

The Printing tab (see Figure 15.8) gives you three options for printing your envelopes:

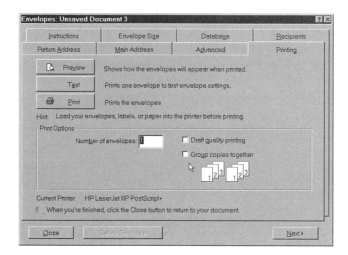

Figure 15.8 Printing your envelopes.

- **Preview** your envelopes—This is a good idea if you think you might have made any errors during your envelope setup. If you spot the problem in an on-screen preview, you won't waste any envelopes. A standard Print Preview screen opens, showing each envelope one at a time. If you find an error, go back to the tab related to that error and change your settings.

- **Test** a single envelope—If you used a custom envelope or want to see how your font choices will look before printing the whole batch, choose this option. Make sure you have an envelope in the printer first, ready to print. If you find an error, go back to the tab related to that error and change your settings.

- **Print** the envelopes—If you've already previewed or tested your envelopes, or if you're confident that you can print all of them without a test or preview, put your envelopes in your printer and then click the **Print** button.

Before printing, choose the number of envelopes per record that you want to print. The default is 1.

CAUTION

Get the Right Envelopes Before you start printing envelopes, make sure the envelopes you have will not jam or melt shut when you use them in your printer or that the paper is so slick or of such heavy weave that the print smears or breaks up. It helps to purchase envelopes marked "suitable for laser printers" or "suitable for inkjet printers." Ask your supplier for samples and try them out when you test your envelope.

The Labels Task Wizard

The Labels Task Wizard takes you step-by-step through the process of printing labels for a large or small mailing. To start the Labels Task Wizard:

1. Open the Works program by clicking the **Start** button on your Taskbar. Choose **Programs, Microsoft Works 4.0, Microsoft Works 4.0**.

2. Works opens the **Task Launcher**. Click the **TaskWizards** tab.

3. Click **Envelopes and Labels** to display the list of related Wizards.

4. Choose **Labels** from the list (use Multiple Copies of One Label when you need to create a page full of the labels with the same address).

5. Click **OK** to start the Wizard and close the dialog box. If an additional dialog box appears asking if you want to create a document using the TaskWizard or use an existing document, select **Yes, Run the TaskWizard**. To avoid seeing this dialog box in the future, deselect the **Always Show This Message** option.

The Labels Wizard appears with the **Instructions** tab as the active tab. This tab shows a list of the six steps involved in selecting, addressing, and printing labels.

TIP **Quick Envelopes** If you're already working in the Works word processor, you don't need to go to the Task Launcher to do envelopes. Choose **Tools, Labels** to open the Labels Wizard dialog box.

Many of the Label Wizard's features look and work the same as the Envelope Wizard. Refer to the Envelope topics earlier in this lesson for more information.

Choosing a Label

The first step is to select the size of the label you'll be using. Click the **Label Size** tab (see Figure 15.9) to see your choices. You can choose from a variety of standard Avery label sizes. If your label isn't listed, click the **Custom** button to enter your label's dimensions. After selecting your label, click **Next** to continue the process. The Wizard directs you to the **Database** tab. Refer to the Envelope topics earlier in this lesson for more information on selecting a database, choosing recipients, and entering fields in your label. You can also lay out the label by selecting the Label Layout tab (see Figure 15.10).

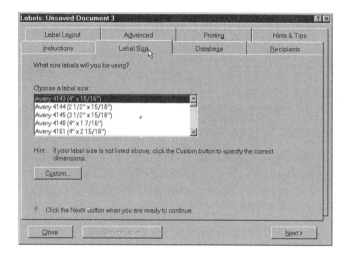

Figure 15.9   Choosing a label.

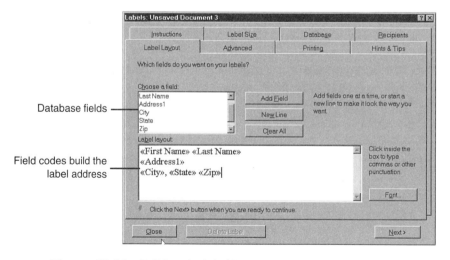

Database fields

Field codes build the
label address

Figure 15.10   Building the label layout.

Printing Labels

The **Printing** tab gives you three options for printing your labels:

- **Preview** your labels—If you think you might have made any errors during your label setup, it's a good idea to preview them. A standard **Print Preview** screen opens, showing each label, one at a time. This can keep you from wasting labels!

- **Test** 2 rows of labels—This is a good idea if you used a custom label or want to see how your font choices will look before printing.

- **Print** the labels—After your preview or test—or if you're skipping those steps—click the **Print** button.

Before printing, choose the number of labels per record that you want to print. The default is 1. If you choose to print more than one label per record, click the **Group copies together** button.

You can also indicate which is the **First row to print.** If you used the first two rows on your sheet of labels in your preprint test, type "**3**" in the box.

Get the Right Labels Before you start printing, make sure the labels you have will not jam or melt and get stuck on the drum of your laser printer when you use them or that the paper is not so slick that the print smears. It helps to purchase labels marked "suitable for laser printers" or "suitable for inkjet printers."

CAUTION

In this lesson, you learned to use the Envelopes and Labels Task Wizards to create envelopes and labels from a database.

Spreadsheets

Spreadsheet Basics

In this lesson, you learn what a spreadsheet is, a few pointers on how to build a spreadsheet, how to launch the spreadsheet tool, the features of the spreadsheet window, how to move around in the spreadsheet, and how to exit the spreadsheet tool.

What Is a Spreadsheet?

A *spreadsheet program* is a software application that organizes data into rows and columns. Numeric values can be calculated, and text can be sorted. The pages or documents these programs create are called *spreadsheets* or *worksheets*. As you'll see, these spreadsheets look very similar to those green ledger sheets used before computers.

Good Spreadsheet Design

Before you create a spreadsheet, you should plan how you want to lay it out. Here are some basic considerations that may help you in setting up your worksheet:

- Include a title for the spreadsheet at the top of the page. This identifies the spreadsheet when it is printed. A title such as "Cash Flow Statement" leaves no question about what information is included in this particular spreadsheet.

- If the spreadsheet information spans a specific period of time, include that time period in the title or create a subtitle for it. For example, a subtitle such as "for First Quarter 1997" makes it clear which time period the spreadsheet covers. Also, leave an empty row between the titles and the first row of information to make it clear which is the spreadsheet title information and which is the data.

- Include a date somewhere on the spreadsheet (and possibly the time) to easily see when the spreadsheet was created or printed. If you print copies of the spreadsheet on different dates, you'll quickly know which is the most recent.

- If you have data in the spreadsheet that you need for calculations but don't want printed, create an area several columns to the right of the spreadsheet as your reference area and enter that data there. Be consistent in where you place this information so you'll be able to locate it easily in any of your spreadsheets.

- If you are going to include a chart, plan where you will place the chart so it will print correctly. Also, decide whether you want the chart to print next to or below the spreadsheet information or on a separate page.

- Create a separate print area if you have data in the main portion of your spreadsheet that you don't want printed. Then you can copy just the information you want printed to this print area.

- Label columns and rows that have totals so readers can understand what is in that row or column. You may want to format your text or cells to differentiate totals from data you entered.

Launching the Spreadsheet

To launch the Microsoft Works spreadsheet tool, follow these steps:

1. Open the Microsoft Works program by double-clicking the **Shortcut to Microsoft Works** icon on your desktop or by clicking **Start** on the Taskbar and then choosing **Programs, Microsoft Works**.

2. From the Works Task Launcher dialog box (see Figure 1.1), click the **Works Tools** tab.

3. Click the **Spreadsheet** button.

Figure 1.1 The Works Task Launcher dialog box with the Works Tools tab selected.

Understanding the Spreadsheet Window

When you open the Spreadsheet Tool of Microsoft Works, you see two windows (see Figure 1.2). The main window is the program window for the Spreadsheet Tool. This window has several parts. Some of them are common to all programs designed to work in Windows 95: the title bar, minimize button, maximize/restore button, close button, and menu bar.

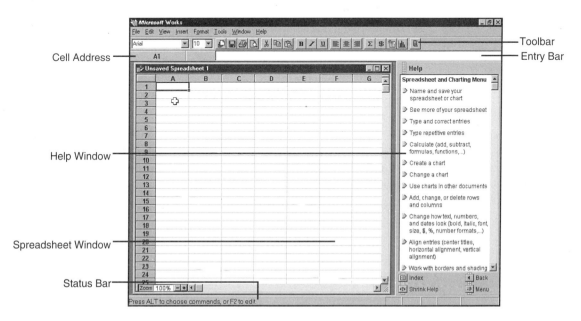

Figure 1.2 The Microsoft Works Spreadsheet Tool window.

There are some parts of this window that are unique to the Spreadsheet Tool, and these parts are explained in the following list:

Toolbar   The Toolbar allows you to quickly access some of the most frequently used menu commands by simply clicking the appropriate button. To find out what each button does, point to it. A small "ToolTip" label will pop up beneath the button to identify it. The Status Bar (see below) also displays a brief explanation of what the tool does. If your Toolbar is not showing, choose **View**, **Toolbar** from the menu bar.

Status Bar   The Status Bar is the horizontal bar that appears at the bottom of your screen. It displays important information such as your location in the spreadsheet, descriptions of menu commands and Toolbar buttons, and keys that are locked (such as the Caps Lock key). If the Status Bar is not showing, choose **Tools**, **Options** from the menu bar, click the **View** tab, and place a check mark in the **Show Status Bar** box.

Cell Address   The name of the current active cell in your spreadsheet is displayed below the Toolbar, to the left of the Entry bar. The active cell is the cell in which your cursor is placed. Cells are referenced by the column name and row number, so cell A1 is in the first row of the first column.

 Cell Addressing   Applies to all spreadsheet programs. All columns are named A, B, and so forth with A starting at the leftmost column. All rows are numbered 1, 2, and so forth, beginning with row 1 at the top of the spreadsheet. The intersection of a column and row is a cell address, named with the column name followed by the row name (A1). This also applies to many tables in word processing programs.

Entry Bar   The area below the Toolbar where you type or edit information to be entered in a cell on the spreadsheet.

Spreadsheet Window   Each spreadsheet you start or open has its own window. The name of the spreadsheet file appears on the title bar of that window (unless you've maximized the spreadsheet window, in which case the file name appears alongside Microsoft Works on the title bar of the program window). If you haven't saved the spreadsheet file, "Unsaved Spreadsheet #" appears on the title bar, where # represents the number of this spreadsheet. The number changes depending on how many spreadsheet files you've opened in this particular session; each one is numbered in order as it's opened.

Help Window   The Help Window appears to the right of the Spreadsheet Window. If you don't need the Help Window, choose **Help**, **Hide Help** from the menu to make it disappear. Choose **Help**, **Show Help** to make it reappear. To make the Help Window smaller without having it totally disappear, click the **Shrink Help** button on the Help Window. Click it again to make the Help Window expand.

In the Spreadsheet Window, you see a grid of small rectangles (see Figure 1.3). Each of these rectangles is called a *cell*. Data is entered in a cell. An *active cell* has a thick border around it and it is the cell in which your cursor currently resides. A cell must be active before you can enter data in it.

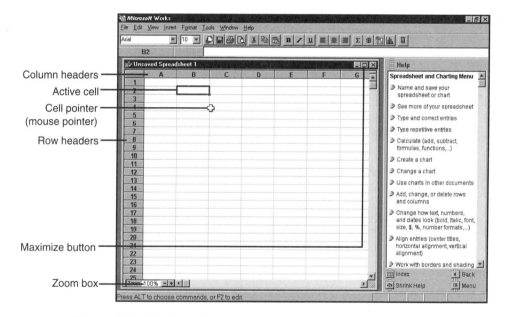

Figure 1.3   The Spreadsheet Window.

A cell occurs at the intersection of a column and a row. Columns are identified by letters of the alphabet (A through IV). There is a gray border above the first row of cells that contains the *column headers* that identify the name of each column.

To the left of the first column is a gray border that contains the *row headers* that identify the name of each row (1 through 16384).

Each cell is referenced by its *cell address*. The cell address consists of the column name plus the row name. Therefore, the cell address of the top cell in the first column is A1; the cell address of the last cell on the spreadsheet is IV16384.

To see more of the spreadsheet, you can do one or all of the following:

- Maximize the Spreadsheet Window by clicking the **Maximize** button to the right of the title bar on that window.

- Shrink the Help Window by clicking the **Shrink Help** button at the bottom of that Window or hide the window by choosing **Help**, **Hide Help** from the menu.

- Click the **Zoom** box at the bottom-left of the Spreadsheet Window and select the magnification level you want, or click the + button to zoom in or the - button to zoom out.

Moving Around the Spreadsheet

One way to move around the spreadsheet is to use the mouse. All you have to do is click the cell you want. If you can't see the cell you want, use the vertical scrollbar to move up and down the spreadsheet or the horizontal scrollbar to move left or right on the spreadsheet. Using scrollbars is explained in Part I, Lesson 2, "Working with a Window."

Another way that is sometimes the easiest and quickest method of moving around the spreadsheet is to use the keyboard shortcuts detailed in Table 1.1.

Table 1.1 Keyboard Shortcuts for Moving Around the Spreadsheet

Press	To
←	Move one cell to the left
→	Move one cell to the right
↑	Move one row up
↓	Move one row down
Tab	Move one cell to the right
Shift + Tab	Move one cell to the left
Home	Move to beginning of row
End	Move to end of row (last cell containing data)

Press	To
Page Down	Move one screen down the spreadsheet
Page Up	Move one screen up the spreadsheet
Ctrl + Home	Go to A1 (the first cell on the spreadsheet)
Ctrl + End	Go to the last cell in the spreadsheet that contains data

To go to a specific cell address, choose **Edit**, **Go To**. In the Go To dialog box (see Figure 1.4), enter the specific cell address or range you want to go to, or select a range name from the ones listed. Click **OK**.

Figure 1.4 The Go To dialog box.

Exiting the Spreadsheet

When you want to exit Microsoft Works, choose **File**, **Exit** from the menu. If you have made changes to the spreadsheet, Works will ask if you want to save it. Click **Yes** if you want to save it, **No** if you want to exit without saving the spreadsheet, or **Cancel** if you decide not to exit Works at this time.

Don't Exit Works If You Only Want to Go Back to the Task Launcher Click the **Task Launcher** button on the Toolbar instead. That way, you don't need to close your spreadsheet file. If you just need to open a file created in another Works Tool, choose **File**, **Open**, select the file from the Open dialog box, and then click **OK**.

CAUTION

In this lesson, you learned what spreadsheets are, what the parts of the Microsoft Works Spreadsheet Tool window are, how to identify the parts of a spreadsheet, how to move around in the spreadsheet, and how to exit Works. In the next lesson, you learn how to create a spreadsheet.

Creating a
Spreadsheet

*In this lesson, you learn how to enter text, numbers, dates, and
times into your spreadsheet. You also find out how to edit or
change any entries you've made and how to undo your
mistakes as well as how to open, save, and close your spreadsheet files.*

Entering Text

To enter text in your spreadsheet:

1. Click the cell (or use the keyboard shortcuts to go to the cell) where you
want the text to appear. That cell then becomes the *active* cell.

2. Type the text. As you type, the text will appear in both the cell and in the
Entry bar at the top of the spreadsheet.

3. Press **Enter** or click the check mark next to the Entry bar to accept your text
entry.

TIP **Quickly Entering Data in One Cell After Another**   If you're entering
data (text, numbers, dates, or times) and you want to enter information in a
series of cells, you don't need to press **Enter** after each entry. Instead, press
the arrow key pointing in the direction you want to go. Works accepts the entry
and moves to the next cell all in one motion. If you're entering data by columns,
use **Tab** the same way, pressing **Tab** after each entry to accept the data and
then move one cell to the right.

Navigating in Spreadsheets   You can move through a spreadsheet or a
table with the use of the arrow and tab keys in most spreadsheet programs and
in most tables in word processing programs.

Entering Numbers

To enter numbers:

1. Click the cell (or use the keyboard shortcuts to go to the cell) where you want the number to appear. That cell then becomes the *active* cell.

2. Type the number. As you type, the number will appear in both the cell and in the Entry bar at the top of the spreadsheet.

3. Press **Enter** or click the check mark next to the Entry bar to accept your number entry.

When entering numbers, you may use dollar signs ($), percentage signs (%), and decimal points (.).

CAUTION

What Happened to My Zeroes? If you're typing figures with decimal points, your trailing zeroes will disappear. For instance, the number 55.10 will appear as 55.1. This is normal. It happens because the spreadsheet is automatically set in the General format. In Part IV, Lesson 12, "Formatting Numbers," you'll learn how to make decimal places appear. Meanwhile, don't worry—the calculations will still be correct even without the zero.

Entering Dates and Times

To enter dates or times in your spreadsheet:

1. Click the cell (or use the keyboard shortcuts to go to the cell) where you want the date or time to appear. That cell then becomes the *active* cell.

2. Type the date or time. As you type, the date or time will appear in both the cell and in the Entry bar at the top of the spreadsheet.

3. Press **Enter** or click the check mark next to the Entry bar to accept your date or time entry.

The best way to enter dates is with slashes (1/12/97), especially if you want to use them for calculations such as figuring ages or length of employment. You can always format it later (see Part IV, Lesson 12) to appear as text (January 12, 1997). However, if you do enter the date as text (January 12, 1997), Works can reformat it later to appear with slashes (1/12/97). What you want to avoid is entering the date with dashes (1-12-97) because Works treats that as text and won't change the date format or recognize it as a date for calculations.

When entering times, add AM or PM for morning or afternoon (10:00 PM) or use the 24-hour or military clock (22:00). You can specify time to the second (10:00:03 PM).

Using Undo

Oops! If you make a mistake in an entry while you are typing it, just backspace and enter the correct text. Don't use the arrow keys to move back and forth, because you'll end up in one of the cells next to the one where you wanted to enter the data and your mistake will appear in the original cell.

Once you accept the entry, the fastest way to fix it is to undo the mistake. Choose **Edit, Undo Entry** from the menu (**Ctrl+Z** is the keyboard shortcut for Undo). However, you must use undo immediately after making the error as you can only undo your most recent action.

Undo Shortcut   Ctrl+Z is a common keystroke used in many programs to *undo* your last entry. Try it in some other programs to see if it works.

Saving the Spreadsheet

To avoid losing the data you entered in your spreadsheet, you must save your file.

When you save your file for the first time, you must name it and locate it in a folder where you can find it later. A file name can be up to 256 characters, including spaces. However, to make it easier to find the file later, you should keep the file name short and simple. Also, put the important part of the name first as files are listed alphabetically. For example, a file called "Report of Monthly Income" will fall under R while one called "Monthly Income Report" would be found under M.

To save your file the first time and give it a name:

1. Choose **File, Save** from the menu. The Save As dialog box appears (see Figure 2.1).

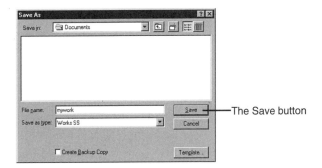

Figure 2.1 The Save As dialog box.

2. From the **Save in** drop-down list, select the drive and/or folder where you want to save the file. Click the down-arrow next to the list to see the choices and then click the one you want. Refer to Part I, Lesson 9, "Viewing Drives, Folders, and Files with the Windows Explorer," to learn more about how drives, folders, and files are organized in Windows 95.

3. In the **File Name** box, enter the name you want to give the file.

4. If you want to save the original version of the spreadsheet as is while also saving the version with your changes each time you modify the file, check **Create Backup Copy**. Just remember that by enabling this option you'll always end up with two files when you save the spreadsheet, and takes up room on your disk.

5. Click **Save**.

Once you've modified a file, you'll need to save it again. You can use one of three methods below and Works will save the file to the name you gave it without opening a dialog box:

- Choose **File, Save** from the menu.
- Click the **Save** button on the Toolbar.
- Press **Ctrl+S.**

You should save your file frequently so you don't lose any valuable information you've entered or waste time entering data over again. If you haven't saved your file and the power goes out or your system crashes, you'll have to re-create it.

On some occasions, you'll want to save a spreadsheet as a new file with a different name so you can make modifications without destroying your current file. For example, if you've prepared an accounts receivable spreadsheet for the first quarter, you may want to use the same form for the second quarter. You don't want to lose your first quarter spreadsheet, so you can save it again but give it a different name. This leaves your old file intact with its original name and creates a duplicate of the first. You can then change the duplicate to meet your needs for the second quarter.

To save a file and give it a different name:

1. Choose **File**, **Save as** from the menu. The Save As dialog box appears.
2. From the **Save in** drop-down list, select the drive and/or folder where you want to save the new file. Click the down-arrow next to the list to see the choices and then click the one you want.
3. In the **File Name** box, enter the name you want to give the file.
4. Click **Save**.

Closing a Spreadsheet

Once you have finished using a spreadsheet, you will want to close it before you go on to other work.

1. Choose **File**, **Close** from the menu.
2. If you have made modifications to the file since you last saved it, Works will ask you if you want to save the file. Click **Yes** if you want to save it, **No** if you don't want to save it, or **Cancel** to stop the closing of the file. You are returned to the Works Task Launcher dialog box.

Opening a Spreadsheet

To work on an existing spreadsheet file, you must first open that file (these instructions assume that you've already launched the Spreadsheet Tool of Microsoft Works).

1. Choose **File**, **Open** from the menu. The Open dialog box appears (see Figure 2.2).

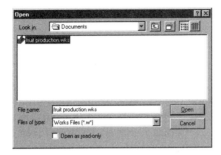

Figure 2.2 The Open dialog box.

2. From the **Look in:** drop-down list, select the drive and/or folder where you stored the file.

3. Select the file name from the list of files.

4. Click **Open**.

Working with the Toolbar

The toolbar is the row of buttons that appears directly below the menu. Each button is a shortcut for a menu command. If you don't see your toolbar, choose **View**, **Toolbar** from the menu. Use the same menu commands to hide the toolbar.

As you point at each button on the toolbar, a small yellow box appears below the tool to tell you what the tool is. The yellow box is called the *ToolTip*. If your Tool Tips don't appear, choose **Tools**, **Customize Toolbar,** check **Enable ToolTips** on the dialog box, and then click **OK**.

When you point at a toolbar button, you'll also see a brief explanation of what that tool does on the Status Bar at the bottom of the screen. Table 2.1 tells you what each tool does.

Table 2.1 The Spreadsheet Toolbar Buttons

Tool	Name	Description
	Font Name	Applies font to selected text or cells
	Font Size	Changes point size of selected text

continues

249

Table 2.1 Continued

Tool	Name	Description
	Task Launcher	Brings up the Task Launcher dialog box that gives you access to TaskWizards, existing documents, and Works tools
	Save	Saves the active document
	Print	Prints the active document using the current defaults
	Print Preview	Displays the active document as it will look when it's printed
	Cut	Cuts the current selection and stores it in the Clipboard
	Copy	Copies a duplicate of the current selection in the Clipboard
	Paste	Pastes the contents of the Clipboard at the insertion point
	Bold	Makes the current text selection bold (or turns bold off if it's already bold)
	Italic	Makes the current text selection italic (or turns italic off if it's already italic)
	Underline	Underlines the current text selection (or turns off underline if it's already underlined)
	Left Align	Left aligns text
	Center Align	Centers text
	Right Align	Right aligns text
	AutoSum	Inserts the SUM function in the current cell and proposes a range of cells to total
	Currency	Applies the currency format to numbers in the selected cell(s)
	Easy Calc	Starts Easy Calc, which helps you create formulas

Tool	Name	Description
![New Chart icon]	New Chart	Creates a new chart
![Address Book icon]	Address Book	Opens the default Address Book

You can customize the toolbar by adding and deleting buttons to suit your own personal needs:

1. Choose **Tools**, **Customize Toolbar** from the menu. The Customize Works Toolbar dialog box appears (see Figure 2.3).

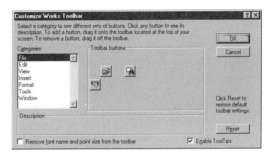

Figure 2.3   The Customize Works Toolbar dialog box.

2. To add a button to the toolbar, select a category from the **Categories** box to view the available tools, click the tool you want, and drag it up on to the toolbar.

To remove a button, drag it straight down off the toolbar.

To remove the Font Name or Point Size buttons, check **Remove Font Name and Point Size From the Toolbar**.

To reset the toolbar to its original set of buttons, click the **Reset** button.

3. Click **OK**.

In this lesson, you learned how to enter information in your spreadsheet, how to undo a mistake, and how to open, save, or close a spreadsheet. You also learned what the buttons on the toolbar are and how to customize the toolbar to suit your needs. In the next lesson, you learn how to edit, delete, move, and copy your data.

Editing Cells

In this lesson, you find out how to select cells, rows, and columns. You learn to edit delete, copy, and move data.

Selecting Cells and Ranges

Before you can delete, move, copy, or format data, you must select the cells to be involved in the operation. The active cell is automatically selected, but if you want to involve additional cells, you must highlight them.

The entries of a highlighted cell have a black background, except for the very first cell in the selection. The first cell in the group (or range) keeps its white background and dark text. The entire highlighted area has a thick border around it. Refer to Figure 3.1 to see an example of highlighted cells.

Table 3.1 lists the methods (both keyboard and mouse) for highlighting cells in your spreadsheet.

Table 3.1 How to Highlight (Select) Cells

To Highlight:	*Mouse Method*	*Keyboard Method*
A cell	Click the cell	Press an arrow key
A group of cells	Starting with the mouse pointer in the first cell, hold down the mouse button and drag to the last cell in the group	Starting with the first cell in the upper-left corner of the group, press F8, and then use the arrow keys to highlight the rest of the cells
A row	Click the row header	Highlight one cell in the row and then press Ctrl + F8

To Highlight:	Mouse Method	Keyboard Method
A column	Click the column header	Highlight one cell in the column and press Shift + F8
The entire spreadsheet	Click the corner header cell where the column headers and row headers meet (upper-left corner of spreadsheet)	Press Ctrl + Shift+ F8

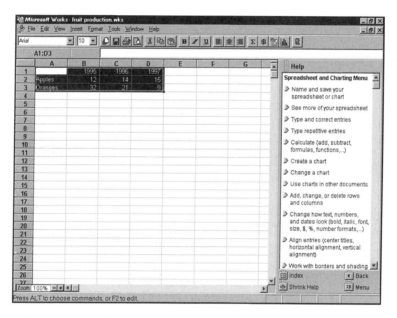

Figure 3.1 A group of highlighted cells.

Selecting Cells The selection of cells and groups of cells is *similar* in all spreadsheet programs as well as tables in word processing documents. Try using the selection controls in Table 3.1 in other spreadsheet programs or word processing tables.

TIP   **Entering a Large Block of Data Quickly**   When you have to enter data
in a large block of cells, highlight the cells first. Then starting in the first cell in
the upper-left corner of the block, enter the data and press **Enter**. Works will
automatically move you to the next cell, first going down one column, then
moving to the top of the next column to the right, down that column, then to the
next column on the right, and so on.

Editing Data

If you have entered data incorrectly and it's too late to undo the entry, you can
correct it by replacing the entry or by editing the entry.

To replace information in a cell, click the cell containing the information you
want to replace, type the new information, and press **Enter**. The new entry will
wipe out the old one.

To edit the data that is already in the cell, follow these steps:

1. Click the cell that contains the data you want to change.

2. Click the Entry bar to place an insertion point (cursor) there (see Figure
3.2).

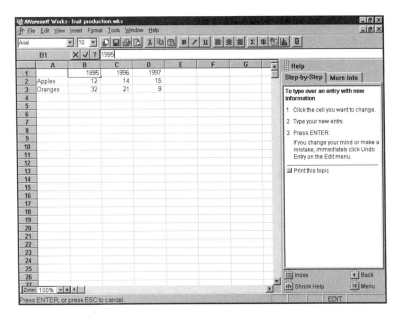

Figure 3.2   This is how the Entry bar appears while you are editing an entry.

3. If you want to add characters, click where you want to insert them or use the arrow keys to move the cursor and then type in the new information.

If you want to remove characters, click immediately after the characters and press **Backspace** until they disappear. To remove a larger number of characters, highlight them and press **Backspace** or **Delete**.

4. Press **Enter** or click the check mark by the Entry bar.

 TIP **Editing in the Cell** Double-click the cell to be edited and make your changes in the cell using the arrow keys to move the cursor and **Backspace** and **Delete** to remove unwanted characters.

Deleting Data

To delete data from a cell or group of cells:

1. Highlight the cell or cells that contain the data you want to remove.

2. Press the **Delete** key or choose **Edit, Clear** from the menu.

If you accidentally delete data in the wrong cell, quickly choose **Edit, Undo Clear**.

Moving Data

You can move data from one part of a spreadsheet to another, or from one spreadsheet to another spreadsheet.

There are two methods of moving data. This first method works well for moving data within a spreadsheet from one area to another:

1. Highlight the cell(s) you want to move.

2. Point to the edge of the highlighted cell or group of cells.

3. When the mouse pointer changes to an arrow with the word "Drag" under it (see Figure 3.3), hold down the mouse button and drag the highlighted cell(s) to a new location. An outline of the cells appears as you drag, and the word Move replaces Drag under the mouse pointer. Release the mouse button and the data is relocated.

255

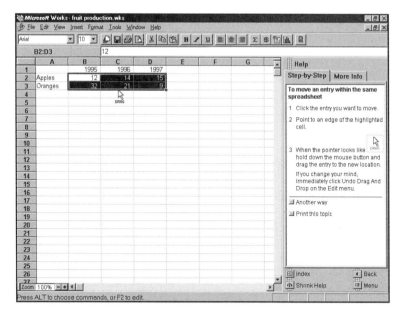

Figure 3.3 The mouse pointer when it's ready to move data.

The second method works well within a spreadsheet but also very well when moving data from one spreadsheet to another:

   1. Highlight the cell(s) you want to move.

   2. Choose **Edit**, **Cut** from the menu or click the **Cut** button on the Toolbar (see Figure 3.4).

Figure 3.4 The Cut, Copy, and Paste buttons on the Toolbar.

   3. Click the cell (or the top-left corner of a group of cells) where you want the data to appear.

   If you want to insert the data in another spreadsheet, you must open that spreadsheet first, then click the cell where you want the data to appear.

   4. Choose **Edit**, **Paste** from the menu or click the **Paste** button on the Toolbar (if you need to switch back to the original spreadsheet file, choose **Window** from the menu and then select the name of the spreadsheet from the bottom of that drop-down menu).

Copying Data

There are two methods of copying data. This first method works well for copying data within a spreadsheet from one area to another:

1. Highlight the cell(s) you want to copy.
2. Hold down the **Ctrl** key.
3. Point to the edge of the highlighted cell or group of cells.
4. When the mouse pointer changes to an arrow with the word Drag under it, hold down the mouse button and drag the highlighted cell(s) to the location where you want the copy placed. An outline of the cells appears as you drag, and the word Copy replaces Drag under the mouse pointer. Release the mouse button and the data is copied.

The second method works well within a spreadsheet but also very well when copying data from one spreadsheet to another:

1. Highlight the cell(s) you want to copy.
2. Choose **Edit**, **Copy** from the menu or click the **Copy** button on the Toolbar (refer to Figure 3.4).
3. Click the cell where you want the data (or the top-left corner of a group of cells) to appear.

   If you want to insert the data in another spreadsheet, open that spreadsheet first and then click the cell where you want the data to appear.
4. Choose **Edit**, **Paste** from the menu or click the **Paste** button on the Toolbar (if you need to switch back to the original spreadsheet file, choose **Window** from the menu and then select the name of the spreadsheet from the bottom of that drop-down menu).

In this lesson, you learned how to select or highlight cells, how to edit data, and how to delete, move, and copy data. In the next lesson, you'll learn how to automate some of your data entry.

Automating Data Entry

4

In this lesson, you learn some techniques to remove the tedium of data entry, making it easier for you than keying in the same data over and over again.

Using Data Fill

When you want to put the same entry in many cells, such as at the top of each column, you can use a feature the Works Spreadsheet Tool calls *data fill*. Type the first cell of information and then have Works fill in the rest of the row.

Copying Entries

To fill in the same information across a row of cells:

1. Enter the data in the first cell.
2. Press **Enter**.
3. Highlight that cell.
4. Drag across the cells you want to fill to highlight them.
5. Choose **Edit, Fill Right** from the menu.

To fill in the same information down a column of cells:

1. Enter the data in the first cell.
2. Press **Enter**.
3. Highlight that cell.
4. Drag down the cells you want to fill to highlight them.
5. Choose **Edit, Fill Down** from the menu.

To use your mouse to fill in the same information in either a row of cells or a column of cells:

1. Enter the data in the first cell. Press **Enter**.

2. Highlight that cell.

3. With your mouse, point at the handle (small black box) in the lower-right corner of the border (see Figure 4.1). The mouse pointer will say `Fill` under it.

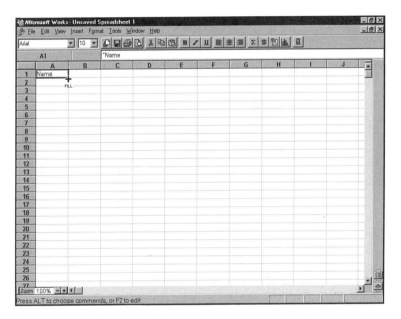

Figure 4.1 The data fill mouse pointer.

4. Drag to the right to fill a row or down to fill a column, highlighting the number of cells you want to fill.

5. Release the mouse button and your data entry will appear in each cell.

To repeat the data in a group of cells, enter the data, highlight all the cells, and then follow instructions 3 through 5.

Filling In a Series

If you want a series of numbers or dates across a row or down a column, you can use data fill to complete the series for you. For example, if you want to list the days of the month down a column, you only have to type "1" in the first cell and "2" in the second cell. Then perform the data fill to fill the next 29 cells.

There are two methods for creating series—you can use the mouse or menu commands.

Using the Mouse

The mouse method is the quickest and fastest method for creating series because it's more intuitive. You can see how many cells you need to fill and know immediately if you did it correctly.

1. Enter the data in the first cell.
2. Press **Enter** or one of the arrow keys.
3. Enter the data in the second cell to set the pattern for the series. The data must be in a logical series (has an obvious next step), or the program only copies the data entries for you.
4. Press **Enter**.
5. Highlight the cells.
6. With your mouse, point at the handle (small black box) in the lower-right corner of the border. The mouse pointer will say Fill under it.
7. Drag to the right to fill a row or drag down to fill a column, highlighting the number of cells you want to fill.
8. Release the mouse button and your data series will appear in the cells.

This type of data fill also works with dates, days of the week, and months of the year. If you type "1/97" in the first cell and "2/97" in the second cell, Works will fill in every month and year when you drag the fill handle. You don't even have to type the full name of the month; if you enter "Jan," Works completes the work when you move to the next cell.

If you enter "January" or "Monday" in the first cell, you don't even have to set a pattern. Drag the fill handle from that one cell and Works automatically fills in every month of the year or every day of the week.

 TIP   **What If You Don't Want Every Month or Every Number?**   Maybe you'd like every other month to show or every fourth number. If you enter this pattern in the cells you select before dragging the fill handle, that's the pattern that will appear. So, if you enter "January" in the first cell and "March" in the second, the data fill will automatically enter every other month.

Autofill   This feature is available in other spreadsheet programs. It may not be called *autofill* but the method used to fill in cells is the same. Try it in Excel or in Lotus 1-2-3.

Using the Menu

You can specify the series pattern you want for filling in cells, even if you only enter the first cell of information. To do this, use the menu choices.

1. Enter the data in the first cell and press **Enter**.

2. Highlight that cell and the remaining cells you want to fill.

3. Choose **Edit**, **Fill Series** from the menu. The Fill Series dialog box appears (see Figure 4.2).

Figure 4.2   The Fill Series dialog box.

4. Select the type of fill you want (**Number**, **Autofill**, **Day**, **Weekday**, **Month**, or **Year**). Depending on what type of data you entered in the cell, some of the choices may be grayed out.

5. If you don't want the data to step one-by-one across or down the cells, enter a number in the **Step by** field. For example, enter a "2" if you want every other one in your series.

6. Click **OK**.

Using AutoSum

Spreadsheets commonly contain row or column totals. You can use a calculator to figure out what those totals are and enter the numbers, you could create a formula to calculate the numbers, or you can have Works automatically calculate the total for you.

261

Formula   A formula is an algebraic expression using cell addresses that tells Works what operations to perform on the contents of the designated cells.

To automatically total columns or rows:

1. Enter the numbers in your spreadsheet.

2. Click inside the next blank cell (at the end of the column or row), then click the **AutoSum** button on the Toolbar (see Figure 4.3).

3. If AutoSum is totaling the numbers in a column, all the cells in the column are highlighted and a formula appears at the bottom of the column (see Figure 4.3) and in the Entry bar.

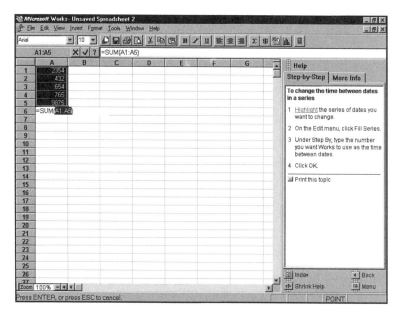

Figure 4.3   The AutoSum formula that automatically appears at the bottom of a column.

If AutoSum is totaling the numbers in a row, all the cells in the row are highlighted and a formula appears at the end of the row and in the Entry bar.

4. Press **Enter** if these are the cells you want to total.

If you don't want to total all the highlighted cells, highlight just those cells you want to include in the total and then press **Enter**. These cells must be contiguous (joined together).

For more information on writing formulas, see Part IV, Lesson 6, "Understanding Formulas."

In this lesson, you learned how to make data entry easier by using the data fill feature, automatically calculating totals for columns and rows, and by copying repeated data to other areas on the spreadsheet. In the next lesson, you learn about ranges.

Working with Ranges

In this lesson, you learn what a range is and how to select ranges and incorporate ranges into your formulas. You also find out how to name a range.

Understanding Ranges

Many calculations in a spreadsheet involve more than one cell. For example, when you total a column of numbers, you need to specify which cells you're totaling. You need to reference the group of cells as a range.

A *range* is a rectangular group of cells connected either horizontally or vertically. It can be as small as one or two cells or as large as the entire spreadsheet. Several cells in a row can constitute a range, as can several cells in a column provided the cells are connected. A range can also include several columns of several rows.

The range is referenced by the first cell in the upper-left corner of the range and the last cell in the lower-right corner of the range. When written, a range reference always has a colon (:) between the cell addresses that define it, such as A1:C9.

To select a range, highlight it by dragging from the first cell in the range to the last.

Applying Range Names

It can be difficult to remember the cell addresses of a range. If you plan to use ranges or cells in formulas, consider giving a name to a range, even if it is only one cell. For example, if cell A32 contains the total sales for the month of January and you need to include that total in a formula, you would have to remember A32 as the cell containing the total sales for January, or point to that particular cell when you are writing your formula. To make things easier, you could name the cell (range) that contains the January total sales, **JanSales**. Then, when you write your formula, you could use the range name **JanSales** eliminating the need to remember the exact cell address.

To learn more about using ranges in formulas, refer to Part IV, Lesson 6, "Understanding Formulas," and Part IV, Lesson 7, "Writing Formulas."

To name a range:

1. Highlight the range you want to name.

2. Choose **Insert**, **Range Name**. The Range Name dialog box appears (see Figure 5.1).

Figure 5.1 The Range Name dialog box.

3. Enter the name you want to give the range (up to 15 characters).

4. Click **OK**.

If you have several range names in a spreadsheet and you want to create a reference table for them, follow these instructions:

1. Click a cell in the area of the spreadsheet where you want the reference table to appear.

2. Choose **Insert**, **Range Name**. The Range Name dialog box appears.

3. Select **List**.

4. Works will ask if you want to overwrite the current data. Click **OK**.

5. A two-column list of range names and references will appear in your spreadsheet (see Figure 5.2). If you change or delete range name references, you must manually rebuild the table following these steps.

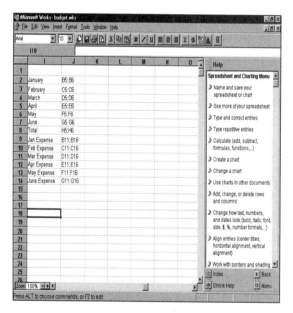

Figure 5.2 A reference table of range names.

To delete a range name, choose **Insert**, **Range Name** from the menu to open the Range Name dialog box. Click the name of the range in the **Select a Name** list, click **Delete**, and then click **Close**. Any places where that range name was referenced revert back to the original cell address references.

To adjust the range reference for a range name, highlight the group of cells you want the range name to refer to, choose **Insert**, **Range Name** from the menu, click the name of the range you want to assign to the highlighted cells from the **Select a Name** list, and then click **OK**.

In this lesson, you learned what a range is, how to select a range, and how to assign names to ranges. In the next lesson, you learn about formulas.

Understanding Formulas

In this lesson, you learn what formulas are, how they should be written, and in what order they operate.

What Is a Formula?

A *formula* is an algebraic expression using numbers, functions, and cell addresses that tells a spreadsheet program what operations to perform on those numbers or the contents of the designated cells.

In algebra, when you're not sure what numbers will be used in the mathematical expression, you substitute letters for numbers (a + b = c). In a spreadsheet, you've already entered values in cells and it's those values that you want to use in your calculations. However, the contents of the cells may change. So, instead of using the actual numbers, the formula uses the cell addresses in calculations. This system tells Works to use whatever value happens to be in that cell when making its calculations.

Cell Address   Each cell in the spreadsheet has a unique address by which you may reference that cell in formulas. Since a cell occurs at the intersection of a column and row, the address consists of the letter of the column the cell is in and the row number. Thus, the cell in the third column, fifth row is referenced as C5.

For example, if you're trying to calculate the amount of commission to pay a salesperson, and you're paying the person 15% of the total sales made in his territory, your calculation would be a multiplication of the total sales times 15%. Let's say that this month Harry's sales were $100,000, so his commission is $15,000. Then at the last minute you find another invoice for sales in Harry's territory for another $20,000. When you change his total sales to $120,000, you want the commission amount to recalculate. If you had entered the actual figure of $100,000 times 15% in the formula, you'd have to change not only the total sales figure but you'd have to change the formula, too. If you used cell addresses instead, the formula would still calculate 15% of the contents of the total sales cell. You would get the correct amount without a lot of work (see Figure 6.1 for an example).

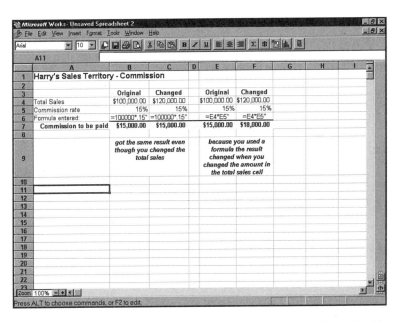

Figure 6.1 A spreadsheet showing the difference between entering cell addresses and entering actual figures in a formula.

Understanding Formula Syntax

A formula can be as simple as adding two numbers. However, if you type **7 + 2** in a cell, all that will display in that cell is 7 + 2. To indicate that the expression you're entering is a formula, include an equal sign (=) at the beginning, such as **= 7 + 2,** and the cell displays the result 9 when you press **Enter.**

Although you can use actual values in a formula, you can also reference cell addresses. The formula **=C5+C9** adds the contents of those cells.

Do not put spaces in your formula. Periods (.) indicate decimal points and colons (:) indicate ranges.

Range   A range is a rectangular group of cells connected vertically and/or horizontally. Since a range can include more than one cell, it is referenced by the beginning cell at the upper left and the ending cell at the lower right of the group. A colon indicates that the two cell addresses mark a range, such as C5:F10.

To indicate the type of operation you want the spreadsheet to perform, you need to use *operators* in a formula. You assign, modify, or combine values into new values by using operators. The most common operators are arithmetic operators, as listed in Table 6.1.

Table 6.1   Arithmetic Operators

Operator	Use To	Example
+	Add two numbers or cell addresses	=C5+C9
-	Subtract two numbers or cell addresses	=C5-C9
*	Multiply two numbers or cell addresses	=C5*C9
/	Divide two numbers or cell addresses	=C5/C9

Understanding the Order of Operations

A formula is calculated from left to right. For example, if the formula is =C6+C9-C10, the contents of cell C6 are added to the contents of cell C9 and the contents of cell C10 are then subtracted from that result.

Arithmetic operators evaluate in the following order: exponents, multiplication and division, and then addition and subtraction. Therefore, the result of the formula =6+4/2 is 8 because the division (4/2) is evaluated first and then added to the 6.

If the formula contains an exponent, it's calculated first so the result of the formula =6+4^2/2 is 14. The exponent (4^2) is calculated first, the result of 16 is then divided by 2 for an answer of 8, and that answer is added to 6.

If your formula is more complicated, you might want to group expressions by using parentheses. For example, in algebra a formula might be (x*y)/(z-y). When parentheses are used in a formula, the calculation within the parentheses is performed first. In this formula, you would calculate the answer to x*y first and then divide it by the answer to z-y. So in a spreadsheet formula such as =(C5*C9)-(D11/D12), the answer to C5*C9 is calculated first, then the answer to D11/D12 is calculated, and finally the two answers are subtracted.

For example, the formula =6+4/2 results in 8 but the formula (6+4)/2 results in 5 because the addition in the parentheses is calculated first and then the division occurs.

In this lesson, you learned what a formula is, how to put a formula together, and in what order the operations in a formula occur. In the next lesson, you learn how to enter a formula in your spreadsheet.

Writing Formulas

In this lesson, you learn how to enter formulas, how to view formulas, how to display formulas in your spreadsheet, and how Easy Calc assists you in creating formulas.

Entering the Formula

To enter a formula in a cell:

1. Click in the cell where you want the result of the formula to appear.

2. Type an equal sign (=) to indicate that you're entering a formula.

3. Type the values, cell addresses, range references or names (enter as A1:A12 or substitute the range name), and operators you need to create your formula as in =(B1/12)*C12. When you enter a range name, enter or insert the name where the range reference normally goes, without any additional punctuation, as in =SUM(Income) instead of =SUM(B3:B9).

 TIP **Using Point and Paint** When you want to use a range reference in a formula, enter the formula up to the point where you need the range reference and then highlight the range of cells you want to reference. Works will automatically display the cell reference on the Entry bar. Type the next character of the formula or press Enter, and the range reference becomes part of the formula. If you've assigned a name to that range of cells, the range name automatically appears in place of the cells' addresses.

4. Press **Enter** or click the check mark next to the Entry bar. The formula results appear in the cell and the formula itself appears in the Entry bar.

For more information on creating formulas, see Part IV, Lesson 6, "Understanding Formulas."

Viewing and Displaying Formulas

When you use a formula in a spreadsheet, the result of the formula appears in the cell. To see the formula itself, click in the cell and look at the Entry bar. The formula appears in the Entry bar (see Figure 7.1).

Formula on Entry bar ——

Result in cell D4 ——

	A	B	C	D	E	F	G	H
1	**Sales by Territory**							
2								
3		Sales	Commission Rate	Commission Due				
4	Harry Block	$100,000.00	10%	$10,000.00				
5	Jeffrey Beane	$250,000.00	16%	$40,000.00				
6	Sally Mumfort	$352,000.00	15%	$52,800.00				
7	Susan Raymond	$112,000.00	5%	$5,600.00				
8	Andres Langley	$432,000.00	20%	$86,400.00				
9	Total	$1,246,000.00		$194,800.00				

Figure 7.1 The formula showing in the Entry bar.

Should you want the formula to appear in a cell, rather than the result of the formula, choose **View**, **Formulas**. Figure 7.2 shows the same spreadsheet as Figure 7.1, but the formulas are displayed. This view is useful for checking your formulas.

To turn off the display of formulas, choose **View**, **Formulas** and remove the check from that menu option.

TIP **Cell Formula** A quick way to see the formula in a cell is to double-click the cell. This action puts you in edit mode, so you must press Enter or click elsewhere on the spreadsheet to see the value again.

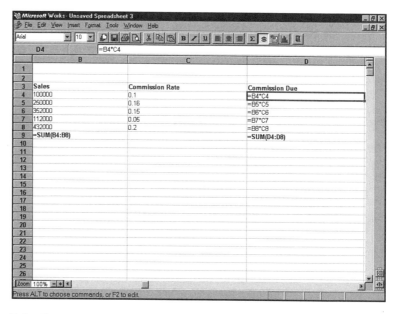

Figure 7.2 Formulas showing in the spreadsheet.

Working with Easy Calc

Easy Calc is a feature of Works spreadsheet that will assist you in writing formulas. Easy Calc is a good tool to use if you are new to spreadsheets.

To use Easy Calc:

1. Click in the cell where you want the results of the formula to appear.

2. Choose **Tools**, **Easy Calc** from the menu or click the **Easy Calc** button on the Toolbar. The Easy Calc dialog box appears (see Figure 7.3).

3. Under Common Calculations, click the button for the type of calculation you want to perform (click **Other** to see a full list of functions).

4. Follow the instructions in the dialog box to build your formula (see Figure 7.4). If you need to click a cell in the spreadsheet and the dialog box is in the way, point to the title bar of the dialog box and drag it out of the way.

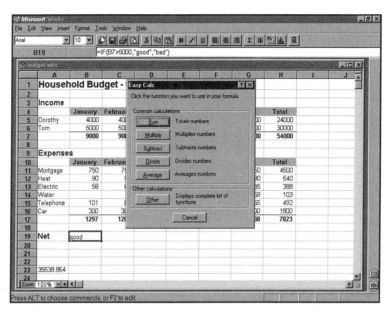

Figure 7.3 The Easy Calc dialog box.

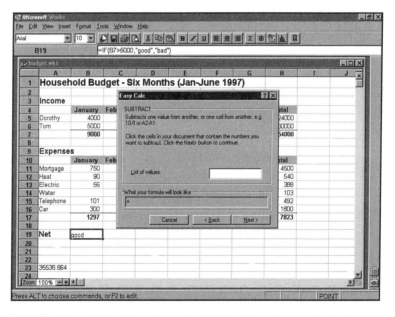

Figure 7.4 The Easy Calc dialog box when Subtract has been selected.

5. Enter whatever values or cell addresses you need to complete your formula (or click the appropriate cells to enter the addresses).

6. Click **Next**.

7. Easy Calc asks you to confirm the cell address where the formula will go (see Figure 7.5). Enter the correct cell address if it isn't already showing in the Result at box.

Figure 7.5   The Easy Calc Final Result dialog box for the Subtract function.

8. Click **Finish**. The results of the formula now appear in the designated cell and the Entry bar shows the formula.

In this lesson, you learned how to enter a formula in the spreadsheet, how to view a formula for a cell, how to display all the formulas in the spreadsheet, and you took a quick peek at Easy Calc to see how it helps you create formulas. In the next lesson, you learn how to modify, move, and copy formulas.

Editing Formulas

In this lesson, you learn how to edit, move, and copy formulas.

Modifying Formulas

When you want to change a formula:

1. Click the cell that contains the formula. The formula appears on the Entry
bar (see Figure 8.1).

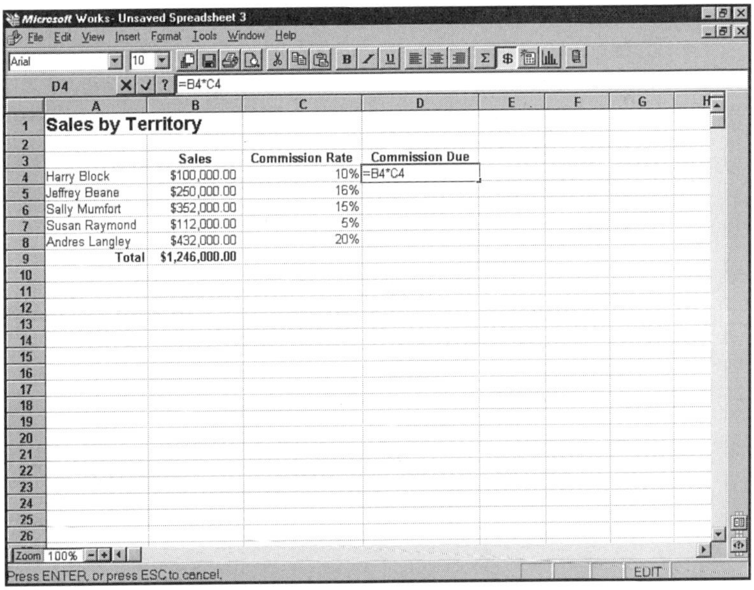

Figure 8.1   Click the Entry bar to change the formula.

2. Click the Entry bar to place your insertion point (cursor) there.

3. Use the left- and right-arrow keys to move your cursor in the formula or click where you want to place the cursor. Once your cursor is in the proper position, type to insert characters.

Use the **Backspace** key to remove characters to the left of your cursor. Use the **Delete** key to remove characters to the right of your cursor.

4. Press **Enter** to accept your changes or click the check mark on the Entry bar.

Moving Formulas

You can move a formula from one part of a spreadsheet to another by using the mouse, Toolbar buttons, or menu commands:

- **Using the mouse**   You can move a formula cell as you would any data cell. Point to the edge of the highlighted cell and drag it to its new location, as shown in Figure 8.2 (see Part IV, Lesson 3, "Editing Cells," for more information on moving cells).

- **Using menu commands and Toolbar buttons**   Choose **Edit, Cut** from the menu or click the **Cut** button on the Toolbar to place a selected formula cell in the Clipboard. Then select the cell where you want to put the formula and choose **Edit, Paste** from the menu or click the **Paste** button on the Toolbar.

TIP **What Happens If I Move the Data Cells?** Your formula may contain cell addresses. If you don't move the formula when you move the cells the formula refers to, you might think that the formula would be pointing to blank cells. You don't need to worry. The formula maintains a link to the cells. When the cells move, the formula registers the move, and changes to match the new addresses of the cells. The same thing happens when you insert or delete rows and columns. The formula changes to reflect the new cell addresses using a feature called *relative* cell addressing. There will be more on relative cell addressing covered later in this lesson.

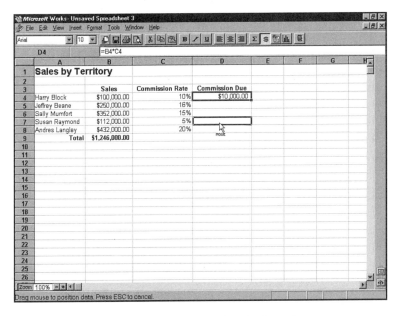

Figure 8.2 The mouse pointer as you are moving the formula.

Copying Formulas

In working with spreadsheets, you frequently need to use the same formula in more than one area. For example, if you want totals at the end of each row, it's easier to create the formula for the top row and copy it down to the following rows.

You use similar methods for copying formulas that you used for copying data (see Lesson 3, "Editing Cells," and Lesson 4, "Automating Data Entry," for a full discussion regarding copying and data fill):

- **Data Fill with the mouse** You can copy a formula cell as you would any data cell. Point at the cell's handle (small black box) in the lower-right corner of the cell border (see Figure 8.3). The word Fill will appear beneath the mouse pointer. Drag to the right to fill a row or down to fill a column, highlighting the number of cells to which you want to copy the formula, and then release the mouse button (see Part IV, Lesson 4, "Automating Data Entry," for more information on using data fill to copy data).

- **Data Fill using menu commands** Highlight the formula cell, and then drag across the cells you want to fill to highlight them. Choose **Edit**, **Fill Right** from the menu for a row or **Edit**, **Fill Down** for a column.

- **Dragging and copying** Highlight the formula cell, hold down the **Ctrl** key, point to the edge of the highlighted cell, hold down the mouse button, and drag the highlighted cell(s) to the location where you want to place the copy. As you're dragging, the word Drag under the mouse pointer changes to Copy. Release the mouse button at the cell where you want to place the copy.

- **Copy and Paste** Choose **Edit**, **Copy** from the menu or click the **Copy** button on the Toolbar to place a selected formula cell in the Clipboard. Then select the cell where you want to put the formula and choose **Edit**, **Paste** from the menu or click the **Paste** button on the Toolbar.

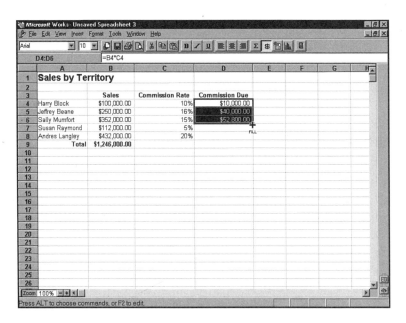

Figure 8.3 The Fill mouse pointer.

Copying with Data Fill Copying information using Data Fill is a feature found in other spreadsheet programs and although the name of this feature may be different, the process of Data Fill is the same.

Relative versus Absolute Addressing

When you copy a formula from one place in the worksheet to another, the formula's cell references change relative to their new positions in the worksheet. For example, let's say row 2 uses the formula =B2*C2. If you copy the formula to row 3, the formula changes to =B3*C3. This happens because of a spreadsheet feature called *relative addressing*.

Relative addressing changes the cell addresses relative to the position of the formula. This is true if you copy the formula from one row or column to the next, or from one side of your worksheet to the other.

All this works beautifully until you want every copied formula to refer to the same exact cell. For example, take a look at Figure 8.4. You have the current sales commission rate in cell C3. In rows 6 through 10, you have values for the total sales for each salesperson. To calculate the amount of commission due each salesperson, you want to multiply the total sales amount by the rate of commission so you enter the formula =B6*C3 in cell C6. However, when you copy that formula down the column, the commission due amounts are obviously incorrect for the remaining salespeople (see Figure 8.4).

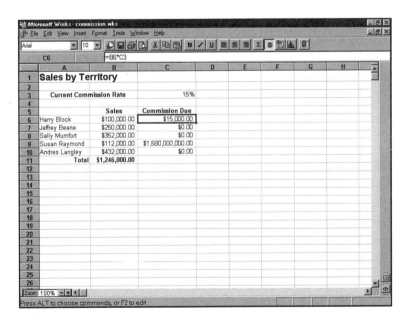

Figure 8.4 Relative addressing could cause a problem in this case.

If you look at the commission due for the Jeffrey Beane, the formula in cell C7 is =B7*C4. Using relative addressing, Works moved the cell references down one cell when you copied the formula down one cell. Although B7 is the correct cell reference, C4 is not where the commission rate is stored. The rate is back in cell C3.

The solution to this problem is to use *absolute addressing*. Absolute addressing marks the exact, original location of a cell in a spreadsheet. To reference such a location in a formula, use dollar signs ($) before the column letter and row number (C3).

For example, in Figure 8.4, the formula entered in cell C6 should have been =B6*C3; the B6 cell address could change as the formula was copied to another cell (it's relative) but the C3 cell address, which is absolute, should remain the same in every copied formula. If =B6*C3 had been the formula that was copied down to each salesperson's row, the formula for Jeffrey Beane's commission would have been =B7*C3 and the correct results would appear in cell C7 (see Figure 8.5).

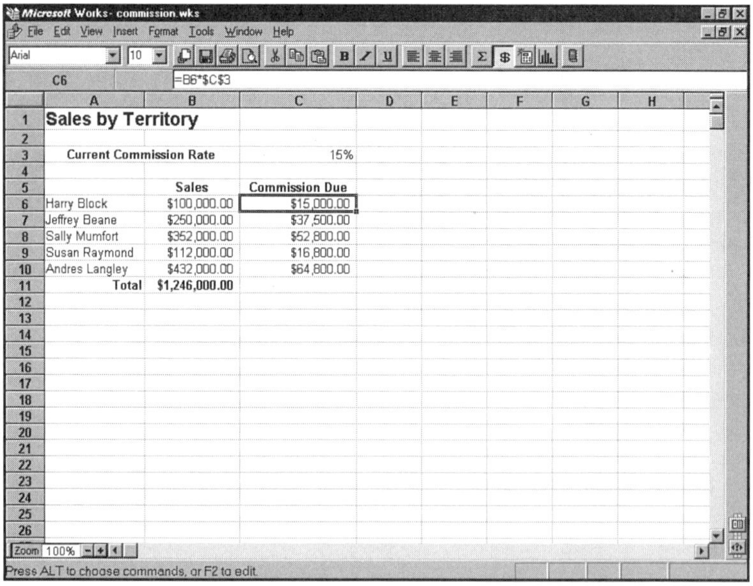

Figure 8.5 Using absolute addressing.

Refer to Table 8.1 to learn where to put the dollar signs in your cell address and how it affects the copied formula.

TIP   **Putting the Dollar Signs In**   Highlight the cell reference in the worksheet to place the cell address in your formula in the Entry bar. Press **F4**, which cycles you through absolute, relative, and mixed reference types each time you press it. Mixed references keep row references absolute while the column references are relative, or row references relative while column references are absolute (dollar signs mark which references are absolute).

Table 8.1   Where Does the Dollar Sign Go?

Type of Reference	Example	How It Acts in a Copied Formula
Absolute column, absolute row	C3	Refers to an exact cell. The cell address doesn't change in the copied formula.
Absolute column, relative row	$C3	The column of the address always remains the same, but the row can change.
Relative column, absolute row	C$3	The row of the address always remains the same, but the column can change.
Relative column, relative row	C3	The row and the column can change.

In this lesson, you learned how to change your formulas, how to move them, how to copy them, and how copying the formulas affects your spreadsheet. In the next lesson, you learn about functions.

Understanding Functions

In this lesson, you learn about functions and how you use them in formulas.

What Is a Function?

Functions are built-in formulas that can save you time when you need to do complicated calculations.

For example, if you need to find the average of five cells of values, you would normally have to add all the values and divide by the number of cells. This could result in a formula like this: =(C1+C2+C3+C4+C5)/5. Works has a function (AVG) that will average for you and write the formula using a function name (=AVG(C1:C5)).

Types of Functions

Functions fall into eight categories:

Financial functions deal with monetary matters, such as calculating interest on a loan or the term of a loan.

Date and Time functions are ones that perform operations to put the current date and time on your spreadsheet or pull out the serial number for the date or time for calculation purposes.

Math and Trig functions help you calculate logarithms, absolute numbers, rounded numbers, integers, exponents, and trigonometric functions (cosine, sine, tangent, cotangent, and so forth).

Statistical functions do many of the everyday calculations such as sums, averages, and counting.

Lookup and Ref functions work with lookup tables that you create within your spreadsheet. They also pull information from those tables into your formulas.

Text functions help you manipulate text strings by pulling out portions or by converting some portions of text for other use.

Logical functions allow you to work with conditional statements (if this, then that).

Informational functions are used to notify of errors in formulas and values.

Function Syntax

There are several rules that apply when writing formulas and these rules are referred to as the *syntax rules*. You must follow syntax rules or your formulas will not work. Those rules that apply specifically to functions are:

- Precede the function formula with an equal sign (=).
- Function names must be capitalized (such as SUM).
- If functions use arguments, the argument must follow the function (see the next section). These arguments must be enclosed in parentheses.
- Arguments must be separated by commas.
- If you use a text string as an argument, the text must be in quotes ("").

Text String   If text in a formula consists of single characters that are not part of a cell address or one or more words, it is considered a text string. For example, in an inventory spreadsheet you might want the words "out of stock" to appear if the inventory of an item is 0. Such a formula might be written **=IF(C7=0,"out of stock",C7)**. The phrase "out of stock" is a text string.

Using Arguments

An argument in a function is the information you provide in order for the function to perform properly. An argument can be a number, a formula, a cell address, a range reference, a text string, or another function.

For example, in the function **=IF(condition,action,else-action)**, "condition", "action", and "else-action" are the arguments.

Arguments are always enclosed in parentheses and separated by commas.

Entering Functions in Cells

You can enter the function manually by typing it in the Entry bar, you can insert the function by using menu commands and then complete the arguments, or you can use Easy Calc to help you enter the function (for more information on Easy Calc refer to Part IV, Lesson 7, "Writing Formulas").

Inserting the Function in the Cell

To insert a function in a cell:

1. Click in the cell where you want to use the function.

2. Choose **Insert, Function**. The Insert Function dialog box appears (see Figure 9.1).

Figure 9.1   The Insert Function dialog box.

3. Under **Category**, choose the type of function you want.

4. Click the function you want to use from the **Choose a Function** list box.

5. Click **Insert**.

6. The function appears in the cell with the first argument highlighted (see Figure 9.2). An overview of the function appears in a Help window.

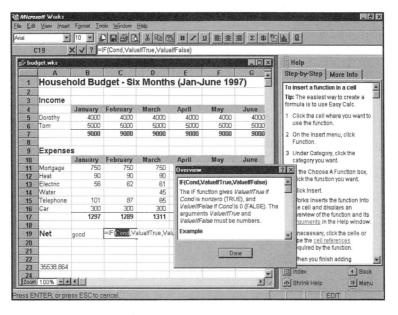

Figure 9.2 The function after it's inserted in the spreadsheet.

7. Click the cells or type in the argument information required by the function.

8. Press **Enter**.

Using Easy Calc to Enter a Function

To enter a function using Easy Calc:

1. Click in the cell where you want the results of the formula to appear.

2. Choose **Tools, Easy Calc** from the menu or click the **Easy Calc** button on the Toolbar. The Easy Calc dialog box appears (see Figure 9.3).

3. Click **Other** to see a full list of functions.

4. The Insert Function dialog box appears (refer to Figure 9.1). Under **Category**, choose the type of function you want.

5. Click the function you want to use in the **Choose a Function** list box.

6. Click **Insert**. A dialog box specific to the selected function appears (see Figure 9.4).

Figure 9.3 The Easy Calc dialog box.

Figure 9.4 The function dialog box.

7. Enter whatever values or cell addresses you need to complete your formula (or click the appropriate cells to enter the addresses).

8. Click **Next**.

9. Easy Calc asks you to confirm the cell address where the formula will go. Enter the correct cell address if it isn't already showing in the **Result at** box.

10. Click **Finish**. The result of the function appears in the cell (you can see the function in the Entry bar).

In this lesson, you learned what functions are, what types of functions are available in Works, and how to write functions, In the next lesson, you see examples of common functions.

Example Functions

In this lesson, you see examples of different types of functions and how to properly use them in your spreadsheet.

Financial Functions

Many of the financial functions deal with figuring interest rates and payment terms for loans. One of the most frequently-used functions is PMT.

```
=PMT(Principal,Rate,Term)
```

You use this function to calculate the periodic payment for a loan or investment. Let's say you want to take out a loan for $25,000 at an interest rate of 7.2% to be paid over 25 years. Your formula would be =PMT(25000, 7.2%, 25).

However, you're trying to figure the monthly payment, not the annual one, so you need to divide the interest by 12 to get the monthly interest (since 7.2% is the annual rate) and multiply the years times 12 to get the number of months over which the payments will be made. Your formula will be =PMT(25000, 7.2%/12, 25*12).

Date and Time Functions

To include the current date or time on your spreadsheet, use the following function:

```
=NOW()
```

Unlike most functions, the NOW function doesn't require any further arguments. It returns the serial number equivalent of the current date and time.

CAUTION

Where's My Date? All I See Is a Big Number   Works translates all dates and times into serial numbers in order to perform mathematical calculations with them. In order to make the date appear "normally," you will have to format it. Formatting dates is explained in Part IV, Lesson 12, "Formatting Numbers."

Math and Trig Functions

You have to figure the circumference of a circle? The circumference of a circle is calculated by multiplying the diameter times the value *pi* (Π). In Works, the PI function provides you with a mathematical approximation of the value of Π (3.1415927).

```
=PI()
```

The PI function requires no arguments and is usually used in conjunction with a larger formula. To find the diameter of the circle cell where the value for the diameter is in A1, the formula is =A1*PI().

Using a number with many decimal places in a calculation can give you an accurate answer but you may need to round that number down to a specific number of decimal places.

```
=ROUND(x,Number of Places)
```

The ROUND function will round off the decimal places for *x*, which can be a number or a cell address. If *number of places* is a positive number, *x* is rounded off to that many decimal places to the right of the decimal point (a 5 or more in the next decimal place makes the number round up one, so 3.155 rounded to 2 digits becomes 3.16 but 3.154 becomes 3.15). If *number of places* is 0, Works returns the nearest integer so 3.155 would round to 3. If *number of places* is a negative number, *x* is rounded off that number of places to the right of the decimal point (761 rounded to -2 digits would appear as 800). Although ROUND can operate up to 14 decimal places, Works displays only 9 decimal places.

Statistical Functions

The most commonly used statistical function is SUM (this is the function used by the AutoSum tool).

```
=SUM(Range)
```

The SUM function adds the values in the cells of the specified range, so the formula =SUM(B12:B15) will add the numbers in cells B12, B13, B14, and B15. You can also use this function to add values in cells that are not in a range by placing commas between them, such as =SUM(B12, B15, B19) which would add the values in cells B12, B15, and B19. When necessary, you can even combine ranges and single cell addresses such as =SUM(A5:A10, B12, E4) which adds the values in cells A5, A6, A7, A8, A9, A10, B12, and E4.

The AVG function averages the values in a range of cells.

```
=AVG(Range)
```

If you have a range of 6 cells, the AVG function totals the values in those cells and divides by the number of cells, such as in the formula =AVG(B1:B6).

Use the MAX function to find the largest value in a range (such as the highest sales) and the MIN function to find the lowest value in a range (such as the lowest number of absences).

```
=MAX(Range)
=MIN(Range)
```

Lookup and Reference Functions

There are times when you need to put tables of important information outside the printing portion of your spreadsheet. Use these tables to look up important data to incorporate in the main portion of the spreadsheet. For example, you might want to include a rate table for insurance or a tax table for sales tax.

To call up the information in these tables you need to use special functions. The HLOOKUP function, for example, searches the top row of the specified range until it finds the lookup value, and then it goes down the specified number of rows to find the value (it starts counting the rows with 0).

```
=HLOOKUP(Lookup Value, Range, Row Number)
```

In Figure 10.1, the formula =HLOOKUP(1996, A1:C21, 12) returns 20. That is the value in the 12th cell under 1996 in the specified range of A1 to C21.

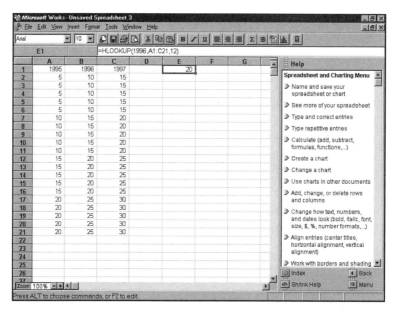

Figure 10.1 Using the HLOOKUP function.

The VLOOKUP function performs a similar operation, only it searches the first column of the range to find the lookup value, and then goes right by the number of columns specified.

```
=VLOOKUP(Lookup Value, Range, Column Number)
```

In Figure 10.2, the formula =VLOOKUP(10, A1:D21, 2) returns 15. That is the value 2 columns across from the entry 10 in the first column of the range A1 to D21.

Both HLOOKUP and VLOOKUP are useful when you have cell addresses in the main portion of your spreadsheet that contain some of the information required. You can then use a cell address as your lookup value.

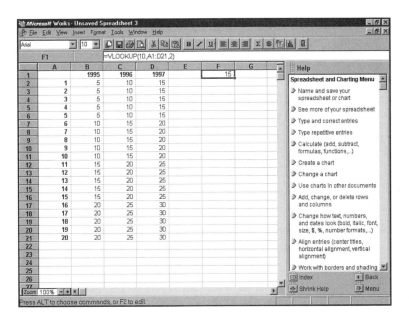

Figure 10.2 Using the VLOOKUP formula.

Text Functions

Text functions manipulate text that you enter. For example, you want to create a portion of your spreadsheet from which you can print an employee phone list. You already have employee phone numbers on one portion of your spreadsheet that were entered as all numbers and no punctuation. You need to adjust that text to put the information in a more presentable format for users.

First, to pull out the area code you can use the LEFT function.

```
=LEFT(Text Value, Number of Characters)
```

If the original phone number is in cell B2, your formula would be =LEFT(B2, 3). The LEFT function returns the number of characters specified, starting from the left side of the text string.

To pull out the rest of the phone number, you can use the RIGHT function.

```
=RIGHT(Text Value, Number of Characters)
```

The formula for that would be =RIGHT(B2, 7). The RIGHT function pulls the number of characters specified starting from the right side of the text string.

But your phone number still doesn't look right. You want it in the format (xxx) xxx-xxxx. To do this, you'll have to use *concatenation*. Concatenation allows you to combine text strings by using ampersands (&) to mark where you want to join them. If you use actual text instead of cell addresses, you must enclose the text in double quotes (""). For example, if you have the first name in cell C1 and the last name in cell C2, you can concatenate the text to appear properly in cell C3 with a formula such as =C1&" "&C2. The double quotes are around a space, which is a text character. If you didn't add that to the concatenation formula, the first name would run right into the last name.

How do you apply concatenation to your phone number? Change your formula to read `="("&LEFT(B2,3)&") "&MID(B2,3,3)&"-"&RIGHT(B2,4)` as shown in Figure 10.3. In this concatenation, you'll see another function, MID, which pulls out the middle set of characters.

```
=MID(Text Value, Offset, Number of Characters)
```

In the MID function, the *offset* is the number of characters from the left that represents the first character of the text you want. MID starts counting the first character as 0 offset. MID returns the number of characters specified going left from that offset point in the text string.

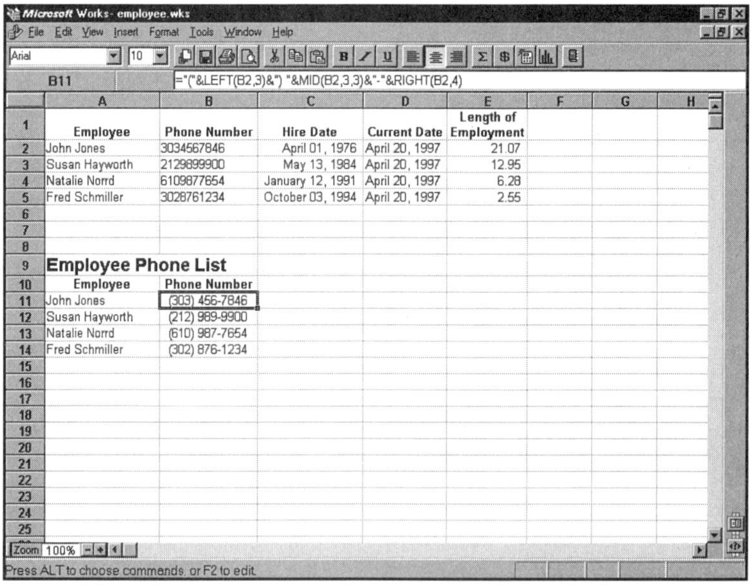

Figure 10.3 Concatenating formulas and text.

There are several useful functions for converting the case of text. =UPPER(Text Value) converts lowercase text to uppercase, =LOWER(Text Value) converts uppercase text to lowercase, and =PROPER(Text Value) converts text to lowercase but capitalizes the first letter of each word.

You may also run into difficulties when someone enters numbers and you need to use them as text. Take the phone number example: The original phone numbers were entered as a string of numbers without punctuation. Works automatically reads that as a number. Unless you edit each number and enter a quotation mark (") at the beginning, you might not be able to extract portions of the phone numbers to concatenate later. You can't mix numbers and text in a concatenated formula. Use the STRING function to convert numbers to text.

```
=STRING(x, Decimal Places)
```

STRING converts the value x to text (puts the double quotation mark in front of it) with the specified number of decimal places. In the case of the phone number, the formula would be =STRING(B2,0) because you don't need decimal places. A quick way to tell if it worked is to check the text alignment. Works always makes numbers align flush right in a cell and makes the text flush left. If you haven't manually changed the default alignment, you can see immediately if the formula worked.

In just the reverse situation, you may have entered a number and then formatted it as text because you needed to use it in a concatenation formula in another cell. Now you find that you also need to use it in a mathematical calculation. Use the VALUE function to convert the text to a number for your formula.

```
=VALUE(Text Value)
```

For example, if you need to multiply the contents of cell B12 times twelve and the number in that cell is formatted as text, use =VALUE(B12)*12.

Logical Functions

Logical functions work with conditional statements to evaluate whether a condition is true or false. Logical functions produce two results: a value of 1 (true) or 0 (false). The logical functions are outlined in Table 10.1.

Table 10.1 The Logical Functions

Function	Syntax	Does This
AND	=AND(Logical0, Logical1,...)	Checks whether *all* the listed arguments are true and returns 1 if they are and 0 if they're not
FALSE	=FALSE()	Gives the value 0 (false) and is used primarily in testing formulas that use logical functions
IF	=IF(Condition, Action, Else-Action)	Determines whether a condition is true or false. If the condition is true the action occurs; otherwise, the else-action occurs.
NOT	=NOT(Logical)	Gives the opposite of the specified argument (if Logical is true it results in 0; if Logical is false it results in 1)
OR	=OR(Logical0, Logical1,...)	Checks whether *any* of the listed arguments is true and returns 1 if any are. If all the values in the listed arguments are false, it returns 0.
TRUE	=TRUE()	Gives the value 1 (true) and is primarily used in testing formulas that use logical functions

The IF function is used frequently to test conditions within spreadsheets. For example, in creating a phone list from an existing employee listing (as in the preceding "Text Functions" section), you may decide to add another column for the dialing prefix. Most of the time the dialing prefix is 1, but you don't need to use a dialing prefix for area code 610. Enter an IF function to test if the area code is 610, and if it is put nothing (entering as "" without a space between the quotes). If it is not 610, you want an entry of 1. The formula reads =IF(LEFT(B2,3)="610", "", 1) as shown in Figure 10.4.

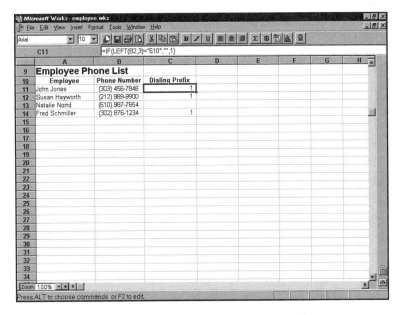

Figure 10.4 Using the IF function.

Information Functions

The information functions are often used in conjunction with other functions. The ERR function displays ERR in the cell or tests formulas that might use erroneous cells.

```
=ERR()
```

What could cause an erroneous cell? The most common cause is division by 0. For example, when you're calculating percentages where you divide the value in one cell by the value in another. That works fine in the original formula. Then you copy the formula down to other cells, where possibly there are blank cells in the row. When a cell is blank, Works automatically uses 0 when its value is asked for in a formula. If that's the cell you're using to divide by, then you're dividing by 0 and an error occurs.

If the cell you're dividing by is C1, use a formula such as =F1/(IF(C1=0, ERR(), C1)). Better yet, to avoid seeing the ERR on your spreadsheet, use a formula such as =IF(ISERR(C12/C1),0,C12/C1) which will put a 0 in the cell rather than ERR if the division C12/C1 is erroneous because C1 is blank or has a 0 in it.

In Figure 10.5, cell J5 has the formula =H5/I5. Because H5 has a 0 in it, ERR appears in J5. Cell J6 shows 0.0% even though H6 has a zero because the formula is =IF(ISERR(H6/I6),0,H6/I6).

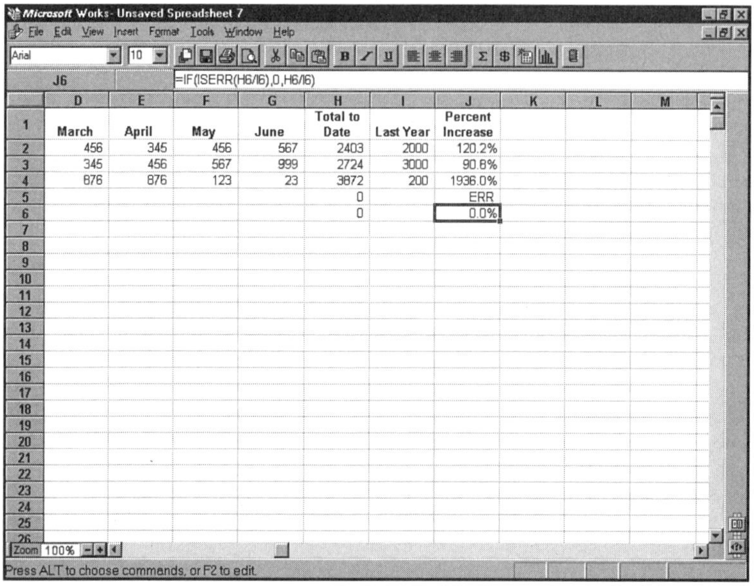

	D	E	F	G	H	I	J	K	L	M
					Total to		**Percent**			
1	**March**	**April**	**May**	**June**	**Date**	**Last Year**	**Increase**			
2	456	345	456	567	2403	2000	120.2%			
3	345	456	567	999	2724	3000	90.8%			
4	876	876	123	23	3872	200	1936.0%			
5					0		ERR			
6					0		0.0%			

Figure 10.5 Using the ISERR function.

In this lesson, you learned about some of the more commonly used functions in each category of function and how they're used. In the next lesson, you'll learn about editing the spreadsheet to add and delete rows and columns, find and replace text, and run spelling checker.

Editing the Spreadsheet

In this lesson, you learn different ways to view the spreadsheet as you work, how to add, delete, and move columns and rows, how to find and replace text, and how to spell check the spreadsheet.

Viewing the Spreadsheet

As you're working with the spreadsheet, you may want to zoom in and magnify one area of the spreadsheet. You do this in one of two ways:

- **Using the menu**, choose **View**, **Zoom** to open the Zoom dialog box (see Figure 11.1). Select the magnification you want, or specify one in the **Custom** box, and click **OK**.

Figure 11.1 The Zoom dialog box.

- **Click the Zoom box** in the lower-left corner of the screen and select the desired magnification from the pop-up list (see Figure 11.2) or click the plus sign (+) to zoom in or the minus sign (–) to zoom out.

Figure 11.2   The Zoom box.

When you have a very long or a very wide spreadsheet, you may no longer be able to see the label you put at the top of the column or the beginning of the row (header text) that tells you what to enter in that column or row. You should split the window vertically or horizontally so you can see the headings in one frame and the data in another (see Figure 11.3).

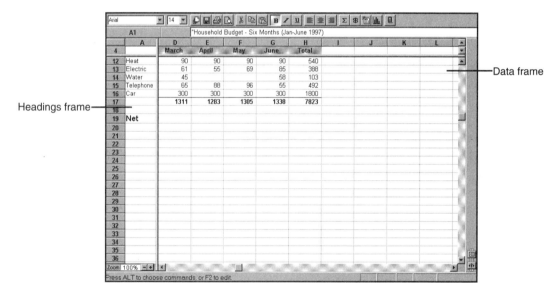

Figure 11.3   Using split windows to view different parts of a spreadsheet.

To split the windows, use one of the following methods:

- From the menu, choose **Window, Split**. A large cross will appear with an Adjust pointer in the middle. Move the cross to where you want the windows to split (see Figure 11.4) and then click. You can then adjust the horizontal or vertical bar by dragging it to the correct position to form up to four frames for the spreadsheet. Individual scroll bars will appear in each frame, so you can scroll up or down, right or left, to the cells you want to see in that frame.

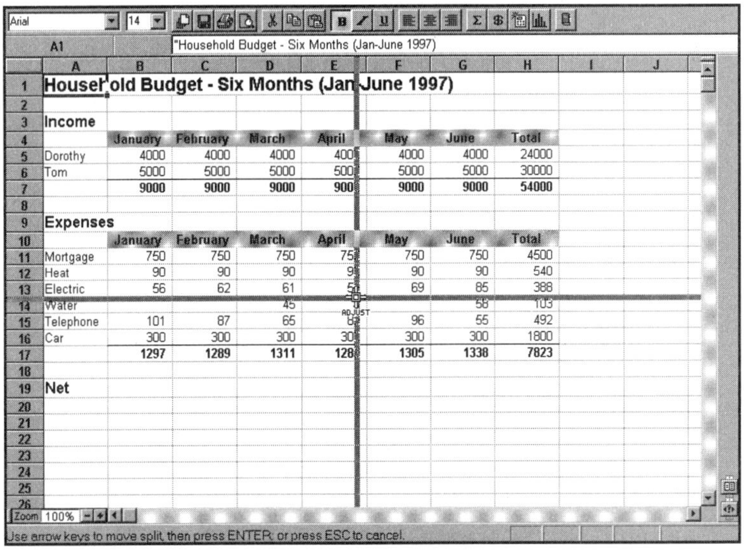

Figure 11.4 A large cross appears with the Adjust pointer in the middle.

- From the Split box at the top of the vertical scroll bar or to the left of the Zoom box (the mouse pointer becomes an Adjust pointer as in Figure 11.5 when it is over the Split box), you can drag a horizontal or vertical frame border to divide the spreadsheet. Individual scroll bars will appear in each frame, so you can scroll up or down, right or left, to the cells you want to see in that frame.

To remove the split, drag the borders back to the top or side of the spreadsheet.

301

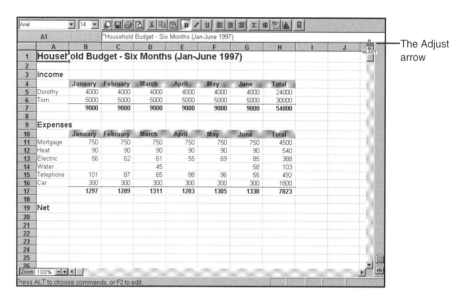

The Adjust arrow

Figure 11.5   The Adjust arrow appears when you point to the Split box.

Inserting Columns and Rows

To add a column to your spreadsheet:

1. Click the column header to the right of where you want to add the column. This will highlight that column.

2. Choose **Insert, Insert Column** from the menu.

3. The columns will move over to make room for the new column.

To add a row to your spreadsheet:

1. Click the row heading below where you want to add the row. That row will be highlighted.

2. Choose **Insert, Insert Row** from the menu.

3. The rows will move down to make room for the new row.

TIP   **Help When You Need It**   You can also right-click the mouse to bring up context-sensitive menus while working in the spreadsheet. When you right-click while in the spreadsheet, you will see a menu that includes an option to insert a column or row.

Right Click Pop-Up Menus A right mouse click will bring up context-sensitive menus in other programs in Works and in some other Windows products.

Deleting Columns and Rows

When you delete a column or row, be sure that no information remains in that column or row that you want to keep. Then do the following:

1. Click the column header or row header of the column or row you want to delete to highlight that column or row.
2. From the menu, choose **Insert, Delete Column** or **Insert, Delete Row**.

Moving Columns and Rows

To move a column or row, you will use the cut-and-paste methods:

1. Click the gray column header to highlight the column you want to move, or click the gray row header to highlight the row you want to move.
2. Choose **Edit, Cut** from the menu or click the **Cut** button on the toolbar.
3. Click the column header to the right of where you want the column to appear or click the row header below where you want the row to appear.
4. Choose **Edit, Paste** from the menu or click the **Paste** button on the toolbar. The moved column is inserted into its new location.

Finding and Replacing

To easily find a word, phrase, or numerical expression in your spreadsheet:

1. Choose **Edit, Find** from the menu. The Find dialog box appears (see Figure 11.6).

Figure 11.6 The Find dialog box.

303

2. In the **Find What** text box, enter the text or numbers you're trying to locate.

3. Under Search, select **By Rows** to have Works search the spreadsheet left to right by rows until it finds a match. Select **By Columns** to search from top to bottom by columns.

4. Select **Formulas** under Look in to search only in formulas. Select **Values** to search only in the values resulting from formulas.

5. Click **OK** to begin the search. Works highlights the cell containing the text or numbers. If Works can't find the text, you see an alert message that the program could not find a match (trying changing your Find entry and going through the process again if you think you should find something).

There are occasions when you want to replace one set of text or numbers with another. For example, when you copy the 1996 income statement form, you might want to change "1996" to "1997."

To replace text or numbers:

1. Choose **Edit**, **Replace** from the menu. The Replace dialog box appears (see Figure 11.7).

Figure 11.7   The Replace dialog box.

2. In the **Find What** box, enter the text or numbers you want to change.

3. In the **Replace With** box, enter the text or numbers with which you want to replace the text.

4. Under Search, select **By Rows** to have Works search the spreadsheet left to right by rows until it finds a match. Select **By Columns** to search from top to bottom by columns.

5. Click **Find Next** to begin the search. Works highlights the cell containing the text or numbers when it finds it.

6. Click **Replace** to replace just that one instance of the text or numbers. If you make this choice, you may continue the search instance-by-instance by clicking **Find Next** again. When Works can no longer find a match, an alert

box appears stating just that. Click **OK** and then click **Close** on the Replace dialog box.

7. Click **Replace All** to replace all the instances of the text.

Spell Checking the Spreadsheet

Although spell checking is usually associated with word processing, you can make spelling errors in spreadsheets, too! It's a good practice to spell check your spreadsheet before closing or printing it.

To check your spelling:

1. Choose **Tools**, **Spelling** from the menu. If there are any spelling errors or unrecognizable words, the Spelling dialog box appears (see Figure 11.8).

Figure 11.8 The Spelling dialog box.

2. The misspelled word appears in the **Change To** box. You may make corrections directly in the box.

3. In the **Suggestions** list box are words that Works offers as the possible correct spellings of the word. Click the right one if it is listed.

4. Under **Spelling Options**, check **Always Suggest** if you want suggested words to appear each time you open the Spell Checker, check **Ignore words in UPPERCASE** if you don't want the Spell Checker to question the spelling when the same word appears in uppercase rather than an upper- and lowercase combination, and **check Ignore Words with Numbers** to avoid stopping for labels such as "1st Qtr."

5. When Works has identified a misspelled word, you can choose one of several commands:

    Click **Ignore** if the word is spelled correctly (such as a proper name).

Click **Ignore All** if you want the Spell Checker to ignore that spelling throughout the spreadsheet.

Click **Change** if you've selected a correction from the Suggestions box or corrected the spelling in the Change to box.

Click **Change All** to change every instance of the misspelling to the correction you selected or made.

Click **Add** to add the word to your personal dictionary for future reference.

Click **Suggest** to get a list of suggestions in the Suggestions box.

Click **Cancel** to end the spell checking process and close the dialog box.

6. After Works finishes finding all the spelling errors, a prompt box appears stating that the spell check is complete. Click **OK**.

In this lesson, you learned to edit your spreadsheet by moving, deleting, and inserting columns and rows. You found out how to zoom, find and replace text, and how to spell check the spreadsheet. In the next lesson, you will learn how to format numbers.

Formatting Numbers

In this lesson, you learn to change fonts to number formats and to apply formatting such as dollar signs, percentages marks, and decimal places. You also learn how to change date and time formats.

Changing Fonts

To change the fonts of the cell or cells where you have placed numbers or dates:

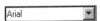

1. Select the cell or cells to which you want to apply the font.
2. Click the **Font Name** button on the toolbar to see the drop-down list of available fonts.
3. Click on the font you want to apply it to the selected cells.

To change the size of the font:

1. Select the cell or cells to which you want to apply the size change.
2. Click on the **Font Size** button on the toolbar to see the drop-down list of available fonts.
3. Select the font size you want to apply to the selected cell or cells.

To make your numbers or dates bold, italic, or underline:

1. Select the cell or cells to which you want to apply the bold, italic, or underline font styles.
2. Click on the **Bold** button, the **Italic** button, or the **Underline** button on the toolbar to apply that style to the selected cell or cells.

To learn more about changing fonts, refer to Part IV, Lesson 13, "Formatting Text."

Changing Number Formats

When you enter numbers into a spreadsheet, you generally enter the digits only. You don't type the dollar signs ($), percentage marks (%), or commas when you are entering data. If you decide later that you want your numbers to have dollar signs and commas, you have to *format* the numbers.

There are several number formats:

General format displays numbers as precisely as possible. The number of decimal places appears as it is typed. Trailing zeroes, however, disappear (if you type 12.30 it appears as 12.3. Larger numbers are shown in exponential format (1.23E+03). Numbers are automatically aligned flush right and text flush left.

Fixed format displays the numbers with the specified number of decimal places (if you specify 3 decimal places and you enter 12.3, it appears as 12.300).

Currency format automatically adds a dollar sign ($) to the beginning of the number and includes a comma separator if the number is over 1,000. You may specify the number of decimal places you want to see, but 2 is the default setting. Negative numbers appear with parentheses around them, and you have the option to show them in red. If you enter a number using the dollar sign, Works automatically formats that cell as currency.

Comma format automatically includes a comma separator if the number is over 1,000. You may specify the number of decimal places you want to see, but 2 is the default setting. Negative numbers appear with parentheses around them, and you have the option to show them in red.

Percent format automatically shows the number as if it had been multiplied by 100 and adds the percentage sign (%) at the end of the number. If you're entering numbers that you intend to later format as percentages, make sure you write them in the correct decimal format (0.15 becomes 15%). You can specify the number of decimal places you want to show. However, if you enter a number with a percentage sign (such as 12%), Works automatically formats that cell as a percentage and puts the number 0.12 on the Entry bar.

Exponential format shows larger numbers as a base number with an exponent. For example, the number 1,000,000 shows as 1.00E+06.

Leading Zeroes format adds zeroes to show the specified number of places (if you enter 1, it appears as 00001 if you specify five places).

Fraction format changes a fraction entered in decimals to a standard fraction preceded by a zero (0.03125 becomes 0 1/32). If you enter 0 1/32 the fraction format is automatically applied to that cell and the number 0.03125 appears on the Entry bar.

True/False format displays all zeroes as FALSE and all non-zero values as TRUE.

Text format lets you specify a numerical entry as text. For example, if you enter a phone number, you want to format it as text.

 TIP **Currency**   You can easily format selected cells with the currency format by clicking the **Currency** button on the toolbar.

Formatting only affects the appearance of the number. Works still uses the unformatted number when calculating. Therefore, when you see a percentage of 75% in a cell you've formatted as percentage with 0 decimal places, the number being used in calculations is 0.751.

To change a number format:

1. Select the cell or cells you want to format.

2. Choose **Format**, **Number** from the menu. The Format Cells dialog box appears (see Figure 12.1).

3. Under **Format**, select the type of format you want to use.

4. Under **Options**, specify any options you want for that format such as number of decimal places. Check the Sample area to see how your choice affects the number.

5. Click **OK**. Any formatting you chose is applied to the cell(s).

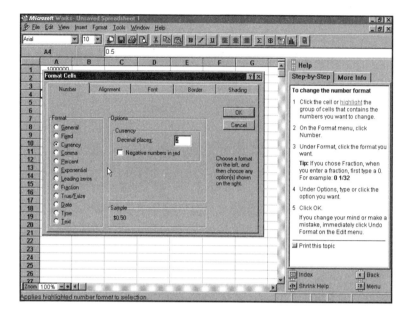

Figure 12.1   The Format Cells dialog box with Currency selected.

Changing Date and Time Formats

You can change the appearance of any dates you entered, so if you entered 4/27/97 you can change it to appear as April 27, 1997.

To format a cell as a date or time:

1. Select the cell or cells you want to format.

2. Choose **Format**, **Number** from the menu. The Format Cells dialog box appears (see Figure 12.2).

3. Under **Format**, select **Time** or **Date**.

4. Under **Options**, specify any options you want for that format.

5. Click **OK**. The formatting you selected is applied to the cell(s).

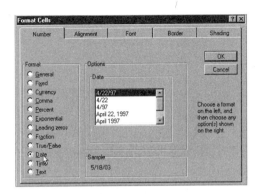

Figure 12.2 The Format Cells dialog box with Date selected.

In this lesson, you learned to change the appearance of numbers, dates, and times by changing the fonts and the number formats. In the next lesson, you learn to format text.

Formatting Text

In this lesson, you learn to format text by changing fonts, font sizes, font styles, and alignment.

Changing Fonts

To change the fonts of the cell or cells in which you have entered text:

1. Select the cell or cells to which you want to apply a new font.

2. Click the **Font Name** button on the toolbar to see the drop-down list of available fonts.

3. Click the font you want to apply to the selected cells.

To change the size of the font:

1. Select the cell or cells to which you want to apply the size change.

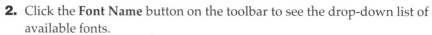

2. Click the **Font Size** button on the toolbar to see the drop-down list of available fonts.

3. Select the font size you want to apply to the selected cell or cells.

To make your text bold, italic, or underline:

1. Select the cell or cells to which you want to apply the bold, italic, or underline font styles.

2. Click the **Bold** button, the **Italic** button, or the **Underline** button on the toolbar to apply that style to the selected cell or cells.

To change more than one font attribute:

1. Select the cell or cells to which you want to apply the font attributes.

2. Choose **Format, Font and Style** from the menu. The Format Cells dialog box appears (see Figure 13.1).

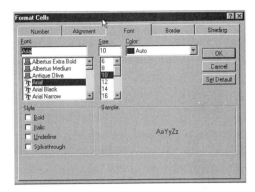

Figure 13.1 The Format Cells dialog box with the Font and Style tab selected.

3. From the **Font** list, select the font you want to use.

4. Under **Size**, select the size you want or enter a number in the **Size** box.

5. From the **Color** drop-down list, select the color you want to apply.

6. Under **Style**, check **Bold**, **Italic**, **Underline**, or **Strikethrough** if you want to use any of those options.

7. Preview your selections in the Sample area. When you have the settings you want, click **OK**.

TIP **Quick Formatting** You can also format text by clicking the right mouse button on your selected cell containing the text. Select **Format** from the pop up menu and then pick the appropriate tab to format your text.

Changing the Default Font

If you consistently find yourself changing the font because you like bigger type or a different typeface in your spreadsheets, you may want to consider setting a new default font. Once you set the new default, that font will be the one that automatically appears when you make an entry in a cell.

To change the default font:

1. Choose **Format, Font and Style** from the menu. The Format Cells dialog box appears with the Font tab open (refer to Figure 13.1).

2. Set your font and size.

3. Click **Set Default**.

4. An alert appears asking if you want to change the default type for all your spreadsheets and database lists to the new settings. Click **Yes**.

Aligning Text

When you enter text in a spreadsheet, Works automatically aligns that text flush left within each cell. You may want to center labels you enter at the head of columns, or make the word "Total" appear on the right side of a cell.

The quickest way to change the text alignment is to use the buttons on the toolbar. Select the cell or cells you want to align and then click on the appropriate cell:

 Left Align aligns the text flush to the left side of the cell but ragged on the right.

 Center Align centers the text between the left and right sides of the cell.

 Right Align aligns the text flush with the right side of the cell but ragged on the left.

To see more alignment options, you need to open the Format Cells dialog box:

1. Select the cell or cells whose content you want to change.

2. Choose **Format, Alignment** from the menu. The Format Cells dialog box appears with the Alignment tab selected (see Figure 13.2).

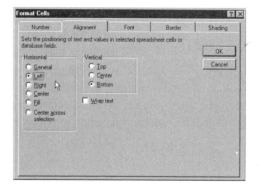

Figure 13.2 The Format Cells dialog box with the Alignment tab selected.

3. Under Horizontal, choose **Left** to align the text on the left side of the cell, **Center** to center the text between the left and right sides of the cell, **Right** to align the text on the right side of the cell, **Fill** to have the characters repeated until they fill the cell from left to right (such as to put asterisks across the cell), or **Center Across Selection** to center the text across the cells you've selected.

4. If your row is deeper than the normal height of your text, select an option under Vertical to align your text with the **Top** of the cell, the **Center** of the cell from top to bottom, or the **Bottom** of the cell.

5. Click **OK**.

Using Word Wrap

When your text overflows the size of a cell, it flows into the cell to the right only if that next cell is blank. If the cell to the right isn't empty, Works will display only the portion of the text that fits inside the left and right borders of your current cell.

Works does have an option that allows the text to wrap within the cell, making multiple lines of text within one cell. When you choose this option you should be aware that the height of the cell increases, affecting the height of the entire row.

To wrap text within a cell:

1. Enter the text in the cell.

2. Highlight the cell.

3. Choose **Format**, **Alignment**. The Format Cells dialog box appears with the Alignment tab selected (refer to Figure 13.2).

4. Select **Wrap Text**.

5. Click **OK**.

Centering Text Across Selected Cells

The ability to center text in a cell does not address centering text across the spreadsheet itself (as in a title). To center text across more than one column, follow these instructions:

1. Enter the text in the first cell you want to include in the group of cells you want to center across.

2. Press **Enter**.

3. Highlight the cells across which you want to center your text including the cell where you entered the text (if your spreadsheet data stretches from column A to column H and you want to center a heading above it in row 2, enter the text in A2, and then highlight cells A2 through H2).

4. Choose **Format**, **Alignment** from the menu. The Format Cells dialog box appears with the Alignment tab selected (see Figure 13.2).

5. Under Horizontal, choose **Center across selection**.

6. Click **OK**.

In this lesson, you learned to change the appearance of your text by changing the font, size, style, and alignment of the text. In the next lesson, you learn how to set margins, insert page breaks, choose a page size, and create headers and footers.

Formatting Pages

14

In this lesson, you learn how to set up your spreadsheet pages so they print properly. You also learn how to set margins, insert page breaks, set the page size and orientation, and create headers and footers.

Setting Margins

The default margins for the Works spreadsheet are 1.0 inch on the top and bottom of the page and 1.25 inch on the left and right sides.

To change the margin settings:

1. Choose **File**, **Page Setup** from the menu. The Page Setup dialog box appears (see Figure 14.1).

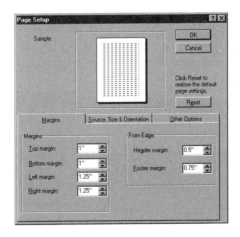

Figure 14.1 The Page Setup dialog box with the Margins tab selected.

2. Under Margins, click the margin you want to change (**Top Margin**, **Bottom Margin**, **Left Margin**, **Right Margin**).

3. Use the small up and down arrows next to the text box to change the current setting by tenths of an inch, or enter an exact measurement in the text box.

4. The Sample area shows an example of what the margin settings will look like for the page. Click **OK** (click **Reset** to return the margins to their original default settings).

Inserting Page Breaks

Works automatically starts a new page when your spreadsheet entries reach the bottom margin of your page. However, that automatic page break may split up an important segment of your spreadsheet. You might rather end the page above this segment so it can be kept together on the next page.

To create a manual page break:

1. Click on the row header of the row you want to begin the next page or on the column header of the column you want to begin on the next page. This highlights that row or column.

2. Choose **Insert, Insert Page Break**. The page break appears as a dashed gridline on your spreadsheet.

To delete a page break:

1. Click on the row header of the row below the page break to highlight that row, or click on the column header of the column to the right of the page break to highlight that column.

2. Choose **Insert**, **Delete Page Break** from the menu.

Determining Page Size and Orientation

When you print your spreadsheet you have several paper sizes available (letter, legal, tabloid, and so forth). It helps in laying out your spreadsheet to select the paper size early in the process. You should also select the orientation (portrait or landscape) of the paper.

What Do You Mean by "Portrait" and "Landscape"? When letter-sized paper is in a vertical, upright position, which is referred to as "portrait," it's 8.5 inches wide and 11 inches tall. When it's in a "landscape" or horizontal orientation, the paper is 11 inches wide and 8.5 inches tall.

To set the paper size and orientation of your page:

1. Choose **File**, **Page Setup** from the menu. The Page Setup dialog box appears (see Figure 14.2). Select the Source, Size & Orientation tab.

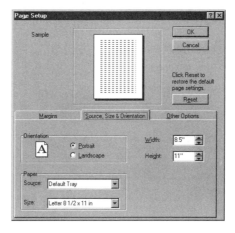

Figure 14.2 The Page Setup dialog box with the Source, Size & Orientation tab selected.

2. Under Orientation, choose **Portrait** or **Landscape**.

3. Under Paper, click on the **Size** drop-down list to select the paper size you want.

4. Click **OK**.

Freezing Titles

With very long or very wide spreadsheets, you may want to have the titles of columns or rows displayed on subsequent pages. You do this by freezing your titles. Then, as you move down or across the spreadsheet you will still see the titles. This works similarly to splitting the window, except that freezing titles also means the titles will print on each page. Splitting the window only displays the titles on each page on your screen.

To freeze titles:

1. Highlight the row below the row you want to freeze, or highlight the column to the right of the column you want to freeze.

2. Choose **Format**, **Freeze Titles** from the menu. A black line appears below or next to the row or column you want to freeze (see Figure 14.3).

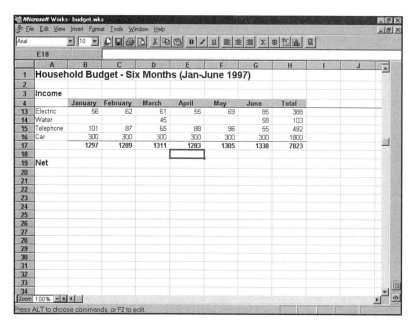

Figure 14.3 Freezing Titles places a black line on the spreadsheet.

To unfreeze the titles, choose **Format**, **Freeze Titles** from the menu to remove the check in front of the option.

Creating Headers and Footers

If your spreadsheet involves more than one page, it is helpful to create headers and footers to print on each page to identify the spreadsheet and add page numbers.

To add headers and footers to your spreadsheet:

1. Choose **View**, **Headers and Footers** from the menu. The View Headers and Footers dialog box appears (see Figure 14.4).

Figure 14.4 The View Headers and Footers dialog box.

2. In the **Header** box enter the text you want to appear at the top of each page. This text automatically centers at the top of the page. If you want any other alignment, you must enter an alignment code (see Table 14.1).

3. In the **Footer** box, enter the text you want to appear at the bottom of each page. This text automatically centers at the bottom of the page. If you want any other alignment, you must enter an alignment code (see Table 14.1).

4. If you don't want the header to appear on the first page of your spreadsheet, select **No header on first page**.

5. If you don't want the footer to appear on the first page of your spreadsheet, select **No footer on first page**.

6. Click **OK**.

To see the headers and footers in your spreadsheet, choose **File**, **Print Preview** from the menu or click the **Print Preview** button on the Toolbar.

Table 14.1 Header and Footer Text Codes

Enter	In Order To
&&	Print one ampersand (&) character
&c	Center characters that follow
&d	Print the current date in "4/27/97" format
&f	Print the filename
&l	Left align characters that follow
&n	Print the current date in "April 27, 1997" format
&p	Print the page number
&r	Right align characters that follow
&t	Print the current time

To print the date on the left and the page number on your right, enter &l&n&r&p.

In this lesson, you learned how to set up your page margins, size, and orientation. You learned how to freeze titles and how to add headers and footers. In the next lesson, you learn how to format the spreadsheet by changing column widths, row heights, borders and shading.

Formatting the Spreadsheet

In this lesson, you explore ways to make your spreadsheet look better with formatting options. You learn to sort data, change column widths and row heights, add borders and shading, and use Works' automatic formatting.

Sorting Data

Many times you enter data as it is given to you or as it comes to you and the data you enter is not in a specific order. Trying to find information out of order can be difficult. Trying to enter information while you are putting it in order can be difficult. Works provides you with the tools you need to sort the data in a spreadsheet *after* you have entered it,

To sort data:

1. Select the data you want to sort.
2. Choose **Tools, Sort** from the menu. The Sort dialog box appears (see Figure 15.1).
3. To sort one column of entries you've highlighted, click **OK**. If you want to sort a range of information based on one of the columns in the highlighted range, select **Sort all the information** and then click **OK**.
4. When the dialog box changes (see Figure 15.2) choose the column you want to use for sorting from the Sort by drop-down list.

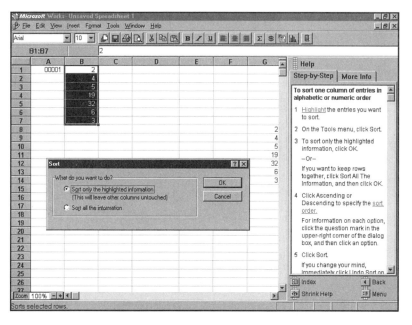

Figure 15.1   The Sort dialog box.

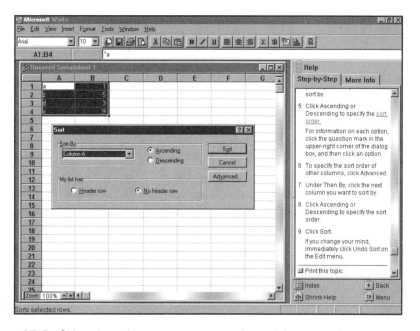

Figure 15.2   Select the column you want to sort by and the sort order.

5. Choose your sort order: Select **Ascending** to sort the column A-Z, 1-100, **Descending** to sort Z-A, 100-1.

6. If the first row of your highlighted sort range has column headings, select **Header Row** under My List Has so Works will ignore that row when it sorts. Otherwise, select **No Header Row**.

7. Click **Sort**.

If you want to sort by more than one column click the **Advanced** button in the Sort dialog box. As you can see in Figure 15.3, you can then specify a second and third column to sort by (This is useful if the first column contains last names and the second column holds first names. You might want to sort first by last names and then by first names in case you have more than one person with the same last name). To start the sort from the Advanced options box, click **Sort**.

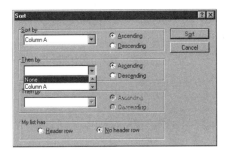

Figure 15.3   Click Advanced to sort by more than one column.

Sorting   Many spreadsheet programs and word processing programs have sorting capabilities. To see how you can sort data in other programs, search for "sort" in the program Help menu.

Changing Column Width and Row Height

By default, the columns in your spreadsheet are set to a width of 10 characters. The row height automatically adjusts based on the font size.

To change the column width or row height, point to the line between the column headers or between the row headers until the Adjust pointer appears, and then drag in the direction you need to increase or decrease the width or height.

To adjust the column width more precisely:

1. Click in one of the cells in the column.

2. Choose **Format**, **Column Width** from the menu. The Column Width dialog box appears (see Figure 15.4).

Figure 15.4 The Column Width dialog box.

3. To specify the exact column width in number of characters enter a figure in the Column width box and click **OK**. The column is resized based on your specifications.

   Click **Standard** to immediately return the column width to 10 characters wide.

   Click **Best Fit** to have Works to automatically select a column width that best fits the text in the column and immediately resize the column.

To precisely specify the row height:

1. Click on a cell in the row that needs adjusting.

2. Choose **Format**, **Row Height** from the menu. The Row Height dialog box appears.

3. Specify the exact row height in point size by entering a figure in the Row height box. Click **OK**; the row adjusts to your specifications.

   Click **Standard** to immediately return the row height to the default text height.

   Click **Best Fit** to have Works automatically select a row height that best fits the text in the column and immediately adjust the row height.

Borders and Shading

Using borders and shading organizes your spreadsheet into definite areas and makes a professional looking printout.

To add borders to cells:

1. Highlight the cells to which you want to apply a border.

2. Choose **Format**, **Border** from the menu. The Format Cells dialog box appears with the Border tab selected (see Figure 15.5).

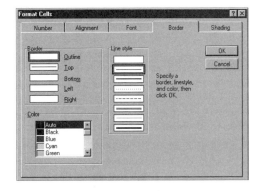

Figure 15.5 The Format Cells dialog box with the Border tab selected.

3. Under Border, select whether you want to apply the border to the **Outline** of the selection, or just the **Top**, **Bottom**, **Left**, or **Right** side.

4. Under Line Style, select the style of line you want to use.

5. From the Color list box, select a color to apply to the line.

6. Click **OK**.

To apply shading to cells:

1. Highlight the cells to which you want to apply shading.

2. Choose **Format**, **Shading** from the menu. The Format Cells dialog box opens with the Shading tab selected (see Figure 15.6).

327

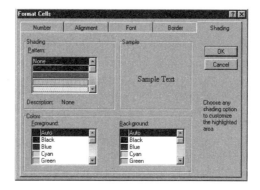

Figure 15.6   The Format Cells dialog box with the Shading tab selected.

3. Under Shading make a selection from the **Pattern** list box.

4. Under Colors, select a **Foreground** color and a **Background** color (for example, you could have blue checks on a yellow background).

5. Preview your selections in the Sample area. Click **OK** to accept your choices and close the dialog box.

Using AutoFormat

Can't make up your mind what colors to use? Don't want to spend time formatting the spreadsheet? Then AutoFormat is for you. AutoFormat offers you a set of predesigned formats that you can apply to your spreadsheet.

To use AutoFormat:

1. Choose **Format, AutoFormat** from the menu. The AutoFormat dialog box appears (see Figure 15.7).

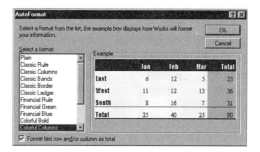

Figure 15.7   The AutoFormat dialog box.

2. Under Select a Format, choose a format from the list. A sample of that format displays in the Example window.

3. Select **Format last row and/or column as total** only if you have totals in the last row or column.

4. Click **OK** to close the dialog box and apply the formatting

In this lesson, you learned how to improve the appearance of your spreadsheet by sorting data, changing column width and row heights, adding borders and shading, or relying on AutoFormat to do it all. In the next lesson, you learn about managing your spreadsheet for use or review by others.

Protecting Data in Your Worksheet

In this lesson, you learn how to protect areas of your spreadsheet so they can't be changed accidentally and so users will be directed to enter data only in specific cells. You also see how to hide information when someone is printing or viewing the spreadsheet.

Protecting the Worksheet

When you want to create a spreadsheet in which someone else might be adding data, you may want to prevent them from changing existing data, formatting cells, or deleting information. In this case, you want to protect your spreadsheet by locking cells.

Normally you can't prevent someone from making changes because the spreadsheet isn't *protected*. In a protected spreadsheet, a user can make modifications only to designated (unlocked) cells. You specify which cells in your spreadsheet are unlocked (all other cells in a protected worksheet are automatically locked), so you effectively keep uneducated users from changing important formulas or data.

To properly protect your spreadsheet, you first designate which cells will be unlocked for user entry or modification. Then you turn protection on for the entire spreadsheet.

To unlock cells:

1. Highlight the cells you want to unlock.
2. Choose **Format**, **Protection** from the menu. The Format Protection dialog box appears (see Figure 16.1).

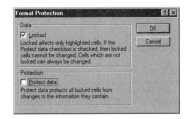

Figure 16.1 The Format Protection dialog box.

3. Remove the check mark from the **Locked** option.

4. Click **OK**.

Follow this procedure for every cell or group of cells you want to have available for data entry or modifications.

To turn protection on for the entire spreadsheet:

1. Choose **Format**, **Protection** from the menu. The Format Protection dialog box appears (refer to Figure 16.1).

2. Check **Protect Data**.

3. Click **OK**.

Protection makes data entry easier. The user can press **TAB** to move from unlocked cell to unlocked cell. If the user attempts to make an entry in a locked cell, an alert appears stating that the cell is locked and that protection must be turned off or the cell must be unlocked. Casual users don't know how to turn off protection or unlock cells, so you've guaranteed that they will change only what you want them to modify.

To turn protection off, remove the check mark from the Protect Data option in the Format Protection dialog box.

Hiding Information

If you need to keep some parts of the spreadsheet confidential, you can hide information so it will not print and casual users will not be able to view it. You might also do this to hide a portion of the spreadsheet you've used for internal calculations that you don't want to appear in the printout.

To hide a column:

- **Drag method**: Point at the right border of the column header until the Adjust pointer appears and drag left until the column is hidden (see Figure 16.2).

- **Command method**: Click in the column to select it or click the column header and drag across several columns to highlight more than one column. Choose **Format**, **Column Width** from the menu. Enter **0** in the **Column Width** box, and click **OK**.

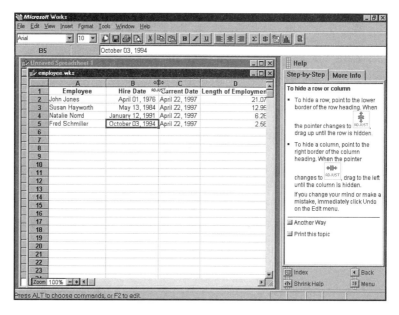

Figure 16.2   Point at the right border of the column until the Adjust pointer appears.

To hide a row:

- **Drag method**: Point to the bottom border of the row header until the Adjust pointer appears and drag up until the row is hidden.

- **Command method**: Click in the row to select it or click the row header and drag up or down several rows to highlight more than one row. Choose **Format**, **Row Height** from the menu. Enter **0** in the **Row Height** box, and click **OK**.

Deleting a row or column would remove the data in that row or column. By changing the row height or column width to 0, the data remains in the spreadsheet even if the row or column isn't displayed.

To show the column or row again, choose **Edit**, **Go To**, enter a cell reference in the column or row you want show, and click **OK**. Choose **Format**, **Column Width** or **Format**, **Row Height** and click the **Standard** button.

In this lesson, you learned how to make data entry easier by protecting the spreadsheet and unlocking the cells where you want data entered. You also found out how to hide columns and rows so they wouldn't print. In the next lesson, you learn how to print your spreadsheet.

Printing a Spreadsheet

In this lesson, you learn how to preview your spreadsheet prior to printing, how to print the spreadsheet, how to print a range, how to set column and row headers, how to print headers and footers, how to print gridlines, and how to print formulas.

Previewing a Spreadsheet

Before you print your spreadsheet, you should see how it will look when it prints. You then have the opportunity to correct any errors, do some formatting, add page breaks, and so forth before you do the actual printing.

To preview your spreadsheet:

1. Choose **File**, **Print Preview** from the menu or click the **Print Preview** button on the toolbar. The Print Preview window opens (see Figure 17.1).

2. The Print Preview window shows your spreadsheet as it will print. If you would like a closer look, click the **Zoom In** button the right side of the screen.

   When in the Preview window, your mouse pointer becomes a Zoom pointer, so you can also magnify your view by clicking the area of your spreadsheet that you'd like to see better.

3. To reduce the magnification, or go back to the full page view, click the **Zoom Out** button.

4. If your spreadsheet has more than one page, click the **Previous** button to go to the page before the current one and **Next** to go to the next page.

5. To start the printing process directly from the Print Preview window, click the **Print** button.

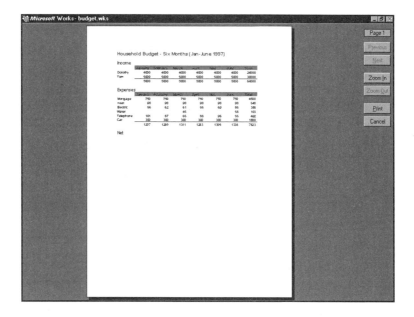

Figure 17.1 The Print Preview window.

6. Click **Cancel** to return to the Spreadsheet window without initiating printing.

 Print Preview   Many Windows programs provide a print preview feature. Search the Help menu in other programs for *Print Preview* for instructions on using this feature.

Printing a Spreadsheet

To print your spreadsheet:

1. Have the spreadsheet open that you want to print.

2. Choose **File**, **Print** from the menu. The Print dialog box appears (see Figure 17.2).

3. Under Print Range, choose to print **All** the spreadsheet pages or select **Pages** and specify the page range you want to print by entering the beginning page number in the **from** box and the ending page number in the **to** box.

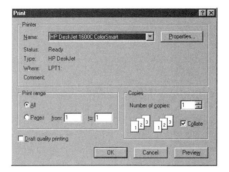

Figure 17.2   The Print dialog box.

4. If you just want a quick printing job and are not worried about quality, check **Draft quality printing**.

5. Under Copies, specify the **Number of copies** by entering a number in the text box or using the up- and down-arrows.

6. If you specify more than one copy, check **Collate** to print each set of pages (1, 2, 3, 1, 2, 3) instead of that number of copies of each page (1, 1, 2, 2, 3, 3).

7. Click the **Preview** button to take a look at the spreadsheet before printing it. If you do, click **Cancel** to return to the Print dialog box or click **Print** to print the spreadsheet from there.

8. If you didn't open the Print Preview window, click **OK** to print the spread-sheet.

 TIP   **Quick Printing**   You can quickly print the spreadsheet by clicking the **Print** button on the toolbar. When you do this, you won't see the Print dialog box. Works accepts all the default settings and sends the spreadsheet to the printer.

Printing a Range

If you don't want to print the entire spreadsheet, you can specify which pages you want to print. If the portion of the spreadsheet you want to print is not an entire page, you can print only a range of cells. To do this, you must set a print area before you open the Print dialog box.

To set a print range:

1. Open the spreadsheet.
2. Highlight the portion of the spreadsheet you want to print.
3. Choose **Format**, **Set Print Area** from the menu.
4. A Works alert box appears asking if it's okay to set the print area to the highlighted cells and warning that it will print only the highlighted cells. Click **OK**.
5. Print as normal (see steps under "Printing a Spreadsheet").

When you no longer want to use the specified area as a print range and would like to go back to printing the entire spreadsheet, you need to remove the print area setting:

1. Choose **Insert**, **Range Name** from the menu. The Range Name dialog box appears (see Figure 17.3).

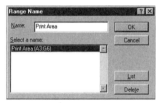

Figure 17.3 The Range Name dialog box.

2. In the **Select a name** box, click **Print Area**.
3. Click **Delete**.
4. Click **Close**.

After removing the Print Area range name, you can now print the entire spreadsheet.

Setting Row and Column Headers

To set up your spreadsheet to print the row numbers (row headers) and column letters (column headers):

1. Choose **File**, **Page Setup** from the menu. The Page Setup dialog box appears (see Figure 17.4). Click the **Other Options** tab.

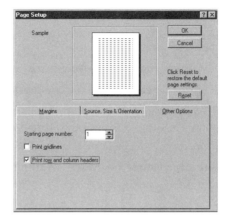

Figure 17.4   The Page Setup dialog box with the Other Options tab selected.

2. Check **Print Row and Column Headers**.

3. Click **OK**.

TIP   **Printing Column & Row Titles, Headers & Footers**   You may want your column or row titles to print on every page. To do this, you need to freeze the column or row titles. Headers and footers will print automatically, but you must create them first. See Part IV, Lesson 14, "Formatting Pages," for more information on freezing titles and creating headers and footers subject.

Printing Gridlines

Even if the gridlines aren't displayed on your spreadsheet (turn them off or on by choosing **View**, **Gridlines** from the menu), you can print the gridlines.

1. Choose **File**, **Page Setup** from the menu. The Page Setup dialog box appears (refer to Figure 17.4).

2. Check **Print gridlines**.

3. Click **OK**.

Printing Formulas

Printing a version of your spreadsheet with the formulas helps you proofread your formulas and/or document your work.

To print the formulas in your spreadsheet instead of the formula results:

1. Choose **View**, **Formulas** from the menu. This makes the formulas appear in the spreadsheet instead of the results.
2. Print the spreadsheet.

In this lesson, you learned about printing the spreadsheet, previewing what you're about to print, printing a selected range of the spreadsheet, and setting some print options. In the next lesson, you learn about some chart basics.

Chart and Graph Basics

In this lesson, you learn about charts and graphs and when and how to use them.

What Is a Chart?

Works uses the word *chart* to refer to both charts and graphs. In most cases, these words are used interchangeably.

What is a chart? It's a pictorial representation of the information on the spreadsheet. A chart makes it easier to understand a series of numbers, to interpret numbers as trends, or compare groups of numbers.

More properly the word *chart* refers to pie charts, diagrams, or organization charts. In a Works spreadsheet, you can prepare pie charts.

What is a pie chart? A *pie chart* is a circle divided into sections that represent percentages of a whole (see Figure 18.1). It's a good way to illustrate how one segment fits into the whole picture, or how a whole is being divided up (such as how your tax dollar is being used).

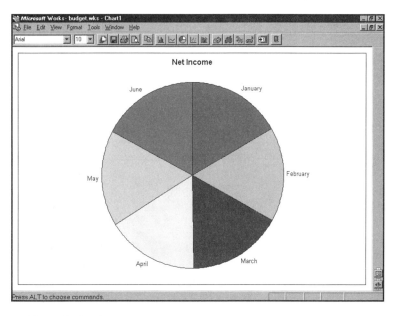

Figure 18.1 A pie chart.

What Is a Graph?

The word *graph* refers to a something that is plotted on an X and Y axis (see the bar graph in Figure 18.2). The X axis is the horizontal line at the bottom of the graph and the labels are categories. The Y axis is the vertical line at the left of the graph and displays the values.

Each value in a graph is plotted against the values on the Y axis. If you're plotting only one piece of data for each category, and the value for the first category is 100,000, the *data point* on the graph for that value is directly above the category and directly across from 100,000 on the Y axis.

You may be plotting several values for each category. For example, in the bar graph shown in Figure 18.2, there are five bars for the 1995 category. For each bar in each category, a data point exists that was plotted against the values in the Y axis.

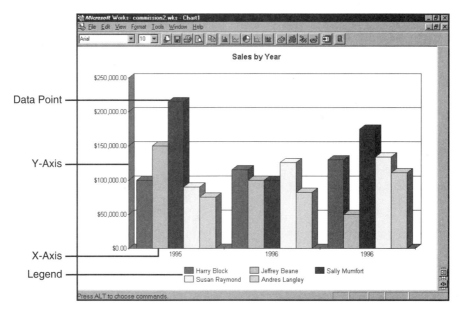

Figure 18.2 This is a bar graph.

Each bar has a different color—one for each salesperson. The *legend* at the bottom of the graph defines which bar belongs to which person. All the red bars, for example, belong to Harry Block. The data for each salesperson represents a *series*.

Figure 18.3 shows you the spreadsheet data used to plot the bar graph in Figure 18.2.

Works has several types of graphs available:

- The **bar** graph is one type and it's useful for comparing information.
- The **line** graph is useful for showing trends.
- Use the **area** graph to show trends versus a quota amount (as in actual sales versus planned sales) over a time period.
- **Scatter** graphs are a favorite tool of statisticians who are plotting populations versus figures by showing just the data points.
- **Radar** graphs are plotted around a center point and are used more by mathematicians.
- Works also has a **combined bar-line** graph.

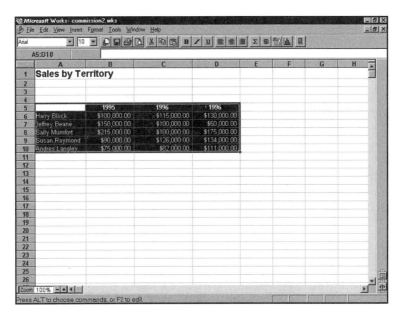

Figure 18.3 The spreadsheet data used to plot the bar graph.

The Practice of Good Charting and Graphing

The number one rule of graphing and charting is KEEP IT SIMPLE! Let the chart speak for itself. The chart is an illustration tool; if it is cluttered up with extraneous information (numbers over bars), it is difficult to read.

Rule number two is to use the correct *type* of chart or graph to illustrate your data. Use a bar graph to show comparisons over time and a pie chart to display parts of a whole, but don't try to use a bar graph to display parts of a whole or a pie chart to show comparisons over time.

Don't use a graph or chart just because it's pretty. If it doesn't have a point, don't bother with it. And, don't spend a lot of time picking colors and line styles. First of all, customizing a graph or chart takes time. Second, a blue bar next to a red bar is just as readable as a blue bar next to a green bar. If the graph gets the point across, changing the appearance isn't really necessary.

In this lesson, you learned what charts and graphs are and a little about how they are used. The next lesson teaches you how to create a chart.

Creating a Chart

In this lesson, you learn how to select the data to chart, how to choose a chart type, how to add a title and border to the chart, how to pick the correction orientation for the data series, and how to save the chart.

Launching a Spreadsheet

Before you can create a chart, you need to have a spreadsheet open that contains the data you want to chart.

To start a new spreadsheet from the Works Task Launcher:

1. From the Works Task Launcher, select the **Works Tools** tab (see Figure 19.1).

Figure 19.1 The Works Task Launcher with the Works Tools tab selected.

2. Click the **Spreadsheet** button.

To start a new spreadsheet from within the Spreadsheet tool:

1. Choose **File**, **New** from the menu.

2. The Works Task Launcher appears. Select the **Works Tools** tab.

3. Click the **Spreadsheet** button.

To open an existing spreadsheet from the Works Task Launcher:

1. Select the **Existing Documents** tab (see Figure 19.2).

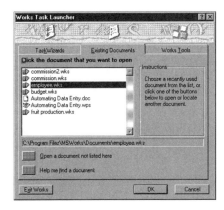

Figure 19.2   The Works Task Launcher with the Existing Documents Tab selected.

2. Select the name of the file you want to open from the list of files.

3. Click **OK**.

To open an existing spreadsheet from within the Spreadsheet tool:

1. Choose **File**, **Open** from the menu. The Open dialog box appears (see Figure 19.3).

2. Select the file you want to open.

3. Click **OK**.

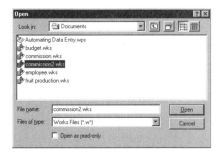

Figure 19.3   The Open dialog box.

Selecting the Data to Chart

Once you've opened a spreadsheet and entered the data , the first step in creating a chart is to select the data to chart. If the chart is a pie chart, this involves only two sets of data: the slice labels and the values each slice represents. If the chart is a graph, the data may involve several columns and rows.

To select the data, highlight the range. If you have rows that end in totals or columns that end in totals, don't include the totals in the chart range (unless you just want to chart the totals).

CAUTION

My Data Is Not All in One Place (Contiguous)!   Use a nonprinting area of the spreadsheet and copy the data to that area. For example, to create a pie chart of the total sales for the year by salesperson, you need only the names of the salespeople and their totals. Copy just the names of the salespeople and their totals to another area of the spreadsheet and highlight that range to create the chart.

Choosing a Chart Type

Using the general information provided in the last lesson, you should know what type of chart you want to make.

To select the chart type:

1. Highlight the data you want to chart.

2. Choose **Tools, Create New Chart** from the menu or click the **New Chart** button on the toolbar. The New Chart dialog box opens (see Figure 19.4).

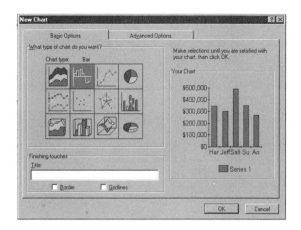

Figure 19.4 The New Chart dialog box.

3. Under **What Type of Chart Do You Want?**, Works displays 12 chart types. Click one of the pictures to select that chart type. The Your Chart area displays the name of the chart and a sample of how your data will look using this chart type.

4. Click **OK** to create the chart. The chart appears on your screen and a Chart Toolbar is now available to use in modifying your chart.

Adding a Title, Border, and Gridlines

You can add a title to the chart, a border around the chart, and gridlines (not for a pie chart).

To add a title, a subtitle, or axis titles:

1. Choose **Edit**, **Titles** from the menu. The Edit Titles dialog box appears (see Figure 19.5).

2. Enter the following information:

Enter the title text in the **Chart** title box.

Enter the subtitle text in the **Subtitle** box.

Enter the text for the X-Axis title in the **Horizontal (X) Axis** box.

Enter the text for the Y-Axis title in the **Vertical (Y) Axis** box.

If you have a second Y-Axis, enter the title for that axis in the **Right Vertical Axis** box.

347

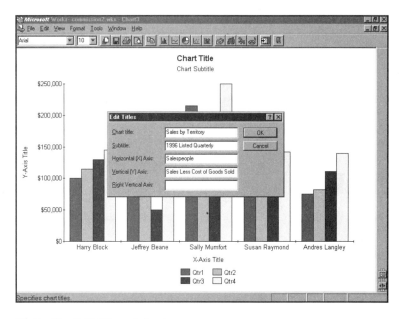

Figure 19.5   The Edit Titles dialog box.

3. As you make these choices, your chart example shows the changes. Click **OK**; the chart now displays the new titles.

To add a border, choose **Format**, **Border** from the menu. To remove the border, use the same menu command.

To show horizontal gridlines, choose **Format**, **Horizontal (X) Axis**. When the Format Horizontal Axis dialog box appears, check **Show Gridlines**, and click **OK**.

To show vertical gridlines, choose **Format**, **Vertical (Y) Axis**. When the Format Vertical Axis dialog box appears, check **Show Gridlines**, and click **OK**.

Understanding Series Orientation

A series is a group of cells, either in a row or column, that falls under each category on the graph. Using the data shown in Figure 19.6, the series are in rows. For example, the information on Harry Block is one series, and Jeffrey Beane is another.

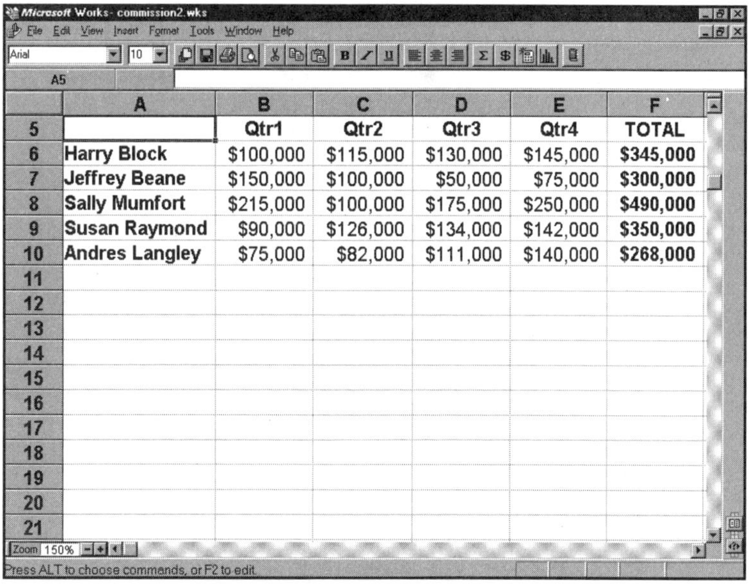

Figure 19.6 Spreadsheet data with series in rows.

When you plot series in rows (across) as a bar graph, the column titles become the categories on the X-Axis and the first column becomes the legend. Each cell of data across the row represents a data point, with each row representing a series. In the bar graph, each cell creates a bar, and each cell in the same row is the same color. For instance, Harry Block's bars are red and Jeffrey Beane's are green. One red bar appears at each category, and one green bar appears at each category.

If you plot your series in columns (down), the first row (your column titles) becomes the legend text and the first column contains the category labels on the X-Axis.

Depending on how you entered your data, you may have to switch the data orientation, although Works may do this automatically for you.

To specify series orientation while still in the New Chart dialog box, follow these steps:

1. Click the **Advanced Options** tab (see Figure 19.7).

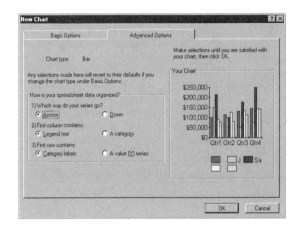

Figure 19.7 The New Chart dialog box with the Advanced Options tab selected.

2. Click Across or Down under Which way do your series go?

3. Make sure you make the proper selection for `First Column Contains` and `First Row Contains` by selecting **Legend Text** or **Category Labels**. Check the Your Chart sample to be sure.

4. Click **OK**.

If you've already created the chart and need to change the orientation, choose **Edit**, **Legend/Series Labels** from the menu (see the Edit Legend/Series Labels dialog box in Figure 19.8). You can then specify which cells are series labels and whether to use them as the legend. Click **OK** to close the dialog box.

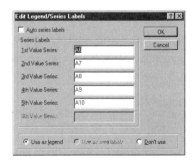

Figure 19.8 The Edit Legend/Series Labels dialog box.

Saving the Chart

Once you have the chart set up, you should save it by saving the spreadsheet. Choose **File**, **Save** from the menu or clicking the **Save** button on the toolbar. Choose **File**, **Close** from the menu to close the chart window; choose **Window** and select your spreadsheet name to switch to the spreadsheet without closing the chart window.

You can have up to eight charts in a spreadsheet.

In this lesson, you learned how to create a chart, pick a chart type, add a title, put a border around the chart, add gridlines, pick the series orientation, and save the chart. In the next lesson, you learn how to change the chart data or chart range.

Changing Chart Data

In this lesson, you learn how to switch between the chart window and the spreadsheet window, how to change the range for the chart data, how to add to the range, and how to delete from the range.

Switching to the Chart Window

When you are in the Spreadsheet window and you want to see one of the charts you made in the spreadsheet, do the following:

1. Choose **View**, **Chart** from the menu. The View Chart dialog box appears (see Figure 20.1).

Figure 20.1 The View Chart dialog box.

2. Select the Chart you want to see.

3. Click **OK**. The chart window opens.

To switch back to the spreadsheet window, choose **View**, **Spreadsheet** from the menu.

To see both a chart and the spreadsheet at the same time, choose **Window**, **Tile**.

Changing the Entry Range

Did you accidentally select the wrong range when you started the chart? You can change the entry range without losing the chart attributes you selected.

To change the entry range for a chart:

1. Open the chart window to the chart you want to modify.
2. Choose **Edit**, **Series** from the menu. The Edit Series dialog box appears (see Figure 20.2).

Figure 20.2   The Edit Series dialog box.

3. Edit the cell address references for the series you want to change.
4. Click **OK**. The chart changes to reflect the values in the new entry range.

Adding to the Entry Range

To add entries to an existing chart:

1. Switch to the chart to which you want to add entries.
2. From the Chart window, choose **Window**, **Tile** to see the chart and the spreadsheet side by side.
3. In the spreadsheet, highlight the entries you want to add to the chart.
4. Point to the border of the highlighted cells. When the word Drag appears beneath the mouse pointer, hold down the mouse button and drag the entries to the chart. As you drag, the word beneath the mouse pointer changes to Move (see Figure 20.3). When you release the mouse over the chart, the chart changes to reflect the additional data.

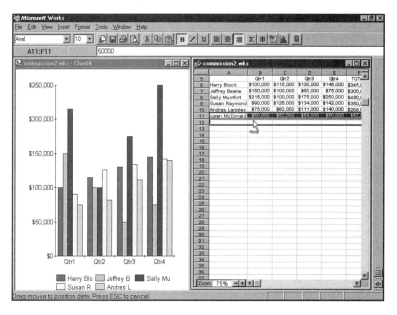

Figure 20.3 The "Move" mouse pointer.

You can also add entries to a chart by copying them from the spreadsheet:

1. From the spreadsheet window, highlight the cells in the spreadsheet that you want to add as entries to the chart.
2. Choose **Edit**, **Copy** from the menu or click the **Copy** button on the toolbar.
3. Switch to the chart window (choose **View**, **Chart** from the menu).
4. Choose **Edit**, **Paste Series** from the menu. The Paste Series dialog box appears.
5. Click the series you want.
6. Click **OK**.

Deleting from the Entry Range

To delete entries from a chart:

1. Switch to the chart you're going to change.
2. From the Chart window, choose **Edit**, **Series** from the menu to open the Edit Series dialog box (refer to Figure 20.2).

3. Highlight the contents of the box for the series you want to delete.

4. Press the **Delete** key.

5. Click **OK**; the chart reflects any deletions you made.

In this lesson, you learned how to switch between the chart and the spreadsheet windows, how to see both windows at the same time, and how to add to, change, or delete from the chart's entry range. In the next lesson, you modify the appearance of the chart.

Modifying the Chart Appearance

In this lesson, you explore ways to change the chart appearance by adding shading and color, editing the chart title, adding gridlines, creating a legend, or changing the chart type.

Adding Shading and Color

If you have color printing capabilities, you may want to change the colors and shading of the elements of your chart. Even if you don't have a color printer, the colors and shades you select affect the gray shades on a black-and-white print job.

To set the shading and color:

1. Open the chart you want to modify.

2. Choose **Format**, **Shading and Color** from the menu or right-click a chart element and choose **Shading and Color** from the pop-up menu. The Format Shading and Color dialog box appears (see Figure 21.1).

3. Click the Series you want to modify.

4. From the Color list, select an appropriate color. (If you're working on an area, bar, or pie chart, avoid putting red and green next to each other as they can't be distinguished by colorblind people. Instead, put a contrasting color like yellow between them.)

5. The choices under Pattern depend on what type of chart you have. For a line chart, the patterns listed are styles of lines. For a bar, pie, or area chart, the patterns listed offer varying intensities of color or cross-hatching choices. Click the pattern you want to use.

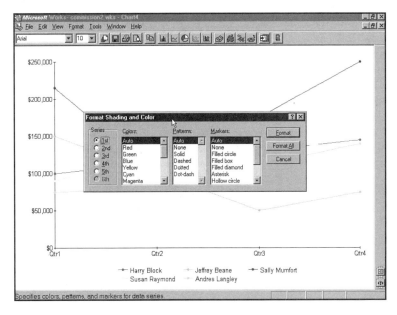

Figure 21.1 The Format Shading and Color dialog box for a line chart.

6. If you are working with a line chart, a list of symbols appears under Marker. The marker appears at the data point on the line. Choose an appropriate one.

7. Click **Format** to change the selected series and the changes are immediately reflected in your chart. Click **Format All** to apply changes to all the value series.

8. Click **Close** to exit the dialog box.

Editing a Chart Title

To modify the Chart Title, Subtitle, X-Axis Title, or Y-Axis Title:

1. Choose **Edit, Titles** from the menu. The Edit Titles dialog box appears (see Figure 21.2).

2. Click in the appropriate text box for the type of title you're changing and make the corrections.

3. Click **OK**. The changes appear on the chart.

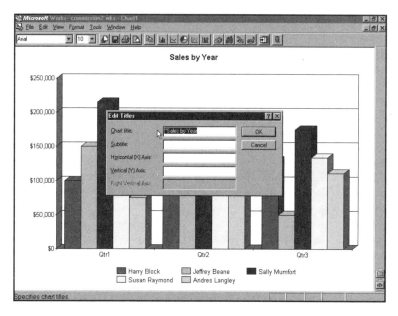

Figure 21.2 The Edit Titles dialog box.

Adding Gridlines

Gridlines are the reference lines that stretch horizontally from the Y-Axis or vertically from the X-Axis.

To show horizontal gridlines, choose **Format, Horizontal (X) Axis** from the menu. When the Format Horizontal Axis dialog box appears, check **Show Gridlines**, and click **OK**.

To show vertical gridlines, choose **Format, Vertical (Y) Axis** from the menu. When the Format Vertical Axis dialog box appears (see Figure 21.3), check **Show Gridlines**, and click **OK**.

Figure 21.3 The Format Vertical Axis dialog box.

Creating a Legend

The legend identifies which colors or lines represent which type of data. If your chart originally started out as a pie chart or had only one bar per category, it may not have a legend.

To create a legend for the chart:

1. Open the chart.

2. Choose **Edit**, **Legend/Series Labels** from the menu to open the Edit Legend / Series Labels dialog box (see Figure 21.4).

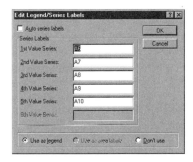

Figure 21.4   The Edit Legend/Series Labels dialog box.

3. Select the **Use a legend** option at the bottom of the dialog box.

4. Click **OK**.

Changing the Chart Type

You may decide at some point to use a line chart instead of a bar graph or to use a stacked bar graph. To change the chart type:

1. Open the chart you want to modify.

2. Choose **Format**, **Chart Type** from the menu or click the Toolbar button for the type of chart you want to use. The Chart Type dialog box appears (see Figure 21.5).

3. Under Chart Type, click the picture of the chart type you want to use. The Your Chart example will show you how the chart will change.

4. Every basic chart type has a series of variations available. To use a variation, select the **Variations** tab, and then click a Chart Type. Your Chart shows how the chart will change.

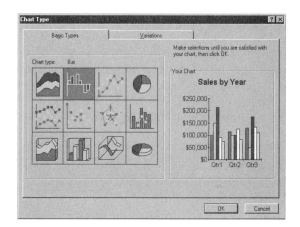

Figure 21.5 The Chart Type dialog box.

5. Click **OK**.

In this lesson, you learned how to change the overall appearance of your chart. In the next lesson, you learn how to format the text on your chart.

Formatting Chart Text

In this lesson, you learn how to change the default font and how to format the title text, the series text, the category text, and the legend text.

Changing the Default Font

To change the default font for your charts, you must set the default font for your spreadsheet. Part IV, Lesson 13, "Formatting Text," explains how to do this.

Formatting the Title Text

To format the text for any title on the chart:

1. Open the chart.
2. Click on the title you want to change.
3. Choose **Format**, **Font and Style** from the menu or right click the title and choose **Font and Style** from the pop-up menu. The Format Font and Style dialog box appears (see Figure 22.1). The dialog box varies depending on the title you selected.
4. From the Font list, select the font you want to use.
5. Choose a point size from the Size list or enter a size in the text box.
6. From the Color drop-down list, select a color.
7. Under Style, check **Bold**, **Italic**, **Underline**, or **Strikethrough**.

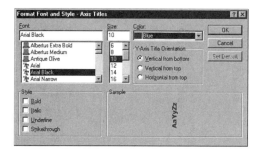

Figure 22.1   The Format Font and Style - Axis Titles dialog box.

8. If you selected the Y-Axis Title, an additional section appears on the dialog box. Under this `Y-Axis Title Orientation` section, you may choose to have the title appear **Vertical from Bottom**, **Vertical from Top**, or **Horizontal from Top**. Select an option and check the appearance in the `Sample` area.

9. Click **OK**.

Formatting Series, Legend, and Category Text

If you click on any series, legend, or category text to select it and then choose **Format**, **Font and Style** from the menu (or right click the text and choose **Font and Style** from the pop-up menu), the selections you make in the Font and Style dialog box are going to affect all the series, legend, and category text.

If no particular piece of text on a chart is selected or highlighted and you make a font change, that font change is applied to the legend text, the data labels, the axis labels, and the categories. It does not affect the titles.

In this lesson, you learned how to format the text on your chart. In the next lesson, you work with axes: learning what they are, changing the scale, and setting the interval of category labels.

Working with Axes

23

In this lesson, you learn about axes—what they are, how to change the scale, how to add a second value axis, and how to set the interval of category labels.

What Is an Axis?

In plotting graphs, there are generally two axes (the plural of axis), or two lines that cross each other. The Y-Axis is the vertical axis where the values appear. The X-Axis is the horizontal axis where the category labels appear. Where the two axes meet is the zero point (the value is 0).

When an entry value is plotted, it's lined up with the values on the Y-Axis and with the category on the X-Axis that it falls into. So, if the figure for January sales is $100,000, the data point is across from the $100,000 mark on the Y-Axis and above the January category.

Changing the Axis Scale

Where the axes meet is usually the zero point, but you can change this by modifying the scale of the axis and specifying a different value as the "minimum" for the axis.

The highest number on the value axis is based on the data entries, being equal to the highest number in the entries. You can also adjust this by changing the "maximum" for the axis.

You can also set how far apart the numbers are by changing the "interval."

To change the axis scale:

1. Open the chart you want to modify.

2. Choose **Format, Vertical (Y) Axis** or **Format, Horizontal (X) Axis** from the menu, depending on which axis scale you want to adjust. The Format Vertical Axis dialog box (see Figure 23.1) or the Format Horizontal Axis dialog box appears.

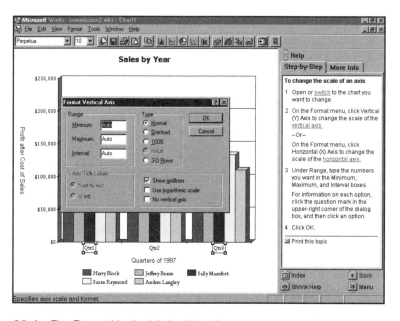

Figure 23.1 The Format Vertical Axis dialog box.

3. Under Range, enter numbers in the Minimum box or Maximum box to set the lowest and highest values on the axis.

4. Enter a value in the Interval box to set how far apart you want the values on the axis to appear (if you enter 100, the values will go up 0, 100, 200, 300, and so on).

5. Under Type, click one of the options to adjust the axis to show values as they are charted for that type of chart.

6. Check **Show Gridlines** to have gridlines appear on the chart.

7. Check **Use Logarithmic Scale** if you have very large numbers (the value intervals go up exponentially) or you need to show a logarithmic relationship.

8. Check **No Vertical Axis** or **No Horizontal Axis** if you don't want the axis to appear.

9. Click **OK**.

Adding a Second Value Axis

When you have dissimilar values (such as dollars and percentages) to show in the same chart, you can create a second value axis to accommodate the different values.

To create a second value axis:

1. Open the chart you want to modify.

2. Choose **Format, Two Vertical (Y) Axes** from the menu (you may have to remove any 3-D effects from your chart if this is grayed out on the menu). The Format Two Vertical Axes dialog box appears (see Figure 23.2).

Figure 23.2   The Format Two Vertical Axes dialog box.

3. For each group of values (series) in your chart that has the same type of values as you're showing on the second ("different") Y-Axis, click **Right**.

4. Click **OK**.

Setting the Interval of Category Labels

There are times when you will have so many category labels that they don't display well on the X-Axis. You may find that having every other label works better for your spacing and is still understandable.

To set the interval of the category labels:

1. Open the chart you want to modify.

2. Choose **Format, Horizontal (X) Axis** from the menu. The Format Horizontal Axis dialog box appears (see Figure 23.3).

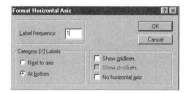

Figure 23.3 The Format Horizontal Axis dialog box.

3. In the Label Frequency box, enter the number for the interval (2 is every other).

4. Click **OK**.

In this lesson, you learned what an axis is, how to change the minimum and maximum numbers on the value axis, how to change the intervals between value numbers and category labels, and how to add a second value axis. In the next lesson, you learn all about data labels.

Adding Data Labels

24

In this lesson, you learn what data labels are and how to create, edit, format, and delete them.

Creating Data Labels

A data label repeats the data entry value right next to the bar, line, or pie slice that represents the number (see Figure 24.1). You can't use data labels on pie, radar, or 3-D charts.

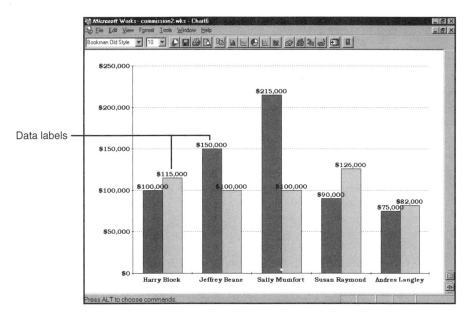

Figure 24.1   A bar chart with data labels.

To add data labels to your chart based on the values in the entry range:

1. Open the chart you want to modify.

2. Choose **Edit**, **Data Labels** from the menu. The Edit Data Labels dialog box opens (see Figure 24.2).

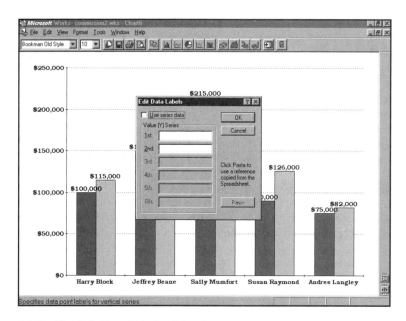

Figure 24.2 The Edit Data Labels dialog box.

3. Check **Use Series Data** at the top of the dialog box.

4. Click **OK** and the series data labels appear on your chart.

To add data labels to your chart using any spreadsheet text or numbers as data labels:

1. Open the spreadsheet window.

2. Highlight the text or numbers in the spreadsheet that you want to use as data labels.

3. Choose **Edit**, **Copy** from the menu or click the **Copy** button on the toolbar.

4. Switch to the chart window (choose **View**, **Chart** from the menu, select the chart you want to open, and click **OK**).

5. Choose **Edit, Data Labels** from the menu. The Edit Data Labels dialog box opens (refer to Figure 24.2).

6. Make sure the Use Series Data check box is deselected.

7. Click the value series text box you want to use for the labels.

8. Click the **Paste** button in the Edit Data Labels dialog box. This inserts the range reference for the cells you copied into the value series text box.

9. Click **OK** to close the dialog box and apply the new data labels to the chart.

To modify your data labels, follow the preceding guidelines to enter the labels but change the range references before clicking **OK**.

Formatting Data Labels

When the data labels appear, the font size may be too large or you might like to use a different color for the labels, so you'll want to change the label format. Be aware that modifying the label format may affect other labels in the chart (you can always undo your settings if you don't like the results).

To change the font size or color:

1. Open the chart window and click any data label.

2. Choose **Format, Font and Style** from the menu (or right-click the data label and choose **Font and Style** from the pop-up menu). The Format Font and Style dialog box appears (see Figure 24.3).

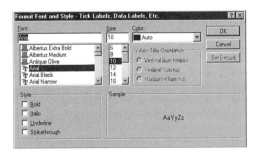

Figure 24.3   The Format Font and Style dialog box.

3. From the Font list, select the font you want to use.

4. Choose a point size from the Size list or enter a size in the text box.

5. From the Color drop-down list, select a color.

6. Under Style, check **Bold**, **Italic**, **Underline**, or **Strikethrough**.

7. Click **OK**.

Deleting Data Labels

To delete data labels:

1. Open the chart.

2. Choose **Edit**, **Data Labels** from the menu. The Edit Data Labels dialog box opens (refer to Figure 24.2).

3. Deselect the Use Series Data check box, if necessary.

4. Highlight the value series you want to delete.

5. Press the **Delete** key on your keyboard.

6. Click **OK**. The data labels are removed from your chart.

In this lesson, you learned how to add data labels to your chart, how to edit them, how to format them, and how to delete them. In the next lesson, you discover how pie charts differ from graphs and what special settings they need.

Working with Pie Charts

In this lesson, you learn how pie charts are different, how to explode a pie chart slice, how to label pie slices, and how to change the appearance of the chart.

What Makes a Pie Chart Different?

The major difference between pie charts and other graphs is that there are no axes. A pie chart consists of a circle sliced into sections that represent percentages of a whole (see Figure 25.1).

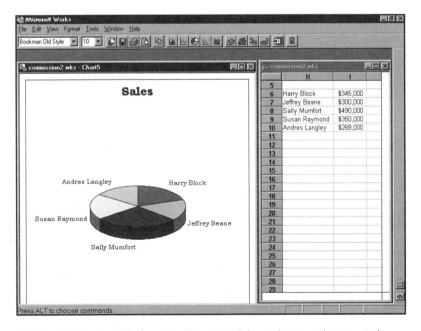

Figure 25.1   A pie chart tiled next to the spreadsheet data used to create it.

A pie chart is simple and easy to read. It's one of the most popular charts used in business presentations. You create your pie chart using the steps outlined in Part IV, Lesson 19, "Creating a Chart."

Exploding a Pie Slice

To emphasize a particular pie slice, you can *explode* or *cut* it. This pulls the one slice out from the center of the pie. To explode the slice:

1. Open the chart you want to modify. Click the slice you want to explode.

2. Choose **Format**, **Shading and Color** from the menu or right-click the slice and choose **Shading and Color** from the pop-up menu. The Format Shading and Color dialog box opens (see Figure 25.2).

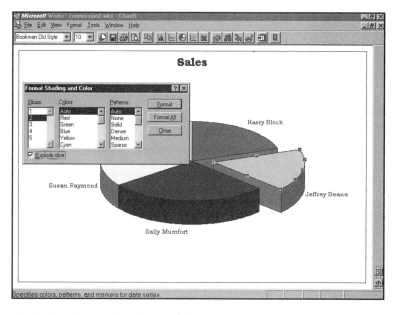

Figure 25.2   The Format Shading and Color dialog box.

3. Under Slices, select the number of the slice that you want to explode (if you clicked the slice before opening the dialog box, that number should already be highlighted).

4. Select **Explode Slice**. This places a check mark in the box.

5. Click the **Format** button (don't choose Format All; you shouldn't explode all the slices in a pie). The chart reflects the new settings you selected (refer to Figure 25.2).

6. Click **Close** to exit the dialog box.

Adding Slice Labels

When you created the pie chart, the data range you highlighted included slice labels. However, you may want a second label for each slice, such as the value or percentage. This second label appears in parentheses after the first label. For example, if the slice label appears as "Retail Sales (50%)," the first label is "Retail Sales" and the second label is "50%."

To add a second slice label:

1. Open the chart you want to modify.

2. Choose **Edit**, **Data Labels** to open the Format Data Labels dialog box (see Figure 25.3).

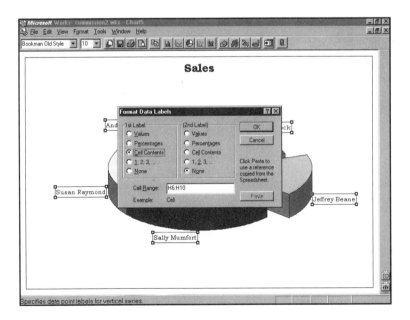

Figure 25.3 The Format Data Labels dialog box.

3. Under 1st Label, Cell Contents is probably selected because the First label is based on the range of cells you selected when you started the chart (if you highlight a range of labels before you open this dialog box, click **Paste** when you make this selection to change the labels). You can change this to **Values** (the numeric contents of the cell), **Percentages** (the percentage of the whole the slice represents), **1,2,3** (the number of the slice), or **None**.

4. Under 2nd Label, you have the same set of choices. Click the one you want to use.

5. Click **OK**.

Formatting Pie Charts

Selecting the format of the chart text is the same for pie charts as it is for other graphs. Changing the colors is only slightly different.

To change the color of the slices:

1. Open the chart you want to modify.

2. Choose **Format**, **Shading and Color** from the menu or right-click the slice and choose **Shading and Color** from the pop-up menu. The Format Shading and Color dialog box appears (see Figure 25.4).

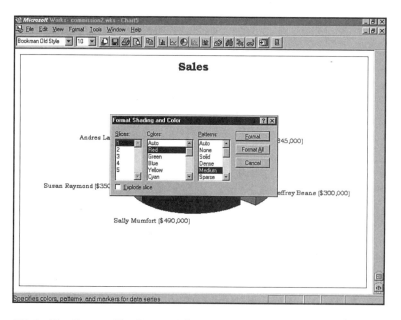

Figure 25.4 The Format Shading and Color dialog box.

3. Under Slices, select the number of the slice you want to modify.

4. From the Colors box, select the color you want to use for that slice.

5. If you don't want to use solid colors, make a choice under Patterns, which include different color densities and hatching options.

6. Click **Format**. The chart reflects your changes.

7. Repeat steps 3 through 6 for each slice you want to change.

8. Click **Close** to exit the dialog box.

In this lesson, you learned what differences exist between pie charts and other graphs and what special settings you have to make to add data labels, change colors, and explode slices. In the next lesson, you learn how to mix chart types.

Mixing Chart Types

In this lesson, you learn how to combine lines and bars on the same chart.

Combining Lines and Bars

You can change any line or bar chart to a combination of lines and bars. Then you can compare some values using the bars but also show a trend using the line.

One method for doing this is to reformat the series as lines or bars:

1. Open the chart you want to modify.
2. Choose **Format, Mixed Line and Bar** from the menu. The Format Mixed Line and Bar dialog box appears (see Figure 26.1).

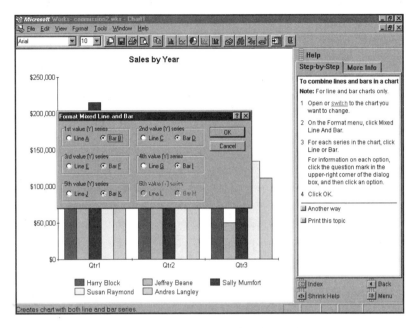

Figure 26.1 The Format Mixed Line and Bar dialog box.

3. For each value series, select **Line** or **Bar**.

4. Click **OK.** Your chart reflects the selections you made.

Another method for combining lines and bars is to change the chart type to a combination chart (you can also select a combination type when you create the chart):

1. Open the chart you want to modify.

2. Choose **Format, Chart Type** from the menu or click the Mixed Chart button on the Toolbar. The Chart Type dialog box opens (see Figure 26.2).

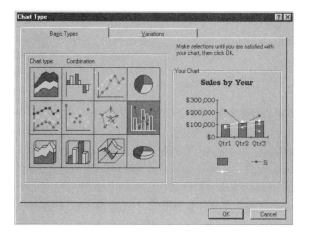

Figure 26.2 The Format Chart Type dialog box.

3. Click the combination chart type.

4. Select the Variations tab to see different formats for the combination (see Figure 26.3).

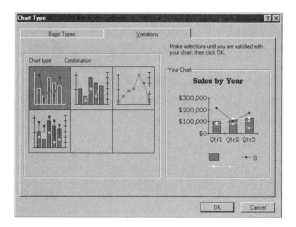

Figure 26.3 The Chart Type dialog box with the Variations tab selected.

5. Click the variation you want to use.

6. Click **OK**.

Because Works automatically makes the first data series the bars and the second data series the lines, you may have to modify the resulting chart. To change which series are lines and which are bars, choose **Format**, **Mixed Line and Bar** (as described at the beginning of this section).

Returning to Line-Only or Bar-Only Charts

When you decide that you want your combination chart to return to a line-only or bar-only chart:

1. Open the chart you want to modify.

2. Choose **Format**, **Mixed Line and Bar** from the menu. The Format Mixed Line and Bar dialog box appears (refer to Figure 26.1).

3. Select **Line** for all the series or select **Bar** for all the series.

4. Click **OK**.

In this lesson, you learned how to change bar or line charts to combination charts and how to specify which series are lines and which are bars. In the next lesson, you find out how to print your charts.

Printing Charts

In this lesson, you learn to print your charts and view how the chart is going to look before you print it.

Displaying the Chart as It Will Be Printed

The way your chart appears on your computer monitor can be quite different than the final printed version, depending on the capabilities of your devices. For example, you may have a color monitor but you may be printing in black-and-white. In this case, the colors become gray shades, and it may not be as easy to distinguish lines, bars, or pie slices without the color.

To display your chart as it will be printed:

1. Open the chart you want to print.

2. Choose **View**, **Display as Printed** from the menu.

3. If you need to make adjustments to colors, shading, or patterns to make your chart print clearly, make them while you can see how it affects your printed version.

4. To return to the original display, choose **View**, **Display as Printed** from the menu.

Printing Charts Only

To print a chart:

1. Open the chart you want to print.

2. Choose **File**, **Print** from the menu. The Print dialog box appears (see Figure 27.1).

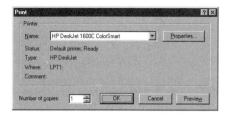

Figure 27.1 The Print dialog box.

3. From the Name drop-down list, select the printer you want to use (if you have more than one).

4. Enter the **Number of Copies**, or use the up and down arrows to set the number.

5. Click **OK**.

TIP **Quick Printing** To quickly print the chart using the default print settings, open the chart and click the **Print** button on the toolbar.

In this lesson, you learned how to display the chart as it will print and how to print the chart. In the next lesson, you learn how linking and embedding enable you to work with multiple applications.

Linking and Embedding Files

In this lesson, you explore two concepts: linking and embedding. You'll learn how these concepts help you work with more than one application.

Sharing Information Between Applications

You can incorporate your spreadsheet data in a Works word processing document, a Works database, or into a non-Works application. You can also "capture" data from other applications and bring it into your spreadsheet.

For example, let's say you're writing a report in a word processing program. Data you need to incorporate in that report is contained in a spreadsheet. You want to capture that spreadsheet data and put it into your report document.

You can share information between applications using:

- **Importing** converts data from its native program so you can include it in your current document. Generally, users import data when they can't open the source document. For instance, if you need a picture in your document, you import the picture from a clip art library into your document. Once you place the picture, you can't open the clip art file and change that picture, and if someone updates the original picture file, those updates do not automatically appear in your document. Your picture remains the same as it was when you imported it.

To learn more about importing, see Appendix A: "Importing and Exporting."

- **Edit**, **Cut** and **Edit**, **Copy** commands allow you to store data temporarily in the Clipboard (a memory holding area created by Windows) and then place it into your document with the **Edit**, **Paste** command.

  To learn more about cutting and pasting, see Part I, Lesson 8, "Copying and Moving Information Between Windows."

- **Linking** utilizes the Clipboard (via the Cut and Copy commands) to bring data from a source document such as an Excel spreadsheet and place it into your Works document or spreadsheet. Any updates to the source information will also appear in your document or spreadsheet. All users of the document must have access to the source file, and the location of that source file cannot change or the link will fail.

- **Embedding** places an "object" created by another program directly into your document. You can edit the object contents by activating the source application directly from your document (all you have to do is double-click the object). Unlike linking, changing an embedded object does not change the source document.

Object An object is a single piece of data such as text, graphics, sound, or animation created by an OLE-supportive application.

Programs that let you share data use one of two methods:

Dynamic Data Exchange (DDE) is a communications protocol that lets you share data between two open applications. DDE is an older technology, so most programs in Windows support it.

Object Linking and Embedding (OLE) extends your ability to dynamically share information between programs and program files. Because of OLE, you can embed or link files from another application into a document; or you can embed a new object and use the object's application to enter data into your document. Not all applications support OLE (especially older ones), so you may not be able to embed files from all your applications.

As a user, you don't have to know if an application supports DDE or OLE. Microsoft Works will automatically employ OLE if the originating application supports it and DDE if it doesn't.

Understanding Linking

When you link data from an application to your document or spreadsheet, the linked object maintains a reference or pointer back to the originating file. Then, when the original file changes, the modifications also appear in your destination document.

For example, if you copy data from a spreadsheet file containing your yearly budget into a word processing document and link the data to its source, any new data you add to the spreadsheet file at the end of the first quarter will also show up in your word processing document. Likewise, anyone else who also linked data to their own documents will receive the updates to the spreadsheet.

As a user, you can't edit or update linked data without using the source application program. You would also need access to the source file and you would need to find the file at the same drive and directory or folder as listed in the reference pointer to the source file. In other words, if the file the data came from was on the server's drive F in the Import directory, you need to specify F:\Import as the source location to access the file from your computer. What are the advantages of linking files?

- You can link files between older Windows programs that don't support embedding.
- You can change the source file and automatically update any documents you linked to it.
- Linked files require less memory than embedded objects.

What are the disadvantages?

- You can't change the location of the source file or delete it entirely because you'll break the link between documents.
- The linked document must be in a shared location.
- Links that update automatically may slow down operations.

Creating Links

To create a link from a source document to the document you have open:

1. Start the application that created the source file, such as the Works Spreadsheet tool.

2. Open the source file (a spreadsheet or document).

3. Select the data you want to copy. Choose **Edit**, **Copy** from the menu.

4. Switch to the document to which you want to add the linked data by choosing **Window** from the menu and then clicking the name of the document or spreadsheet.

5. Position your cursor (insertion point) where you want to place the data or item.

6. Choose **Edit**, **Paste Special**. The Paste Special dialog box appears (see Figure 28.1).

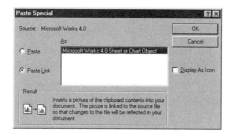

Figure 28.1 The Paste Special dialog box.

7. Select **Paste Link**.

8. Choose a display format in the As box.

9. If you'd rather see an icon in your document instead of the linked data, select the **Display as icon** check box. Figure 28.2 shows an example of an icon in a document.

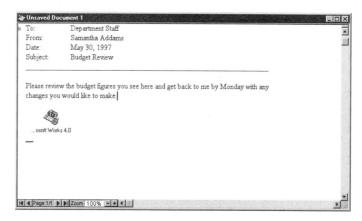

Figure 28.2 The data displayed as an icon.

10. Click **OK**. The linked object appears in your document, similar to Figure 28.3.

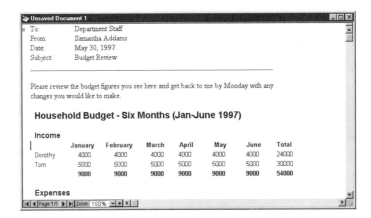

Figure 28.3   The linked data shown in the document.

Some applications support the newer OLE 2.0 technology, which lets you link data by using the drag-and-drop method. To do this:

1. Start up both applications—the application where you want to put the data (the destination application) and the application that created the data (the source application).

2. In the source application, open the file that contains the data you want to copy. In the destination application, open the document where you want to put the data.

3. Choose **Window, Tile** from the menu to make both windows appear on-screen at the same time.

4. Starting in the source application window, select the data you want to link.

5. Hold down the **Control** key, and drag the selected data to your destination document.

6. Release the mouse button to drop the data where you want it to appear in the document. An alert box may ask if you want to create a link to the original data (this happens when you drag spreadsheet data to a word processing document). Click **Yes**.

Once your linked data appears in a document, your application tries to update that information each time you open that document. A dialog box appears asking if you want to refresh the information. Answer **Yes**.

Understanding Embedding

When you embed a file or object, a copy appears in your destination document. An embedded file maintains no connection to the source application file, so updates to the source file don't change your document.

What are the advantages of embedding?

- Since the document and the data are stored together in the same file, you don't need to maintain links, path names, and source files.
- You don't even have to keep the source data because the embedded object becomes part of the destination document.
- To update the embedded object, you can stay right in your document. You don't have to close or minimize the window and open the source application.

What are the disadvantages?

- The documents that contain embedded objects are larger than other documents, so they may take longer to open and they take up more storage space.
- If you update an embedded graphic, it may print at a lower resolution than the original (not as clear a copy).
- The embedded document has no connection to the original source document. If you want to update the object in both the destination and the source files, you'll have to open each file to make the update.

Embedding Objects

To embed a file:

1. In the source application, select the data you want.
2. Choose **Edit**, **Copy** to copy it to the Clipboard.
3. Switch to the destination application and open the document where you want to place the embedded object.
4. Position your cursor in the document where you want the embedded object to appear.
5. Choose **Edit**, **Paste Special**. The Paste Special dialog box appears (refer to Figure 28.1).

6. Select **Paste**.

7. Pick the source from which you copied the data from the As box.

8. If you want to display an icon instead of showing the embedded data, check **Display as icon**.

9. Click **OK**.

To edit the data in an embedded object, double-click it to open the file in the source application, as shown in Figure 28.4. Make your changes and click the document outside the embedded object selection border.

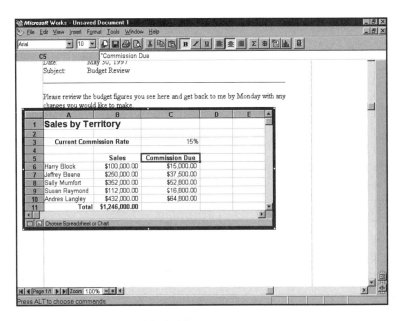

Figure 28.4   Editing the embedded object.

In this lesson, you learned about linking and embedding and how to place linked data and embedded objects into your application documents.

Databases

Database Basics

In this lesson, you learn what a database is, when you need a database, how to identify the parts of a database, and how to plan a database.

What Is a Database?

The term *database* itself has a dual meaning: It is used to describe a type of program as well as the type of file you create in the program. This is similar to the way we use the term *spreadsheets.*

A database program automates the process of creating, collecting, sharing, and managing almost any kind of information. That information might be a list of names and addresses, used for club membership and for tracking dues.

Databases can also be referred to as *applications.*

Works provides many Wizards to help you build databases. It's very possible that you will find most of what you need in the TaskWizard list.

If you have experience with other databases, can't find a TaskWizard that meets your needs for a database, or you enjoy creating files from scratch yourself, you can use the Database Tool to build your own database as described in this section of the book.

When Do You Need a Database?

You'll need a database when you need to keep large lists of data, track status, sort, or extract information from that data. Typical database applications include:

- **An address book** This is a list of names and addresses which can be sorted by name, address, ZIP code, or phone number. You can also extract a list of people in a particular area code or ZIP code.

- **An inventory**   This a list of personal or business items which can be sorted by status (on hand, on order) location (dining room, warehouse), ordering information, vendor, value, or price of an item.
- **A customer list**   This is a list of customers which can be sorted by location, salesperson, status (active or inactive), or contact name.

The Parts of a Database

As you build a database, you are building a table of information. Like a spreadsheet, a table has rows and columns. The primary components of any database are fields and records.

Fields   The smallest piece of data in the database. Fields represent such information as first name, last name, address, city and so forth.

Records   A record is a set of fields. In a customer database, each customer is a record.

Fields are displayed in columns in the database table, and the field name appears at the top of the column. Records are displayed in rows in the database table. In the example of a club membership database, each person in the club would be a record. Figure 1.1 shows a database table with records and fields.

You can add information to the database by typing directly into the table, or you can create forms for entering data. Input forms are easier to read than tables. Figure 1.2 represents an input form in an employee database.

You create reports when you want to print information from your database. With a report, you can print all or some of your data, and you can sort, extract, and format the appearance of that data. Figure 1.3 is a report created in an employee database, listing all employees whose retirement year is 1997, sorted by employee number.

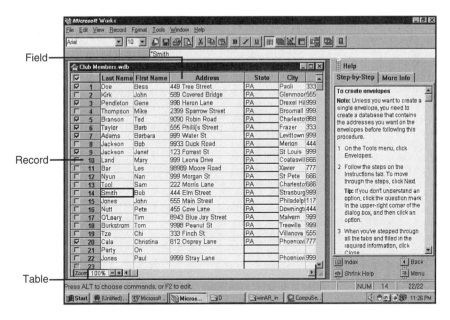

Figure 1.1 The database table displays information in columns and rows.

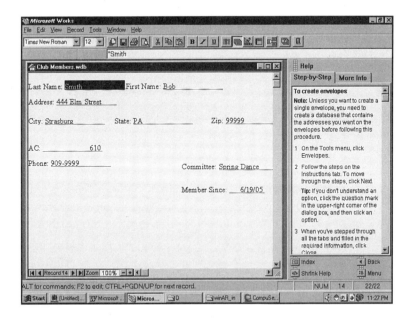

Figure 1.2 You can design forms for inputting data.

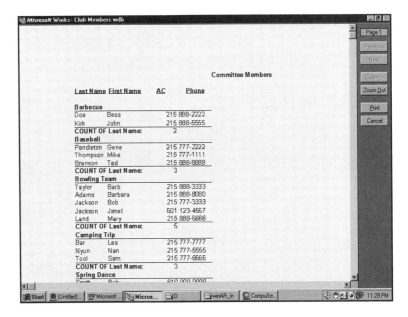

Figure 1.3 Create reports and print your data. Data can be sorted, manipulated, or extracted using Reports.

Planning a Database

Planning is the first stage in creating a database. There are three basic steps to planning:

1. **List the fields you need**   List the fields you want to include in your database. The fields you need are determined by how you need to sort and extract data. If you plan to sort by last name, you'll need a separate last name and a first name field, rather than one field called Name. If you plan to use this database as a mailing list or to generate letters from this database, you'll need a salutation, or title field (such as Mr. or Ms.).

2. **Plan your input forms**   If you don't mind working in a table, you won't need input forms. When you add or edit a new record in your database, you can work in the table. However, if others will be adding to your database, why not make this process attractive by providing a form for adding new records? Determine what information will be on that form and in what order you want the fields to appear on the form. Will you want graphics or color in your forms? Plan for all foreseeable needs now.

3. Plan your output needs (reports)   Make a list of how you want to print your data. You need this information for creating reports. Determine how many reports you will need, how you want the data to appear, and which fields you want on each report.

 TIP   **Plan on Reports No Matter What!**   Even if you think you won't *need* printed reports, you should *plan* for reports. Report planning can help assure you that you have included all fields you will need in your database (step 1 of planning). For example, if you plan a report listing club members who are on the *grounds* committee of your club, it can act as a checklist against your field planning. Did you remember to create a field that identifies members by their committees? You can't extract grounds committee members if there is no field containing that data!

You should sketch out the database on paper. Decide what kinds of information you need to include, and how you would like the information to appear on the screen when you (or others) are filling in the data, or *populating* the database.

If others will be using your database, interview them during your planning stage. Often referred to as interviewing *the field*, any and all information you can gather to include in your planning process will save you redesign time later.

Once you have collected all of your information and sketched out the information on paper, you can begin the creation of your database.

In this lesson, you learned what a database is and when you need to use a database program. You also learned how to plan a database. In the next lesson, you learn how to use the Works Database Tool.

Using the
Database Tool

In this lesson, you learn how to create a database file and how to enter fields. You also learn about naming fields and selecting formatting and appearance options.

Creating a Database File

To start a database from scratch, start Microsoft Works. When the Task Launcher appears:

1. Click the **Works Tool** tab.
2. Select **Database**.
3. The First-time Help dialog box appears as shown in Figure 2.1. You can take the quick tour (this will take about six minutes), after which you will be returned to this dialog box. Once you finish the tour, or should you decide to skip it, click the **To Create a New Database Icon**.

TIP You Can Turn Off First-Time Help   If you don't want to see the First-time Help screen in the future, click the **Don't Display This Message in the Future** check box. To access the Quick tour after you've disabled it, choose **Tools, Options** from the menu. On the **View** tab, click the **Show First-time Help** check box.

4. The **Create Database** dialog box appears (see Figure 2.2). You are now ready to begin entering the fields for your database.

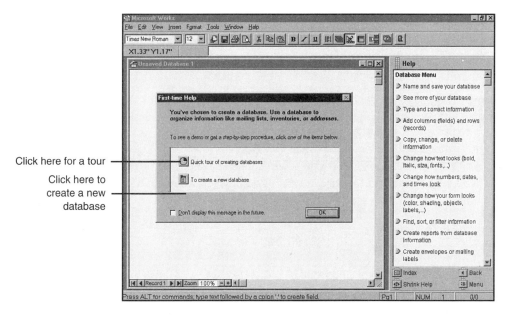

Click here for a tour

Click here to create a new database

Figure 2.1 The First-time Help dialog box.

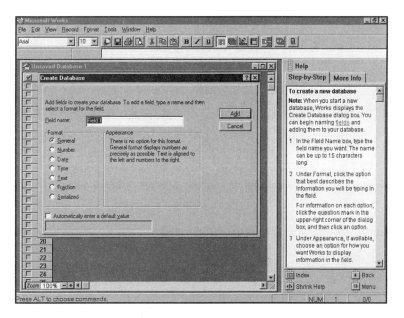

Figure 2.2 The Create Database dialog box. Enter fields here for your new database.

The Help screen is also visible on the right side of the screen. You can use Help during the creation of your database. For more information on Help, see Part II, Lesson 2, "Using Works Help."

About Fields

Each field in the database must have a unique name and a format. The format indicates what type of field this is (text, date and so forth). Some formats (see Table 2.1) also require that you select an appearance for the field, or how the field will appear on the screen when you have entered the data. The steps to creating a database are:

1. Name the field.

2. Select the field format.

3. Choose the field appearance (this option is not available for all field formats).

4. Click **Add** in the Create Database dialog box.

 TIP   **Create Fields Based upon Your Sorting Needs!**   If you create only one address field which includes street, city, state, and ZIP, you will not have the ability to locate people by their state or ZIP code. Use a separate field for each piece of information that you will need to extract or sort by later.

Naming Fields

Field names must be unique. You can't have two fields with the same name. You can accept the default names of Field1, Field2, and so on or you can name the fields yourself with a more descriptive name. We recommend you name your fields using descriptive names such as *First name* and *Last name*. Field names can be up to 15 characters long and may include spaces, symbols, or special characters.

 Unique Field Names   In all databases, field names must be unique. Different database programs will allow for different field name lengths and may have different field formats (types) than you find in Microsoft Works.

Field Types and Formats

After you type a name for your field, you should pick a field format. Choose the format that best describes the data you will enter into this field. Some fields can then be formatted for appearance. Table 2.1 lists the field types available in Works and their formatting options:

Table 2.1   Field Formatting Options

Type of Field	Uses	Formatting Options
General	Text (such as first name or city) or for numbers that have no numeric value (such as ZIP code)	Text is left-aligned, numbers right-aligned. You cannot add, subtract, or do any calculations on numbers that you type in a *general* field type.
Number	Use for numbers that have numeric value and numbers that you need to perform calculations on. Number formatting will not permit any entry except numbers.	Several choices are available for appearance, including decimal places and dollar signs.
Date	For dates only. Date formatting will not permit any entry except dates.	Select from the drop-down list of available formats. Choices include month only, month and day, and month, day, and year.
Time	For time only. Time formatting will not permit any entry except valid times.	Choose from several formats in the appearance list.

continues

399

Table 2.1 Continued

Type of Field	Uses	Formatting Options
Text	Good for text and numbers that have no value such as ZIP codes and telephone numbers. Any characters can be entered when Text is the field type.	No formatting is available at this step for text. You can format your text fields after you have created them and closed this dialog box.
Fraction	Rounds off numbers and displays as fractions.	Options include 1/2, 1/8, and so forth.
Serialized	For record numbers or when you need automatic numbering.	Select an increment for your numbering as well as the next value.

CAUTION

Be Careful Not to Select Field Type *General* When You Really Need *Text* General has no formatting options, while Text allows you to sort data. Use Text for names and ZIP codes or area codes if you will need to sort these fields or if you need to display values as text.

Adding Fields

Add fields to the database by typing the field name in the Create Database dialog box. Select the formatting option and click the **Add** button as shown in Figure 2.3.

After you add a field, Works will automatically place the next field default name in the Field Name text box. For example, if you type First Name as your first field name and click the **Add** button, *Field2* will appear in the Field Name text box. You don't need to delete it; simply type your next field name.

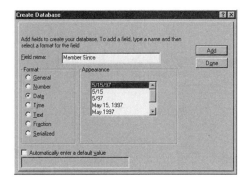

Figure 2.3 Adding Fields.

TIP   **Plan Well Now Save Data Entry Time Later!**   Select **Automatically Enter a Default Value** for fields that will contain the same information in all, or most records. This is helpful if all people in your club membership database live in the same state. When you select this option, a text box appears to enter the default value. You can overwrite this value when you are entering records.

When you have finished adding fields to your database, click the **Done** button. The Done button will appear after you click the **Add** button. Don't be concerned if the default name Field*x* is displayed in the Field Name text box. This field will not be added unless you click the **Add** button.

I've Made a Mistake in My Field Name!   While working in the Create Database dialog box, you cannot return, or go back to a field you have entered. If you've made a typing error in your field name, forgotten to add a field, selected the wrong field format or would like to change the order of the fields, don't worry. You can edit any or all of this information after you have clicked the **Done** button and are in the List view.

CAUTION

Once you have clicked the Done button, the database is displayed in List view mode. It's a good idea to save and name your database now, even if you plan to make changes to your fields. Once you have saved the database, the database name appears in the title bar as shown in Figure 2.4 with the file extension .wdb, which stands for Works Database. Depending on your version of Windows and Works, the .wdb files extension may or may not be shown in the title bar.

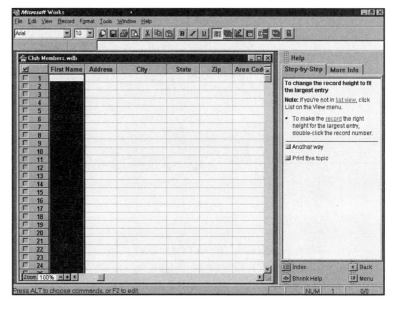

Figure 2.4 The Works Database List View.

Saving a File

It's a good idea to save your work early and often. To save your database, choose **File**, **Save** from the menu, or press **Ctrl+S**. You can also save by clicking the **Save** icon on the toolbar. If you're not familiar with this icon, see Lesson 3 in this part, "Understanding the Database Window," to learn about the toolbar icons.

Exiting the Database

When you want to exit Microsoft Works, choose **File**, **Exit** from the menu. If you have made changes to the database since you last saved it, Works will ask if you want to save it. Click **Yes** if you want to save it, **No** if you want to exit without saving the database, or **Cancel** if you decide not to exit Works at this time.

TIP **But I Only Wanted to Get to the Task Launcher** Don't exit Works if you only want to go back to the Task Launcher. Click the **Task Launcher** button on the toolbar instead. That way, you don't need to close your database file. If you just need to open a file created in another Works Tool, choose **File**, **Open**, select the file from the Open dialog box, and then click **OK**.

In this lesson, you learned how to create a database and add fields to the database. In the next lesson, you learn how to navigate the database window.

Understanding the Database Window

In this lesson, you learn about the database window and how to use the menus and toolbar of the Database tool. You also learn how to move around the Database window.

Database Window Contents

The Database window will open once you have finished creating and entering new fields into a new database or when you open an existing database. If you have just completed Part V, Lesson 2, you should have completed entering your database fields, saved your database, and the database window remains open. If you have left Works and want to reopen a database file, start Microsoft Works. In the Works Task Launcher, click the **Existing Documents** tab. Locate your database in the document list and click **OK**.

Figure 3.1 shows the Database Window which contains two windows, the main window (in List view) on the left and the Help window on the right. Databases can be viewed in List mode, Form mode, and Report mode. The default mode is List view. You'll learn more about views later. Like all Microsoft windows, the Database window has a title bar, Minimize button. Maximize/Restore button, Close button, a Menu bar, a Toolbar, and a Status bar.

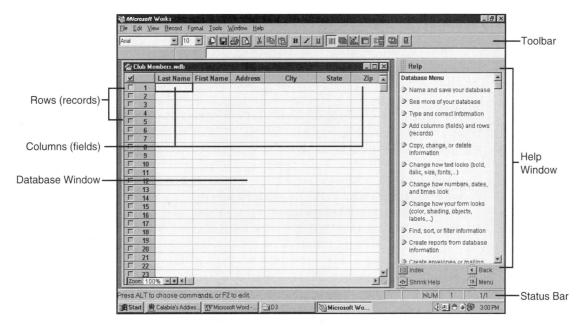

Figure 3.1 The Microsoft Works Database Tool Window.

The Database window in List view is laid out much like a spreadsheet or table. Rows in the database window represent records in your database and columns represent fields. The intersection of a row and a column is called a *cell*, the same as it is called in a spreadsheet. As you can see in Figure 3.1, no data has been entered into the database; therefore, the cells are blank.

The Database Menu Bar

The Database Menu bar contains the features and functions of the program; commands such as **File**, **Open** and **Edit**, **Cut** can be accessed by clicking once on the menu item. A drop-down menu will appear showing options within that category. You can also access the menu by holding down the **Alt** key while pressing the underlined letter in the menu. Most of the functions of the program are found in the menu and the menu is context-sensitive; that is: It will change depending upon the view and function you are performing while in the Database Tool. If you take a moment to read the menu options by clicking each item in the menu bar, it will help you to become familiar with the features of the Database Tool.

The Database Toolbar

Like all Windows products and programs, the Database Toolbar represents shortcuts for menu commands. You can click an icon in the toolbar in lieu of selecting a menu item. Not every menu item is represented on the toolbar.

Displaying the toolbar is optional. If your toolbar is not displayed as shown in Figure 3.1, choose **View**, **Toolbar** from the menu. Use the same commands when you want to hide the toolbar.

As you point with your mouse to each button on the toolbar, a small yellow box appears below the tool to tell you what the tool is. The yellow box is called the *tool tip*. If your tool tips don't appear, choose **Tools**, **Customize Toolbar**, check **Enable Tool Tips** on the dialog box and then click **OK**.

When you point at a toolbar button, a brief explanation of what that tool does is displayed on the Status bar at the bottom of the screen. Table 3.1 lists each icon found on the Database toolbar. Figure 3.2 displays the toolbar.

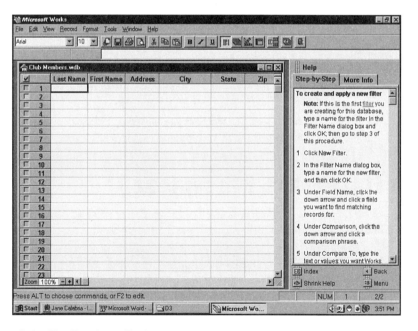

Figure 3.2 The Database Toolbar.

Table 3.1 The Database Toolbar Buttons

Tool	Name	Description
Arial ▾	Font Name	Applies font to selected text or cells.
10 ▾	Font Size	Changes point size of selected text.
	Task	Brings up the Task Launcher dialog box Launcher and gives you access to TaskWizards, existing documents, and Works tools.
	Save	Saves the active document.
	Print	Prints the active document using the current print defaults.
	Print	Displays the active document as it will Preview look when it's printed.
	Cut	Removes the current selection from the document and stores it in the Clipboard.
	Copy	Stores a duplicate of the current selection in the Clipboard.
	Paste	Inserts the contents of the Clipboard at the insertion point (where the cursor is positioned).
B	Bold	Makes the current text selection bold (or bold off if the selection is already bold).
I	Italic	Makes the current text selection italic (or turns italic off if the selection is already italic).
U	Underline	Underlines the current text selection (or turns off underline if the selection is already underlined).
	List View	Displays the current selection in List, or table View. This is the default view.
	Form View	Displays the database records, one at a time, in a form instead of a table. Uses the default form created by Works if you have not designed a form.
	Form Design	Displays the forms design view, allowing you to change the order and appearance of fields, and to add fields, objects, or labels.

continues

407

Table 3.1 Continued

Tool	Name	Description
	Report View	Runs the Report Wizard to create a new report, or displays the last active report.
	Insert Record	Creates a new, blank row in the table at the insertion point so that you can create a new record between existing records.
	Filters	Runs a Wizard to create a filter, applies existing filters, or allows modification of existing filters.
	Address Book	Opens the default Address Book.

You can customize the toolbar by adding and deleting buttons to suit your own personal needs:

1. Choose **Tools**, **Customize Toolbar** from the menu. The Customize Works Toolbar dialog box appears (see Figure 3.3).

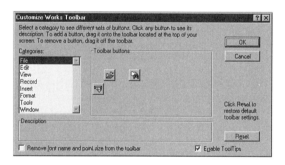

Figure 3.3 The Customize Works Toolbar dialog box.

2. To add a button to the toolbar, select a category from the Categories box to view the available tools, click the tool you want, and drag it up on to the toolbar.

To remove a button, drag it straight down off the toolbar.

To remove the Font Name or Point Size buttons, check **Remove Font name and point size from the toolbar**.

To reset the toolbar to its original set of buttons, click the **Reset** button.

3. Click **OK** to save your changes and close the dialog box.

Moving Around the Database

Although you may not yet have added data to your database, you can still move around the database window. Move to a field by clicking the cell. Use the vertical scroll bar to move up and down the database or the horizontal scroll bar to move left or right on the database table.

For more information on using scroll bars, see Part I, Lesson 2, "Working with a Window."

Another way to move around the database is to use the keyboard shortcuts detailed in Table 3.2.

Table 3.2 Keyboard Shortcuts for Moving Around the Database Window

Press	To
←	Move one cell to the left
→	Move one cell to the right
↑	Move one row up
↓	Move one row down
Tab	Move one cell to the right
Shift + Tab	Move one cell to the left
Home	Move to beginning of row
End	Move to end of row (last cell containing data)
Page Down	Move one screen down the database
Page Up	Move one screen up the database
Ctrl + Home	Go to A1 (the first cell on the database)
Ctrl + End	Go to the last cell in the database that contains data

To move to a particular field, choose **Edit, Go To** from the menu. In the Go To dialog box (see Figure 3.4), select the field you want. Click **OK**.

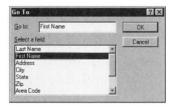

Figure 3.4   The Go To dialog Box.

In this lesson, you learned how to navigate the Database Tool Window. You also learned what the icons on the toolbar represent. In the next lesson, you learn how to enter data into a database.

Populating a Database

In this lesson, you learn how to enter data into your database, or populate the database. You will also learn how to edit data.

Entering Records

The most cumbersome part of creating a database is populating, or adding records to the database. When you add records, you don't need to be concerned about the order in which you add them. The very purpose of a database program is that it will allow you to sort, filter, and manipulate data when you need to rearrange or find information.

To add records, simply position your cursor in the field of the database in which you want to add information. In the default *list* view, the database is displayed as a table as shown in Figure 4.1. Enter records by filling out each field in the database, then moving down the table to the next record. Use the **Tab** key to move from field to field and from record to record if you have reached the last field in a record.

As you begin to enter records into the database, you may discover that the display width in the list view is not wide enough to display all of the information you have added in a field. Change the display width by placing your cursor in a field column header, on the separator line between columns. The cursor changes, displaying two arrows and the word ADJUST (as shown in Figure 4.2). Holding down the mouse button, click and drag the column header to expand or shorten the column width.

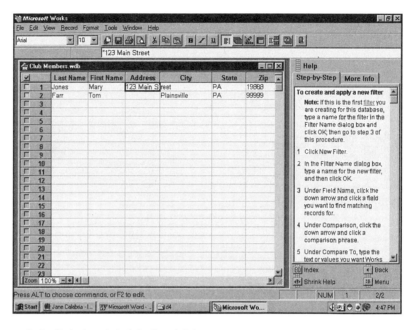

Figure 4.1 Entering data into the database.

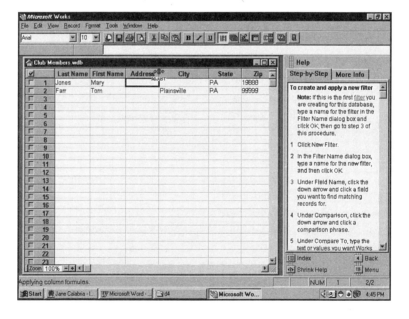

Figure 4.2 Adjusting the column width.

Editing Data

Editing features and skills you use in the Database Tool are similar or the same as the other Works Tools. In particular, note that the Entry bar appears below the toolbar and like the Works spreadsheet, you can edit data in the entry bar or in a cell of the database described as follows:

To change the value of a field:

1. Position your cursor in the cell you want to change and type the new information.
2. Press **Enter**.
3. The new information will replace the existing values in the cell.

To search and replace text:

1. Choose **Edit**, **Replace** from the menu.
2. The Edit dialog box appears. Type the text or numbers you want to find in the **Find What** box.
3. Type the text or numbers you want to replace it with in the **Replace With** box.
4. Select **Replace All** to replace all occurrences in the database, or **Find Next** to work through the database one occurrence at a time.

For more information on Find and Replace, see Part III, Lesson 3, "Editing Text."

To delete the contents of a field, place your cursor in the field and press the **Del** key.

To delete a record, select the record by clicking the record number (the first column on the left of the table) and press the **Del** key. You can also select the record and choose **Record**, **Delete Record** from the menu.

To insert a new record (row) between two existing records (rows):

1. Place your pointer on the record below where you want to insert the new record (row).
2. Right-click with your mouse and select **Insert Record** from the pop-up menu or, select **Record**, **Insert Record** from the menu.

3. The new, blank record will appear *above* your current cursor position.

4. Using the tab key to move between fields, enter the field information in the new record.

 TIP **Is It Necessary to Insert a Record Between Existing Records?** The answer here is no. If you have properly designed your database, you will be able to sort records in the order you need them. See Part V, Lesson 9, "Manipulating Data," for more information on sorting records.

You may want to insert multiple records at one time to your database. For example, if the Jones family has joined your organization and you maintain a record for each family member, you may want to insert three records for the three members of the Jones family at one time.

To insert multiple records between two existing records:

1. Position your cursor below the record where you want to insert multiple blank records.

2. Dragging down the database list, highlight the number of existing records that represents the number of blank records you want to insert. For example, if you want to insert three new records, highlight three existing records.

3. Right-click with your mouse and select **Insert Record** from the pop-up menu.

4. The new, blank records will appear *above* your current cursor position.

5. Using the tab key to move between fields, enter the field information in the new records.

To move a field, click the field name to highlight the field. Click a second time; the pointer will change to a Move pointer. Drag the field to a new position.

To undo your last revision, entry, move, or change: Choose, **Edit**, **Undo** or press **Ctrl+Z.**

In this lesson, you learned how to enter and edit data while in List view. In the next lesson, you learn ways to automate your data entry.

Automating Data Entry

In this lesson, you learn how to automate data entry by using the Copy and Fill commands and by using Formulas and Functions.

About Automating Data Entry

There are several tools available for automating your data entry. You can copy field contents to and from fields by using the Copy command or the Fill command. You can create a series of numbers that will be automatically filled in for you with the use of Autofill. You can also create formulas that will automatically fill in fields. Since data entry is the most time-consuming part of creating a database, you should take advantage of these tools to help to save time and reduce typing errors.

Copying Data

If several records contain the same information (such as area code), you can copy the information to help speed your data entry. To copy information:

1. Select the field containing the data you want to copy by clicking it once.
2. Choose **Edit**, **Copy** from the menu, *or* press **Ctrl+C**. This copies the information in the clipboard.
3. Click once in the cell in which you want to paste the copied information.
4. Choose **Edit**, **Paste** from the menu, or press **Ctrl+V**. This pastes the information from the clipboard.
5. Continue to paste (step 4 above) the information into all of the cells you need to. There is no need to recopy the data. The contents of the clipboard remain the same until you overwrite them by copying something new or when you close Works.

TIP

Save Time!   To copy more than one field at a time, select the fields before you copy them. This method works for contiguous, or adjacent fields only.

To copy an entire record, first click once on the record number (the first column on the left). This selects the entire record. Then, copy the record.

SKILLS
TRANSFER

Use This in Other Windows Programs!   You can cut, copy, and paste information in all Windows programs by using one of these methods:

- Use the Edit menu selections.

- Use shortcut keystrokes (such as **Ctrl**+**C** for copy).

- Use the icons found on the toolbar.

- Right-click the mouse button and select from the pop-up menu.

CAUTION

I Pasted It into the Wrong Place!   When you paste into a cell that contains information, the pasted information will replace the original. You can undo the paste by holding down the **Ctrl** key and pressing the letter **Z** on the keyboard. **Ctrl**+**Z** is the Undo feature of Works and will undo the last change you made in the database, whether it was a cut, paste, move, formatting change, and so on. This Undo feature functions in all of the Works tools.

Using Fill Down and Fill Right

Another way to copy data is to use the Fill Down and Fill Right menu selections. These work the same as copying and pasting, but they are faster. These features work for contiguous, or adjacent fields only. For example, if all of the people in your database are located in one state, you can fill that state into other records by using the Fill Down feature. Adjacent fields can be fields below, or to the right of the field containing the information you want to copy. To copy by using Fill Down or Fill Right:

1. Select the field entry you want to copy.

2. Holding down the mouse button, drag down or to the right of the field, highlighting the adjacent fields you want to copy the information to.

3. Select **Edit**, **Fill Down** or **Fill Right** from the menu.

Using Fill Series

Fill Series can automate your process of entering numbers or dates if the numbers or dates need to step or increase by a fixed value. For example, suppose you are creating an inventory database and want to assign parts numbers to each item in your parts database. After you create a parts number field and enter one record in the field, you can use Fill Series to fill in the parts numbers in the rest of the fields, increasing the part number by one for each part in your database.

To type a series of numbers or dates using Fill Series:

1. In List view, select the field where you want to start the series and type the starting number or date. Press **Enter**.
2. Drag the field down the database, highlighting the remaining fields in the records in which you want to fill the series of numbers or dates.
3. From the menu, choose **Edit**, **Fill Series**. Figure 5.1 shows the resulting Fill Series dialog boxes—for number series and date series.

Figure 5.1 The Fill Series dialog boxes.

4. Select the unit you want to use for the series under Unit in the Fill Series Dialog Box.
5. In the Step By box, type the number you want the series to increase by.
6. Click **OK**.

CAUTION

Fill Series Doesn't Work! Fill series can work only if the first field contains a number or date, and the field is *formatted* as a number or date field. If the first field does not contain a number or date or is formatted incorrectly, a message appears telling you this. You can choose to learn more information about series, or click the **OK** button to close the message box. Go back to the first field and fix the formatting problem.

417

Before you decide to copy records using Fill Series, consider using a serialized field format. By formatting the field with serialized number, Works will automatically fill in the value and you don't need to use Fill Series. You can add a new serialized field to your database or edit a field format type, changing it to Serialized.

Wrong Series?   If you don't like the series you've assigned, or you want to delete the series, choose **Edit**, **Undo Fill Series** on the menu or press **Ctrl+Z**. You must do this immediately after completing the series or the Undo feature will not work.

CAUTION

Automating with Default Values

Default values for fields can help you to automate data input. For example, if most of the people in your database are in the state of Pennsylvania, assign a value of PA to that field. Works will enter that value each time you create a new record. If you need to change the value, click in the field and type in the new information.

Default values can be text or numbers. To assign a default value to an existing field:

1. Select the record you want to change to serialized format and select **Format**, **Field** from the menu.
2. The Format dialog box appears.
3. On the **Field** tab, click the **Automatically Enter a Default Value** check box. A new text box appears as shown in Figure 5.2. Enter the default value in the text box.
4. Click **OK** to save your changes and close the dialog box.

Use Default Values Wherever You Can   Default values are commonly used in database programs. They not only help to speed data input, they reduce typing errors in a database.

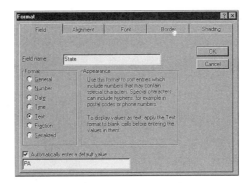

Figure 5.2 Entering a default value can speed data input.

Automating Data Input with Formulas and Functions

Formulas and functions can be used in the Works database just as they are used in a spreadsheet. You can use formulas and functions to:

- Perform arithmetic operations in a formula. For example, you can total the number of parts in an inventory with the formula +Sum(In Stock) where In Stock is a field name.

- Calculate a field's contents by creating a formula. For example, Price + Sales placed into a field named Total would calculate the total amount due, when Price and Sales are the names of fields.

- Use a function. For example, creating a formula that says =avg(Jan Stock, Feb Stock, Apr Stock) would calculate the average of inventory items in stock for the 1st quarter.

To enter a formula in your database:

1. In List View, click the field name to select the field which will contain the formula.

2. Press the = key . The entry bar is activated as shown in Figure 5.3. Type your formula or function.

3. Press **Enter**. The result of the formula appears in the field and the formula appears in the entry bar.

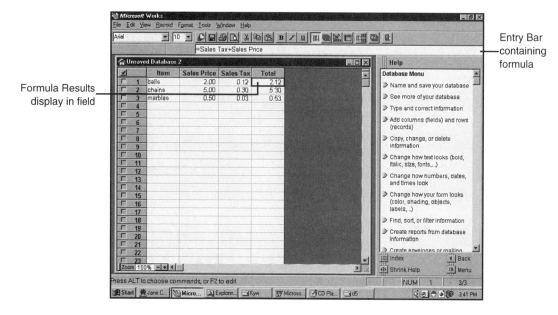

Entry Bar
containing
formula

Formula Results
display in field

Figure 5.3 Entering a formula or function in a field.

To clear a formula, highlight the field name and choose **Edit, Clear Formula**.

For more information on writing formulas, see Part IV, Lesson 7, "Writing Formulas."

For more information on using functions, see Part IV, Lessons 9 and 10.

In this lesson, you learned how to automate data entry by using Copy, Fill, and Default Values. In the next lesson, you learn how to edit and format fields.

Editing and Formatting Fields

In this lesson, you learn how to edit field names, move fields, and delete and change field size. You also learn how to change field formatting.

Editing Field Names

It's not unusual to want to change a field name after you have completed the initial design of your database. For example, you might find that you want to shorten the field named *Area Code* to *AC*.

To edit a field name:

1. In your opened database, select the field you want to edit by clicking its name. Choose **Format**, **Field** from the menu. The Format dialog box appears with the Field tab in front, as shown in Figure 6.1.

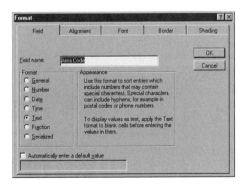

Figure 6.1 The Format dialog box.

2. In the Field name text box, change your field name by typing your new field name. The new text will replace the old field name.

3. Click **OK** to save your changes and close the dialog box.

Moving Fields

Fields appear in your database View list in the order in which you entered them when you first created the database. To change the position of a field:

1. Click once on the field to select it.

   2. Click again on the field, this time holding down your mouse button. The pointer will indicate that the field is ready to be moved by changing to a Move pointer.

3. Drag the field to the position you desire and release the mouse button.

Deleting Fields

You can delete a field in one of several ways. Remember that when you delete a field, you delete all of the data that is contained in that field for every record. When you cut or delete a field, Works will display a dialog box asking if you want to permanently delete this information. This is a safety measure designed to make you pause and think before you delete. When you see the dialog box and you are certain you want to delete the field, click **OK** to close the box and delete the field.

To delete a field, do one of the following:

- Select the field and choose **Edit**, **Cut** from the menu.
- Select the field and press **Ctrl+X**.
- Right-click the field and choose **Delete Field** from the pop-up menu.

CAUTION

I Didn't Mean to Delete This Field!   If you accidentally delete a field, or delete the wrong field, you can undo the delete as long as it is the very next step you take. To undelete, press **Ctrl+Z,** or choose **Edit**, **Undo Delete field** from the menu.

Changing Field Size

When your field contains more data than the display width of the field, information will be truncated in views. The display of information in the Database tool is similar to the display of information in a spreadsheet. For example, Figure 6.2 shows a field (City) that contains more characters than the display width of the field itself. Since the field to the right of this field (State) is blank, the information spills over into the second field.

Figure 6.2   Data displays in columns to the right if the fields are blank.

In Figure 6.3, the State field contains information; therefore, the City field is truncated and you cannot read its entire contents. Whether or not a blank field follows a field not wide enough to display its contents, you should always widen fields so that their entire content is visible.

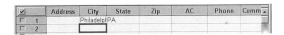

Figure 6.3   Data in fields is truncated if the field width is insufficient.

To widen or shorten the field width:

1. Click once on the column separator of the field you want to adjust.

2. The pointer will indicate that the field is ready to be sized by changing to an Adjust pointer (a two-directional arrow).

3. Holding down the mouse button, drag the field to the desired new width (left or right) and release the mouse button.

Changing a Field Format

You can change the format of a field, remembering that this kind of change might affect your data. For example, if you change a field format from number to text, you can no longer calculate on that field. Alternately, changing a text field to a number field would allow you to calculate totals.

To change a field format:

1. Click once on the field you want to change. Select **Format**, **Field** from the menu.

2. On the **Field** page, change the field format by selecting a different **Format**.

3. Click **OK** to save your changes and exit the dialog box.

Changing Field Alignment

By default, Works assigns a *general* alignment to all fields as you create them in your database. The general alignment options results in all text fields aligning left, all number fields aligning right, and all fields vertically center-aligned. You can change the field alignment on a field-by-field basis. Word wrap is also available as an alignment option, causing the field contents to display within a cell, regardless of the field display width.

To change a field alignment:

1. Click once on the field you want to change. Select **Format**, **Alignment** from the menu.

2. Change the field alignment by selecting a **Horizontal** or **Vertical** format (see Figure 6.4).

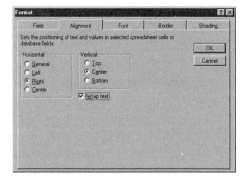

Figure 6.4   The field alignment options.

3. To enable word wrap, click the **Wrap Text** check box.

4. Click **OK** to save your changes and exit the dialog box.

Adding a Border

You can add borders to your fields. Keep in mind that these borders have nothing to do with your forms design, which is covered later in this part. Borders you add here will be displayed in your database while in List View.

To add borders:

1. Click once on the field you want to add a border to. Select **Format**, **Border** from the menu.

2. The Format dialog box appears.

3. Select the **Border** position (right, left, top, bottom), the **Line Style**, and the **Color** of the border (see Figure 6.5).

4. Click **OK** to save your changes and exit the dialog box.

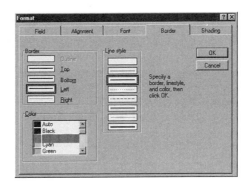

Figure 6.5   Adding Borders.

Adding Shading

You can add shading to your fields. Keep in mind that this shading has nothing to do with your forms design, which is covered later in this part. Shading you add here will be displayed in your database while in List View.

To add shading:

1. Click once on the field you want to add shading to. Select **Format**, **Shading** from the menu.

2. The Format dialog box appears.

3. Select the shading **Pattern, Foreground**, and **Background** of the border.

4. Click **OK** to save your changes and exit the dialog box.

In this lesson, you learned how to edit and format fields, add borders and shading, and delete and move fields. In the next lesson, you learn how to work with a form.

Working with a Form

In this lesson, you learn about the two views of a Form. You will also learn how to populate your database while in Form view and how to delete records from Form view.

Understanding Form and Form Design View

 When you create a database, Works automatically creates a form from your database fields. To see this default form, open your database and choose **View, Form** from the menu, or click the **Form View** Icon.

The default form lists all of your fields, in the order in which they appear in your table, or list view. All fields were aligned as you formatted alignment (see Lesson 6 in this part). If you did not apply any alignment formatting, then the default alignment is used (general) and text is left-aligned; numbers, right-aligned. Database information appears on the form one record at a time (see Figure 7.1). The form can be used to display, print, or enter data.

You can modify the form by switching to Form Design view. Choose **View, Form Design** from the menu to see this view. Figure 7.2 shows the Form Design view. You will learn how to work in this view later in this lesson.

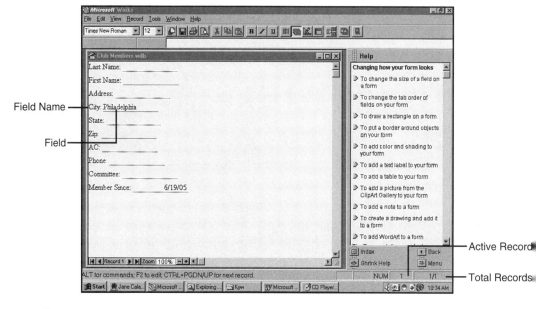

Figure 7.1 Use Form view to enter data.

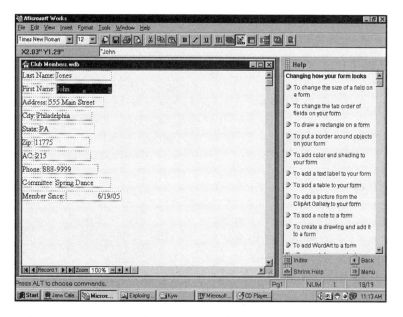

Figure 7.2 Use Form Design view to modify a form.

Adding and Deleting Records in Form View

You may find it easier to populate your database from the Form View rather than the List View. Using the Form View, you can see one record at a time, or one empty form ready to be filled in. The status bar of the Form view indicates which record is currently being displayed, and you can move forward or backward through the database one record at a time, or go to the first record or the last record. Figure 7.3 shows the Form View status bar.

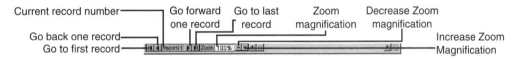

Figure 7.3 The Form View Status Bar.

To enter records in Form View:

1. Start in Form View by selecting **View, Form** or click the **Form View** icon on the toolbar.

2. Click the last record indicator on the status bar (see Figure 7.3).

3. A new, blank form appears ready to be filled in. Fill in each field, using the **Tab** key to move from field to field.

4. When you are finished filling in the record, use the **Tab** key to bring up a new, blank form. Continue until you have finished adding your new records.

To delete a record in Form View, go to the record you want to delete and then choose **Record**, **Delete Record** from the menu.

Viewing and Finding Records

You can use the arrow keys on the status bar to move from record to record in Form View or you can go to a specific record by using **Find**.

To find a specific record:

1. Choose **Edit**, **Find** from the menu.

2. The Find dialog box appears as shown in Figure 7.4.

3. Fill in the information you want to find, such as the name Jones, in the Find What box.

4. Click **OK**.

Figure 7.4   Use the Find dialog box to locate a record.

Works will display the next Jones it finds in the database. If you want to see *all* Joneses in the database, click the **All Records** option in the Find dialog box (see Figure 7.4). When you select this option, works will display all occurrences of Jones, one record (form) at a time. Click the next record indicator to move through the records.

Changing the Window Size

You can zoom in and out of the Form View, making your form appear larger or smaller. You can also make the form full screen.

To change the Zoom, click the **Zoom** plus and minus keys on the status bar.

To make the form full screen, first shrink the help screen by clicking the **Shrink Help** icon at the bottom of the help screen. Click the Zoom plus button on the status bar until the zoom magnification reaches 150% and the broken line indicating the margin disappears.

In this lesson, you learned how to enter records while in Form view and how to work within the Form view. In the next lesson, you learn how to modify a form.

Modifying a Form

In this lesson, you learn how to manage fields while in Form Design view and how to enhance your form with borders, shading, and rectangles. You also learn how to change the Tab order of fields.

Adding Fields in Form Design View

Database Form Design view (or Design view for short) looks very much like Form view, except that dotted lines appear around fields and graphics. Form Design view is the view you work in when you want to edit a form. One editing function that you can perform in Design view is adding fields. In Lesson 4 of this part, you learned how to add a field to a database while in List view. To add a field while in *Form Design* view:

1. Open the database and choose **View**, **Form Design** or click the **Form Design** icon on the toolbar.

2. Position your cursor and click where you want the new field to appear.

3. Choose **Insert**, **Field** from the menu.

TIP **Field Names** You can also insert a field with the right mouse button. Position your cursor where you want the new field to appear and click with the right mouse button. Choose **Insert Field** from the pop-up menu.

4. The Insert Field dialog box appears. Fill in a **Field name** and select a **Format**. Select any Appearance options that apply.

5. Click **OK**. The new field now appears on your form.

Moving Fields

You can move fields in Form Design view by dragging a field to its new location. As you design your form, you may find you want to change the order of fields. Or, you may want to put all input fields first, all fields with default or calculated values last. To move a field:

1. Click the field to select it.

2. The mouse pointer changes to a **Drag** pointer.

3. Holding down the mouse button, drag the field to its new position. As you drag, you will see the pointer change to a **Move** pointer. When you have positioned the field where you want it, release the mouse button.

 TIP **Move Several Fields at Once!**   To move several fields at one time, select them by holding down the **Ctrl** key, click each field you want to move, then drag them into place. You can also select a group of fields by drawing a *selection box* around them. To draw a selection box, press and hold down the mouse button and drag over the group of fields. You can see a selection box surround the fields. Release the mouse button. The selection box disappears, but the group of items remains highlighted, ready for you to move.

 Use Selection Skills in Other Programs!   Selection box methods you learn here are applicable to many Windows programs. Selection boxes are commonly used in graphics programs.

Changing the Tab Order of Fields

The tab order is the path that the cursor takes when moving from field to field. In Works, the default order of the tab is top to bottom and right-to-left on your form. If you move a field, the tab order changes. Figure 8.1 shows the tab order Works will take in a sample form.

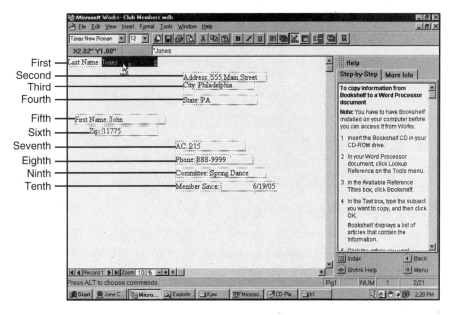

Figure 8.1 The Works default tab order.

Prompt Order The tab order in a form or table is often referred to as the *prompt order*. The ability to change the prompt order in a form is a feature found in many database and some word processing programs.

You can change the tab order without changing a field's position. You might want to do this if your database has a field that is rarely populated, and often skipped over. You can make that field last in the tab order, but keep it third or fourth or wherever you want it in the form itself. To change the tab order:

1. From Form Design view, choose **Format**, **Tab Order**. The Format Tab Order dialog box appears as shown in Figure 8.2.

2. Select the field you want to move in the tab order. Use the **Up** or **Down** buttons to reorder the field.

3. When you have the order you want, click **OK** to save your changes and close the dialog box.

4. To test the new tab order, press the tab key to move through your fields in Form View or Form Design view.

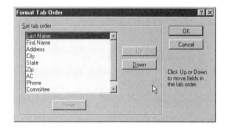

Figure 8.2   Changing the Tab order.

Adding Labels

In Works, a *label* is descriptive text added to your database form. Unlike other databases, a label does not show on the form in lieu of the database field name. You might want to create a label to assist others when they are filling in your database. For example, descriptive text such as "Enter Mr. or Mrs. or Miss" next to a field called "Title" helps others to understand that you do not want them to enter "President."

To create a label:

1. In Form Design view, place the cursor in the position where you want to place the label. Be certain that your cursor is not on an existing field, but in a blank area of the form.

2. Type the text and press **Enter**.

Figure 8.3 shows labels added to a form in Form Design view. One label acts as a header; another is used to provide instructions to users when they are filling out a field. Notice that the form name is formatted with a different font. The following section teaches you how to format text.

Edit labels as you would edit any text. Delete by selecting the label and pressing the **Del** key. Place your cursor within the text to correct or change letters, or format the text as explained in the following section.

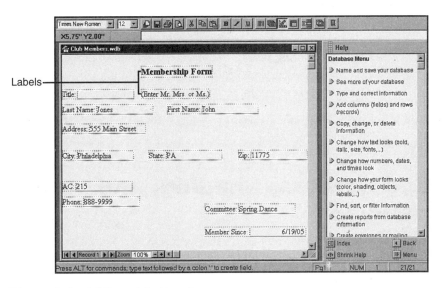

Figure 8.3 Adding a label to a form.

Formatting Text

You can format the font, color, and size of text in your form. The formatting can be applied to labels, fields, or field names. Although there are several ways to format text, we have listed the quickest methods:

- **To format field names** In Form Design view, right-click the field name you want to format. From the pop-up menu, select **Font and Style**. The Format dialog box appears with the Font tab displayed. Select font formatting options in this dialog box.

- **To format field contents** In Form Design view, right-click the field contents you want to format. From the pop-up menu, select **Font and Style**. The font dialog box appears. Select font formatting options in this dialog box.

- **To format labels** In Form Design view, right-click the label you want to format. From the pop-up menu, select **Font and Style**. The font dialog box appears. Select font formatting options in this dialog box.

435

- **To format multiple field names, contents, or labels at one time**   Select the items you want to format by holding down the **Ctrl** key while you click each item. Staying within the black region of any of the selected items, click the right mouse button. From the pop-up menu, select **Font and Style**. The font dialog box appears. Select font formatting options in this dialog box.

For more information on selecting fonts and working with styles, see Part III, Lesson 1, "Word Processing Basics."

Adding Borders, Shading, and Rectangles

Borders, shading, and rectangles that you apply in Form Design view will display in Form Design and Form views only (not in List view). Borders and shading can be applied to fields, field names, and labels.

To add borders:

1. Select the items(s) you want to border. Choose **Format**, **Border** from the menu. The **Format** dialog box appears.
2. On the **Border** tab, select the **Border** position, the **Line style**, and the **Color** of the border.
3. Click **OK** to save your changes and close the dialog box.

To add shading:

1. Select the item(s) you want to shade. Choose **Format**, **Shading** from the menu. The **Format** dialog box appears.
2. On the **Shading** tab, select the **Pattern** and the **Background** and **Foreground Colors**.
3. Click **OK** to save your changes and close the dialog box.

Rectangles differ from borders in that they encompass more than one field, field name or label. Rectangles can be used on forms to highlight areas of the form, or create sections on the form.

To create a rectangle:

1. Position the cursor where you want the rectangle to begin.
2. Choose **Insert**, **Rectangle** from the menu.

3. Works places a square on your form as shown in Figure 8.4. The square is ready for you to move into position and size. To move the square, position your mouse on the square and your pointer will change to a **Drag** pointer. Hold down the mouse button and drag the square to position it on your form. As you drag it, your pointer will change to a **Move** pointer.

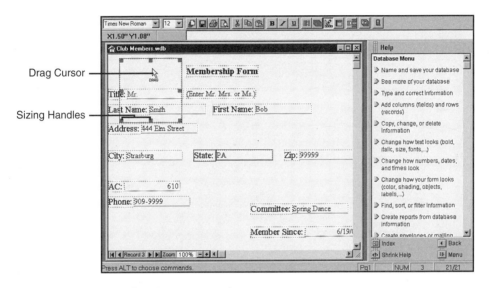

Drag Cursor —
Sizing Handles —

Figure 8.4 Creating a rectangle.

4. To size the square, position your mouse on one of the sizing handles (see Figure 8.4) and your pointer will change to a **Resize** pointer. Once the Resize pointer appears, drag the sizing handle to the new size.

CAUTION

My Label or Field Has Disappeared! When you add a rectangle, the rectangle will be layered on top of existing text or fields. If the rectangle has no shading, you can still see your existing text. But, if you apply shading, your text may be placed in the background of the shading. To bring your text to the foreground, select the rectangle and choose **Format**, **Send to Back** from the menu.

Add Graphics and Other Objects   You can add clip art, WordArt, a Note-It, and an MS Draw Object to your form. The instructions for working with each of those items are in Part III, Word Processing.

In this lesson, you learned how to modify and enhance your form. In the next lesson, you learn how to manipulate your data by searching, filtering, and hiding.

Manipulating Data

9

In this lesson, you learn how to work with a populated database. You learn how to hide fields and records, sort data, extract data by using filters, and how to protect data so that no one can change it.

Hiding Fields

You can hide *fields* in List view and you can hide field *names* in Form view. You may want to hide a *field* in List view (which also hides the field title) if the field information is important only to you and not to others using the database, if the information is confidential, or if you want to display less information on the screen. You may want to hide a field *name* in a form to display a cleaner, less cluttered form.

Hiding *fields* is performed in List view and hiding field *names* is performed in Form Design view.

Hiding Fields in List View

To hide a field from List view, start in List view by selecting **View**, **List** from the menu (or press **Shift+F9** or click the **List View** button on the toolbar). Then:

1. Select the field you want to hide by clicking once on the field name in the column title.
2. Choose **Format**, **Field Width** from the menu. The field width dialog box appears as shown in Figure 9.1.
3. Set the **Column Width** to 0.

4. Click **OK** to save the change and close the dialog box. The field is now hidden in List view.

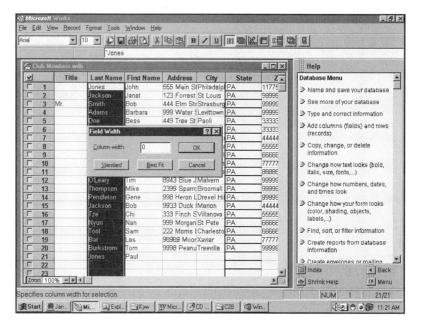

Figure 9.1 Hiding a Field from List View.

CAUTION

Hiding in One View Does Not Hide in Another View Hiding a field in List view does *not* hide the field in Form view. A hidden field in List view will still display in Form view. Unless it is protected, it can also be populated in List view. For more information on protecting a field, see "Protecting Fields" later in this lesson.

When Works hides a field, you may see a heavy black line on the screen where the field was displayed prior to hiding it. To redisplay a field:

1. Choose **Edit, Go To** from the menu. The Go To dialog box appears.

2. Select the field name that is hidden and click **OK**.

3. Your cursor is now positioned in the border of the hidden field as shown in Figure 9.2.

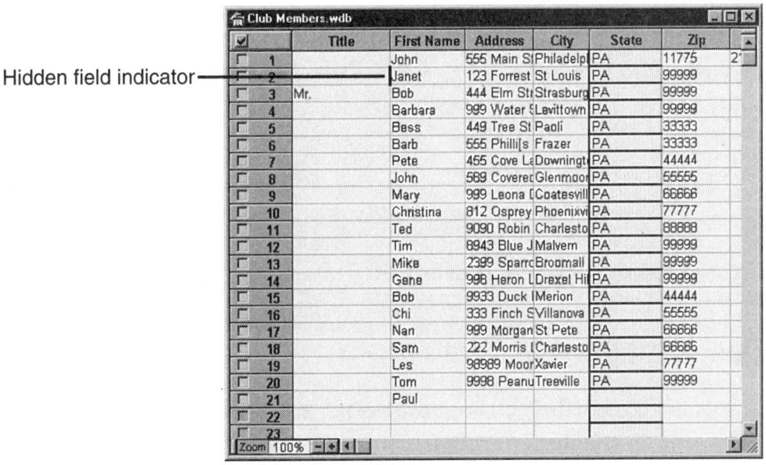

Figure 9.2 Finding a hidden field.

4. Unhide the field by choosing **Format**, **Field Width** from the menu. The Field Width dialog box appears. Reset the field width by clicking the **Standard** or **Best Fit** buttons or by indicating the exact number of characters you want for the **Field Width**.

5. Click **OK** to save your changes and close the dialog box. Your field now displays again in List view.

Hiding Field Names in Form View

To hide a field name in a Form, start in Form Design view by selecting **View**, **Form Design** from the menu (or press **Ctrl+F9,** or click the **Form Design** button on the toolbar). Then:

1. Select the field name you want to hide.

2. Choose **Format** from the menu. Remove the check mark beside **Show Field Name**.

3. The field name disappears from the Form but not the data contained in the field. To show the field name again, choose Format and place a check mark beside **Show Field Name**.

Hiding Records

Unlike hidden fields, hidden *records* will *not* display in *any* view. If you hide a record in List view, it will not be seen in Form View.

To hide a single record:

1. In List view, select the record you want to hide.

2. Choose **Record**, **Hide Record** from the menu.

3. The record is now hidden. To display the record again, choose **Record**, **Show 1. All Records** from the menu.

To hide multiple records, you first mark the records by placing a check mark in the box located in the item number column. Figure 9.3 shows the item number column and the box to check. If you change your mind about a record, click again on the box to remove the check mark.

Mark records here

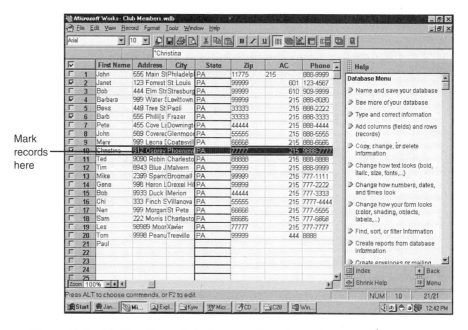

Figure 9.3   Marking Records in the record number column.

TIP **Try Another Way!** You can also use the box in the item number column to mark records for printing. For more on printing, see Lesson 13, "Printing Database Information," in this part.

To hide multiple records:

1. In List view, mark the records you want to hide.

2. Choose **Record, Show, 2 Unmarked Records** from the menu.

3. The records you marked will now be hidden from the List view.

You can use the **Record, Show** submenu to view:

- **All Records**: Displays all records in the database which are not hidden.
- **Marked Records**: Displays only marked records in the database.
- **Unmarked Records**: Displays only records which are not marked in the database.
- **Hidden Records**: Displays only hidden records in the database.

Protecting Data

Different from hiding data, protecting data enables you to lock fields so that a field's contents cannot be changed. A protected field can be viewed, but not edited. No information can be added to a field once you have protected it. When you add a new record that contains a protected field, no one can enter data into that field because the tab order will skip over the field. Protected fields cannot be deleted.

You might want to protect a field when you are finished populating your database. This will prevent the data from being edited or deleted. Protection is not permanent. You can remove protection on fields.

To protect a field:

1. Select the field you want to protect.

2. Choose **Format, Protection** from the menu. The Format Protection dialog box appears as shown in Figure 9.4.

3. Check the **Protect Field** box.

4. Click **OK** to save your changes and close the dialog box.

Figure 9.4 The Format Protection dialog box.

To disable protection, follow the previous steps but remove the check in the **Protect Field** box.

To protect every field in the database, choose **Edit**, **Select All** from the menu (or press **Ctrl+A**) to select the entire database, then follow the previous steps 1 through 4.

Sorting Records

A key feature of any database program is the ability to sort records. Sorting records enables you to populate the database without concern for alphabetical or numeric order. Once you have populated the database, you can sort on any of your fields. To refine your sort order, you can sort on up to three fields, giving you the ability to sort a database by committee, last name, and first name, for example.

Although you can sort while in Form Design or List views, it is easier to see the effects of sorting if you work in List view. The List view shows multiple records. Form Design view displays only one record at a time.

TIP **Work in List View When Sorting!** Sorting changes the order of *records*, not *fields*. If you sort by fields named *committee*, *last name*, and *first name*, but the first field in your List view is last name, the sort order may not be effective on first glance since the first sort field is somewhere in the database other than the first position. Save yourself confusion by repositioning the fields in List view (see Lesson 6 in this part) to match the order you want to sort by.

To sort a database:

1. In List view, choose **Record**, **Sort Records** from the menu.

2. The Sort Records dialog box appears (see Figure 9.5). Using the drop-down lists, select the fields you want to sort on, in the order you want them sorted.

3. Choose **Ascending** or **Descending** for each field as the order to sort.

4. Click **OK** to save your sort preferences and close the dialog box.

5. Your database now appears in the order you indicated in the Sort Records dialog box.

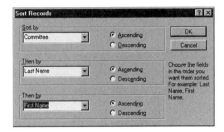

Figure 9.5 Sort up to three fields using the Sort Records dialog box.

In this lesson, you learned how to hide fields, records, and field names. You also learned how to protect data and sort records. In the next lesson, you learn about filters.

Working with Filters

In this lesson, you learn how to create, apply, edit, and delete filters.

What Is a Filter?

A filter has greater capabilities to locate information than a simple search you would perform with the Find command. You use the Find command when you want to search for John Jones, but you use a filter when you want to search for members in your database who have joined your organization after December 31, 1996, and before December 31, 1997 (see Figure 10.1).

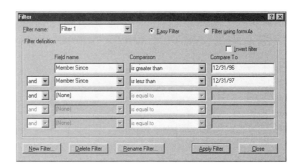

Figure 10.1 Creating an Easy Filter.

Works has two kinds of filters, the Easy Filter and the Filter Using Formula. This book concentrates on the Easy Filter. An Easy Filter uses a comparison when searching for records. At a minimum, you must supply three pieces of information for the easy filter.

The three pieces of information you must supply for a Filter are:

1. *Field Name*   The name of the field whose contents you are searching.

2. *Comparison*   Comparison phrases are selected from a drop-down list. They contain phrases representing operators, such as *is less than*, *is equal to*, and *does not contain*.

3. *Compare to*   The search criteria.

Column two of Table 10.1 lists the Comparison choices available in the Filter dialog box. This table shows examples of Comparison choices and the results of the Filter when using these comparisons in a club membership database.

Creating a Filter

When you create a filter, the filter results are displayed in List view as well as Form view. It is easier to see the results and effects of the filter if you work in List view. Once you apply the filter, you will see only those records that match the filter criteria. The other records in your database are not deleted; they are simply filtered from the view.

To create and apply a filter:

1. From List view, choose **Tools**, **Filters** from the menu -or- click the Filters button on the toolbar

2. If this is the first time you have created a filter in Works, the First-Time Help dialog box will appear. Click **To Create and apply a new filter** to close this dialog box. The Filter Name dialog box appears as shown in Figure 10.2. A default name of Filter 1 is supplied. If you do not want this name, type a descriptive name for your filter. Click **OK** to save your filter name and close the dialog box.

Figure 10.2   Name your Filter in the Filter Name dialog box.

3. The Filter dialog box appears as shown in Figure 10.3. Use the drop-down menus to select a **Field name** and **Comparison**.

4. In the Compare to text box, type the value for your filter criteria.

5. If you need to add a second filter, you must choose **and** or **or** from the drop-down list on the left of the second line. Use *or* to search for records which match any of your comparisons; use *and* for records which match all of your comparison criteria.

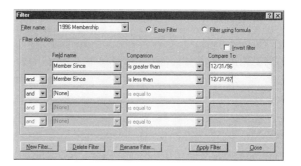

Figure 10.3 Creating a filter to find all members who joined in 1996.

6. Click the **Apply Filter** button to close the dialog box and finish your filter. Works will display the search results. If no match was found for your filter, you will see the message shown in Figure 10.4. If you see this message, click **OK** and try different criteria for your filter.

Figure 10.4 Message displayed when no records match your filter criteria.

Works saves every filter you create, unless you click the Cancel button in the Filter dialog box.

CAUTION

Deleting Filters Works saves every filter you create, even if you click the **Close** button on the Filter dialog box before you finish or apply the Filter. If you are practicing or learning about filters, you could end up with filters you don't want or can't use. To rid yourself of practice filters or filters that don't give you the results you were looking for, delete them as described later in this lesson.

To redisplay all records in the database, effectively removing the filter, choose **Record**, **Show**, **1 All Records** from the menu.

To reapply the filter, choose **Record**, **Apply Filter** from the menu and choose a filter from the list.

Creating Additional Filters

Filters are very useful, particularly when you are working with a large database. To work with filters effectively, descriptive names are important. For example, in a large database of club members, you might create filters called "1996 members," "Paid memberships," and "Out of State."

Works saves every filter you create and you can apply the filters at any time. To create additional filters:

1. In List view, choose **Tools**, **Filters** from the menu.

2. The Filter dialog box appears. Click the **New Filter** button.

3. In the **Filter Name** dialog box, type a name for your new filter.

4. The Filter dialog box appears. Complete the information for your new filter and click the **Apply Filter** button to apply the filter now, or click the **Close** button to save, but not apply the filter.

Selecting Filters

All filters that you create will be displayed in the Apply Filter submenu (see Figure 10.5). To see a list of available filters and select a filter to run or edit, choose **Record**, **Apply Filter** from the menu. Pick the filter you want to apply from the submenu. Works applies the filter immediately.

Figure 10.5   Filters you create display in the Apply Filter menu.

To clear the filter and see all records, choose **Record**, **Show**, **1 All records**.

Editing, Renaming, and Deleting Filters

You can edit a filter after you have created it. You might want to edit it to further refine your results.

To edit a filter:

1. Choose **Tools**, **Filters** from the menu.
2. The Filter dialog box appears. Use the drop-down menu in the **Filter Name** field to locate the filter you want to edit (see Figure 10.6).
3. Make changes to your filter and click the **Apply Filter** button to run the filter, or the **Close** button to close the dialog box without applying the filter.

   If you select **Close**, Works will prompt you to save your changes.

   If you select **Apply Filter**, Works saves your changes to the filter.

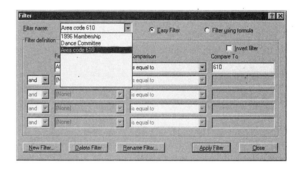

Figure 10.6 Selecting a filter in the Filter dialog box.

To rename a filter:

1. Choose **Tools**, **Filters** from the menu. The Filter dialog box appears.
2. In the **Filter Name** drop-down box, select the filter you want to rename.
3. Click the **Rename Filter** button.
4. The **Filter Name** dialog box appears. Type your new name for the filter, and click **OK**.
5. Click **Close** to close the Filter dialog box. Works saves your change.
6. To see your filter's new name, choose **Record**, **Apply filter** from the menu. The new filter name displays in the menu.

To delete a filter:

1. Choose **Tools**, **Filters** from the menu. The Filter dialog box appears.

2. In the Filter Name drop-down box, select the filter you want to delete.

3. Click the **Delete Filter** button.

4. A message appears as shown in Figure 10.7, confirming that you want to delete the filter, and displaying the filter name. Click the **Yes** button to delete the filter or the **No** button if you have changed your mind or selected the wrong filter to delete.

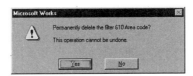

Figure 10.7 Make certain you have selected the correct filter to delete.

In this lesson, you learned how to create, edit, rename, and delete Easy filters. In the next lesson, you learn how to create reports.

Creating Reports

In this lesson, you learn what a report is, what it is used for, and how to create one.

What Is a Report?

A report is like a form, in that you control its appearance, adding borders and rectangles, and selecting fonts and colors. It is *unlike* a form in that you can select which fields appear on a report. The primary use of a report is to produce printed output.

For example, suppose that Barbara is your club member responsible for recruiting other club members into committees, such as the spring dance committee or the fundraising committee. Supplying Barbara with a list of club members who are not active committee members and their phone numbers would help Barbara recruit new committee members. Other member information contained in your database, such as dues and addresses, would not be contained in your report to Barbara, as this is information she doesn't need.

Reports can also contain calculated information. In an inventory database, for example, you can total the number of blue widgets, red widgets, yellow widgets, and the total number of all widgets.

Figure 11.1 shows a list of club members grouped by committee, with a summary of the number of members per committee.

When you create a report, you can apply filters or create new filters during the report creation process. After the report is created, you can edit or fine-tune it in the Report View.

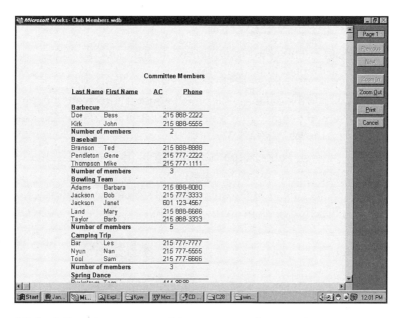

Figure 11.1 A Sample report containing groups and summaries.

Planning a Report

It's a good idea to plan your report on paper first. This could save you time during the creation process. When planning the report, answer the following questions:

1. What Report Title do you want to display at the top of the report?

2. How do you want to categorize your report? Works calls categories *groups* and you can have up to three groups. For example, in a report of club members, you might want to group them by State, then by City.

3. What fields do you want to print on your report? Make a list. If you are grouping information, do you really want to repeat that field in every record? If not, don't include the fields that you will be grouping by.

4. Do you want to show the field names at the top of the report? If you do not, make a note of it before you begin the report generation process. The default is to include them. Refer to your handwritten list during the report creation process so you don't forget to hide field names.

5. Determine whether you want the report to print portrait or landscape. This is your paper orientation.

Creating a Report

You can create up to eight reports per database. To create a report, you will use a Wizard called ReportCreator:

1. Open the database for which you want to create the report. Choose **File**, **Open** to open your database or select it from the **Existing Documents** page of the Works Task Wizard.

2. Choose **Tools**, **ReportCreator** from the menu. The Report Name dialog box appears as shown in Figure 11.2.

3. You can accept the default report name from Works or supply your own, descriptive name in the Report Name dialog box. Click **OK**.

Figure 11.2   Give a descriptive name to your Reports.

4. The ReportCreator dialog box appears as shown in Figure 11.3. Your report name appears in the title bar of the dialog box and the Title tab is displayed. The Report Title default is the database name followed by a dash, followed by the report name you have assigned. The Report Title will print on the report itself, and you might want to change it from the report name. In this example, we are going to change the Report Title from Club Members.wdb - By Committee to Committee Members.

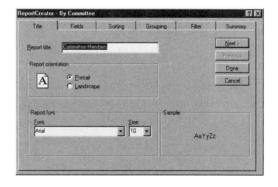

Figure 11.3   The Title page is the starting page of ReportCreator.

5. Select an Orientation for your report and a Report Font. You can change the font on a field-by-field basis later (see Editing Reports) if you want.

6. Click the **Next** button to continue.

7. Works displays the **Fields** tab. Here, you will indicate which fields appear on your report and the order in which they appear. Highlight the field in the **Fields available** list and click the **Add** button as shown in Figure 11.4. You must do this for each field you want to add to your report, unless you are adding all of the fields in the database. To add all of the fields in the database at one time, click the **Add All** button. If you add a field by mistake, highlight the field in the Field Order box and click the **Remove** button.

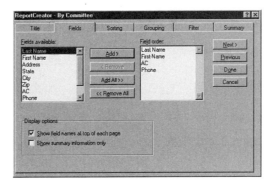

Figure 11.4 Adding Fields to the Report.

TIP **Save Space!** Do not add a field to the report if you intend to group by that field. For example, if you are grouping by the *committee* field, you don't need to see the committee field in each record.

8. In the Display Options section of the Fields tab, remove the check mark in the box next to Show field names at top of each page if you do not want the field names to print. If your report contains summary information only and you do not want any of the records to display, check the **Show summary information only** box.

9. When you have finished selecting your records, click the **Next** button to continue.

10. The Sorting tab appears next. Select the order in which you want your records to appear in the report. You can sort by up to three fields. Beginning with the Sort By box, select the field name from the drop-down list and then choose Ascending or Descending for the sort order as shown in Figure 11.5.

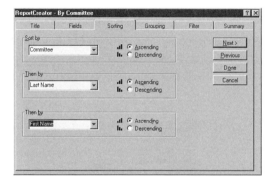

Figure 11.5   Specify the sort order of your report on the Sort tab.

TIP   If you intend to group your report, choose the field you are grouping by, in the Sort by box on the Sorting tab. This will place your groups in order. For example, if you are going to group by committee, choose **committee** as the first Sort by field and choose **Ascending** as the order. This will result in a report grouped by committee and the committees will be in alphabetical order. Your Then By choices might be last name and first name.

11. When you have finished selecting your sorting preferences, click the **Next** button to continue.

12. The **Grouping** tab appears as shown in Figure 11.6. The fields which you have selected in the Sorting tab appear here, in the sort order you indicated. Placing a check mark in the box next to the selection turns the selection on; clicking a checked box removes the check mark, turning the selection off. You can choose from the following options for each field:

> **When contents change**   Inserts a blank line in the report between categories. For example, if you group by committee, a blank line will appear between each committee type. If you leave this check box blank, you will not be able to select from the other options which follow.

Use first letter only Inserts a blank line in the report whenever the first letter of the field changes. For example, if you are grouping by last name, a blank line will be inserted between all of the last names beginning with A and the last names beginning with B, and so forth.

Show group heading Specifies that the field contents appears as a group header on the report. For example, sorting by committee, each committee type, such as "Spring Dance," will appear as a group heading.

Start each group on a new page Forces a page break each time this group changes, resulting in one group type per page.

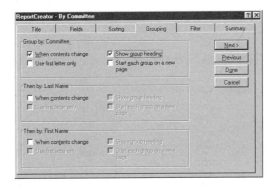

Figure 11.6 Selecting the display options for sorted records.

CAUTION

Why Can't I Group? The Grouping tab will be grayed out if you have not selected any fields on the Sorting tab. If you want to change or add the sorting information, click the **Sorting** tab, make your changes, and click the **Grouping** tab to return to the preceding step 12.

13. Select your grouping options and click **Next** to continue.

14. The `Filter` tab appears in Figure 11.7. Here, you can select the filter to use in the `Select a filter` box. The default filter selection is (`Current Records`), which includes all records in your database except hidden records. To include hidden records in your report, select **(All Records)**. To use an existing filter, choose it from the list of filters. To create a new filter, click the **Create New Filter** button.

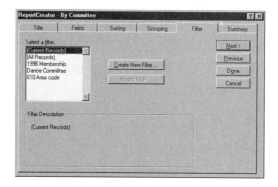

Figure 11.7   Apply filters to your report on the Filter tab.

For more information on creating new filters, see Lesson 10 in this part, "Working with Filters."

15. When you have completed your filter choices, click the **Next** button to continue.

16. The Summary tab appears as shown in Figure 11.8. Summaries generally apply to number fields, not text fields. For example, you should not elect to sum the contents of a field called First name because there is no number to sum in that field. You can, however, elect to count the number of items in a field. Choose the field you want to calculate (or count) in the Select a field box and check off your options in the Summaries box.

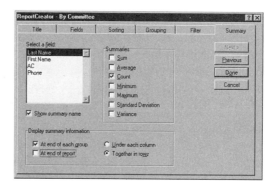

Figure 11.8   Use the Summary options to perform calculations on your report.

17. Select from the following options to further refine your report:

Show Summary Name This option is checked by default. With this item checked, the summary option you choose will be labeled in your report. For example, if you choose Sum in the Summaries section, the word Sum will appear on your report, followed the number representing the sum total. If you remove the check, no label will appear on your report.

At End of Each Group This option prints the summary information for each group on your report.

At End of Report Placing a check in this box prints the summary information at the end of the entire report. You can select this and a Group summary if you wish.

Under Each Column This option prints summary information in the fields column.

Together in Rows This box prints summary information in rows, at the end of the report or the end of a group, whichever you have selected.

TIP **You Can Change This Later** Summary names or labels can be changed in Report view after you have finished running the ReportCreator. If you want your report to say *Total* instead of *Sum*, you can change it later. See, Part V, Lesson 12, "Editing and Enhancing a Report," for more information.

18. When you have completed your summary options, click **Done**.

19. A message appears indicating that the ReportCreator is finished. Click **Preview** to see your report in Print Preview. You can select **Modify** to modify the report, but you will see the report without data. It is much more useful to see the report with data in Print Preview mode.

When you have finished previewing your report in Print Preview mode, click the **Cancel** button. Works will display your report in Report view. For more information on printing, see Part V, Lesson 13.

In this lesson, you learned how a report is used, how to plan for a report, and how to create a report using ReportCreator. In the next lesson, you learn how to edit and enhance a report.

Editing and Enhancing a Report

In this lesson, you learn how to edit a report and how to edit report settings. You also learn how to add headers and footers.

Working in Report View

Just as you can edit a Form in Form Design view, you can edit a report in Report view. To open a report, choose **View**, **Report** (or click the Report View icon on the toolbar) from the menu, select your report title in the View Report dialog box, and click the **Modify** button. The report displays in Report view as shown in Figure 12.1.

Report view does not show the contents of the report, only the report design. To see the contents of the report, click the **Print Preview** icon on the toolbar. When you have finished previewing your report, click the **Cancel** button to return to Report view.

Report view contains text that appears as field names and instructions that are displayed as labels. Report view contains a column that shows the label definition. Table 12.1 lists labels and their definitions.

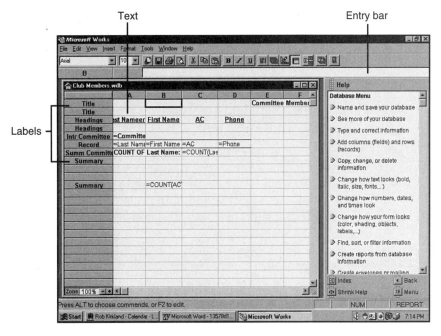

Figure 12.1 Report view shows the report design.

Table 12.1 Report Label Definitions

Label	Definition
Title	Displays the Report Title you defined in the ReportCreator
Headings	Displays field names at the top of each page, if you elected to do so
Intr<filename>	Inserts a blank line or heading above each group
Record	Indicates which records to print
Summ<filename>	Prints the summary information for groups
Summary	Prints the summary information for the report

Changing Text and Settings

You can change the way the report looks and the report contents by changing the sorting, filtering, grouping, or summary information on a report. You can also change the text in a report by typing the text or changes on the report itself.

Editing or changing text in Report view is done in the same manner as editing or changing text in Form view. For example, you can change the word Sum in your report to Total.

To change text:

1. Highlight the text you want to change.
2. Click the Entry bar, or press **F2**.
3. Edit the text and press the **Enter** key when you are finished.

You can change text or field fonts, borders, shading, alignment, or field numbers by right-clicking the text or field and selecting Format from the pop-up menu. The Format dialog box appears. See Part V, Lesson 8, "Modifying a Form," for more on using the Format dialog box.

To change a report sorting:

1. Choose **Tools**, **Report Sorting** from the menu.
2. The Report Settings dialog box appears. On the **Sorting** tab, change your sorting preferences.
3. Click **Done** when you are finished to save your changes and close the dialog box.

To change to a different filter, or create a new filter:

1. Choose **Tools**, **Report Filter** from the menu.
2. The Report Settings dialog box appears. On the **Filter** tab, choose a different filter in the Select a Filter box, or click **Create New Filter** to create a new filter.
3. Click **Done** when you are finished to save your changes and close the dialog box.

To change the grouping settings:

1. Choose **Tools**, **Report Grouping** from the menu.
2. The Report Settings dialog box appears. On the **Grouping** tab, change the grouping preferences.
3. Click **Done** when you are finished to save your changes and close the dialog box.

To add a summary calculation:

1. Position your cursor in the cell in which you want the summary information to appear. Choose **Insert**, **Field Summary** from the menu.

2. The Insert Field Summary dialog box appears. Select the **Field** and the **Statistics** for the summary information.

3. Click **Insert** when you are finished to save your changes and close the dialog box.

Copying, Renaming, and Deleting Reports

Reports are available only in the database in which you created them, so you can't access a report created in Database One, for use in Database Two. Although you can work around this restriction with the Copy and Paste commands, you must remember that if your fields are not exactly the same in both databases, the report will not copy properly.

The most common reason for copying a report is to generate the same report for different regions, or different committee members. You can copy a report and change the filter and title so that the report is customized for each filter.

To copy a report:

1. Choose **Tools**, **Duplicate Report** from the menu.

2. The Duplicate Report dialog box appears. In the `Select a Report` box, select the report you want to copy.

3. In the `Type a Name Below` box, type a new name for the report. Report names must be unique.

4. Click the **Duplicate** button.

5. Click **OK** to close the dialog box.

Should you find that the report name you've given a report is not descriptive enough, or that you made a typing error, you may want to rename your report. To rename a report:

1. Choose **Tools**, **Rename Report** from the menu.

2. The Rename Report dialog box appears. Select the report you want to rename in the `Select a Report` box and type the new name for the report in the `Type a name below` box.

3. Click the **Rename** button.

4. Click **OK** to close the dialog box.

You can delete a report by choosing **Tools**, **Delete report** from the menu. Select the report you want to delete and click the **OK** button in the Delete Report dialog box. A message appears asking if you are sure you want to delete the report. If you are sure, click **Yes** to delete the report and close the dialog box.

Creating Headers and Footers

If your report is large, adding headers, footers, and page numbers is a helpful way to keep the report in order. To create a header or footer:

1. Choose **View**, **Headers and Footers** from the menu.

2. The View Headers and Footers dialog box appears as shown in Figure 12.2. In the Header box, enter the text you want to appear at the top of each page. The text will automatically center at the top of the page. If you want any other alignment, you must enter an alignment code (see Table 12.2).

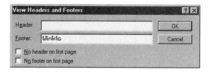

Figure 12.2 Create Headers and Footers for long reports.

3. In the Footer box, enter the text you want to appear at the bottom of each page. This text automatically centers at the bottom of the page. If you want any other alignment, you must enter an alignment code (see Table 12.2).

4. If you don't want the header to appear on the first page of your report, check **No header on first page**.

5. If you don't want the footer to appear on the first page of your report, check **No footer on First page**.

6. Click **OK** to save your changes and close the dialog box.

Table 12.2 Header and Footer Text Codes

Enter	To
&&	Print one ampersand (&) character
&c	Center characters that follow
&d	Print the current date in "4/27/97" format
&f	Print the file name
&l	Left-align characters that follow
&n	Print the current date in "April 27, 1997" format
&p	Print the page number
&r	Right-align characters that follow
&t	Print the current time

To print the date on the left and the page number on your right, enter &l&n&r&p.

In this lesson, you learned how to edit report contents and text and how to enhance your report with headers and footers. In the next lesson, you learn about printing reports.

Printing
Database
Information

In this lesson, you learn how to print database information, forms, and reports.

Printing a Database

From List view, you can print an entire database or you can print selected records in a database. When you print from List view, your printout looks very much like the database you see on the screen. By default, Works will print all records in the database without Field names if you print from List view.

Using Page Setup

Use Page Setup to include field names and to set margins and orientation for printing. To set up a page for printing:

1. Choose **File**, **Page Setup** from the menu.
2. The Page Setup dialog box appears as shown in Figure 13.1. You see three tabbed pages in this dialog box: Margins; Source, Size & Orientation; and Other Options.
3. Click the **Margins** tab to set the **Top**, **Bottom**, **Left**, and **Right** margins if the defaults are not to your liking. In the From Edge box, indicate the amount of space you want between the header and footer of your document and the edge of the paper.

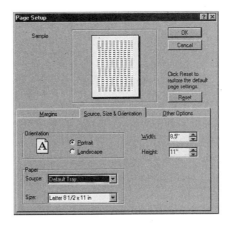

Figure 13.1 The Page Setup dialog box.

4. Click the **Source, Size & Orientation** tab and select the Orientation, Paper Source, and Size. You should have to adjust only the Width and Height if your printing paper varies from the standard size (such as legal or letter).

5. Click the **Other Options** tab and indicate your starting page number (the default is 1). Place a check mark in the **Print gridlines** box if you want gridlines to print on your paper. Check the box next to **Print Record and Field Labels** if you want the field names and other labels to print.

6. When you have finished setting all of your preferences, click **OK** to close the dialog box and save your changes. To change all of the settings back to their original default values, click the **Reset** button.

The selections you made in the Page Setup dialog box will affect the printing of your document.

TIP **Preview in Other Programs, Too!** Like most Windows programs, Works allows you to preview a document before printing it. Reports, Lists, and Forms can be previewed quickly by clicking the **Print Preview** icon on the toolbar. You can also preview documents from some dialog boxes. Look for a button labeled Preview in dialog boxes.

Selecting Data to Print

There are times when you want to print some but not all of the records in your database. You can select individual records to print by first applying a filter to your database, then printing the results of the filter. Alternately, you can select records in List view by placing a check mark in the item number column (the first column on the left of the database). To print selected records from List view:

1. Place a check mark next to the records you want to print as shown in Figure 13.2.

2. Choose **Record, Show, 2 Marked Records** from the menu. The List view now displays only those records that you have checked.

3. Select **File**, **Print** from the menu or click the **Print** icon in the toolbar to print the selected records.

Place checks here to mark records

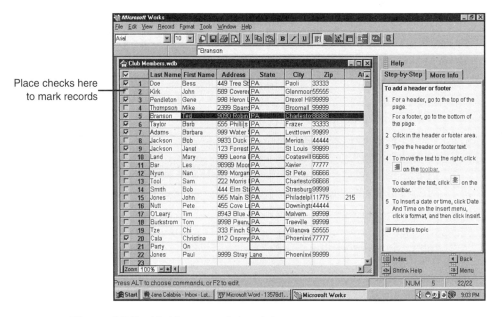

Figure 13.2 Marking records to print.

Setting Print Parameters

Once your Page setup is complete, you may want to set some print parameters at the time you print. If you use the Print icon on the toolbar to print, Works will always print one copy of your list, report, or form.

If you need multiple copies or want to print only certain pages of a list or report, you will need to print using the **File**, **Print** command. When you choose **File**, **Print** from the menu, the Print dialog box appears as shown in Figure 13.3.

Indicate the number of Copies and Print Range (All or Page numbers) in the Print dialog box and click **OK** to print.

CAUTION

Collating Could Slow You Down! The Print dialog box contains the check box **Collate**. Placing a check mark in this box results in Works sorting your copies as it prints. It may seem only natural that you would want your report copies sorted, but be aware that this can slow down the printing process considerably, depending upon your printer.

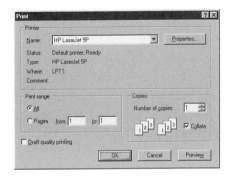

Figure 13.3 Indicate the number of copies to print in the Print dialog box.

Printing Forms

When you want to print a form, it's a good idea to preview it first. There is an extra step in the preview process of Forms. If you click the **Print Preview** icon on the toolbar, you will see the form displayed in print preview. But the image you see is not totally accurate, that is, it is not really displayed as it will be printed.

To see how your form will look when it is printed:

1. Start in Form design view by selecting **View**, **Form Design** from the menu.

2. Open the View menu and place a check mark next to **Format for Printer**.

3. Now when you choose Print Preview, your form will be displayed exactly as it will print from your printer.

469

In Form view, each record is displayed in its own form. By default, when you click the Print icon, every record in the database will be printed, one record per form, one form per page.

You can print a single record, multiple records, or blank forms.

To print a single record:

1. Start in Form view by choosing **View**, **Form** from the menu.
2. Select the record you want to print by clicking the arrow keys at the bottom of the document window until you see the record you want to print displayed on the screen.

 TIP **To Print One Record** If you want to print only one record, you may find it easier to start in List view. Highlight the record you want to print in List view, then change to Form view. When you make the change to Form view, the record you had highlighted in List view is displayed on the screen in your Form.

3. Choose **File**, **Print** from the menu.
4. The Print dialog box appears. Select **Current Record Only** in the What to Print Section.
5. Click **OK**.

 Use Shortcut Keystrokes Instead of choosing **File**, **Print**, you can use **Ctrl+P** to display the Print dialog box in Works as well as most Windows programs.

To print multiple records, but not all the records in the database, apply a filter first, then click the **Print** icon on the toolbar. Only the records that meet the filter criteria will print, one record per form, one form per page.

To print a blank form, you must start in Form Design View. Once in Form Design View, click the **Print** icon on the toolbar. A single, blank form will print.

Printing Reports

It's important to preview your report before printing it. For example, if your report is wider than the paper you are printing on, Works will break the information into two pages and you'll have to tape them together to see all of your columns!

When you Print Preview your report, if you find that it is too wide for your paper, use your formatting skills to adjust font sizes or consider printing the report in Landscape mode. If the report is just too wide for any paper size, consider putting a column break in the report. Inserting a column break enables you to tell Works which columns should appear on the first page of the report, and which columns should appear on the second. You can break the information in a more sensible manner than if you let Works determine the break.

Report printing is pretty straightforward. In a report, you cannot select a record to print. If the report is designed correctly, it contains only the records it should contain.

You can insert a row break to start a new page. For example, you might want to insert a row break after a grouping so that each group in your report prints on its own separate page(s).

To insert a page break (row or column):

1. In Report view, highlight the row below the row in which you want a page break or highlight the column to the right of the column where you want a page break.
2. Choose **Format**, **Insert Page Break** from the menu.

To delete a page break, follow step 1 in the previous list and choose **Format**, **Delete Page Break** from the menu.

In this lesson, you learned to print database information, forms, and reports.

Real World
Solutions

Creating Calendars

In this lesson, you learn to use a TaskWizard to develop and maintain a daily, weekly, and monthly calendar of activities.

About the Works Calendars

The Works Calendars are simple to use and set up. You can keep track of your business and personal commitments in one calendar, or keep separate calendars for the separate parts of your life. In either case, you'll find that maintaining your appointments on a daily, weekly, or monthly basis helps keep you organized!

Starting Your Daily Calendar

To begin creating a daily calendar:

1. From the Works Task Launcher, display the TaskWizards tab. In the TaskWizards list, select either **Business Management** or **Household Management**. A list of items appears (see Figure 1.1).

2. Choose **Calendar** from the list, and click **OK**.

3. A dialog box appears, asking whether you want to use the TaskWizard or work with an existing document. Select **Yes, Run the TaskWizard** (deselect **Always Display This Message** to avoid seeing this dialog box in the future). The **TaskWizard** screen appears (see Figure 1.2), offering three calendar choices:

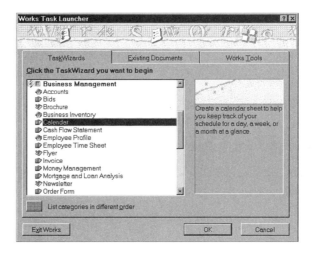

Figure 1.1 The Task Launcher.

- **Today's Events** helps you plan your schedule one day at a time.
- **This Week's Events** lets you see one week's events at a glance.
- **One-Month Calendar** shows accurate dates for any month.

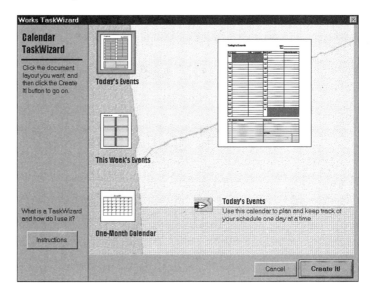

Figure 1.2 The Calendar TaskWizard.

TIP **Quick Help** If you want a quick overview of the **TaskWizard** and how to use it, click the Instructions button.

4. Choose **Today's Events** (you see an example of the Today's Events calendar at the right side of the dialog box). Click the **Create It!** button. A Today's Events calendar opens on-screen.

Using the Daily Calendar

When the TaskWizard creates an empty calendar in a new window on your screen (see Figure 1.3), this calendar is actually a large spreadsheet with cells that have been formatted to house your daily activities. You may choose to print out blank calendars for handwritten entries or enter your activities into the calendar on-screen. To start filling in calendar data, follow these steps:

1. In the upper-right corner of the calendar, enter the date and day into the specified cells. For example, click inside the Date cell and type today's date.

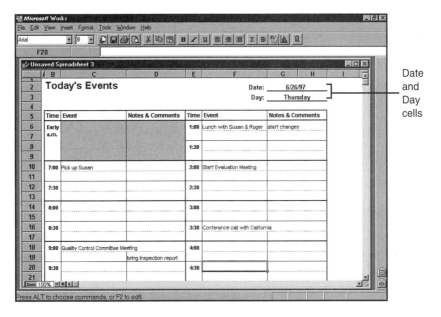

Date and Day cells

Figure 1.3 The Daily Calendar window.

2. Starting on the left side of the calendar, enter your activities into the cell next to the time appointed for that task. The day is broken down into half-hour segments, for Events and Notes & Comments.

3. Below the half-hourly breakdown of the day (use the scroll bar to move down), the calendar contains three large boxes for other information:
   - Today's Priorities
   - Phone Calls
   - Expenses

4. Enter any items that fit these categories by typing into the cells within each category (see Figure 1.4).

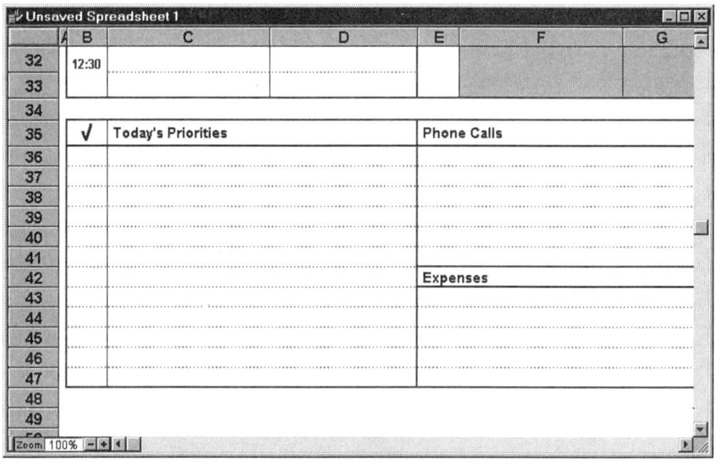

Figure 1.4 Today's Priorities, Phone Calls, and Expenses.

Customizing Your Calendar

If the default layout and categories are not appropriate for you, you can change them by selecting the cell and typing the new category or other information. Some simple ways to change the calendar:

- Change the start time from 7:00 A.M. (the default) to whatever time you prefer. Enter the remaining half-hour increments accordingly.

TIP **Editing Cells** To change a cell's contents, click the cell you want to change and type the replacement text or numbers. Press the **Enter** or **Tab** key to commit to the new cell contents.

- Change the increments from half hours to full hours (or any other increment you want) by selecting the cell and retyping the times in each cell.
- Change Notes & Comments to some other classification that is more useful for you.
- If you track mileage rather than expenses, change the word Expenses to Mileage.

CAUTION

Locked Cells When you try to change the entries in many of the cells, you receive a warning from Works that you must first turn off the cell protection or unlock the cell. To unlock a cell or groups of cells, select the cells, choose **Format, Protection** from the menu, deselect the **Locked** option, and click **OK**.

You can also change the font, size, style, and color of your text, by choosing **Format, Font and Style** from the menu or clicking the Font Name, Font Size, Bold, Italic, or Underline buttons on the toolbar.

Using the Weekly Calendar

The Weekly Calendar gives you a view of a whole week at one glance. To create a weekly calendar:

1. From the Task Launcher, select the TaskWizards tab and then choose either **Household** or **Business Management**.

2. From the drop list, choose **Calendar**. If a dialog box appears asking whether you want to run the TaskWizard or work with an existing document, select **Yes, Run the TaskWizard** (deselect **Always Display This Message** to avoid seeing this dialog box in the future).

3. In the **TaskWizard** window (refer to Figure 1.2), choose **This Week's Events**. An example of the This Week's Events calendar is displayed on the right side of the window. Click the **Create It!** button.

The TaskWizard creates the empty This Week's Events calendar in a new window. You may choose to print out blank calendars for handwritten entries or enter your activities into the calendar on-screen. To use the calendar on-screen:

1. In the upper right corner of the calendar, enter the starting (scroll to the right to see this portion of the calendar, or click the **Shrink Help** button to have your calendar window expand to full-screen width). When you press **Enter**, the ending date for the week automatically appears.

2. Each day of the week is contained in a block of ten rows per day. The hours of the day appear between the blocks. Scroll to the left to see Monday, and then starting with Monday at 8 A.M., enter your weekly activities.

3. Once you have completed your entries, save the file. Print the calendar if you want a written copy, and then close the file.

Customizing Your Weekly Calendar

Your weekly calendar can be changed to meet your needs. Some simple changes you can make:

- Change the starting and ending times for each day by entering new numbers in the shaded column between the days. Before you can change these entries, you must first unlock the cell(s). To unlock a cell or group of cells, select the cells, choose **Format, Protection** from the menu, deselect the **Locked** option, and click **OK**.

- Add more rows to each day. To do this, click a cell in the row above which you want the new row to appear and then choose **Insert, Insert Row** from the menu. If Insert Row is not available, you must remove the cell protection from the calendar by choosing **Format, Protection** from the menu, deselecting **Protect Data**, and then clicking **OK**.

- Change the fonts, sizes, and color of the text.

Using the One-Month Calendar

The third Calendar TaskWizard creates is a monthly calendar with a small block for each day. To create a One-Month calendar:

1. From the Task Launcher, select the **TaskWizards** tab and then choose either **Household** or **Business Management**.

2. From the drop-down list, choose **Calendar**. If a dialog box appears asking whether you want to run the TaskWizard or work with an existing document, select **Yes, Run the TaskWizard** (deselect **Always Display This Message** to avoid seeing this dialog box in the future).

3. In the **TaskWizard** window, choose **One-Month Calendar** (see Figure 1.5) and click the **Create It!** button.

The one-month calendar is displayed here →

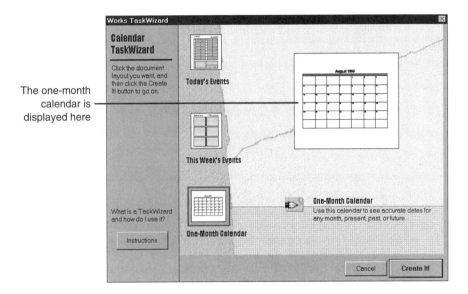

Figure 1.5 Monthly Calendar TaskWizard.

The TaskWizard creates a 30/31-day month calendar (see Figure 1.6). You may choose to print out blank calendars for handwritten entries or enter your activities into the calendar on-screen. To use the calendar on-screen:

1. To change the month or year, click in cell B2 (automatically selected when you open a new calendar).

2. Type the month or year and press **Enter**. The text you type replaces the previous cell contents. The dates automatically change to the correct dates for that month and year.

Cell B2 Is Empty!   No, it's not really empty. The Month and Year text were originally entered into that cell by the TaskWizard, and then the text was centered across the columns that make up the calendar's days.

CAUTION

Cell B2

Figure 1.6   The One-Month Calendar.

For more information about formatting spreadsheet columns, see Part IV, Lesson 15, "Formatting the Spreadsheet."

3. Enter events into the blocks for each day. Each block consists of two cells— one contains the date (number) and the other is an empty cell for your information.

4. Print the calendar if you want a copy of it. Then save and close the file.

Customizing Your One-Month Calendar

Using the Format menu and toolbar, you can change the appearance of the One-Month calendar:

- Change the font, size, and color of the calendar text and numbers, as well as formatting your own text that you enter into the daily blocks (you must first unlock the cell(s): select the cells, choose **Format, Protection** from the menu, deselect the **Locked** option, and click **OK**).
- Shading and border styles can be added or changed.

In this lesson, you learned to create a daily, weekly, and monthly calendar. In the next lesson, you learn to create and maintain a home inventory.

Maintaining a Home Inventory

In this lesson, you learn how to maintain a home inventory by entering, editing, saving, and printing a database of household items.

What Is a Home Inventory?

Your household inventory is a database of the items you own—appliances, jewelry, furniture, and other personal possessions. Microsoft Works provides a TaskWizard that allows you to maintain this database, with information on each item such as where it was purchased, how much you paid for it, its current condition, and any repair and warranty data. When the inventory list is printed, each item has its own page, on which there is a square to affix a photo of the item.

If you have a small business, or perhaps own rental property in addition to your home, you should maintain a separate inventory database for each residence or business. Just use the tasks in this lesson to create separate files for each.

Starting Your Home Inventory

The Task Launcher appears as soon as you open Works. Click the TaskWizards tab, if it's not in front (see Figure 2.1). If Works is already running and the Task Launcher is not displayed, choose **File**, **New** from the menu and the Task Launcher appears.

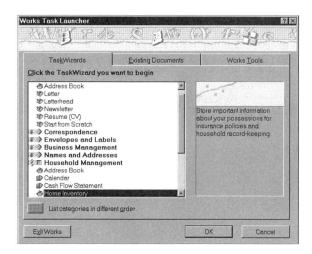

Figure 2.1   The Task Launcher dialog box.

1. From the list of TaskWizards, expand Household Management, and choose **Home Inventory** from the list. Click **OK**.

CAUTION

TaskWizard or Existing Document?   Every time you choose an item from the TaskWizard list, a dialog box appears asking whether you want to run the TaskWizard or a list of existing documents. Choose **Yes, Run the TaskWizard**. To avoid seeing this dialog box in the future, deselect **Always Display This Message**.

2. The TaskWizard begins by offering three choices—**Home Inventory**, **Library**, or **CDs and Tapes** (see Figure 2.2). Choose **Home Inventory**. An example of the Home Inventory database form is displayed on the right side of the screen.

3. Click the **Create It!** button to create the database.

The Home Inventory screen opens, with two windows within it. On the right, the TaskWizard displays the Help window. On the left, you see the Home Inventory database (see Figure 2.3).

TIP   **Shrink Help**   To view the Inventory database without the accompanying help, click the **Shrink Help** button in the lower-right corner of the Help window. If you need Help back again, click the same button in the right margin of the screen.

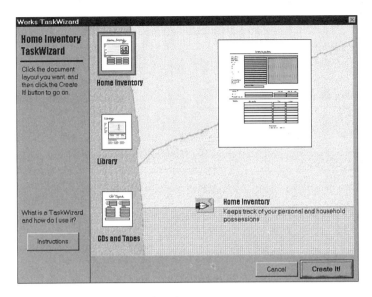

Figure 2.2 Home Inventory TaskWizard.

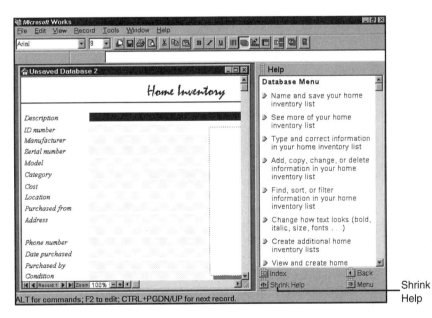

Figure 2.3 The Home Inventory and Help Windows.

The Home Inventory database window contains a series of fields, with the field name on the left and a blue rectangle on the right. Scroll bars allow you to move through the long list of fields.

Database   A database consists of records—one record for each item in the database. Each record is made up of fields. Fields are the "pieces" of data that you enter about each item, such as First Name, Last Name, Address, and Phone Number in a personal address book.

For more information about database concepts, see Part V, Lesson 1, "Database Basics."

Entering and Editing Records

To begin entering your list of household items:

1. Click the blue rectangle next to **Description**, which is the first field in the database (see Figure 2.4).

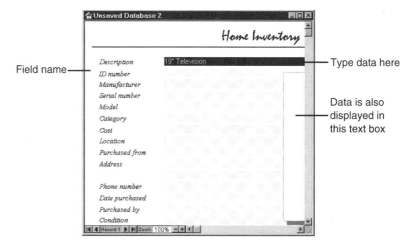

Figure 2.4   The Database fields.

2. The rectangle is highlighted (turns black). Begin typing the item's description.

3. To move to the next field, press the **Tab** key. **Shift**+**Tab** will take you backward to fix any errors or skipped fields.

CAUTION

What If I Make a Mistake While I'm Typing? As you enter text into the fields, the text also appears in a box above the database window. This is where you edit the text that has already been typed into a field.

To make changes, place your cursor in this text box and add or delete existing characters. Press the **Enter** key to commit to your changes and return to the database.

4. Continue to enter data for your item in each of the fields.

5. Scroll down to the second section of the database, which is for Warranty information. You move from left to right in these fields. If the item isn't under warranty, you can skip this section.

6. The third section of the database is for the item's repair history (scroll down to see it). The cost of repairs is entered for each repair incident, and the database totals your repairs automatically. If there have been no repairs on this item, you can skip this section.

TIP **Skip the Warranty and Repair Information?** For items with no Warranty or Repair information, you can go quickly to the next item by choosing **Record**, **Insert Record** from the menu. This places you at the top of the next blank record, and you can begin entering data for the next item.

7. When you're finished entering the data for the current item, press **Tab** on the last field, and you are automatically placed at the top of the database, with a new blank record. Continue repeating steps 1 through 7 to fill out records for each item in your household inventory.

To go backward or forward through your entered records, use the buttons in the lower-left corner of the database window. The display shows your current record number and the black triangles allow you to scroll forward and backward through your records (see Figure 2.5).

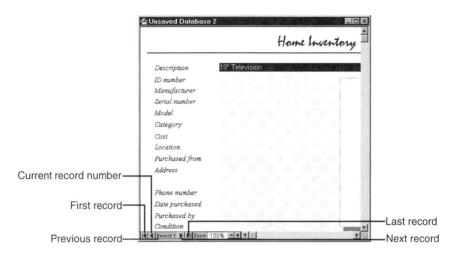

Current record number─┐

First record─┐

Previous record─┘

Last record

Next record

Figure 2.5 Record navigation buttons.

Copying and Deleting Records

Your inventory will change, and occasionally you'll buy an item that is similar to one you already own (like another VCR). You can copy the first record, paste it into a new record, and then make a few adjustments to match the information on the new equipment.

To copy and paste a record:

1. Make sure the record you want to copy is displayed as the current record.

2. Choose **Edit**, **Copy Record**.

3. Use the record navigation buttons (see Figure 2.5) to display a blank record and choose **Edit**, **Paste Record**. An identical record appears.

4. In the pasted record, make any changes to the data that are unique to each item, such as serial number and date of purchase.

To delete a record:

1. Go to the record you want to delete.

2. From the **Records** menu, choose **Delete Record**.

Delete a Record by Mistake? If you catch your mistake immediately, choose **Edit**, **Undo Delete Record**. If you didn't notice your error right away, you'll have to reenter the record from scratch.

CAUTION

488

Viewing the Inventory

You can work in one of two views as you enter your data: Form view and List view. The default view is Form view because it is designed to make entering the data easier. List view is more concise, and allows you to see more than one record at a time. In List view, you can hop from one record to another by clicking the mouse anywhere on the desired record's row (see Figure 2.6).

Column headings contain field names

Each record in its own row

Number of records in your inventory

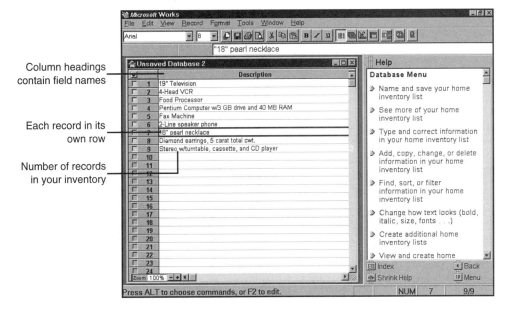

Figure 2.6 List View.

To switch between these two views, open the View menu, and choose either **List** or **Form**.

CAUTION

How Do I Keep My Field Names Visible in List view? As you enter data for each record in List view, the field names in the first column disappear. To prevent that, select the second column and choose **Window, Split** from the menu. Now as you scroll to the right, your field names remain in view.

TIP

How Many Records? To find out how many records are in your inventory, switch to List view and read the row numbers on the left side of the list.

Sorting Your Inventory

After you've completed your inventory, you can sort the records. Sorting refers to the order in which the database records are presented. The order in which you choose to display or print your inventory depends on your perspective—which aspect (field) of your data contains the information that's most important to you?

To sort your inventory:

1. Open the inventory file you want to sort. In either Form or List view, choose **Records**, **Sort Records** from the menu.

2. A dialog box opens with three levels for sorting (see Figure 2.7). In each level, the field names appear in a drop list.

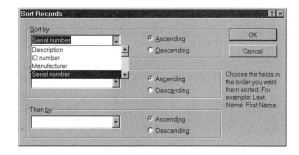

Figure 2.7   The Sort Records dialog box.

3. In the Sort By drop-down list, choose a field on which to sort, and select **Ascending** or **Descending** order.

4. (Optional) If you want to sort information using additional fields, in the Then By drop-down list, select a second field on which to sort. Choose whether to sort by ascending or descending order, and click **OK**.

Filtering Your Inventory

At times, you may not want to see your entire inventory. You may only want to see a certain category of items (such as jewelry), or only the items in a particular location (such as in the bedroom where you had the fire). When you apply a "filter," you filter out the items you don't need to see at this time.

To see only certain records from within your inventory database:

1. Choose **Tools, Filters**. The Filter dialog box is displayed, along with a Filter Name box.

2. In the Filter Name box, enter a name for your filter and click **OK**. Naming filters allows you to keep track of the filters you've used before, so you can run them again without setting them up from scratch.

3. In the Filter Definition area (see Figure 2.8), choose the field that has the information you want to filter by clicking the down-arrow in the Field Name box and selecting the field name.

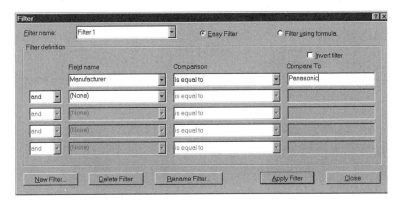

Figure 2.8 The Filter dialog box.

4. Choose a comparison phrase such as **is equal to**, **begins with**, or **is greater than** from the Comparison drop-down list.

5. In the Compare To text box, enter the value (field content) for which you are looking. For example, if the field name is Category, the Compare To text might be Furniture. If you selected is equal to as the Comparison phrase, then the result should be a list of all the records that have "Furniture" in the Category field.

6. Click **Apply Filter**. The records that meet your criteria will appear one at a time in Form view, or as a numbered list in List view.

TIP **Can You Look for More than One Field?** Before you click Apply Filter, click the down-arrow in the small box to the left of the Field Name box on the second row. Select **And** to look for this criterion in addition to the first one; select **Or** to seek one criterion or the other.

Creating Inventory Reports

After creating an inventory database, you can print out the records. In addition to printing a simple one-page-per-record report, you can design a customized report that shows only the fields you need.

To create and print a customized report:

1. Choose **Tools**, **ReportCreator**. The Report Name box appears.
2. Give your report a name, and click **OK**.

 TIP **Don't Like the Report Name?** The name you choose when creating the report isn't carved in stone. You can change a report's name later by choosing **Tools**, **Rename Report**.

3. The ReportCreator dialog box opens, with six tabs across the top (see Figure 2.9). Each tab represents part of the report that you can customize:

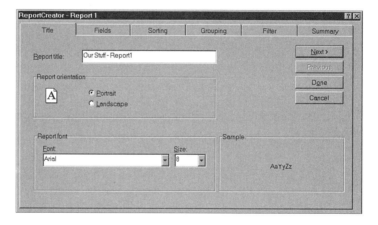

Figure 2.9 The ReportCreator dialog box.

- **Title** This tab contains options for the name of the report, the paper orientation, and the font of the title text.
- **Fields** Choose this tab to select which fields will show on the report.
- **Sorting** This tab allows you to choose the order in which the records will print.

- **Grouping** This tab gives you the option to have records grouped by common data.

- **Filter** You can choose from filters you named previously or create a new filter. Only those records meeting your filter criteria will show on the report.

- **Summary** To set up your report so that it displays such things as a count of items, sum totals, or average values under each group of records, choose this tab.

4. Click the tab for the part of the report you want to customize and make your changes. Click **Next** to move to the next tabbed page. When your report customization is complete, click **Done**.

5. A dialog box appears stating that the report definition has been created and it gives you a choice of previewing or modifying the report definition. Choose to **Preview** your report. The report appears in a Print Preview window (see Figure 2.10). You can move from page to page by clicking the **Next** and **Previous** buttons in the Preview window. To enlarge your preview, click **Zoom In**.

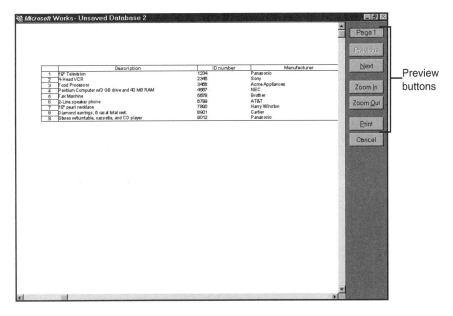

Figure 2.10 Looking at your report in Print Preview.

6. To print the report as it appears in the preview, click **Print**. If you don't want to print at this time, click **Cancel** to close the Preview window.

 TIP **What About Reports that You Don't Need Anymore?** Once you've created a report, you can delete it by choosing **Tools**, **Delete Report**.

In this lesson, you learned to create and maintain a Home Inventory. In the next lesson, you learn to create an Address Book.

Creating an Address Book

In this lesson, you learn how to create, edit, maintain, and print an address book.

Starting Your Address Book

A major benefit of maintaining an electronic Address Book is that unlike the manual version, you can keep many different books for all the different types of contacts you have, both personal and business. Each Address Book is a separate file, but all the files can be in one location—your computer. In addition, you can customize the Address Book that you create with Works to include the extra information you want to keep about your contacts.

You can access the Address Book TaskWizard (see Figure 3.1) from the Task Launcher:

1. Choose **Address Book** from the **Common Tasks** or **Household** wizards and click **OK**. A dialog box appears asking if you want to run the TaskWizard or see a list of existing documents. Click **Yes, Run the TaskWizard**. If you deselect **Always Show This Message**, you won't see this dialog box in the future.

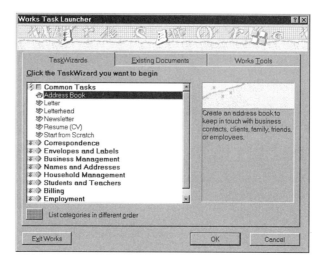

Figure 3.1   The Task Launcher.

2. The Wizard begins. Choose the type of Address Book you want to create (see Figure 3.2). Your options are:

- Personal
- Business
- Customers or Clients
- Suppliers and Vendors
- Sales Contacts
- Employees

3. For the purposes of this lesson, choose **Personal** and click **Next**. (You access the other types of Address Books in the same way.)

4. The next window shows what fields you'll see in your Address Book. Click **Next** to move to the next step.

5. The TaskWizard lets you customize your Address Book in three areas (see Figure 3.3):

- **Additional Fields**   You can add extended phone numbers, personal information about the contact, and a notes area.
- **Your Own Fields**   This dialog box gives you the ability to create up to four new fields. Simply click the field check box and type in a name that is no more than 14 characters long.
- **Reports**   Choose either an alphabetized book or a categorized one. You can also choose both options, to allow either type of printout later.

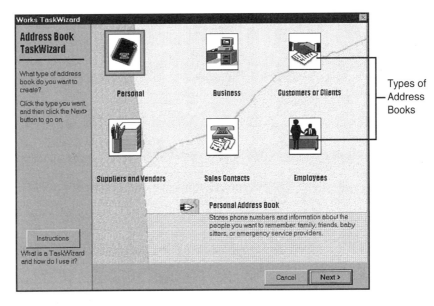

Types of
Address
Books

Figure 3.2 The Address Book TaskWizard.

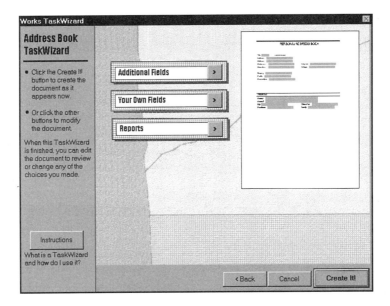

Figure 3.3 Customize your Address Book.

6. To customize your address book, click the desired button. Another box opens with options for customizing the database. Select the options you want to apply, then click **OK**.

7. Click **Create It!** to begin the TaskWizard's creation process.

8. Next, you see a check list of the options you chose in the previous steps. To confirm them and create the Address Book, click **Create Document**.

Entering Your Data

The TaskWizard creates a database entry form (see Figure 3.4), containing the basic Address Book fields for the type of book you chose to create, as well as the optional fields you added.

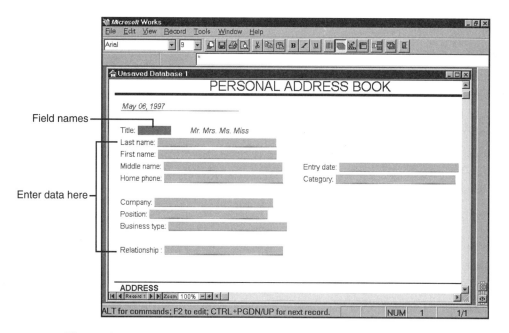

Figure 3.4   The Address Book Entry Form.

Database   A database consists of records, one record for each item in the database. Each record is made up of fields. Fields are the "pieces" of data that you enter about each item, such as First Name, Last Name, Address, and Phone Number in a personal address book.

For more information about database concepts, see Part V, Lesson 1, "Database Basics."

To begin entering your Address Book records:

1. The shaded box to the right of the **Title** label is already highlighted, ready for you to enter data (if it isn't, click in the shaded box).

2. Type the contact's title.

3. To move to the next field, press the **Tab** key. If you want to move backward, press **Shift+Tab**.

4. Enter information into all the fields for which you have data.

CAUTION

What If I Make a Mistake While I'm Typing?   As you enter text into the fields, the text also appears in a box above the database window called the Entry Bar. This is where you edit the text that has already been typed into a field.

To make changes, place your cursor in the Entry bar and add or delete existing characters. Press the **Enter** key to commit to your changes or click the **Enter** button (the check mark) and return to the database.

TIP

Enter Data Correctly the First Time!   When entering dates, be sure to type the slashes between the month, day, and year, for example: 5/17/97.

5. When you reach the last field in your record, press **Tab** to move to the first field in a new, blank record. You can also jump out of the current record and go to a new, blank record by choosing **Record, Insert Record**. Continue following steps 1 through 5 to enter data for each record you want to include in the address database.

Copying and Deleting Records

If you have contacts in one Address Book that you want to duplicate and use in another, you can copy their records from their current location and paste them into the new location. This will save you from typing redundant information.

To copy and paste a record:

1. Make sure the record you want to copy is the currently displayed record. Use the record navigation buttons at the bottom left corner of the screen to move from record to record.

2. Choose **Edit, Copy Record**.

3. Go to a blank record and choose **Edit, Paste Record**. An identical record appears.

4. In the pasted record, make any changes to the data that are unique to that record.To delete a record:

- Display the record you want to delete.
- Then, from the **Records** menu, choose **Delete Record**.

CAUTION

What If I Delete the Wrong Record?   If you catch your mistake immediately, choose **Edit, Undo Delete Record**. If you didn't notice your error right away, you'll have to reenter the record from scratch.

Address Book Views

You can work in one of two views as you enter records into your Address Book. The default view is the Form view. You can also work in List view (see Figure 3.5), which shows each record horizontally. List view looks like a spreadsheet with each field in a column, and each record in a row.

		Last name	First name	Middle nam	Home phor	Category	Company	Po
	1							
	2	Malone	Leva		:234-5678	personal		
	3	Fender	Denton	A.	:555-3456	business	Granite Countertops,	Own(
	4	Haste	Marion		:555-1234	business	Engle, Stuart, and Fre	Offic
	5	Kendall	Jerry	B.	657-1224	personal		
	6	Jamison	Marilyn	G.	555-0987	personal	Trader General Stores	
	7	Malone	Leva		:234-5678	personal		
	8	Fender	Denton	A.	:555-3456	business	Granite Countertops, Inc.	
	9	Haste	Marion		:555-1234	business	Engle, Stuart, and Freidkin	
	10	Kendall	Jerry	B.	657-1224	personal		
	11	Jamison	Marilyn	G.	555-0987	personal	Trader General Stores	
	12							
	13							
	14							
	15							
	16							
	17							
	18							
	19							
	20							

Figure 3.5   This is the List view.

To switch between these two views, use the **View** menu, and choose either **List** or **Form**.

TIP   **Which View Is Right for You?**   It's a matter of personal preference. The default view is Form view because it is designed to make entering the data easier. List view is more concise, and allows you to see more than one record at a time. In List view, you can hop from one record to another by clicking the mouse anywhere on the desired record's row.

CAUTION

How Do I Keep Your Field Names Visible in List View?   As you enter data for each record in List view, the field names in the first column disappear. To prevent this, select the second column and choose **Window**, **Split** from the menu. Now as you scroll to the right, your field names remain in view.

TIP   **How Can You Tell How Many Records You've Entered?**   Switch to **List** view and read the row numbers on the left side of the list.

Create as Many Address Books as You Need!   To keep your personal and business Address Books separate, give them names that indicate the nature of the contacts they contain. Windows 95 allows up to 255 characters including spaces, so be as descriptive as possible!

Sorting Your Address Book

After you've completed your Address Book, you can sort the records. Sorting refers to the order in which the database records are presented. The order in which you choose to display or print your Address Book depends on your perspective—which aspect (field) of your data contains the information that's most important to you?

To sort your Address Book:

1. In either Form or List view, choose **Records**, **Sort** Records from the menu.
2. A dialog box opens with three levels for sorting. In each level, the field names appear in a drop list (see Figure 3.6).

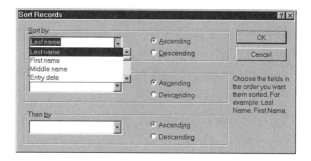

Figure 3.6 The Sort dialog box.

3. Choose a field on which to sort, and select **Ascending** or **Descending** order.

4. Use the Then By drop-down list to choose fields for second- or third-level sorts, and click **OK**. The records appear in the order you specified.

Filtering Your Address Book

You may want to see a listing of only specific people, perhaps those who work for a specific company or live in a particular state. To do this, you must filter out the people who don't meet these criteria.

To see only certain records from within your Address Book database:

1. Choose **Tools, Filters** from the menu. The Filter Name box appears.

2. Name your filter and click **OK**. Naming filters allows you to keep track of the filters you've used before, so you can run them again without setting them up from scratch.

3. From the Field Name drop-down list, choose the field that contains the information you want to use as a filter (see Figure 3.7).

4. Choose a method of filtering by selecting a phrase from the Comparison drop-down list—such as **is equal to**, **begins with**, or **is greater than**.

5. In the Compare To text box, enter the value (field content) you want as your filter. For example, if you want to find all the residents of Philadelphia in your address book, the field name you want to select is City, the comparison phrase is "is equal to," and "Philadelphia" is the text you enter in the Compare To box.

Field to be filtered

Comparison

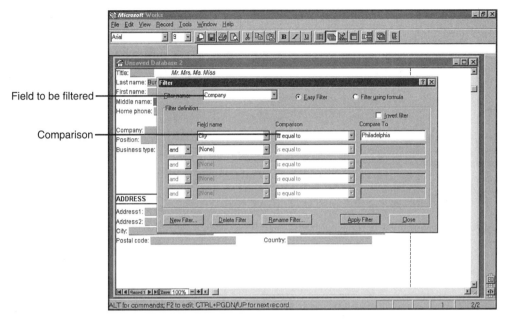

Figure 3.7 This is the Filter dialog box.

6. Click **Apply Filter**. The records that meet your criteria will appear one at a time in Form view, or as a numbered list in List view.

Creating Address Book Reports

In addition to printing a simple one-page-per-record report, you can design a customized report that shows only the fields you need.

To create and print a customized report:

1. Choose **Tools, ReportCreator**.

2. In the Report Name dialog box, give your report a name, and click **OK**.

TIP **Do You Want a Better Report Name?** The name you choose when creating the report isn't carved in stone. You can change a report's name later by choosing **Tools, Rename Report**.

3. The Report Creator dialog box appears as shown in Figure 3.8. Each of the six tabs represents part of the report that you can customize (click **Next** to move to the next tab, **Previous** to return to the last tab):

- **Title**   This tab contains options for the name of the report, the paper orientation, and the font of the title text.

- **Fields**   Choose this tab to select which fields will show on the report.

- **Sorting**   This tab allows you to choose the order in which the records will print.

- **Grouping**   This tab gives you the option to have records grouped by common data.

- **Filter**   You can choose from filters you named previously or create a new filter. Only those records meeting your filter criteria will show on the report.

- **Summary**   To set up your report so that it displays such things as a count of items, sum totals, or average values under each group of records, choose this tab.

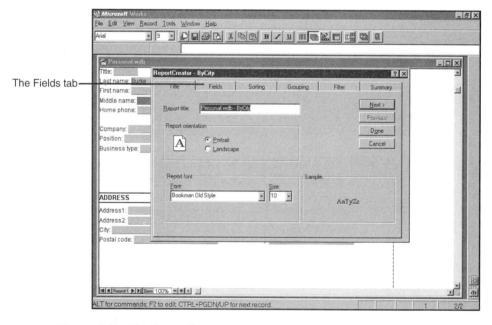

Figure 3.8   The ReportCreator dialog box.

4. When your report customization is complete, click **Done**.

5. A dialog box appears offering the option to preview the report or modify it. Choose to **Preview** your report. The report appears in a Print Preview window. You can move from page to page by clicking the **Next** and **Previous** buttons in the Preview window. To enlarge your preview, click **Zoom In**.

6. To print the report as it appears in the preview, click **Print**. Click **Cancel** to exit the Preview window without printing.

TIP   **What About Reports that You Don't Need Anymore?**   Once you've created a report, you can delete it by choosing **Tools**, **Delete Report**.

In this lesson, you learned to create, maintain, edit, and print a personal address book. In the next lesson, you learn to create a résumé.

Creating a Résumé

In this lesson, you learn to use the Résumé TaskWizard to create and update your résumé.

Using the TaskWizard to Create a Résumé

When you first open Works, you see the Task Launcher (see Figure 4.1). If you're already in Works and the Task Launcher is not displayed, choose **File, New**. To begin creating a résumé:

1. From the Works Task Launcher, click the TaskWizards tab and then expand the **Common Tasks, Employment,** or **Business Management** icon. Choose **Résumé (CV)** from the list. Click **OK**.

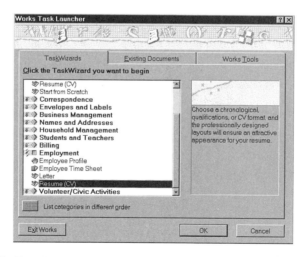

Figure 4.1 The Task Launcher.

2. A dialog box appears asking if you want to use the TaskWizard to create a new document or work with an existing document (deselect **Always Display This Message** to not see this dialog box in the future). Select **Yes, Run the TaskWizard**. The Résumé TaskWizard dialog box opens where you can view the three résumé types (see Figure 4.2):

- **Chronological**   This is a traditional listing of jobs and employers.
- **Qualifications**   This is a résumé which focuses on skills and strengths.
- **Curriculum Vitae (CV)**   This is a document which describes your professional experiences in a particular field and describes your professional and personal experiences, strengths, and skills in a specific field. This type of résumé is used primarily by people in the Education field.

For our example, choose Chronological, although the following steps are the same for any type of résumé you choose to create.

3. Click the **Next** button.

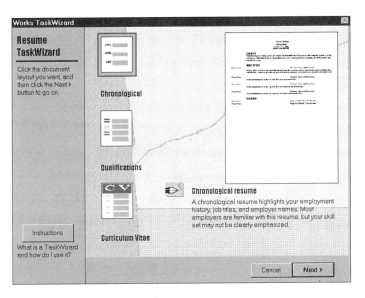

Figure 4.2 The Résumé TaskWizard.

4. In the next screen, the TaskWizard offers four areas to customize your résumé (see Figure 4.3). Each area is represented by a button:

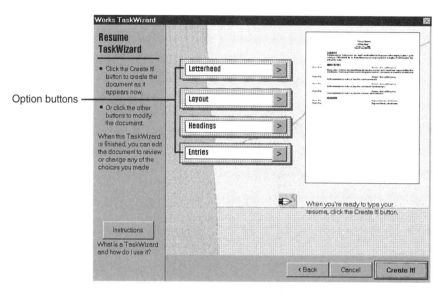

Figure 4.3   Résumé TaskWizard options.

• **Letterhead**   Choose from seven letterhead styles for your résumé, as shown in Figure 4.4.

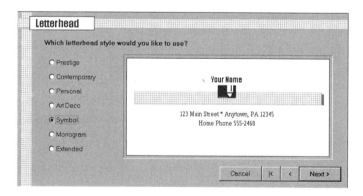

Figure 4.4   Letterhead options.

- **Layout** Choose from four styles of type for your headings and body text (see Figure 4.5).

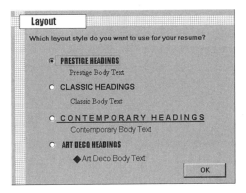

Figure 4.5 Layout options.

- **Headings** This dialog box lists the sections that you can have in your résumé (see Figure 4.6). Click next to the items you want to include. These headings will vary depending upon which résumé type you are creating.

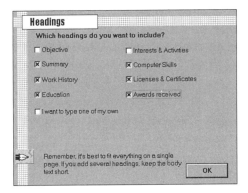

Figure 4.6 Headings options.

- **Entries** Choose how many jobs and educational listings you want to include in your résumé (see Figure 4.7).

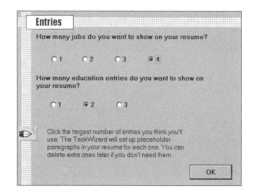

Figure 4.7   Entries options.

5. Click the **Option** button for the areas you want to change. Make the changes in the dialog box and click **OK**. After you've made all the changes you want, click **Create It!**.

6. The TaskWizard then asks you to confirm your choices. If they are correct, click **Create Document**; if not, click **Return to Wizard**. The TaskWizard then creates your résumé, and presents the document in its own window (see Figure 4.8).

What If I Change My Mind About My Setup Choices?   You can always rethink your choices. At each stage of the TaskWizard process, you can choose to **Cancel**, **Go Back**, or **Return to Wizard**.

CAUTION

Entering Your Information

The TaskWizard's version of your résumé contains instructional text that tells you where to put your own personal and professional information.

To replace the instructional text:

1. Highlight the text you want to replace.

2. Type your text. This will replace the instructions with your content.

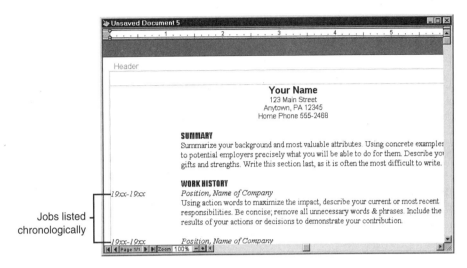

Jobs listed
chronologically

Figure 4.8   A sample Chronological résumé.

Formatting Your Résumé

The TaskWizard creates your résumé with the fonts and layout you selected in the Letterhead and Layout boxes in the Résumé Wizard. You can make changes to these formats by using Works' Format menu and toolbar.

Wow Them, Don't Overwhelm Them   If you decide to make formatting changes, be careful not to make your résumé too "busy" with too many fonts, too many font sizes, or too many different styles. Keep it simple!

For more information on formatting text, see Part III, Lesson 6, "Formatting Text."

TIP   **More than One Version**   Once you've created a basic résumé with all of your information, you can make as many versions as you like (for different types of jobs) and save each one with a different name by using **File**, **Save As**.

In this lesson, you learned to create a résumé by using the Résumé TaskWizard. In the next lesson, you learn to use Works' Mortgage and Loan Analysis Wizard.

Using the Mortgage and Loan Analysis

In this lesson, you learn how to determine the monthly payment on a mortgage or loan.

What Is a Mortgage and Loan Analysis?

The Mortgage and Loan Analysis TaskWizard allows you to enter an amount to be borrowed and to determine the monthly payment. By adjusting the length of the loan and interest rates, you can set up various "what-if" scenarios to determine payment amounts in different situations.

The Task Launcher appears as soon as you open Works. If Works is already running and the Task Launcher is not active, choose **File**, **New** from the menu.

Starting Your Analysis

To begin using the Mortgage and Loan Analysis TaskWizard:

1. From the list of TaskWizards in the TaskWizards tab of the Works Task Launcher, expand **Business Management** or **Household Management** (see Figure 5.1).

2. Choose **Mortgage and Loan Analysis** and click **OK**. A dialog box appears asking if you want to create a new document using the TaskWizard or if you want to work with an existing document. Click **Yes, Run the TaskWizard** (deselect **Always Show This Message** to avoid seeing this dialog box in the future).

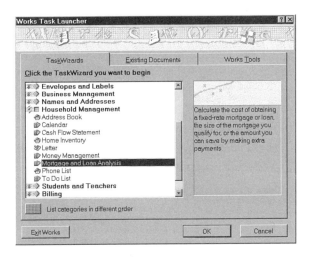

Figure 5.1 The Task Launcher.

3. The TaskWizard begins by offering three choices: Standard Loan to calculate fixed-rate mortgages and loans, Extra Payments to calculate the effect of extra payments on a fixed-rate mortgage or loan, or Qualification Worksheet to calculate the maximum amount you might qualify for when applying for a mortgage. Choose **Standard Loan** (see Figure 5.2).

4. Click the **Create It!** button to create the loan analysis.

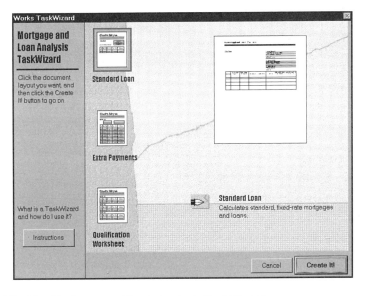

Figure 5.2 The Mortgage and Loan Analysis TaskWizard.

513

Using Standard Loan Analysis

On the left side of the screen, you see the loan analysis window (see Figure 5.3). On the right, you see the Help window.

TIP   **Seeing More of the Loan Window**   To view the Mortgage and Loan Analysis without the accompanying Help, click the **Shrink Help** button in the lower-left corner of the Help window. Click the same button again to expand Help when you need it.

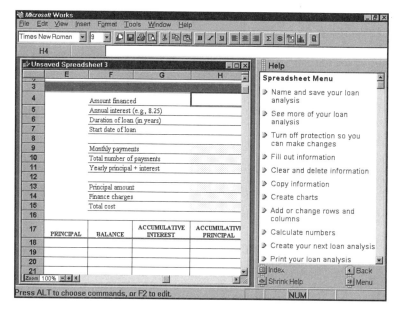

Figure 5.3 The Loan Analysis and Help Windows.

The Mortgage and Loan Analysis spreadsheet has been designed to determine a monthly loan payment based on a series of variables:

- The amount to be borrowed
- Annual interest rate
- Duration of loan
- Start date of loan

As you supply the data for each of these areas (see Figure 5.4), Works automatically calculates following information :

- Monthly payments
- Total number of payments
- Yearly principal and interest
- Principal amount
- Finance charges
- Total cost

Resulting payment amount

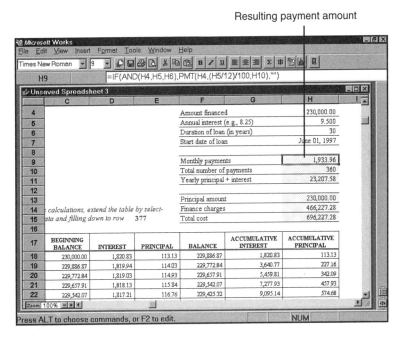

Figure 5.4 Payment Amounts.

The bottom section of the spreadsheet displays how each monthly payment will affect your principal and interest amounts (see Figure 5.5).

To see what effect a change in interest rate or length of loan will make in your monthly payments, change the information in the cell containing the current interest rate or length of loan. The monthly payment amount will change automatically.

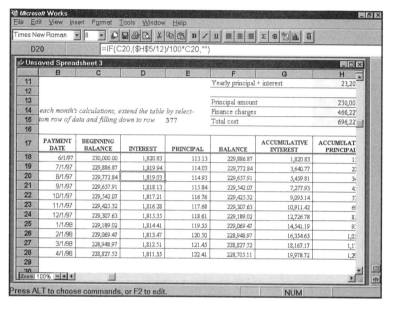

Figure 5.5 Monthly payment details.

Changing Spreadsheet Values Spreadsheet formulas are based on cell addresses within the spreadsheet, not on actual numbers. For this reason, changing a cell's contents will change any results for any formulas that refer to that cell address.

For further information on spreadsheet concepts, see Part IV, Lesson 1, "Spreadsheet Basics."

Entering Your Loan Information

To place your loan information in the appropriate cells:

1. Click in the cell to the right of **Amount Financed**. Enter the amount of the loan.

2. Use the down-arrow on the keyboard to move to the cell directly below the previous entry, or simply click inside the cell by using the mouse. You need to enter only the first four items for the loan analysis, ending with **Start Date of Loan**.

Editing Your Analysis

To move to a cell and change the value, you can use one of the following methods:

- Click directly in the cell
- Use the arrow keys to go to the cell

Type your new entry in the cell. This replaces the cell's previous contents.

You can edit a cell's contents in the Entry bar (text box found just below the toolbar) by clicking there. Use the arrow keys to move the cursor back and forth; use the **Backspace** and **Delete** keys to remove unwanted characters. You can also double-click in a cell to edit the entry there.

Formatting Your Analysis

The TaskWizard creates a spreadsheet with the fonts, colors, column widths, and layout already designed for you. This is the nature of a Wizard—to take the formatting and design decisions out of your hands. You can, however, make changes to the appearance of the spreadsheet by using the Format menu and toolbar buttons.

To change the general appearance of a spreadsheet quickly, select the cells to be modified and then choose **Format**, **AutoFormat**. You can choose from several predesigned formats that apply font, color, and layout formats, in one command (see Figure 5.6) and see the new format in the Example area of the dialog box before you commit to any changes. Click **OK** when you've found the format you like best.

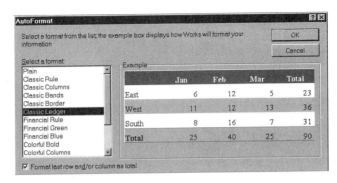

Figure 5.6 The AutoFormat dialog box.

Using the Qualification Worksheet

The loan analysis spreadsheet allowed you to determine what your payment would be for an amount borrowed, at a specific rate, for a specific length of time. The Qualification Worksheet will help you to figure out if the bank will allow you to borrow the money in the first place!

Starting the Qualification Worksheet

To start the Qualification Worksheet:

1. From the list of TaskWizards in the TaskWizards tab of the Works Task Launcher, expand **Business Management** or **Household Management**.

2. Choose **Mortgage and Loan Analysis** and click **OK**. A dialog box appears asking if you want to create a new document using the TaskWizard or if you want to work with an existing document. Click **Yes, Run the TaskWizard** (deselect **Always Show This Message** to avoid seeing this dialog box in the future).

3. From the three choices the TaskWizard offers, choose **Qualification Worksheet**.

To begin using the worksheet:

1. Choose **Qualification Worksheet**.

2. Click the **Create It!** button.

3. View the spreadsheet that opens in the new window (see Figure 5.7). This spreadsheet contains cells for entering your financial information:
   - **Income**   Your salary, interest on investments, and any other sources of income
   - **Debts**   Your car payments, leases, credit cards, and other loans

4. Enter your information in the appropriate cells.

5. Scroll to the right to see your qualification numbers—the amounts you could qualify for in terms of your ability to pay (see Figure 5.8).
   - The **First Qualifying Number** is the monthly amount you could afford without considering your long-term debts.
   - The **Second Qualifying Number** takes your long-term debts into account.

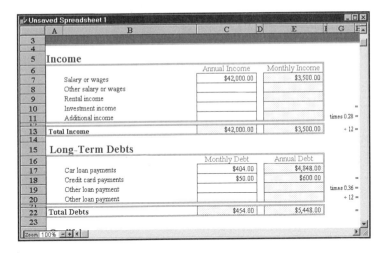

Figure 5.7 The Qualification Worksheet.

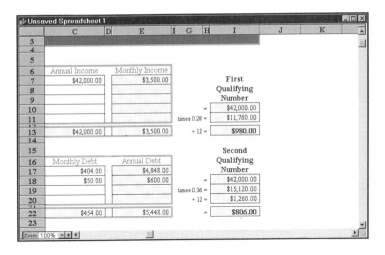

Figure 5.8 Your Qualifying Amounts.

6. As you scroll down the spreadsheet, more information is available (see Figure 5.9). Between the sections asking for information, you see instructions and explanations of terms and mortgage concepts.

7. Enter your escrow, insurance, and fee information. Your total qualifying loan amount will appear in the last box on the spreadsheet.

519

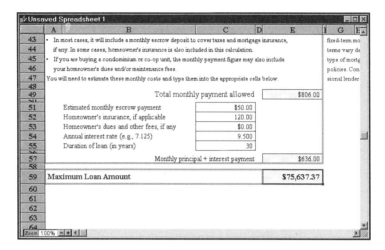

Figure 5.9 Final Loan Amount.

In this lesson, you learned to use the Mortgage and Loan Analysis TaskWizard to figure out monthly payments on a loan by entering variables. In the next lesson, you learn to keep track of your money and investments.

Money Management

In this lesson, you learn to use the Works TaskWizard to forecast investment values—the amount a current investment will be worth in the future, as well as how much you need to invest now to reach a specific financial goal.

Using the Money Management TaskWizard

The Money Management TaskWizard offers three types of management tools: Investment Projections to project the future value of an investment or to help you set an investment goal, Loan & Credit Planner to calculate monthly payments and balances on a loan and pay down the balance on a credit account, and Leasing versus Purchasing to work out the terms of a potential lease and compare the cost of purchasing with a loan versus leasing the item. This lesson will cover the Investment Projections TaskWizard.

To begin using the TaskWizard:

1. From the Works Task Launcher, click the **TaskWizards** tab and display the **Household** or **Business Management** category. Select **Money Management** (see Figure 6.1) and click **OK**.

2. A dialog box appears asking whether you want to create a new document using the TaskWizard or work with an existing document. Select **Yes, Run the TaskWizard** (deselect **Always Display This Message** to avoid seeing this dialog box in the future).Then the TaskWizard begins. Choose **Investment Projections** (see Figure 6.2) and click the **Create It!** button.

Figure 6.1 The Task Launcher.

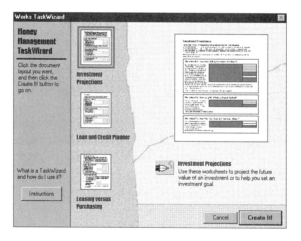

Figure 6.2 The Money Management TaskWizard.

3. A new window opens, containing the Investment Projections worksheets
(see Figure 6.3). Each worksheet begins with a question and an explanation
of what the user needs to do:

- How much will my investment be worth?

- How long will it take to reach my goal?

- How much do I need to invest each month?

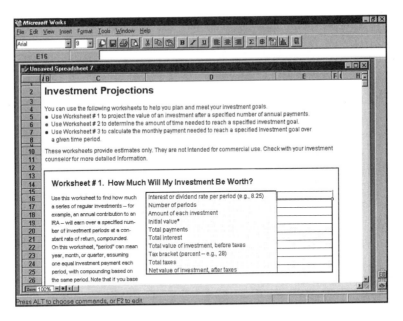

Figure 6.3 The Investment Worksheets.

Entering Your Worksheet Information

1. To work in any of the three worksheets, use the scroll bar to find the worksheet, then click in the first cell (for example, click in the blank cell next to **Interest or dividend rate** in Worksheet #1).

I'm Not Sure What All These Terms Mean! The TaskWizard provides a lot of help for you inside each worksheet. Read the fine print next to and below the worksheet cells for clarification of terms and concepts.

CAUTION

2. Type your numbers. Press **Tab** to move to the next cell.

3. As you enter your numbers, the Total and Net value of investment after taxes cells will fill in automatically (see Figure 6.4). These numbers are the result of the TaskWizard's calculations.

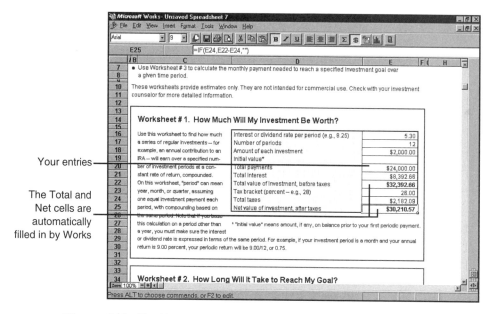

Your entries

The Total and
Net cells are
automatically
filled in by Works

Figure 6.4   The Worksheet Results.

Formatting Your Worksheets

The TaskWizard creates a spreadsheet with the fonts, colors, column widths, and layout already designed for you. This is the nature of a Wizard—to take the formatting and design decisions out of your hands. You can, however, make changes to the appearance of the spreadsheet by using the Format menu and toolbar buttons.

To learn more about formatting in spreadsheets, refer to Part IV, Lesson 13, "Formatting Text."

Other Money Management Tools

The Loan and Credit Planner and the Leasing versus Purchasing TaskWizards work the same way as the Investment Projections TaskWizard. You will work within a predesigned worksheet, answering questions about your loan/credit or potential lease/purchase. The TaskWizard will analyze your entries and provide monthly payment projections based on your information.

In this lesson, you learned to use the Money Management TaskWizard to analyze a current investment and plan future values. In the next lesson, you learn to create your own letterhead.

Creating Your
Own Letterhead

*In this lesson, you learn to use Works' TaskWizard to create
customized letterhead for your personal or business use.*

Using the Letterhead TaskWizard

The Works TaskWizard allows you to design your own letterhead. To begin
creating your letterhead:

1. From the Task Launcher, display the **TaskWizards** tab, and choose **Letterhead** from the list of **Common Tasks** (see Figure 7.1). A dialog box appears
that asks if you want to create a new document using the TaskWizard to
use an existing document. Select **Yes, Run the TaskWizard**. Deselect the
Always Show This Message option to hide this dialog box in the future.

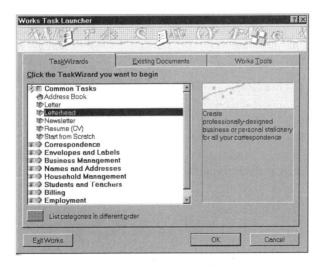

Figure 7.1 The Task Launcher.

2. The TaskWizard begins, offering three letterhead choices (see Figure 7.2):

- **Professional**   This letterhead is a typical business format.
- **Simple**   Described as crisp, this letterhead is a very basic layout with a minimum of features.
- **Formal**   In this variation on the Professional letterhead, the topic of the letter replaces the salutation.

3. Choose **Professional** and click **Next**.

4. The TaskWizard continues, and the next dialog box offers five areas of customization (see Figure 7.3):

- **Letterhead**   Choose from a variety of styles, such as Prestige, Contemporary, and Art Deco, and then enter your address and other content in a series of dialog boxes. As you choose a style, you can view it on the right side of the screen. Creating a letterhead creates your logo at the top of the paper.
- **Address**   Choose to type your recipient's address or select one from a Works database (see Lesson 3, "Creating an Address Book," in this part).
- **Content**   A list of business documents appears. The first choice is a blank document. The remaining choices are for introductions, proposals, invitations, and other business documents. If you choose one of these documents, the TaskWizard will insert sample text to assist you.

TIP   **Can't Find Your Content?**   If you don't immediately recognize the document you wanted to create among the content choices, choose Blank Document. This option gives you the most flexibility.

- **Text Style**   Choose from a variety of fonts to set the tone of your letterhead document.
- **Extras**   You can add typical document items such as cc:, typist's initials, and enclosure.

5. For each area you want to customize, click the appropriate option button, make your choices in the option areas, then click **OK**. In this example, the Blank document is chosen from the Content option area.

6. Click **Create It!**.

7. The TaskWizard asks you to confirm your selections. Click **Create Document**.

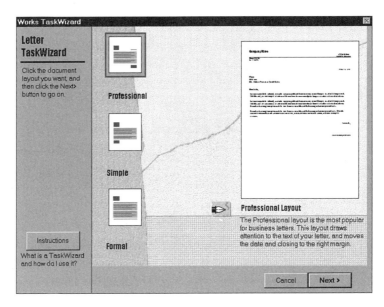

Figure 7.2 The Letterhead TaskWizard.

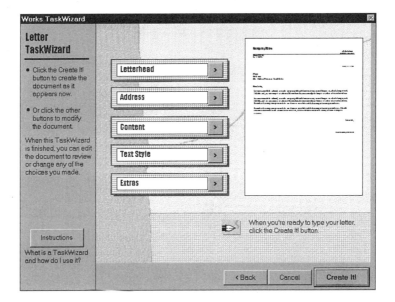

Figure 7.3 Letterhead Options.

Editing Your Letterhead

Even in the blank document, there is some instructive sample text: Start typing your letter here (see Figure 7.4) to indicate where your document text should begin. There is also sample text to indicate where you should place the date and recipient address. To complete the document:

1. Select the Date and type the date of your letter (you may have to scroll to the right to see it or click the Shrink Help button to remove the Help window).

2. Select the sample recipient address and type the real address for your recipient.

3. Replace the **Dear John** salutation with yours.

4. Select **Start typing your letter here** and begin typing the real content of your letter (your text replaces the instructional text). Continue typing until the end of your letter and insert your own closing.

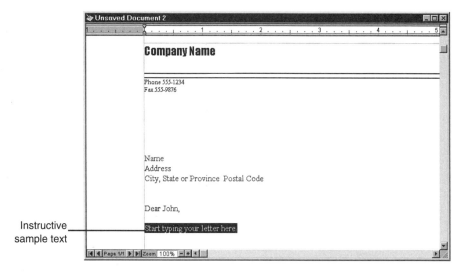

Instructive sample text

Figure 7.4   The Blank Document with Instructive Text.

What If I Just Want a Sheet of Blank Letterhead? Rather than replacing the instructive sample text, delete it. This leaves a blank document with your name, address, and phone information logo across the top of the paper.

CAUTION

In this lesson, you learned to use a TaskWizard to create your own letterhead for a business document. In the next lesson, you learn to create a newsletter.

Creating a Newsletter

In this lesson, you learn to create, edit, save, and print a newsletter.

What Is a Newsletter?

A newsletter is an informative publication, containing text (articles) and graphic images (clip art, graphs, or photographs) usually arranged in one, two, or three columns per page. Newsletters are published to share important information with colleagues or to market a company's services to potential customers. Most organizations publish a newsletter to serve both of these purposes.

Microsoft Works provides a TaskWizard in the Common Tasks category, specifically designed for creating newsletters (see Figure 8.1). This list of tasks appears as soon as the Works program is started.

1. The Task Launcher appears when you start Works (if you're already using Works and want to begin a Newsletter, choose **File**, **New** from the menu, which displays the Task Launcher). Select the **TaskWizards** tab.

2. Choose **Newsletter** from the list of Common Tasks and click **OK**.

3. A dialog box appears that asks if you want to create a new document by using a TaskWizard or if you want to work with an existing document. Click **Yes, Run the TaskWizard**. To avoid seeing this dialog box the next time you use a TaskWizard, deselect **Always Display This Message**.

4. The Newsletter TaskWizard starts.

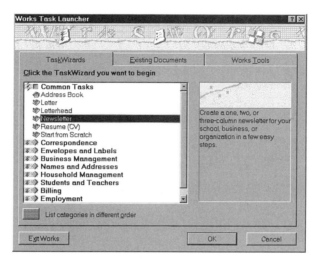

Figure 8.1 Works Task Launcher.

Creating a Newsletter

Follow the steps in the Newsletter TaskWizard to create your newsletter:

1. In the first TaskWizard screen, specify the number of columns you want for your newsletter (see Figure 8.2). To preview the one-, two-, or three-column layouts, click the button for each alternative.

TIP **I'm Not a Designer!** · Let the TaskWizard help you! The TaskWizard makes suggestions with each layout, indicating the best applications for each choice. For example, the three-column newsletter is the most traditional and professional layout, while the one and two column layouts are rather informal—good choices for schools and social organizations.

2. Click the **Create It!** button.

3. A two-sided screen is displayed. On the left, a newsletter appears in the layout you selected in the previous step. On the right, the TaskWizard offers a Help window (see Figure 8.3).

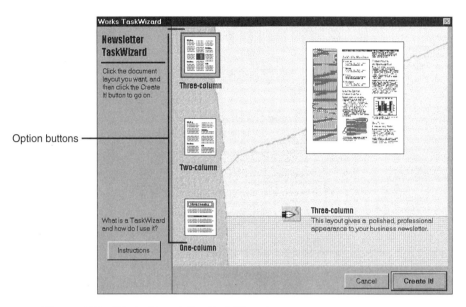

Figure 8.2   Works Newsletter TaskWizard.

Option buttons

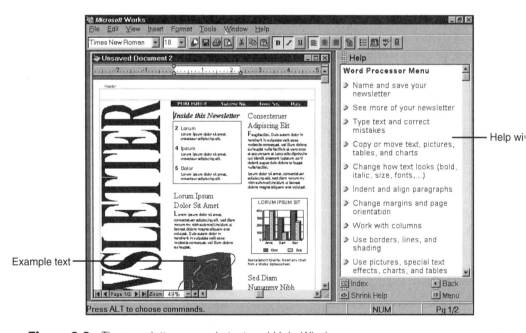

Figure 8.3   The newsletter example text and Help Windows.

Example text

Help wi

TIP **Seeing More of the Newsletter** To view the newsletter without the accompanying help, click the **Shrink Help** button in the lower-right corner of the Help window. If this is the first time you are creating a newsletter in Works, however, it is advisable to keep the Help window open. Once you are comfortable with the newsletter-creation process, this window can be closed (shrunken) to provide a larger work area for the newsletter itself. If your Help window doesn't show, click the Shrink Help button in the right margin to bring it back.

Editing Your Newsletter Layout

The newsletter contains example text in columns, and a collection of graphic objects—the headline, the volume/edition and date information, and any clip art, graphs, or photographs. Each object can be selected for moving and resizing by clicking it once with the mouse. When an object is selected, it appears with a thin gray line around it, and small gray boxes, called handles, in each of the four corners. Handles also appear centered on each side of the object (see Figure 8.4). Your mouse is the most important and informative tool at this stage in the process. Depending on where the mouse is located on the surface of the newsletter's graphic objects, you can either drag (move) or resize any object:

- If the mouse is pointing to a handle, the pointer changes to Resize mode. Just click the button and drag the handle toward the center of the picture or away from the center. The gray outline shows you the size of the object. Release the mouse button when the object is the size you want it.

- If the mouse is pointing to anywhere on the object itself (within the border of the selected object), the pointer changes to Drag mode. Hold the left mouse button down and drag the object to a new location.

CAUTION **What If I Don't Like the Layout?** If you chose a three-column layout and you wish you'd chosen a two-column layout, simply close the document and start over with the TaskWizard. If you do decide to start over, do so before you've put in a lot of work on the newsletter—you can't change the layout later without having to redo your work!

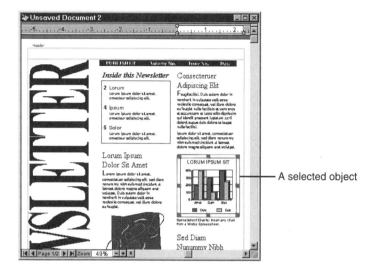

A selected object

Figure 8.4   Graphic objects.

Inserting Text into the Newsletter

The newsletter's sample text is gibberish and appears only to indicate where you should insert your content. As with a newspaper, the text goes down one column and when it reaches the bottom of the page (or a graphic object at the bottom of the page), it continues at the top of the next column.

To replace the example text that the Wizard created with your own content:

1. Select the example text with your mouse.
2. Begin typing the text that will replace it. The selected text will disappear, and the text being typed will begin to flow into the column.

Text can also come from other documents. If the text you want to use in your article already exists in another file or document, merely copy it in the source location, and paste it into the newsletter.

To copy and paste text:

1. Open or switch to your source document (if the source document is already open, you can use **Alt**+**Esc** or click the appropriate button on the Taskbar). The source document is the document containing the text you want to use in your newsletter.

2. Select the text you want to use. Choose **Edit**, **Copy** from the menu, or press the shortcut keys **Ctrl+C**.

3. Return to your newsletter, and select the example text which you want to replace. From the **Edit** menu, choose **Paste**, or press the shortcut keys **Ctrl+V**.

Using WordArt to Create the Headline

The headline object is inserted by the TaskWizard with the example text NEWSLETTER in it. This headline is a WordArt object. WordArt is an additional program that ships with Microsoft Office and Microsoft Works that you may use in other programs besides Works. It makes it possible to use words as graphic objects and change them into banners, wrap them around circles, and so on. When you use WordArt, it embeds an object in your document. The NEWSLETTER text is an embedded object, so if you double-click it, the WordArt program opens and you can edit the object.

To insert your own headline:

1. Double-click the headline object.

2. The WordArt tools appear on-screen, including a small box with the word **NEWSLETTER** selected (see Figure 8.5). Whatever you type in this box will replace the text in the object box.

3. Use the other WordArt tools for changing the size, color, shape, and font of the text.

For more information on using WordArt, see Part III, Lesson 6, "Formatting Text."

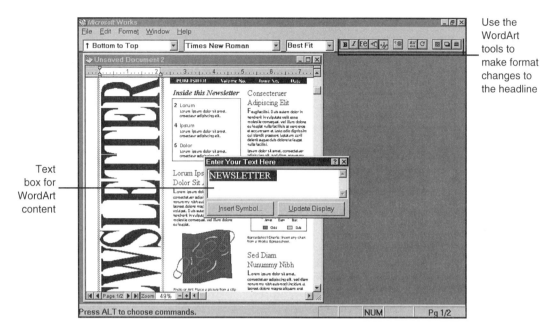

Use the WordArt tools to make format changes to the headline

Text box for WordArt content

Figure 8.5 Enter your text here.

Special Formatting

As the TaskWizard creates the newsletter, certain formats are imposed: the fonts and color of the text, and the space between lines and paragraphs. This is done so that you don't have to be a graphic artist to create a newsletter. Use the format menu and the toolbar to apply your own formats to selected text. Here are some ideas you might want to try:

- Lines between columns (**Format, Columns**).
- Putting text in a shaded box (**Format, Borders and Shading**). Or even try white text on solid shading.
- Adding borders around text or pictures (**Format, Borders and Shading**).
- Insert ClipArt or graphs to illustrate your articles (**Insert, Clip Art or Insert, Chart**).

For more information on Works' formatting tools, see Part III, Lesson 6, "Formatting Text."

Headers and Footers

Headers and footers perform the same function as they do in a word processing document—they're a good place to put the page number, the title, the date, and any other information you want to appear on each page of the document.

 TIP **Number Your Pages** Most newsletters are more than one page, so you might need to number your pages.

In a traditional newsletter, page numbers appear on the outside corners of each page. The page numbers appear on the left on even-numbered pages, and on the right on odd-numbered pages.

Cover pages are not numbered in most traditional business documents.

To edit your header or footer:

1. Click inside the header or footer box and see your cursor activate within the box.

2. If the Ruler isn't displayed, choose **View, Ruler** from the menu. You can see the preset tabs on the ruler bar. Reset or remove these tabs as needed.

3. Type your text.

4. Remember that the border that appears around the header and footer boxes on-screen will not actually print. If you want to place a full or partial border around the text, choose **Borders and Shading** from the **Format** menu.

 TIP **Add a Border as a Visual Separator** To help visually separate your header and footer text from the main text of your document, apply a bottom border to the header, and a top border to the footer.

For further information about Headers and Footers, see Part III, Lesson 9, "Formatting Pages." For more information on Borders and Shading, see Part II, Lesson 10, "Working with Tables" (borders and shading options are the same for tables as for paragraphs).

In this lesson, you learned how to create and edit a newsletter. In the next lesson, you learn to use the Start from Scratch TaskWizard to create a word processing document, a spreadsheet, and a database.

Using the Start from Scratch Wizard

In this lesson, you learn to create a word processing document, a spreadsheet, and database file from a TaskWizard.

Using the Start from Scratch TaskWizard

The Start from Scratch TaskWizard takes the customization and simplicity of a TaskWizard and combines it with Works' three basic programs: Word Processing, Spreadsheets, and Databases. By automating the layout and design aspects of generating a document, the TaskWizard frees you to concentrate on the file's content and functionality. You want to use this TaskWizard when none of the other TaskWizards seem to quite fit your needs.

1. When you start Microsoft Works, the Task Launcher appears (see Figure 9.1). Select the **TaskWizards** tab (if it's not already selected).

2. From the list of **Common Tasks**, select **Start from Scratch**.

3. Click **OK**. A dialog box may appear asking if you want to use the TaskWizard to create a new document or if you can work with an existing document. Click **Yes, Run the TaskWizard** (to avoid seeing this dialog box each time you select a TaskWizard, deselect the **Always Display This Message** option).

4. The Start from Scratch TaskWizard begins (see Figure 9.2), giving you a choice of three types of files:
   - Word Processor
   - Spreadsheet
   - Database

5. Select the type of file you want to create, and then click **Next**.

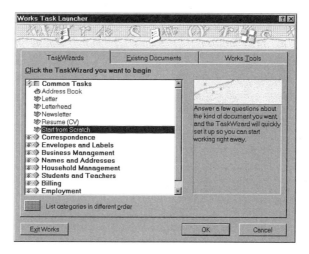

Figure 9.1 The Task Launcher.

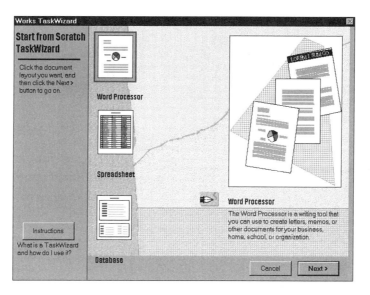

Figure 9.2 The Start from Scratch TaskWizard.

Word Processing from Scratch

Once you have selected the **Word Processor** option:

1. In the first word processing screen (see Figure 9.3), you see two option buttons—one for selecting your **Text Style** and another for selecting **Page Borders**. To change either of these attributes, click the option button, make the desired changes, then click **OK**.

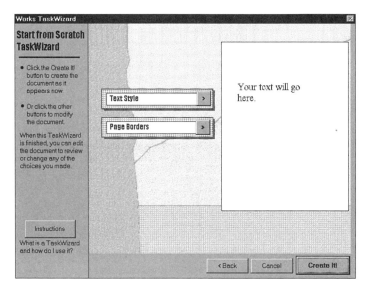

Figure 9.3 Document options.

2. After making your selections, click **Create It!**

3. The TaskWizard asks you to confirm your selections. If the selections are correct, click **Create Document**. If not, click **Return to Wizard** and make the appropriate modifications before returning to this screen.

4. A blank document opens in a new window (see Figure 9.4). If you selected a border for your document, you see it on the perimeter of your page. Your document also contains:

- A header section
- A footer section
- Standard formatting—margins set at 1" all around, .5" tabs, and single line-spacing

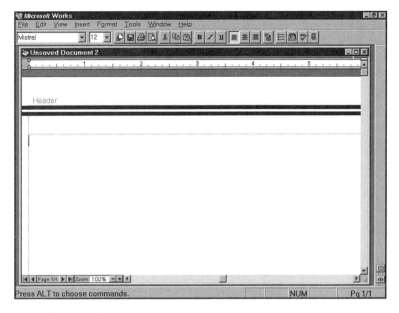

Figure 9.4   The Start from Scratch document.

Using Your Document

To use your blank document, simply begin typing. Your cursor will already be at the top of the document, below the header section. The document works the same as any normal document.

For more information about word processing, see Part III, Lesson 1, "Word Processing Basics."

Formatting Your Document

The TaskWizard creates your document with the fonts, styles, and layout already designed for you; you'll see them as soon as you begin typing. This is the purpose of a Wizard—to take the formatting and design decisions out of your hands. You can, however, make changes to the appearance of the document by using the Format menu and toolbar buttons.

For more information about formatting a word processing document, see Part III, Lesson 6,"Formatting Text."

Creating a Spreadsheet from Scratch

Once you have selected the spreadsheet option:

1. The next TaskWizard screen (see Figure 9.5) gives you three areas to customize:

- **Page Header & Footer**   Choose the content (if any) of the header and footer sections
- **Text Style**   Choose the font for your spreadsheet
- **Page Orientation**   Choose **Portrait** or **Landscape**

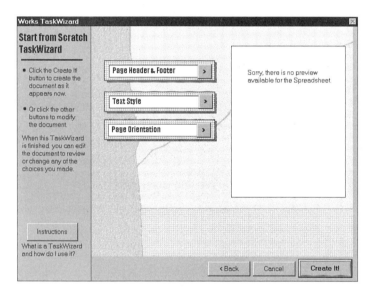

Figure 9.5   Spreadsheet options.

2. Click each of these option buttons and enter the requested information and then click **OK**. After making your selections, click the **Create It!** button.

3. You'll be asked to verify your selections. If they're correct, click **Create Document** to create the spreadsheet. If they're not correct, click **Return to Wizard**, make the appropriate adjustments using the directions in step 2 to return to this screen.

4. The TaskWizard creates a blank spreadsheet. You can begin making your entries in the appropriate cells. The content of the spreadsheet is up to you—no text, numbers, or formulas are inserted by the TaskWizard.

For more information about spreadsheets, see Part IV, Lesson 2, "Creating a Spreadsheet."

Creating a Database

Once you have selected the database option:

1. The first database TaskWizard screen (see Figure 9.6) gives you two areas to customize:
   - **Fields** Choose from a name and address format, or a list of five generic fields, which you name (see the task below).
   - **Text Style** Select the font for your database.

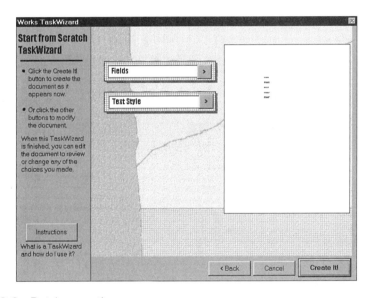

Figure 9.6 Database options.

2. Based on your entries into these option dialog boxes, the TaskWizard creates a database form. Click **Create It!** to begin the process.

3. You'll be asked to confirm your selections. Click **Create Document**. The TaskWizard will create a blank database entry form in a new window.

Customizing Your Database

When you choose the generic fields option, the database form contains five empty fields (with the name and address fields option, there are more fields and all are named appropriately to enter full name and address data). To assign names to the fields:

1. From the **View** menu, choose **Form Design**. You'll see a dotted border appear around the field names and the data boxes next to each one (see Figure 9.7). You don't enter data in the Form Design view; you only create the spaces where you want the data to be entered in the Form view.

2. Click once on the generic field name, and type the replacement field name plus a colon (if you don't, an alert appears asking if you want to delete this field and all its contents; click **Cancel** and type the colon after the field name). Repeat this for each of the five fields.

Click and type a field name here

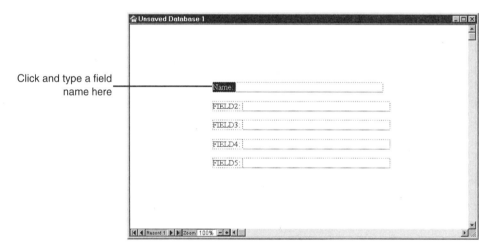

Figure 9.7 Form Design view.

3. To add fields, place your cursor on the form where the new field should be. Type the field name, followed by a colon. Press **Enter** when you've finished typing the name.

4. The Insert Field dialog box opens. Choose the type of field, such as number, text, or date. Click **OK**.

5. When you've finished customizing your database, return to Form view by choosing **View**, **Form** from the menu to begin entering data. You can also switch to List view, if you prefer.

You can begin entering your data in either Form or List view.

 TIP   **Reordering Your Fields in List View**   When in List view, you'll find that your fields will default to the order in which they were created—the first five generic fields will be first, even if you added your own fields in front of or between them in Form view.

To reorder your fields, **Edit**, **Cut** and **Edit**, **Paste** your columns in List view so that they appear in the order that makes the most sense for data entry.

In this lesson, you learned to use the Start from Scratch TaskWizard to create a word processing document, a spreadsheet, and a database. In the next lesson, you learn to create a Form letter.

Creating Form Letters

In this lesson, you learn to create a Form letter by using a TaskWizard and Works database.

The Form Letter TaskWizard

The Form Letter TaskWizard takes you step-by-step through the process of creating a business letter and inserting names and addresses from a Works database. To start the Form Letter TaskWizard:

1. Open the Works program by clicking the **Start** button on your Taskbar.

2. From the Programs menu, choose **Microsoft Works**, **Microsoft Works**.

3. When Works opens, your screen displays the **Task Launcher** (see Figure 10.1). Click the **TaskWizards** tab.

4. Click **Correspondence** to display the list of related Wizards.

5. Choose **Form Letter** from the list.

6. Click **OK** to start the Wizard. A dialog box appears asking if you want to create a new document using the TaskWizard or if you can work with an existing document. Click **Yes, Run the TaskWizard**. To avoid seeing this dialog box every time you choose a TaskWizard, deselect the **Always Display This Message** option.

7. The Form Letter Wizard (see Figure 10.2) begins by offering three types of form letters for you to create: **Professional**, **Simple**, or **Formal**. Choose the type of letter you need and click **Next**.

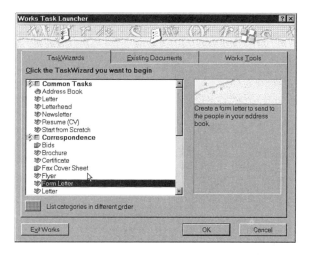

Figure 10.1 The Task Launcher.

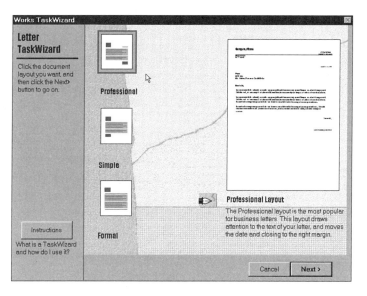

Figure 10.2 The Form Letter Wizard.

8. Use the customizing option buttons to select the layout, list of addresses, and so on that you'll need for the form letter (see "Setting Up Your Form Letter" for more assistance). Then click **Create It!**.

9. When the Checklist appears, click **Create Document** if all is listed correctly (click **Return to Wizard** if not).

TIP   **Form Letters**   To create a Form Letter from a blank Works word processor document, open a blank document and choose **Tools, Form Letters** from the menu. A six-tab dialog box opens, offering you options for choosing the database, selecting the records you want to use for your mailing, inserting your database fields, and printing your letters. Review the Envelope and Label Wizards in Part III, Lesson 15, for more information on this approach.

Setting Up Your Form Letter

When the customizing options appear in the TaskWizard (see step 8 previously) you can make decisions about the content and style of your letter through a series of five option buttons, as shown in Figure 10.3:

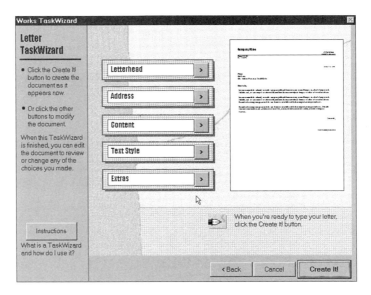

Figure 10.3   Letterhead Options.

- **Letterhead**   Choose to use preprinted stationery or to create your own letterhead.
- **Address**   You can choose to address a single letter or use a Works database to generate a group of form letters.
- **Content**   Select a type of letter from a list of typical business letters, proposals, and reports.

- **Text Style**   Choose a style or look for your letter. The choice you make will dictate the font and layout of your letter.

- **Extras**   You can add items like a carbon copy recipient (cc:) or typist's initials to your letter.

Once you select an option, you'll work through a series of screens where you supply information or make decisions about what you want to put in your letter. To continue each step of the process, click **Next**. Once the option is completed, click **OK**.

For more information on using the Letter Wizard's style and content options, see Part VI, Lesson 7, "Creating Your Own Letterhead."

Choosing a Database

In the Form Letter **TaskWizard**'s **Address** option, choose to use a Works database and then click **Next**. Select your database from the list and click **Next** again.

If you haven't created a Works database, refer to Part VI, Lesson 3, "Creating an Address Book."

TIP   **Documents Folder**   If your database isn't listed, it means you didn't save it to the Documents folder. If you choose **The file I want isn't in the list**, Works tells you that it can't find any databases for you and suggests you use another Wizard to create one. If you already have a Works database that you want to use, **Cancel** the Wizard and use **My Computer** or the **Windows Explorer** to move your database to the **Documents** folder. Then, go back to Works and restart the Wizard.

Inserting Address Fields

The Form Letter TaskWizard opens a dialog box that contains the fields from your database. The fields appear in a box on the left, and you build the recipient address for your letter by adding these fields to the box on the right (see Figure 10.4).

To add fields, select them in the box on the left, and click the **Add** button. To move to the next line (to insert your Address fields, for example), click **New Line**. If you add a field in error, click **Remove**. There is also a **Comma** button to use between the City and State fields. Spaces will be automatically inserted when the Wizard creates your letter.

When you have added all the fields you need, click **Next**.

549

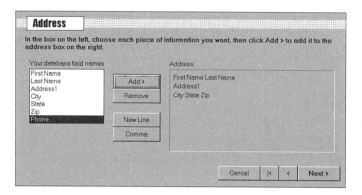

Figure 10.4   Inserting your recipient address field codes.

The last field you have to insert is for your salutation or greeting (see Figure 10.5). You can choose fields such as **First Name**, or **Title** and **Last Name** to create the complete greeting. Click **Next** to complete the Address settings, and then click **OK** to accept your selections and close the dialog box.

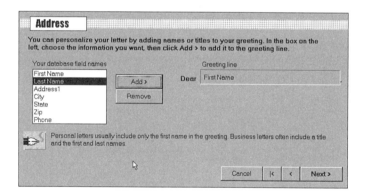

Figure 10.5   Create your salutation.

The **TaskWizard** now returns to the Letterhead options dialog box. Click **Create It!**. You are then asked to confirm your settings—click **Create Document** to accept your form letter settings and close the **TaskWizard**.

Works opens a new document window, and you have the beginnings of a form letter on-screen. The field codes for your database fields appear on the letter (see Figure 10.6), and you can begin to type the content of your letter.

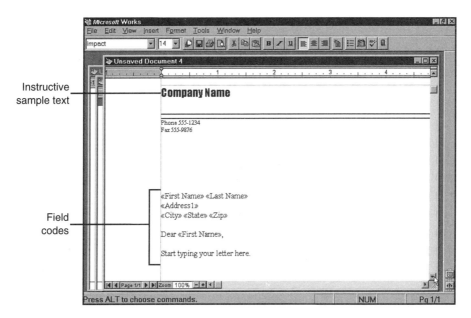

Instructive
sample text

Field
codes

Figure 10.6 The Form Letter.

Selecting Recipients

When you've completed the body of your letter, it's time to choose who will receive it. You can choose to send it to everyone in your database, or to only certain people.

To select your recipients:

1. In your open Form Letter window, choose **Tools**, **Form Letters**.
2. A six-tab dialog box opens (see Figure 10.7). Click the **Recipients** tab. You can choose from four selection options:

   - All records
   - Current visible records
   - Currently marked records
   - Filtered records

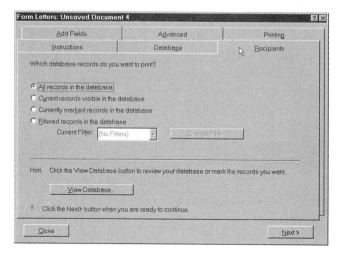

Figure 10.7   Selecting recipients.

If you want to **Filter** your database, see Part V, Lesson 10, "Working with Filters." To mark your records, click the **View Database** button and click the box next to each record you want to use. Click **Go Back** to return to the Labels dialog box.

To print a label for every record in your database, leave the default option (**All Records**) selected.

It's a good idea to save your Form Letter as soon as you've begun entering your content. This will save your database and field selection, as well as the work you've done on the body of the document.

TIP   **Storing Form Letters**   If you'll be using the Form Letter Wizard in the future, be sure to save all form letters and databases to the **Documents** folder. This is the default location where the Wizard looks for your files.

Printing Form Letters

Printing a form letter is different than printing a regular document. To print a form letter, you must first merge the letter with the associated database.

To merge and print your form letter:

1. If your form letter isn't open, choose **File**, **Open** from the menu or select the file from the **Existing Documents** tab on the **Task Launcher**.

2. With your form letter open on-screen, choose **Tools**, **Form Letters** from the menu. The Form Letters dialog box opens.

3. Click the **Printing** tab. You can choose to **Preview** your letters (one for each record you chose in the Recipients tab), or go directly to the printer by clicking the **Print** button.

In this lesson, you learned to create a Form letter by using a TaskWizard and a Works database.

User-Defined Templates

In this lesson, you learn how to create documents using user-defined templates.

What Are User-Defined Templates?

Microsoft Works includes a wide range of user-defined templates not available in previous versions of Works. Those templates include (but are not limited to) templates to create the following:

- Gift Tags
- Home Budget
- Graph Paper
- Travel Planner
- Conversion Tables
- Lawn and Garden Planning and Worksheets
- Fitness Tracker
- Move Planner
- Menu Cards
- Grocery List
- Meal Planner
- Certificate of Achievement
- Sports, Team Roster
- Gift Certificates
- Floral Stationery

- Vehicle Maintenance Checklist
- Personal Medical History
- Return Address Labels

When you select from the User Defined Templates category, a template appears on your screen ready for you to customize to your needs. User-defined templates do not use Wizards to help you create documents. It is recommended that you understand the Database, Spreadsheet, and Word Processing Tools in Works before you attempt to customize one of these templates. Figure 11.1 shows the Return Address Label template.

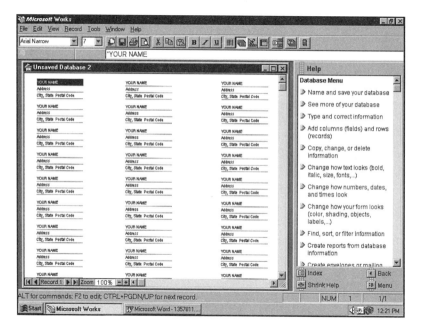

Figure 11.1   The Return Address Label found under User Defined Templates.

After you customize the work, you don't have to worry about changing the original template when you save your work, as Works will save your work as a document, spreadsheet, or database, depending on which tool the current template is using. Figure 11.2 shows a customized version of the Return Address Label template.

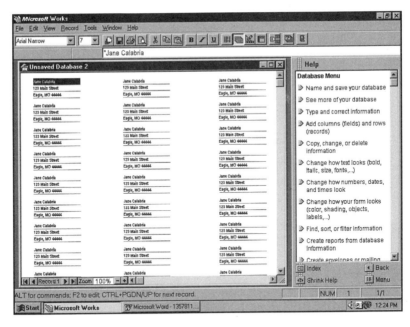

Figure 11.2   The Return Address Label template creates a new database with the database tool.

The tool used by each template is identified by the icon located to the left of the template. Figure 11.3 shows that the Move Planner templates use the Works Word Process Tool, the Place Card templates use the Works Database Tool, and the Meal Planner uses the Works Spreadsheet tool.

Figure 11.3   A partial list of templates available in User Defined Templates.

Creating Work With User-Defined Templates

To create work using User-Defined Templates:

1. Start Works by clicking the **Start** button and choosing **Microsoft Works**, **Microsoft Works** or by double-clicking the Microsoft Works shortcut icon on your desktop.

2. On the Task Wizard tab, click **User Defined Templates**.

3. Select the template you want to use and click **OK**.

4. Modify the template with your information.

5. When you are finished with your changes, choose File, Save and give your work a name. Works will apply the appropriate file extension.

You will find over 100 templates listed under the User Defined category. Once you understand the basics of Works' database, word Processing, and spreadsheet tools, you'll find the templates are quite useful and provide professional-looking results with a limited amount of design effort on your part.

Appendixes

Importing and Exporting

In this appendix, you learn how to export files from Microsoft Works to other applications and how to import files from other applications into Works.

Importing from Other Applications

Occasionally, you'll need to bring data or complete files into a Works document or spreadsheet from applications other than Microsoft Works. If these files are on your hard drive and you can open them in the application that created them, then you will copy and paste the data or items into your document or spreadsheet.

To learn more about copying, pasting, linking, and embedding files, see Part IV, Lesson 28, "Linking and Embedding Files."

But what do you do when the file was created on another computer and you don't have that application? For example, let's say that a coworker created the file at work using Lotus 1-2-3 but at home you don't have 1-2-3. How do you use that 1-2-3 spreadsheet in Works? You *import* the file.

Although Works imports many types of files from many different applications, you should check Works first to see which file formats it will import.

For instance, Works will import Lotus 1-2-3 files but only if the files have an extension of WK1 (the file extension follows the file name and defines what type of file it is), such as Budget.wk1. The Lotus 1-2-3 program has been in existence for several years and has been improved many times. Each time the program is improved, Lotus releases a new version. The WK1 extension means the file was created in version 2.0, 2.1, 2.2, or 2.4. However, later versions of the Lotus 1-2-3 program saved their files as WK3 or WK4 files. If your coworker hands you a disk with a file created by Lotus 1-2-3 for Windows, version 5.0, the file on that disk has a WK4 extension, such as Budget.wk4. Works may not be able to import it. Ask your coworker to save the spreadsheet file as a WK1 file type instead and give you a copy of that file (all your coworker has to do is use the File, Save As command and specify wk1 from the Save As Type drop-down list). Although you may lose a few of the more recent features that may have been incorporated into the file, at least you'll be able to open the file in Works without losing the basic data.

Make sure the file you want to import has been saved in one of the formats listed in Table A.1 before attempting to open it in Works.

Table A.1   Importable File Formats

File Extension	Type of File
b*	Backup file (in general)
db	Microsoft Works 3.0 or 4.0 for Macintosh database
dbf	dBase database file
doc	Microsoft Word 3.x-6.0 for MS-DOS document Microsoft Word 2.x for Windows document Microsoft Word 6.0/95 for Windows & Macintosh document Microsoft Word (Asian versions) 6.0/95 document Microsoft Word 97 document WordPerfect 5.x file
rtf	Rich text format file
slk	SYLK file
ss	Microsoft Works for Macintosh spreadsheet
txt	Text file
w*	Microsoft Works file (in general)
wcm	Microsoft Works communication document
wdb	Microsoft Works database
wk1	Lotus 1-2-3 spreadsheet
wks	Microsoft Works spreadsheet
wp	Microsoft Works for Macintosh word processing document

File Extension	Type of File
wps	Microsoft Works word processing document
wri	Windows Write document
xl*	Microsoft Excel spreadsheet
	* represents a wildcard (substitutes for any combination of letters)

Saving the File You Want to Import

Before you save a file that you intend to bring into Works, check to see in what file format the original application saves it. If it is not a format Works accepts, do the following:

1. Open the file you want to import in its original application.

2. Choose **File**, **Save As** from the menu (see Figure A.1).

Figure A.1   Save As dialog box from Microsoft Excel.

3. Select the location where you want the file saved from the Save in drop-down list (use 3_ Floppy A: to put a copy of the file on a floppy disk).

4. Enter a name for the file in the File Name box.

5. From the Save as type drop-down list, select the format in which you want to save the file (choose one of the formats Works accepts, as listed in Table A.1).

6. Click **Save**.

Working with Macintosh Files   To open Macintosh files on your PC, you must use PC Exchange or Apple File Exchange on the Macintosh to copy the file to a PC disk before you can put the disk into your PC. Then follow the procedures to import the files from that disk.

CAUTION

563

Importing the Files into Works

In order to import a file into Works, you must first open it:

1. Click the **Existing Documents** tab on the Works Task Launcher.

2. Click **Open a document not listed here**. The Open dialog box appears (see Figure A.2).

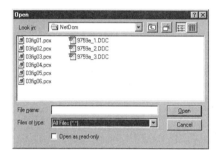

Figure A.2 The Open dialog box.

3. From the Look in drop-down list, select the location where you stored the file.

4. Works looks for a Works file, so you may not immediately see the file you want to import. Click the down-arrow next to the Files of type box and select the appropriate file format.

5. Select the file you want to import.

6. Click **Open**.

Once the file opens, you can format it using Works tools and save it. If you only need a portion of the data to add to a current Works document, spreadsheet, or database, copy that portion using the **Edit**, **Copy** command from the menu. Open the Works document to which you want to add the data, position your cursor where you want the data to go, and choose **Edit, Paste** from the menu.

Importing Graphics Files

Although Works supplies you with some pictures (called *clip art*) that you can place in your word processing documents, you can also bring in pictures from outside sources.

For more information on adding clip art to your word processing documents, see Part III, Lesson 12, "Adding Clip Art and Charts."

As with importing data files, the clip art you import must be available in a format acceptable to Works. For example, if you want to include a Microsoft PowerPoint slide in a document, PowerPoint saves all the slides in a presentation together as one file, with a PPT extension. Works cannot import a slide using that file format. However, you can save the current slide in PowerPoint as a WMF (Windows Metafile) format that is acceptable to Works. Use the same method as outlined in Saving the File You Want to Import, earlier in this appendix.

Works imports graphics files saved in the following formats:

> Encapsulated Postscript (EPS)
>
> Macintosh PICT
>
> Windows Metafile (WMF)
>
> Enhanced Metafile (EMF)
>
> Tagged Image File Format (TIF)
>
> JPEG File Interchange Format
>
> GIF
>
> Portable Network Graphic
>
> Windows Bitmap (BMP)
>
> WordPerfect Graphic (WPG)
>
> Computer Graphics Metafile (CGM)
>
> PC Paintbrush (PCX)
>
> Photo CD

To import a graphic into a Works document:

1. In the Works Task Launcher, either choose the Word Processor tool, to start a new word processing file, or select the **Existing Documents** tab and then double-click the name of the document file you want to open.

2. Position your cursor where you want the graphic to appear in your document.

3. Choose **Insert, Clip Art** from the menu. The Microsoft Clip Art Gallery appears (see Figure A.3).

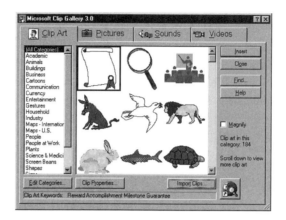

Figure A.3 The Microsoft Clip Art Gallery.

4. Click **Import Clips**. The Add Clip Art to Clip Gallery dialog box opens (see Figure A.4).

Figure A.4 Add Clip Art to Clip Gallery dialog box.

5. From the Look In drop-down list, select the location where you stored the file.

6. From the Files of Type drop-down list, select the type of file you want to import. The dialog box displays a list of files of that type that are stored in the location you selected.

7. Select the file name you want and click **Open**. The Clip Properties box appears (see Figure A.5).

8. Check a category where you want to reference this graphic for later use (Works adds it to the Clip Art Gallery). Click **Category** to create a new category name.

9. In the Keywords box, enter a word or two that will help you identify this graphic.

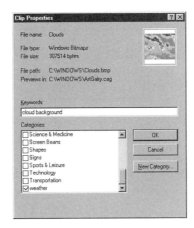

Figure A.5 The Clip Properties box.

10. Click **OK**.

11. Click the thumbnail picture of your graphic in the Clip Art Gallery to select it.

12. Click **Insert**.

Exporting Works Files

You may need to share the work you've done in Works with people in your office who do not have Microsoft Works. To do this, you need to save your files in formats that can be recognized by other applications.

Works can save your files in the formats listed in Table A.2.

Table A.2 Exportable File Formats

Word Processing Documents	Spreadsheet Files	Database Files
RTF (Rich Text Format)	Excel	dBase III or dBase IV
Text	Lotus 1-2-3	Text & Commas
Text (DOS)	Text & Commas	Text & Tabs
Windows Write 3.0	Text & Tabs	Text & Tabs (DOS)
Word 2.x for Windows	Text & Tabs (DOS)	Works for Macintosh database

continues

Table A.2 Continued

Word Processing Documents	Spreadsheet Files	Database Files
Word 3.x-6.x for DOS	Works for Macintosh spreadsheet	Works for DOS database
Word 6.0/95		Works for Windows 2.0 or 3.0 database
WordPerfect 5.x for DOS		
WordPerfect 5.x for Windows		
Works for Macintosh word processing		
Works for DOS word processing		
Works for Windows 2.0 or 3.0 word processing		

To save a Works file in the format, you need to open it in another application:

1. Choose **File**, **Save As** from the menu. The Save As dialog box appears.
2. Select the location where you want the file saved from the Save in drop-down list.
3. Enter a name for the file in the File Name box.
4. From the Save as type drop-down list, select the format in which you want to save the file.
5. Click **Save**.
6. Follow the import instructions for the application in which you want to open the file.

In this appendix, you learned how to export files from Microsoft Works to other applications, how to import files from other applications into Works, and how to save files from other applications in formats acceptable to Works.

Using the Communications Tool

This appendix gives you an overview of the Works Communications Tool and how to set up your computer to communicate with other computers.

Setting Up the Communications Tool

The Communications Tool enables you to send mail and documents to other computers via your modem.

To establish a connection with another computer, on the Works Tools tab in the Task Launcher, click **Communications**.

When you open the Communication Tool for the first time, the Easy Connect dialog box appears (see Figure B.1). Easy Connect lets you set up your communications by entering the name of the service or computer with which you want to connect and the phone number your modem needs to dial.

CAUTION

Not Ready to Go Yet? Make sure that your devices have been set up and that you have adjusted the communications settings before you try to communicate with another computer. See the instructions in "Setting Up for Communications" later in this appendix if you need to do this or check with your system administrator.

To use Easy Connect:

1. From the Country Code list box, select the code for the country that you are dialing. These are the codes for international calling, so you can connect to computers outside the United States.

2. In the Area Code box, enter the area code for the computer you want to reach.

3. In the Phone Number box, enter the telephone number of the computer you want to call. Works ignores any dashes, parentheses, and spaces you enter. Type a comma where you need to pause, and be sure to enter any prefixes you need to dial to get an outside line (such as 8 or 9).

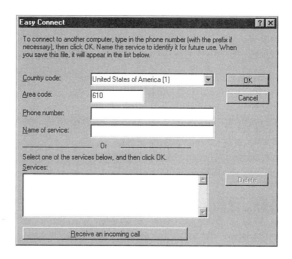

Figure B.1 The Easy Connect dialog box.

4. To be able to call this computer again without keying the information every time, give this setup a name by entering one in the Name of Service box. Then, when you want to connect to this computer in the future, you select the service name from the Services list when the Easy Connect dialog box appears.

5. Click **OK**. The Dial dialog box opens (see Figure B.2).

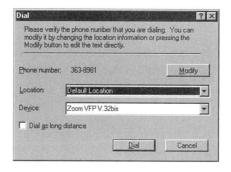

Figure B.2 The Dial dialog box.

6. In the Dial dialog box, you're asked to verify the phone number you want to dial. If you need to change the phone number, click **Modify** and enter the new number. Click **Done**.

7. The Default Location choice automatically appears in the Location box. The location tells Works where your computer is (Works needs to know what your local area code is, for example), and the default location is the site from which you normally dial. You can create other locations (useful for traveling with a laptop), and they will appear on this list. In that case, select the correct location from the drop-down list.

8. The name of your modem appears in the Device box. If you have more than one modem available, select the one you want to use from the drop-down list.

9. Check **Dial as Long Distance** if you need to dial 1 and an area code to reach the other computer.

10. Click **Dial**. Your modem dials the phone number of the other computer and opens a communication session.

11. When your communication session is complete, choose **Phone**, **Hang up** from the menu.

When you start up the Communication Tool or begin a new communication, the Easy Connect dialog box automatically appears. To bring up this dialog box at any other time, choose **Phone**, **Easy Connect** from the menu.

Setting Up for Communications

You need to set up your devices and enter information regarding how you want the system to dial out and receive calls.

Adding a Modem

Your modem should already be set up for you through the Windows 95 Control Panel unless you just added a modem to your system.

To add a new modem:

1. Click the **Start** button on the Taskbar.

2. Choose **Programs, Microsoft Works, Microsoft Works** from the Start menu. The Works Task Launcher appears.

3. Click **Communications**. When the Easy Connect dialog box appears, click **Cancel**.

4. Choose **Settings, Modem** from the menu. The Modems Properties box appears.

5. On the **General** tab, click **Add**. The Install New Modem wizard appears (see Figure B.3).

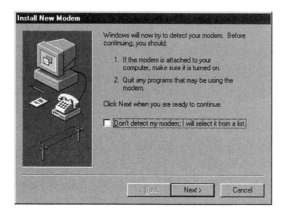

Figure B.3   Install New Modem wizard

6. To have Windows 95 automatically detect your new modem, turn the modem on and click **Next**.

If Windows 95 cannot detect your computer, an alert appears in the dialog box asking you to pick your modem from a list. Click **Next**. Select the correct modem from the list and click **Next**.

7. Click **Finish**.

To check on the settings for your current modem, follow the previous steps 1 through 4. Then click **Properties** and view the settings. Click **OK** to close the Properties box.

Configuring Phone Settings

The phone settings tell the Communication Tool what type of effort to make in calling a number—whether or not to redial, how many times to redial, and what interval you need between dialing attempts.

1. On the Works Tools tab in the Task Launcher, click **Communications**. When the Easy Connect dialog box appears, click **Cancel**.

2. Choose **Settings, Phone** from the menu or click the **Phone Settings** button on the toolbar. The Settings dialog box appears (see Figure B.4).

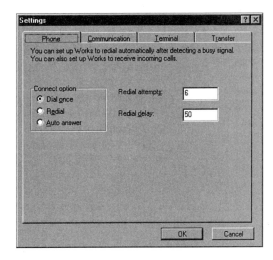

Figure B.4 The Settings dialog box with the Phone tab selected.

3. In the `Connect option` section, choose **Dial Once** to have your modem dial only once to reach another computer, **Redial** to have your modem dial the number again if it doesn't get through on the first try, or **Auto Answer** to have your modem automatically respond to incoming calls.

4. If you selected Redial, enter the number of times you want the modem to attempt reaching the other computer in the `Redial Attempts` box.

5. In the `Redial Delay` box, enter the time interval in seconds that you want the modem to wait before it dials again.

6. Click **OK**.

Changing the Communications Settings and Dialing Properties

To select the modem you're going to use for communications and to add locations from which you'll be dialing, you need to change the communications settings.

1. On the Works Tools tab in the Task Launcher, click **Communications**. When the Easy Connect dialog box appears, click **Cancel**.

2. Choose **Settings, Communication** from the menu or click the **Communications Settings** button on the toolbar. The Settings dialog box appears with the Communication tab selected (see Figure B.5).

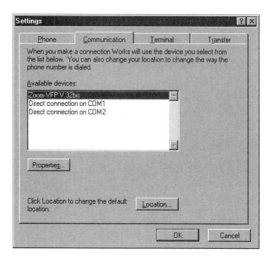

Figure B.5 The Settings dialog box with the Communication tab selected.

3. From the `Available Devices` list box, select the modem you want to use to make connections.

4. To change the settings for the default location or to add a new location, click **Location**. The Dialing Properties dialog box opens (see Figure B.6).

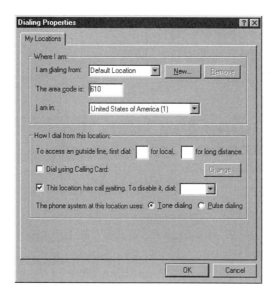

Figure B.6 The Dialing Properties dialog box.

5. The Default Location automatically appears in the I am dialing from box. If you want to create a new location, click **New**, enter a name for your new location, and click **OK**.

6. Enter the area code at your location in The area code is box.

7. Select the name of the country where you're working from the I am in drop-down list.

8. If you have to dial a prefix code to get an outside line, enter the codes in the for local and for long distance boxes.

9. To use a calling card for dialing, check **Dial using Calling Card**. Click **Change** to enter the phone prefix and Calling Card number.

10. Because Call Waiting can disconnect your modem, you need to disable it before using the phone line. If you have Call Waiting, check **This location has Call Waiting** and select the code that disables it from the dial drop-down list.

11. Select **Tone dialing** or **Pulse dialing**, depending on the phone service you have.

12. Click **OK** to return to the Communication settings.

13. Click **OK** to close the Settings dialog box.

Viewing Terminal and Transfer Settings

When you're connecting to a service like an Internet Service Provider (ISP), that service may ask you to choose a particular set of terminal and/or transfer settings. The terminal settings specify the terminal emulation, or how your connection controls your display so you can read the characters coming from the other computer. The transfer settings define the language the two computers will use when transferring data or files. You occasionally will need to select a different transfer protocol.

 TIP   **Protocol**   A protocol is a set of rules for how a computer sends and receives files. To successfully transfer files, both computers must be using the same set of rules or protocols.

CAUTION **Changing the Terminal and Transfer Settings** Unless you receive instructions from a service provider, systems administrator, or your modem manufacturer's customer support, don't start changing these settings. The default settings should work, and you could cause communication problems if you change the settings without knowledgeable instruction.

To view the terminal and transfer settings:

1. On the Works Tools tab in the Task Launcher, click **Communications**. When the Easy Connect dialog box appears, click **Cancel**.

2. Choose **Settings**, **Terminal** or **Settings**, **Transfer**. The Settings dialog box opens.

3. Select the **Terminal** tab to see the terminal settings or the **Transfer** tab to see the transfer settings.

4. Click **OK** to close the Settings box.

Saving Your Settings

To save your communications settings for use another time:

1. Choose **File**, **Save** from the menu. The Save As dialog box appears .

2. In the Save in box, select the folder where you want to save the file.

3. Enter a name for the settings file in the File Name box.

4. From the Save As Type list box, choose **CM Settings**.

5. Click **Save**.

Communicating with Another Computer

Once you make the connection to the other computer, you can send text, transfer files, or capture text.

TIP **Call Ahead** If you're sending a file or text to an individual rather than a service, call first and ask if they're ready to receive your communication.

Sending Text

To send text by typing text in the Communications window:

1. On the Works Tools tab in the Task Launcher, click **Communications**.

2. Enter the necessary information in the Easy Connect dialog box or select the service to which you want to connect.

3. Click **OK**. The Dial dialog box appears.

4. Make any necessary changes to the settings in the Dial dialog box and click **Dial**.

5. Once you connect to the other computer and that computer responds, type your text in the open Communications window.

6. To let the person you've called know you've finished your message, type "over" or some other signal that lets that person know to respond.

7. When you want to end the session, choose **Phone**, **Hang Up** from the menu.

To send a text file:

1. Follow steps 1 through 4 above.

2. Choose **Tools**, **Send Text** (see Figure B.7).

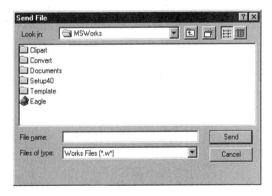

Figure B.7   The Send dialog box.

3. In the Look in box, select the folder where the file is stored.

4. From the File Name list, select the file.

5. Click **Send**.

6. When you want to end the session, choose **Phone**, **Hang Up** from the menu.

577

Receiving Files or Text

When you're receiving text or files from another computer, be sure first that you use the correct protocol by contacting the source and asking which one to use. Check your transfer settings (see Viewing Terminal and Transfer Settings in this lesson) to see what protocol you're using and select the correct one.

To receive a file:

1. On the Works Tools tab in the Task Launcher, click **Communications**. When the Easy Connect dialog box appears, click **Cancel**.

2. Tell the person sending the file to send it.

   If you're online with a service and you want to "download" (have them send you) a file, follow the instructions from the service on selecting the file.

3. Choose **Tools**, **Receive File** from the menu.

4. Enter a file name of up to eight characters if the protocol you're using is "Xmodem." Otherwise, the file name will match the name of the file you're downloading so you don't need to enter your own file name.

5. When the transfer is complete, click **OK**.

In this appendix, you learned about the Works Communications Tool and how your computer can communicate with other computers.

Index

W

MACMILLAN COMPUTER PUBLISHING USA

A VIACOM COMPANY

Technical ----- Support:

If you need assistance with the information in this book or with a CD/Disk
accompanying the book, please access the Knowledge Base on our Web
site at **http://www.superlibrary.com/general/support**. Our most
Frequently Asked Questions are answered there. If you do not find the
answer to your questions on our Web site, you may contact Macmillan
Technical Support **(317) 581-3833** or e-mail us at **support@mcp.com**.

Check out Que® Books on the World Wide Web
http://www.quecorp.com

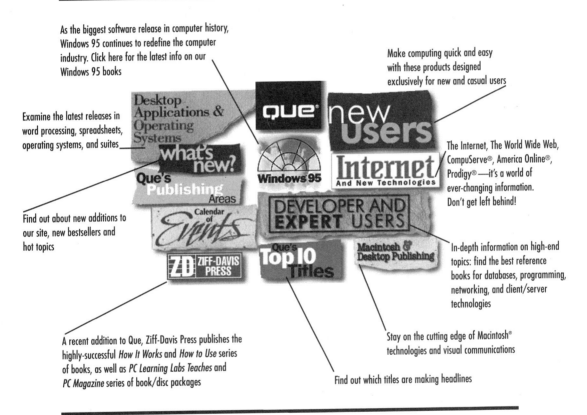

As the biggest software release in computer history, Windows 95 continues to redefine the computer industry. Click here for the latest info on our Windows 95 books

Make computing quick and easy with these products designed exclusively for new and casual users

Examine the latest releases in word processing, spreadsheets, operating systems, and suites

Desktop Applications & Operating Systems

que® new Users

what's new?

Windows 95

Internet And New Technologies

The Internet, The World Wide Web, CompuServe®, America Online®, Prodigy® —it's a world of ever-changing information. Don't get left behind!

Que's Publishing Areas

Calendar of Events

DEVELOPER AND EXPERT USERS

Find out about new additions to our site, new bestsellers and hot topics

ZD ZIFF-DAVIS PRESS

Que's Top 10 Titles

Macintosh & Desktop Publishing

In-depth information on high-end topics: find the best reference books for databases, programming, networking, and client/server technologies

A recent addition to Que, Ziff-Davis Press publishes the highly-successful *How It Works* and *How to Use* series of books, as well as *PC Learning Labs Teaches* and *PC Magazine* series of book/disc packages

Stay on the cutting edge of Macintosh® technologies and visual communications

Find out which titles are making headlines

With 6 separate publishing groups, Que develops products for many specific market segments and areas of computer technology. Explore our Web Site and you'll find information on best-selling titles, newly published titles, upcoming products, authors, and much more.

- Stay informed on the latest industry trends and products available
- Visit our online bookstore for the latest information and editions
- Download software from Que's library of the best shareware and freeware

Que®

Complete and Return this Card
for a *FREE* Computer Book Catalog

Thank you for purchasing this book! You have purchased a superior computer book written expressly for your needs. To continue to provide the kind of up-to-date, pertinent coverage you've come to expect from us, we need to hear from you. Please take a minute to complete and return this self-addressed, postage-paid form. In return, we'll send you a free catalog of all our computer books on topics ranging from word processing to programming and the internet.

Mrs. ☐   Ms. ☐   Dr. ☐

(first) ☐☐☐☐☐☐☐☐☐☐☐☐ (M.I.) ☐ (last) ☐☐☐☐☐☐☐☐☐☐☐☐☐☐☐

ss ☐☐☐☐☐☐☐☐☐☐☐☐☐☐☐☐☐☐☐☐☐☐☐☐☐☐☐☐☐☐

☐☐☐☐☐☐☐☐☐☐☐☐☐☐☐☐☐☐☐☐☐☐☐☐☐☐☐☐☐☐

☐☐☐☐☐☐☐☐☐☐☐☐ State ☐☐ Zip ☐☐☐☐☐ ☐☐☐☐

☐☐☐ ☐☐☐☐ Fax ☐☐☐ ☐☐☐☐

any Name ☐☐☐☐☐☐☐☐☐☐☐☐☐☐☐☐☐☐☐☐☐☐☐☐☐☐☐

l address ☐☐☐☐☐☐☐☐☐☐☐☐☐☐☐☐☐☐☐☐☐☐☐☐☐☐☐

ase check at least (3) influencing factors for rchasing this book.

or back cover information on book .... ☐
al approach to the content .... ☐
leteness of content .... ☐
r's reputation .... ☐
sher's reputation .... ☐
cover design or layout .... ☐
or table of contents of book .... ☐
of book .... ☐
al effects, graphics, illustrations .... ☐
(Please specify): _____ ☐

w did you first learn about this book?

n Macmillan Computer Publishing catalog .... ☐
nmended by store personnel .... ☐
he book on bookshelf at store .... ☐
nmended by a friend .... ☐
ved advertisement in the mail .... ☐
n advertisement in: _____ ☐
book review in: _____ ☐
(Please specify): _____ ☐

w many computer books have you rchased in the last six months?

book only .... ☐   3 to 5 books .... ☐
ks .... ☐   More than 5 .... ☐

4. Where did you purchase this book?

Bookstore .... ☐
Computer Store .... ☐
Consumer Electronics Store .... ☐
Department Store .... ☐
Office Club .... ☐
Warehouse Club .... ☐
Mail Order .... ☐
Direct from Publisher .... ☐
Internet site .... ☐
Other (Please specify): _____ ☐

5. How long have you been using a computer?

☐ Less than 6 months   ☐ 6 months to a year
☐ 1 to 3 years   ☐ More than 3 years

6. What is your level of experience with personal computers and with the subject of this book?

	With PCs	With subject of book
New	☐	☐
Casual	☐	☐
Accomplished	☐	☐
Expert	☐	☐

Source Code ISBN: 0-7897-1357-8

7. Which of the following best describes your job title?

Administrative Assistant .... ☐
Coordinator .... ☐
Manager/Supervisor .... ☐
Director .... ☐
Vice President .... ☐
President/CEO/COO .... ☐
Lawyer/Doctor/Medical Professional .... ☐
Teacher/Educator/Trainer .... ☐
Engineer/Technician .... ☐
Consultant .... ☐
Not employed/Student/Retired .... ☐
Other (Please specify): _____ ☐

8. Which of the following best describes the area of the company your job title falls under?

Accounting .... ☐
Engineering .... ☐
Manufacturing .... ☐
Operations .... ☐
Marketing .... ☐
Sales .... ☐
Other (Please specify): _____ ☐

Comments: _____
_____
_____

9. What is your age?

Under 20 ....
21-29 ....
30-39 ....
40-49 ....
50-59 ....
60-over ....

10. Are you:

Male ....
Female ....

11. Which computer publications do you read regularly? (Please list)

_____
_____
_____
_____
_____
_____
_____
_____
_____
_____

Fold here and scotch-tape to